COUNSELING FAMILIES

An Introduction to Marriage, Couple, and Family Therapy

FOURTH EDITION

David L. Fenell

University of Colorado - Colorado Springs

LOVE PUBLISHING COMPANY®
Denver • London • Singapore

 Published by Love Publishing Company
P.O. Box 22353
Denver, Colorado 80222
www.lovepublishing.com

Library of Congress Catalog Card Number 2010936997

Copyright © 2012 by Love Publishing Company
Printed in the United States of America
ISBN 978-0-89108-350-4

Contents

3   The Emergence and Evolution of Marriage, Couple, and Family Therapy   37

4   Current Issues, Ethics, and Trends in Marriage, Couple, and Family Therapy   57

5   The Family as a Living System: Essential Concepts   99

6   Making the Paradigm Shift: Building Bridges from Individual to Family Systems Theory   121

7   Using Core Counseling Skills in Marriage, Couple, and Family Therapy   139

Part Two
Helping Couples Change with Individual and Systems Theories 165

11 Helping Families Using Cognitive and Behavioral Systems Theories   267

12 Helping Families Using Humanistic Individual Theories   311

13 Helping Families Using Humanistic Interpersonal Systems Theories   341

16   Research in Marriage, Couple, and Family Therapy   445

Figures

Tables

Case Studies

Preface

Marital, couple, family, and other relationship conflicts are ubiquitous. Unresolved relational problems often lead people to seek professional help. Typically, one member of a family seeks counseling while others remain disengaged. Through the process of individual counseling, the therapist often discovers that other family members are involved in creating and maintaining the presenting problems. As the individual client gains insight into the contextual nature of the problem, the therapist may ask the client to invite the nonattending family members to join the therapeutic enterprise (Wilcoxon & Fenell, 1983). When the other family members enter therapy, the process of traditional family systems therapy, which includes the entire family, commences.

In actual practice, marital, couple, and family therapy is often delivered by mental health professionals who have received the majority of their clinical training in providing individual and group counseling, including professional counselors, social workers, psychologists, medical professionals, and clergy. This book is designed for these therapists. It has been developed to ensure that all mental health professionals may be as fully prepared as possible to provide effective treatment to couples and families. Introductory coursework in family therapy has become more commonplace in academic training programs. However, most programs provide only one or two courses focusing specifically on family systems therapy (Gladding, Burggraf, & Fenell, 1987).

According to a survey ("Training of Clinical Psychologists," 1981), clinical psychologists in private practice provide couple and family therapy approximately 40% of the time, yet fewer than 5% of the therapists surveyed had any formal coursework in couple and family therapy. Over the years, the number of therapists with this formal training has increased, but even today many mental health professionals treat couples and families with only a minimum of family therapy preparation. Conversely, therapists trained in graduate programs focused specifically on couple and family interventions reported that their programs emphasize system-based and, to some extent, postmodern, collaborative approaches to treatment, with little attention given to individual and group counseling theories and procedures. In either case, a more comprehensive therapist training program that implements a planned and sequential curriculum focusing on individual counseling, group counseling, *and* couple and family counseling will produce more highly qualified therapists who are equipped to provide services to the full spectrum of presenting client problems in family, group, or individual therapy.

In *Counseling Families,* I have attempted to address this task by providing the reader with information about how the basic individual core counseling skills such as empathy, respect, genuineness, and reflection of content and feelings taught in most graduate programs are useful for individual, group, and couple and family counseling. Moreover, I describe how traditional individual counseling theories such as person-centered therapy, gestalt therapy, transactional analysis (TA), cognitive and behavioral therapy, and other individual approaches may be applied to marital, couple, and family therapy.

In this book, I hope to bridge the gaps between individual, group, and family therapies. The helping professions are too fragmented, as each struggles for its place in the managed care marketplace in what seems to be perceived as a zero sum game with winners and losers. Mental health professionals from virtually all types of professional training programs, including professional counseling, social work, psychology, psychiatry, psychiatric nursing, the clergy, and couple and family therapy, will serve clients who present with relationship problems. I hope that all mental health professionals will be as broadly prepared and competent as possible. One important goal of this book is to encourage counselors and other mental health professionals with individual and group training to recognize that they already posses the theoretical knowledge and clinical skills to be effective with many of the problems presented by couples and families. In addition, I hope this book will help readers develop an increased array of helping skills by incorporating family systems theories and interventions as well as recent constructivist and other nonsystemic family approaches into their therapeutic repertoire.

Too often, I hear of counselors avoiding the use of systems theories that may be beneficial to their clients because of the misperception that the systems approach to problem resolution is often too clinical or manipulative and does not focus sufficiently on the therapeutic relationship between clients and the therapist. This misconception is confronted by the significant body of research literature incorporated throughout this book that emphasizes the importance of the therapeutic relationship in family, group, and individual counseling sessions. Moreover, counselors and other mental health professionals who are not able to integrate the key concepts and skills of general systems theory into their counseling practice may not be able to provide the most effective help to certain couples and families. While family therapy is not necessarily the answer to all presenting problems, it does offer an alternative paradigm that is often effective when nonsystemic interventions have been applied without success. Thus, I hope this book encourages counselors to deepen their exploration of family systems theories and interventions and integrate them into their counseling repertoire as an adjunct to their individual and group counseling skills.

Family therapy has evolved in significant ways since the third edition of this text was published. Well-established systems theories have been refined and their application expanded and postmodern and collaborative treatment approaches have emerged. In this book, I have attempted to present the latest developments in couple and family theory and techniques as well as significant changes to the profession of family therapy, including recent developments in licensure and professional recognition.

A Note on Language Use

I have alternated the use of male and female personal pronouns in order to avoid the perspective of the "universal he" while also avoiding awkward sentence construction. Every effort is made throughout the text to be mindful to use language that is inclusive of and respectful to all forms of the changing modern family.

A Personal Comment

My own recent experiences as a family therapist have been focused on helping combat veterans and their families reconstitute after combat deployments. I have presented workshops throughout the country to help mental health professionals develop the necessary skills to effectively help families from the "military culture" (Fenell, 2008). I have been mobilized and deployed in support of the Global War on Terrorism as a US Army Behavioral Sciences Officer to Afghanistan (2002–2003) and later to Iraq (2007). During and after those deployments, I helped soldiers, spouses, and children confront the personal and family-related issues inherent in deployments and in reestablishing their relationships.

As a result of my combat deployments to Afghanistan and Iraq, I needed to work through many of the same concerns and issues as other returning combat veterans. Reestablishing my relationship with my wife, Ruth Ann, and resuming the normal life of a college professor presented personal challenges for me. Like the families I counseled, my transition back from the combat zone to "civilization" was a challenge for my own family. My personal experiences in reintegrating with my own family after multiple deployments made it easy for me to empathize with the struggles of the military families I counseled. Ruth Ann, a professional school counselor, kept the home fires burning during my deployments and was a constant source of support for me and for our two adult children, Nathan and Maija, who were each serving overseas as well. Our daughter Maija Lawler served in the Mediterranean as a surface warfare officer in the Navy, and our son Nathan continues to serve as an infantry officer in the Marine Corps. Nathan has served two combat tours in Iraq. Thus, I had the role of a deployed soldier and the role of the father of deployed children. The role of father was the most personally stressful for me. A new chapter has been added to this book devoted specifically to counseling military families, influenced by my combat deployments and experiences serving as a military family counselor.

In addition to the new chapter on counseling military families, the fourth edition of *Counseling Families* has been significantly revised in other ways. Revised chapters elaborating on the history and nature of marital, couple, and family relationships and an expanded description of the history and founding of the family therapy profession has been added. Other important additions to the fourth edition include a review of evidence-based practices in family therapy and a review of the common factors approach to treatment.

This discussion is important in providing information to emerging family therapists that will inform their choices of theoretical orientation in their future work. Recent efforts by the American Association for Marriage and Family Therapy (AAMFT) to identify core competencies required to be an effective family therapist are reviewed. Finally, the fourth edition has added sections describing evidence-based approaches to treatment including cognitive–behavioral couple and family therapy, integrative behavioral couple and family therapy, multisystemic therapy with families, and emotionally focused couple therapy.

Acknowledgements

My career as a professional counselor and family therapist has spanned more than 30 very good years. During that time, I have drawn knowledge, support, and friendships from mentors, colleagues, students, family, and friends. All of these relationships have brought me to the place I stand today. I would especially like to acknowledge my mentors and professors at Purdue University, Bruce Shelter, Wallace Denton, Doug Sprenkle, Dick Hackney, and Dick Nelson. I am also grateful for the support and friendship of my colleagues, Alan Hovestadt, Brian Canfield, Fred Piercy, Jerry Junke, Pat Love, Gay Hendricks, Bev Snyder, Rhonda Williams, Joe Wehrman, Julaine Field, Colonel (retired) Gary Greenfield, and Colonel Morgan Banks. I am especially indebted to Barry Weinhold, my coauthor for the first three editions of this book. He has embarked on other writing projects with Love Publishing. Sections of our collaborative work remain in this fourth edition.

Special thanks to those who made this book a reality including my publisher and friend Stan Love and editor Carrie Watterson. They made sense of my writing and helped clarify the thoughts I wanted to communicate to the reader. I would also like to thank the professional colleagues who reviewed the manuscript for this book and made important suggestions for improving it. Thanks also to the professors who have adopted this text and to all the students who have used it. The suggestions received from professors and students who used this book were invaluable in identifying important new areas to include in this edition of the text and in improving the format and presentation of ideas to make the book even more reader friendly.

Finally I want to acknowledge the support of my own family. I am the proud father of two remarkable adults, Nathan and Maija. I am eternally grateful for all their love and support. Over the years, I have drawn much of my strength from these relationships and more recently from my special relationships with my three granddaughters Greta, Meredith, and Cate Lawler and my two grandsons Maddox and Zachary Fenell.

Most importantly I want to acknowledge my wife Ruth Ann for her patience and wisdom while I was revising this text and throughout our 38 years of marriage. She exemplifies all the qualities of an outstanding counselor and can empathize, encourage, and confront as each situation requires. In short, "she believes in me."

About the Author

David L. Fenell is the interim Dean of the College of Education and professor of counselor education in the Department of Counseling and Human Services at the University of Colorado at Colorado Springs. He received his BS in physiology from Oklahoma State University in 1968, his MA in Education (Counseling emphasis) from the University of Southern California in 1976, and his PhD in Counselor Education (Family Therapy emphasis) from Purdue University in 1979. He completed a postdoctoral internship in Counseling Psychology at Texas A&M University (College Station) in 1980.

Dr. Fenell has been a practicing family counselor for more than 30 years, most recently serving on active duty as a Behavioral Sciences Officer in Afghanistan and Iraq, providing therapy services to the military families impacted by the Global War on Terrorism. He received the Bronze Star Medal for his service in Afghanistan and the Bronze Star Medal (1st Oak Leaf Cluster) for his service in Iraq. He retired from the Army Reserve as a Colonel in January 2007 and was awarded the Legion of Merit for his 26 years of honorable military service to the nation.

Dr. Fenell has published and presented in the following areas:

- Effectiveness of marriage enrichment program
- Comparison between delayed and immediate supervisory feedback in family therapist training
- Characteristics of satisfactory long-term marriages
- Critical issues experienced in long-term marriages
- Family therapy in rural settings
- Predictable crisis in military deployments
- Therapy with combat veterans and their families
- School counselor support of deployed military families

He is a clinical member, approved supervisor, and fellow of the American Association for Marriage and Family Therapy (AAMFT), a National Certified Counselor, and Licensed Psychologist. He is member of the American Counseling Association (ACA), Association for Counselor Educators and Supervision (ACES), the International Association for Marriage and Family Counseling (IAMFC), and the American Psychological Association (APA). He received the ACA's Presidential Award in 2008 for his service to the counseling profession. He serves as a consultant to the US Army and Marine Corps in the assessment and selection of personnel for special missions.

Dr. Fenell is married to the former Ruth Ann Hemingway, a licensed professional counselor and school counselor. They have two grown children, Nathan and Maija, and five grandchildren. Ruth Ann publishes and collaborates with David on writing projects and presentations involving military families and school counseling.

Part One

Understanding Family Therapy

Chapters

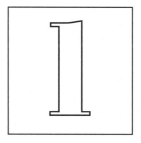

Families and
Family Therapy:
An Introduction

This chapter describes the evolution of the contemporary Western family. It is the contemporary Western family that is most likely to make use of family therapy services. Definitions are provided for important terms used throughout this book describing the nature of the family, marriage, and other committed relationships. Finally, the organization of this book will be described and strategies are suggested for effect use of the information provided.

Key Concepts

- ○ Functions served by the family—today and in the past
- ○ Traditional and nontraditional families
- ○ Definition of marriage
- ○ Definition of the family
- ○ Therapy for the trainee
- ○ Counseling and psychotherapy

Questions for Discussion

1. Why is it important for counselors and other mental health professionals to have the knowledge and skills necessary to work with couples and families?
2. What are your reactions to the definitions of family, marriage, and committed relationships provided in this chapter? Do you believe these definitions are important for the family therapist? Why or why not?
3. Do you believe it is important for family counselors in training to participate in their own therapy? Defend your answer.
4. The terms family therapist, counselor, and psycho-therapist are used interchangeably throughout this book. Do you agree with this usage? Why or why not?

Evolution of the Family

Families in one form or another have existed since humans began populating the earth. The earliest prehistoric family groups have evolved into the modern family forms that exist today. The family forms that exist today will likely evolve even further in the future. Since the beginning of human existence, people have come together to form social organizations. In the earliest times, these family groups were formed to meet basic safety and security needs, such as protection from enemies, obtaining and sharing food and water, and providing support in raising offspring and ensuring their survival (Maslow, 1968). Before the Middle Ages and through the 19th century, men and women who married and produced offspring were essential to the economic well-being of the family. Parents and children alike contributed to the economic survival of the family, working together to raise crops and livestock or to operate small enterprises. The industrial revolution influenced further change as families evolved from self-supporting, self-regulating farmers and ranchers to urban employees of emerging industries with a set schedule and work routine.

Today's family has evolved in a variety of ways. It is increasingly likely that both parents in a family are employed outside the home and that much of the care, education, and socialization of young children will occur in daycare centers and schools while parents are at work (Olson & DeFrain, 2006).

A *traditional family* is composed of a wife, husband, and children. In traditional families, it is usual for the husband to work outside the home as primary breadwinner and the mother to work in the home and as primary caretaker for the children. Recent Census Bureau data report that fewer mothers are full-time homemakers than in the past. In the 1950s, more than 70% of US families had a mother working in the home. Twenty years later, in approximately 51% of families, both spouses worked outside the home in full- or part-time employment (Olson & DeFrain, 2006).

There are several *nontraditional family* forms. These families include unmarried, cohabitating heterosexual couples (with and without

"You are not to play with those Jetson kids! Their parents
are very strange... They're in their <u>first</u> marriage."

children); single parent families, child-free families, homosexual unions, communal families, and plural marriages. The political discussions generated by the emergence of many of the nontraditional family forms are often contentious. Some groups advocate that the family must be based upon a legal union, marriage, between a woman and a man. Other groups argue that nontraditional family forms, such as marriages between same-sex couples, are just as valid as the traditional forms and should be recognized and afforded the same rights and privileges as traditional families.

Whether in traditional or nontraditional unions, the percentage of married couples is declining, from 68% in 1970 to 60% in 2006 (US Bureau of the Census, 2001).

Irrespective of the politics embedded in the definitions of marriage and the family, counselors should be aware that that they will be providing family therapy to both traditional and nontraditional couples and families in their practices. Therapists should be ethically prepared to provide competent treatment, or effective referral, to all who seek their services.

Family Defined

As the reader has discovered, defining today's families is a challenging undertaking. Olson and DeFrain (2006, p. 5) compiled a series of definitions of the family:

- The *American Heritage Dictionary of the English Language* (2000) defines *family* as
  - ○ a fundamental social group in society typically consisting of one or two parents and their children;
  - ○ two or more people who share goals and values, have long-term commitments to one another, and reside in the same dwelling place;
  - ○ all members of a household under one roof; or
  - ○ a group of persons sharing a common ancestry.

- The US Bureau of the Census (2002) defines a family as two or more persons related by birth, marriage, or adoption residing together in a household.
- The American Association of Family and Consumer Sciences (2004) defines a family as two or more persons who share resources, share responsibility for decisions, share values and goals, and have a commitment to one another over time.
- Irving (2003, p. 6) reported that throughout history all societies have developed some type of family organization. But what is a family? He believes that term family generally refers to a group of people related to one another by birth, marriage, or adoption. In contemporary society, the term may be applied to any group that declares itself a family and feels a sense of kinship and a family connection.
- Finally, Howard (2002) took a different approach and stated that the group of individuals can be called a unit, network, or a tribe, or a family. But whatever you call it, and whoever you are, he emphasized that you need one.

For the purposes of this text, the definition of family developed by Olson and DeFrain (2006) will be used. They defined family as "two or more people who are committed to each other and who share intimacy, resources, decision-making responsibilities and values; people who love and care for each other" (p. 6). Each of the previous definitions defines the family broadly. As family therapists, we will be called upon to respond to Howard's (2002) important message emphasizing that we, our clients, and everyone else in our society needs a family. Our job is to try to help those families to be as healthy, supportive, loving, and functional as possible.

Marriage Defined

Olson and DeFrain (2006) defined marriage as "the emotional and legal commitment of two people to share emotional and physical intimacy, various tasks and economic resources" (p. 3). The most prominent difference between the definition for marriage and the definition for family is that marriage is a legal as well as emotional commitment. Broderick (1992) identified several characteristics of marriage:

- Marriage creates a relational unit that is a "building block" and part of a larger society.
- Marriage creates a new and larger social network as the family and friends of each spouse become part of the network.
- Marriage in the United States is a legal contract, with laws in each state specifying the rights and responsibilities of the spouses.
- Marriage creates an economic unit, as most couples merge financial resources.
- Marriage is the living arrangement of choice for most adults. Most men and women have been married at least once by the age of 35.
- Marriage is socially sanctioned for, and is the context for, most human sexual activity.
- Marriage provides the context for reproduction and socialization of children.
- Marriage provides an opportunity for spouses to mature and develop psychologically and interpersonally through the intimacy in their relationship.

After considering this list, the reader may be wondering if these characteristics are valid today. While most adults do marry, increasing numbers are choosing cohabitation or are remaining single. Marriage continues to produce a social economic unit; however, more dual-income couples have agreed to keep their finances separate. Marriage remains the socially accepted context for sexual activity; however, premarital and extramarital sexual activities appear to be more acceptable to contemporary society (Olson & DeFrain, 2006). Moreover, many marriages are unsatisfactory and end in divorce. Based on recent trends, some 50% of marriages fail, and, of those that do survive, some are unsatisfactory or dysfunctional (Popenoe & Whitehead, 2004). Most divorces involve children, with more than 1 million children affected by divorce each year. Even, so, most divorced people remarry a second or even third time. However, the probability of a woman remarrying decreases as the number of children she has increases (Olson & DeFrain, 2006).

It is clear the marriage and the family are evolving. Yet in many ways these institutions remain the foundation of society by providing a stable and supportive context for meeting life's challenges and carrying out life's developmental tasks. Despite all the changes and the current debates about the marriage and about the family, these institutions still provide stability and continuity for our society. As family therapists, we are called upon to help marriages and families that are not effectively supporting their members change and become more loving and purposeful.

Becoming a Family Therapist

Most counselors and mental health professionals receive training in basic helping skills including empathy, respect, warmth, genuineness, concreteness, self-disclosure, and immediacy. Most counselors are trained to use these skills with individual clients or with small groups. Although many counselor training programs offer one or two academic courses in marriage, couple, and family therapy, few offer practicum or internship experiences of significant enough duration to allow the counselor in training to develop effective skills working with couples and families (Gladding, Burggraf, & Fenell, 1987).

Most generalist counselor training programs have little room in their curricula for marriage and family therapy coursework and training because of the significant accreditation requirements for courses in support of the preparation of individual and group psychotherapists. Only 34 of approximately 230 colleges and universities have masters degree marriage, couple, and family counseling training programs that have been accredited by the Council for Accreditation for Counseling and Related Educational Programs (CACREP, 2011). Thus, many graduates of counselor training programs who are interested in family therapy must receive their formal training in marriage, couple, and family therapy beyond the masters level through continuing professional education (Fenell & Hovestadt, 1986).

A further obstacle for students desiring to develop marriage and family therapy skills is the perception that marriage and family therapy, practiced from a systems perspective, is radically different from the theories and techniques taught in a masters program that focuses on individual and group therapies. Because of the mystique and different terminology surrounding marriage and family therapy, counseling professionals often believe they are not adequately prepared to work with couples and families. This book demonstrates ways in which counseling students can begin to apply many of the basic skills learned in individual and group work to work with couples and families. Further, this book demonstrates how these skills can be used to construct bridges linking individually-oriented counseling theories to systems theories while increasing the readers' confidence in their ability to help couples and families.

In their preface to Volume I of the *Handbook of Family Therapy,* Alan Gurman and David Kniskern (1981b) justified their decision to exclude certain approaches to family therapy, including cognitive, rational–emotive, behavioral, person-centered, Adlerian, gestalt, and transactional analysis (TA) therapies. They acknowledged that these approaches have exerted significant influences on the practice of individual and group therapy and that specific aspects of these approaches have been incorporated in the work of some family clinicians. Nonetheless, Gurman and Kniskern concluded, "These therapeutic approaches have not yet exerted a significant impact on the field of family therapy" (p. ix). Although they recognized Virginia Satir's tremendous impact on the family therapy field, they opted to exclude her approach because they determined that no clearly discernable school or therapeutic methods have evolved from her important contributions.

Volume II of the *Handbook for Family Therapy* (1991) addressed the evolution of the theories presented in Volume I and introduced several new systems-based theories. The authors continued to exclude individual theories (except behavioral theory) that are employed with success in treating family and other relationship problems.

Gurman and Kniskern recognized that in order for family therapy to emerge as an autonomous, coequal, and respected member of the mental health care delivery system, it was essential to clearly distinguish family therapy from long-accepted individual and group approaches to treatment. Gurman and Kniskern and other family therapy pioneers envisioned family therapy as a distinct profession, separate and equal to counseling, psychology, social work, and psychiatry. The early leaders of the field were committed to ensuring that family therapy would be recognized as a new and radically different paradigm for treating psychological problems and would not be regarded as simply another theory to be subsumed by psychology, social work, professional counseling, or any of the other helping professions. The issue of whether the family therapy exists as a distinct mental health profession or as a specialty area of other professions such as psychology, social work, or counseling is the most significant issue facing the field today (Bowers, 2007).

Therapy for the Counselor in Training

Many training programs in marriage, couple, and family therapy; professional counseling; and other mental health professions strongly encourage their trainees to undergo personal counseling during the training program. Based on my 30 years of experience preparing professional marriage and family counselors, I recommend undergoing voluntary counseling. This experience greatly enhances trainees' ability to become effective therapists, especially if they have not been in counseling previously. By participating in personal growth–oriented therapy, trainees will gain the opportunity to examine their own family patterns and histories and the personal values, assumptions, and beliefs that will inevitably impact their approaches to family treatment. Through personal therapy, trainees often increase their *self-awareness*, remove blind spots, reveal unfinished business, identify and build upon personal strengths, identify weakness, and develop plans to minimize the impact of those weaknesses when serving clients. Trainees will also develop enhanced *adaptability*. Therapist adaptability means that the self-aware trainee is able to adapt to the situations presented by clients in therapy and chooses the best response from a number of possible treatment alternatives. Without participating in personal therapy, many trainees habitually rely on the familiar response that fits the counselor's, but probably not the client's, value and belief systems. Moreover, therapy for the therapist allows the trainee to experience the thoughts, feelings, and actions associated with being a client. This awareness increases the trainees' empathy for clients seeking family counseling services.

Clarifying Terminology

Distinguishing between the terms counseling and psychotherapy can be confusing for students. Gladding (2009), as well as other authors, distinguished between the two terms by defining *counseling* as a relationship-based treatment for clients with problems in daily living. Counseling is viewed as developmental, focused on personal growth, wellness, or career issues. Of course, counselors also treat psychopathology, but this aspect of the profession is usually not emphasized. Psychotherapy, on the other hand, treats more serious mental health problems. *Psychotherapy* is defined as a specific clinical treatment based on psychiatric diagnoses such as those identified in the *Diagnostic and Statistical Manual of Mental Disorders* (APA, 2000).

Certainly, there is significant overlap between psychotherapy and counseling. For the purposes of this book, counseling and psychotherapy will be used interchangeably, as will the terms family counseling and family therapy. Counseling and therapy both provide supportive treatments in dealing with problems of daily living and both provide clinical treatment of diagnosed disorders. In my judgment, the difference, if any, between a trained professional counselor and a trained psychotherapist is minor. Both have the task of helping individuals,

Advantages of therapy for the trainee

- Examine family histories and patterns
- Identify blind spots and unfinished business
- Critically examine personal values, beliefs, and assumptions
- Enhance empathy by discovering what it is like to be a client
- Increase self-awareness
- Increase adaptability

couples, and families alleviate human suffering and are accorded equal status in this book.

Furthermore, throughout this book, marriage, couple, and family therapy may be referred to as *family therapy, family counseling, marriage and family counseling (MFC), or marriage and family therapy (MFT)*. While marriage counseling is reemerging as a specialization within the family therapy profession, most family therapists consider the marital dyad to be a part of the larger family system. Thus, family therapy implies treatment of the couple (married or in a committed relationship), children, and any other members of a particular family system. Treatment may be with the entire family system or may be with members of various subsets of the family, such as the children, the marital dyad, or committed partners. These subsets of individuals within the family are usually referred to as *subsystems*. Some practitioners have specialized in marital and couple counseling and only see clients with problems related to their dyadic relationships. Others specialize in child or play therapy and treat the children of the family system. These specialists are often referred to as family therapists, especially if they view the problems treated in therapy as being precipitated and maintained by the behaviors of all members of the family system.

Because contemporary families are increasingly composed of unmarried adults with children and because homosexual unions are gaining legal and social recognition, many scholars and practitioners have expanded the title of the profession from *family therapy* to *marital, couple, child and family counseling* or *therapy*. This title is inclusive and recognizes many current family forms. For simplicity, in this book I will usually refer to marital, couple, family, and child counseling as *family counseling* or *family therapy*. When referring to the treatment of married and unmarried, gay or straight couples I will refer to this as *couple counseling or therapy* and treatment of children alone as *child counseling or play therapy.*

Navigating This Book

The fourth edition of *Counseling Families: An Introduction to Marriage, Couple, and Family Therapy* has been organized in a way that is designed to assist mental health professionals in developing basic knowledge and skills in family therapy. Moreover, this edition has been expanded to include many of the most recent and respected family therapy theories.

Part One of this book introduces the field of family therapy and describes how family therapy is important as a mental health treatment approach. The history and evolution of the profession of family therapy is documented along with the most significant professional issues and trends. A chapter is devoted to introducing the terminology required to effectively read and understand the family therapy literature and to presenting a set of core counseling skills that may be used effectively in counseling families, groups, or individuals.

In Part Two of the fourth edition of *Counseling Families,* the student is reintroduced to familiar individual theories such as gestalt, person-centered, and TA. The reader then learns how these individual theories and their associated counseling skills may be used in providing therapy to families. After studying the familiar individual theories and applications, readers will be able to construct a theoretical bridge linking these familiar theories to their most closely related family systems theories. For example, after reviewing the chapter describing psychodynamic *individual* theories, the student will be introduced to a companion chapter describing the related psychodynamic *family systems* theories. The student will know from the review of the individual theories that individual psychodynamic theories rely heavily on the examination of past experiences, parental relationships, and unconscious processes. The student will then be prepared to apply the relevant knowledge gained in studying the individual theories to the newly introduced psychodynamic systems theories, facilitating the understanding and application of the systems theories. The developmental process of moving from familiar theories to new and unfamiliar theories will help the student comprehend and apply the skills associated with the new theories. The theories covered in this book are introduced in three major classifications:

1. Theories based on *psychodynamic* concepts
   - Individual theories:
     - Sigmund Freud—psychodynamic theory
     - Alfred Adler—Adlerian theory
     - Eric Berne—transactional analysis (TA)
   - Family theories:
     - Murray Bowen—family systems theory

- James Framo—family of origin theory
- Richard Schwartz—internal family systems theory

2. Theories based on *cognitive–behavioral* concepts
   - Individual theories:
     - Albert Ellis—rational–emotive behavior theory (REBT)
     - Frank Dattilio—cognitive–behavioral couple and family therapy
     - Gerald Patterson—behavioral therapy: the social learning approach
     - Andrew Christensen—integrative behavioral couple therapy
   - Family theories:
     - Salvador Minuchin—structural family therapy
     - James Barton and colleagues—functional family therapy
     - Mental Research Institute—brief strategic therapy

3. Theories based on *humanistic/interpersonal* concepts
   - Individual theories:
     - Carl Rogers—person-centered theory
     - Fritz Perls and Walter Kempler—gestalt theory
     - J. L. Moreno—psychodrama
   - Family theories:
     - Virginia Satir—communications theory
     - Carl Whitaker—symbolic–experiential family therapy
     - Michael White and David Epston—narrative therapy
     - Susan Johnson—emotionally focused therapy

Part Three of this book features a new chapter developed to help therapists counsel military families. Other chapters in Part Three are focused on treating families with special needs and research in family therapy. Information pertaining to professional issues and ethical concerns in family therapy is included in Chapter 4 in this edition.

The overall purpose of the fourth edition of *Counseling Families* is to provide mental health professionals who are trained and experienced using individual counseling theories and techniques with the knowledge and skills to work with couples and families using systems concepts under the supervision of a qualified therapist. The book demonstrates how students may employ the basic counseling skills taught in most counselor training programs in clinical work with couples and family systems.

Summary

Marriage and the family have evolved from the days when children were needed to help the family function to the present day where families serve a more relational and less utilitarian function. Family therapists should be familiar with the controversies and debates about the definition of marriage and the family because they will be treating clients with very differing views on these two institutions. Family therapy for the counselor in training is beneficial because the experience will increase the person's awareness of family issues that could interfere with the counseling process and provides the counselor in training with the experience of being a client. Both reasons will contribute to the making of an effective family therapist.

The question is not whether counselors will work with couples and families. Because of the tremendous demand for family therapy services, practicing professional counselors will certainly encounter clients experiencing family-related problems. The important question is: Will counselors be adequately prepared to help clients who seek help with marriage and family related problems? This book is designed to provide counselors with information they need to begin to provide supervised therapy to couples, families, and others experiencing relationship difficulties. Each chapter will bring the reader closer to the goal of being able to begin to work with couples and families under the supervision of a competent marriage and family counselor.

The Need for Family Therapy

This chapter describes several frequently occurring family and relationship problems that family therapists are called upon to treat. Further, this chapter explains why treatment of these problems from a family systems perspective provides the therapist with an expanded array of strategies for effective helping.

Key Concepts

- ○ Two-career families
- ○ Marital problems
- ○ Cyber relationships
- ○ Single-parent families
- ○ Drug and alcohol abuse
- ○ School-related problems
- ○ Families with a gifted child
- ○ Families with a child with disabilities
- ○ Child management problems
- ○ Adolescent depression and suicide
- ○ Problems with adult children leaving home
- ○ Care of elderly parents
- ○ Elderly family members with Alzheimer's disease
- ○ Rural families
- ○ Families with chronic medical problems
- ○ Families with an HIV-positive member

Questions For Discussion

1. What are some specific counseling problems that may best be treated with family therapy? What aspects of the family systems approach do you think make it helpful?
2. Which specific family-related problem discussed in this chapter would you consider most difficult to treat? Why? Which would be the easiest? Why?
3. What affect do you think frequent online activities can have on marriage, couple, and family relationships?
4. How might family members support the addictive behavior of an alcoholic or drug-abusing member even though they report that they want the member to change?
5. Think about your own family relationships. How might family therapy be helpful for you and your family?

Over the past 45 years, marriage, couple, and family therapy has evolved in to an important mental health treatment approach. The social, economic, and political demands placed on families today far exceed those of previous generations and can create considerable stress for family members. Helping professionals have recognized that counseling an individual without considering or including other family members makes lasting change less likely. The family member who is exhibiting symptoms is called the *identified patient* (IP) by most family therapists. The IP is thought to be the symptom bearer for a family that is not functioning well, and it is that patient's acting out that often draws therapeutic attention to family dysfunction. Often families send the IP to therapy for treatment without recognizing the roles of family members in maintaining the client's symptoms. It is the responsibility of the therapist to engage the family members in treatment with the IP (Wilcoxon & Fenell, 1983, 1986).

Because societal pressures have increased family stress and because more families are seeking help through therapy, counselors and therapists need to be prepared to treat psychological problems that occur within the family context. Specific areas of contemporary concern include the pressures of families in which both parents work; the unique stresses experienced by single-parent families; and problems with school-related issues, ranging from problems with gifted students to those with developmental disabilities. Other issues include escalating numbers of family members engaging in alcohol and drug abuse; higher suicide rates in the teenage population; and increased life expectancy, resulting in worries about caring for elderly parents, including those with Alzheimer's disease. Family therapy can also be effective in working with families who have a member who is HIV-positive or has other chronic medical problems.

These are a few of the emerging issues of which effective counselors must be aware and able to handle successfully. Counselors must understand how these issues and other family problems not mentioned here *affect every member of the family unit*. This awareness enables therapists to help the family by broadening the focus of treatment beyond the IP to the family system and implementing intentional change strategies that influence *all* family members. A fundamental concept of systems theory that family counselors need to remember is that changes in one family member affect the entire family and changes in family relationships affect each and every individual in the family. Much more will be said about this important concept throughout this book.

Influence of the Family on Problem Formation

A practicing counseling professional is presented with numerous client problems that other members of the client's family may cause, encourage, or support. Experienced therapists recognize the difficulty of successfully treating individual clients with problems that have their basis in difficult family relationships. Individual therapy with an IP who is experiencing family-related problems is often initially successful. However, when the IP who has made changes in therapy returns to the family system without the support of therapy, the client is likely to revert to former patterns of dysfunctional behavior. Regression to problematic past behaviors occurs because, even though the IP has made changes, the rest of the family has not. Thus, the family's unchanged behavior creates an environment that slowly returns the client to the old problematic ways of functioning. This predictable family phenomenon introduces another important concept in family therapy: The family system can be powerful enough to thwart individual psychological growth. Consequently, change is best implemented when all family members participate and all engage in making changes that support improved family functioning.

To reiterate, if the behaviors of the rest of the family members remain constant, individual clients are likely to revert to former dysfunctional behaviors that have been supported and reinforced by the family system. This concept leads to a third important family therapy concept: All client behavior makes perfect sense when the therapist understands the clients' family relationships and other client contextual variables. In other words, *all behavior makes sense in its context*.Therefore, the well-trained counselor has to understand how to effectively treat psychological problems that the family reinforces and supports. This treatment often involves participation of all the family members in therapy. Several of the most commonly encountered family problems are described in this chapter.

Two-Career Families

Economic pressures and changes in the role of women in society have contributed to an increase in the number of women in the workforce and the number of two-career families in the United States. Developing an effective two-career lifestyle raises many issues and questions for the couple. Frequent issues that dual-career couples raise in therapy are the following (Fenell, 1982):

1. How will the necessary household duties be divided with both partners working?
2. How will young children be cared for?
3. How will finances be managed?

When these concerns are not resolved, couple or family counseling may be indicated. If only one partner enters treatment, the therapeutic alternatives would be limited, because the counselor would deal with the perceptions and feelings of only one person. With both partners present in treatment, however, new rules can be negotiated that identify and respond to the needs and concerns of each person. If both partners' needs are considered, there is a better chance that mutual agreements can be made and that lasting change will take place.

Marriage and Couple Relationship Problems

One of the most common reasons for seeking psychotherapy is for support in resolving problems in couple relationships. Therapy is needed because couples have complex and serious disagreements and do not have the communication and problem-solving skills necessary to resolve them (Sperry, Carlson, & Peluso, 2006). When treating one partner alone, the therapist is limited to only that person's perceptions of the problem. Moreover, when one person is treated for marital problems, deterioration in the couple's relationship is more likely (Gurman & Kniskern, 1978a) than if both partners are treated together. Thus, the counselor should possess the skills necessary to engage both partners in the counseling process (Whitaker & Keith, 1981; Wilcoxon & Fenell, 1983, 1986) and should be capable of treating the couple conjointly as well as individually.

A client treated for relationship problems in individual therapy is likely to achieve personal therapeutic growth. The partner not in treatment is likely to observe positive change in the other. This improvement occurs because the client is no longer trying to ineffectively process and resolve emotional issues with the nonattending partner. The issues are being processed in therapy and the emotional energy surrounding those problems dissipates in the therapy session rather than at home. Thus, the client in treatment comes home a happier person and the nonattending person is happier as well. Demands for support and open communication with the person at home decrease because these needs are being met by the counselor in the therapy sessions. However, when therapy is concluded, it is likely that the old problems will resurface and emotional intensity will reappear because the client will no longer have an accepting place to openly process concerns. When therapy ends with no real change in the couple's interaction pattern, the differences between the partners may actually increase and make resolution of the relationship difficulties even less likely in the future. The anger and disappointment the couple may experience with each other when their problems return may complicate the situation and perhaps lead to dissolution of the relationship if successful couple therapy is not initiated.

If the presenting concern is a couple's relationship problem and the goal is to resolve this problem, the counselor should attempt to involve both partners in treatment. Conjoint couple therapy is the treatment of choice for relationship problems, because it offers the therapist a more realistic picture of the role each person plays in creating and maintaining the difficulties. Also, because the partners work together to resolve their problems in conjoint treatment, they do not grow farther apart as could be the case if only one person was in treatment (Gurman & Kniskern, 1978a).

Cybersex Relationship Problems

The incredible popularity of internet chat rooms, social networking, and specialized information available on the internet has created a new and insidious cybersex phenomena that can cause or exacerbate relationship problems. Recent surveys have estimated that more than 69 million people use the internet for sexual purposes, and more than 18 million may be have problems controlling their use (Goldberg, Peterson, Rosen & Sara, 2008). I use the term insidious here because a partner can chat with another person or lose himself in a specialized web page of interest any hour of the day or night, withdrawing from the personal relationship. Insidious also because a social consensus has not yet formed around this new phenomenon: One member of the couple may view it as infidelity while the other considers it innocent. Nonetheless, as one partner takes energy from the couple's relationship and devotes it to cybersex, difficulties are likely just as if an actual affair was in progress.

Meanwhile, helping professionals may be unprepared to address the problem. In a survey conducted by Goldberg et al. (2008) and published in the *Journal or Marital and Family Therapy*, one of the top journals in the family therapy field, 39% of 164 responding family therapists viewed cybersex as problematic for a marriage. In that study, 18% of the respondents stated that cybersex was the same as infidelity if the activity is kept secret from the other partner, while 19% reported that they would not be concerned about clients engaged in cybersex if they were open with each other and agreed to the activity. However, open-ended responses to the survey indicated that these therapists would be concerned if the cybersex activity was addictive, illegal, or led to relationship or intimacy problems. More than 75% of the respondents would be concerned if young or adolescent children viewed the materials. More than 90% of the respondents believed that cybersex may be addictive and expressed varying opinions about whether the internet could be used adaptively for sexual purposes (Goldberg et al., 2008).

The survey further revealed that most family therapists did not receive adequate training in their graduate programs to deal with cybersex problems. Most have learned through attending workshops and through clinical experience with their clients. No evidence-based treatment protocol has been identified for treating this problem.

Finally, it is important that family therapists examine their own values concerning the topic of cybersex treatment. Some therapists may be comfortable assessing and treating this problem while others may not be comfortable doing so. Appropriate referral is important in these instances (Goldberg et al., 2008).

Single-Parent Families

Because of the high divorce rate in the United States, the number of single-parent families has continued to increase. Single mothers head nearly 6 million households in the United States (Goodrich, Rampage, & Ellman, 1989), and single fathers, nearly 2 million (Davis & Borns, 1999). Thus, counselors must be prepared to respond to the problems experienced by both men and women who are single parents.

The parent with custody of the children faces a myriad of problems that must be resolved to effectively support and nurture the family. Single parents frequently feel the pressures of time while trying to meet the needs of the children, their own personal needs, and work responsibilities. This stress can spill over on the children and create difficulties. Although some children of single parents do fine, one study suggests that children of single-parent families may have more problems than children from two-parent families in adjusting, handling challenges at school, and forming stable relationships with others (Wallerstein, 1992).

When single parents experience increased stress levels, they may begin to lose a sense of control of their children, families, and perhaps of themselves. Often, children sense the lack of control experienced by the parent and respond by becoming symptomatic, frequently developing health problems or beginning to act out at school and home. Counseling with the single parent, the children, and available support persons is an effective way to help moderate the tension and stress in this difficult situation. If the former partner is available and willing to enter family therapy with the single parent and children, this participation can often enhance the chances for successful outcome.

Another serious issue the single parent may face involves issues of custody, child support, and parenting time. These issues are rarely resolved successfully without the participation of all concerned parties in the counseling process.

Families with Drug and Alcohol Problems

When a family member has a problem with drug and alcohol abuse or addiction, all other members of the family are affected by the abuser and affect the abuser for better or for worse. In addition to assisting the substance abusing client, counselors must help other family members deal with their feelings about the abusing client and about their ineffective attempts to support change in the abuser's behaviors. Furthermore, some family members may inadvertently engage in specific behavior patterns that support the continuation of the drug or alcohol abuse. Family therapy can help identify these dysfunctional patterns.

Children may become overly responsible and handle duties that a parent would normally perform. These youngsters are referred to as *parentified children*, as the family system has assigned them the role of overfunctioning and acting as an adult in order to maintain family's operation. The actions of parentified children allow the parents to continue their irresponsible substance abuse and often have the effect of eroding the child's self-esteem, because no matter how hard they try, they are not able to "fix" the family. Moreover, this family pattern deprives the child of normal developmental experiences that can impact his significant relationships later in life.

The partner or children of the substance abuser often behave in a way that has been described as *codependent*. This term describes a person who has a tremendous irrational need to maintain the relationship that she is unwilling to seriously challenge the substance-dependent partner's dysfunctional behavior. Children can be codependent when they assume parentified roles and do whatever they can to deny or cover up the hurtful actions of the substance abuser. Thus, codependent family members help perpetuate the problem of dependency or addiction.

In addition to parentification and codependency, other roles may be identified in the families of alcohol and drug abusers. These roles may even be found in families with other symptom patterns (Murphy, 1984; Stevens & Smith, 2001):

- The *enabler*—often called codependent—allows the substance abusing behavior to continue by serving as a rescuer for the abusing family member.
- The *scapegoat* is the child who gets into trouble to distract the family members from the pain caused by the substance abuser.
- The *hero* is the family member who continues to function well. The hero may serve to demonstrate to others and to himself that the family is a good family despite the substance abuse.
- The *lost child* is often marginalized by the other family members. The pain felt by the lost child is rarely recognized and, if recognized, not acknowledged.

- The *clown* is the family member who distracts family members from the substance abuse problems through humor and cute antics.

   George (1990) summarized several "rules" that are characteristic of most families with a substance-abusing member:

- Resist any change and remain the same. This is accomplished by not talking about the problems in the family.
- Do not trust family members and do not trust yourself.
- Ignore and deny your feelings.
- Vigorously uphold the myth that all of the family's problems are caused by some factor other than substance abuse.

   Maintaining these rules, rather than attempting to achieve health, becomes the primary goal of all family members unless they receive help. A great deal research demonstrates that all family members play a role in maintaining the problem. Treatment should include family sessions that identify the family roles and the family rules in effect that serve to sustain the family's problems. Thus, counseling with the entire family is an important component of effective drug and alcohol abuse treatment (Edwards & Steinglass, 1995; George, 1990; Stevens & Smith, 2001).

   Research compiled by the Substance Abuse and Mental Health Services Administration (SAMHSA, 2010) reported that family-oriented treatment programs are widely available and effective:

- 82% of individuals who participated in family treatment programs describe significantly improved mental health and well-being.
- 73% described their functioning at work, school, and home to be greatly improved.

School-Related Problems

Teachers and principals often encourage children who are having difficulty in school to begin counseling. When the difficulties are related to problems at home or conflicts between the school and home, counseling the child alone is rarely effective. Parents, siblings, teachers, school counselors, and administrators should be involved to gain a complete and accurate contextual assessment of the problem. Participation of the family as well as school personnel with significant relationships with the student is important to establish effective cooperation between the school and the family. The goal is to identify ways that both systems—the school system and the family system—might be contributing to the problem through their ineffective efforts to change the child's behaviors. The school counselor should be prepared to help school personnel and family members change their behaviors toward the child at the same time as the child is changing her problematic behaviors. The counselor must have excellent skills to enlist the cooperation of these three important systems, child, school, and family, in initiating and sustaining the change process (Lambie, 2008).

School Phobia

The National Education Association (NEA) estimates that 160,000 students miss school every day because of phobias (Fried & Fried, 1996). Nichols and Schwartz (2001) reported that children who experience school phobia frequently live in families that have weak, overprotective parental structures and an inability to control their children. When it is time for the children to go to school, they rebel, either by refusing to go to school or by going to school but creating significant turmoil for the parents and school staff.

School-related problems such as these are rarely handled effectively by working with the child alone. Family therapy is required. Integrating the school counselor and other school personnel and the family in treatment is extremely important. Minuchin and Fishman (1981) described structural family therapy techniques that are helpful with these problems. They focus on strengthening the parents' relationship to each other and developing agreement on how to handle the child's problems consistently. School personnel are informed of the parents' strategies and are asked to support them. With parents and school personnel working together in a caring fashion, the school phobic child can no longer play one system off against the other and is likely to improve. Structural family therapy will be described more fully later in this book.

School counselors are trained to respond effectively to children's problems. More often the than not, these problems involve the family, teachers, and/or peers. Therefore systems-based family therapy training is essential for school counselors. All school counselor trainees in our program at the University of Colorado at Colorado Springs must complete a course in introductory family therapy theory and techniques and a skills training laboratory course that emphasizes the application of systems theory interventions in order to graduate. Graduates of our program have reported that the family therapy module of instruction has contributed to their effectiveness as school counselors in resolving peer, family, and teacher problems experienced by their students, staff, and parents. School counselors who are comfortable with the skills introduced in an introductory family therapy course are more willing to engage teachers, administrators, families, and peers in the treatment of individual students. School counselors are more likely to make successful interventions with their student with the support of all involved parties. If the child is changing his behavior and those changes are intentionally supported by parents, teachers, and peers, the changes are more likely to persist.

Gifted Students

School counselors are involved in the education of gifted students. The parents of gifted students are frequently highly involved with their student and the educational system, trying to ensure that the child's giftedness is appropriately recognized and nurtured. Parents who protectively hover over their children to ensure all goes well for them have been dubbed *helicopter parents*. This parental hyper-concern can have a negative effect on the child leading to rebellion, underachievement, withdrawal, or acting out. Conversely, some parents are not aware of their child's abilities and do not provide support for the child's optimal educational and social development. The school counselor is most effective in helping the gifted family by meeting with the student, parents, and teachers. Working collaboratively, she can determine how to maximize the educational experience for the student while attempting to develop an appropriate level of involvement by the parents. Without the participation of key elements of the family, teachers, and counselors from the educational system, a successful outcome is less likely. The effective school counselor will need family systems skills to respond most successfully to the concerns presented by families with gifted children.

Students with Disabilities

Students with disabilities and their families present unique challenges for the school counselor. Working collaboratively with the special education teacher, the counselor will want to engage all relevant parties in an effort to provide an optimal education for the child with a disability. Convening a meeting of all members of the family, educational, and, when necessary, medical systems usually results in the most productive planning for providing a developmentally appropriate education for the student. Parents, siblings, and school personnel all want the best for their student with a disability. However, the sincere attempts made by the family to be helpful to the student can contribute to the student's lack of improvement. When family, friends, and school personnel do "too much" for the student, it robs her of the initiative to try new behaviors and engage in suitable activities. Thus, the student does not develop and may even lose headway. Family meetings involving the school counselor, student, parents, special education teacher, and other involved school personnel can be the key to helping students with disabilities reach their full potential (Fenell, Martin, & Mithaug, 1986).

Child Management Problems

Family counseling is helpful when parents have difficulty managing their children's behavior (Minuchin & Fishman, 1981). It is quite common for the annoying behavior of an acting-out child to create disagreement between the parents about how to manage and discipline the child. Failure to resolve the disagreement quickly may result in increased stress and instability in the relationship and lead to discord in the family. The child may be blamed for the family problems and becomes the scapegoat (Barker, 1992). This stress, in turn, escalates the child's acting out. The parents typically respond by increasing their ineffective attempts to correct the acting-out child rather than examining their conflict about how to best deal with the child. The longer the parents ignore their own conflict, the more likely it is that the child will continue to act out. The child then becomes worse, because he senses the escalating tension in the relationship and the increased focus on his behaviors. Contributing to this problematic cycle is the parents' narrow focus on the child's behaviors rather than examining how their couple disagreements and strained relationship may be contributing to the continuation of the problem.

Family therapy is the most effective way to accurately identify the roles enacted by each family member when a child begins acting out. It is the only method of treatment that identifies behaviors of each family member that maintain, decrease, or increase the symptoms. Family therapy can help change the dysfunctional interactional patterns among the acting-out child, parents, and siblings and thereby help all family members identify the issues present in the family that maintain or exacerbate the symptoms of the acting-out child. When the roles and interactional patterns are identified in therapy, the family typically develops a more functional and pleasant family life, and the child's symptoms decrease or become more accepted and less problematic for the parents and other family members.

Adolescent Depression and Suicide

The number of adolescents suffering from depression and, in the most severe cases, contemplating suicide has increased alarmingly in the last decade. More and more pressure from peers and the media is placed on adolescents to engage in adult behaviors they are not physically or psychologically prepared to handle. Moreover, parents may put pressure on their children through excessively high expectations they hold for their teenagers, demanding excellence in academics, sports, and other extracurricular activities. Or parents may signal to their teens that they are not competent and trustworthy by becoming helicopter parents, hovering over and doing things for their children that they could easily do for themselves. These parent behaviors can create feelings of incompetence in their offspring that can develop into depression. Furthermore, the counselor must be aware that sometimes these pressures are self-inflicted. The adolescent perceives that her parents hold unreasonable expectations when, in fact, they may not. Family therapy is especially effective in helping families sort out these issues and perceptions, identifying the sources of the pressure adolescents feel. In any case, when adolescents do not live up to real or perceived parental expectations, they may develop depression. When the depression is severe, the adolescent might consider suicide.

Family therapy is an excellent treatment modality for problems of adolescent depression in reaction to perceived parental, school, and social pressures because it sensitizes all family members to causes of the depression and, in cases of suicidal potential, educates family members about warning signs and ways to deal with the problem. Family therapy can assist all members of the family discover what each can do to support the improvement of the depressed member and what behaviors are not particularly helpful and should be decreased or eliminated.

The therapist will encourage all family members to be present in treatment and ensure that each is able to discuss the impact the depressed member is having on him and on the family as a unit. All members are given the opportunity to think of ways to support the depressed member and the opportunity to check out their ideas to see whether they are, indeed, helpful. As each family member makes small but significant changes in behavior, often by remembering and acknowledging the depressed adolescent's strengths, improvement often follows.

If the depressed member does not improve or worsens, consultation with a psychiatrist who has family systems training may be required. The psychiatric consultant might prescribe medication or, in the most serious cases, hospitalization for the depressed member. All ethical standards require that the counselor respond to imminent suicidal behavior in ways that ensure the client's welfare (AAMFT, 2001; IAMFC, 2001). When harm to the client is likely, this imperative takes precedence over the ethical requirement to maintain confidentiality (Jurich, 2001). This topic will be addressed more specifically in Chapter 4.

Launching Adult Children

A relatively recent phenomenon in our society arises in facilitating the departure of adult children from the parents' home. On the one hand, parents want their adult children to become autonomous, but, on the other hand, some parents do not believe that their children will be able to succeed financially or emotionally on their own. These parents send subtle and indirect messages to their children suggesting that they will not be successful. Noted family therapist Murray Bowen (1978) believed that the negative messages transmitted by parent to child result from anxiety parents have about themselves. Rather than deal with their own anxiety, parents often transmit it to the child. These children grow into adults who doubt their own ability to succeed without their parents' support and may eventually project the same anxiety onto their own children, perpetuating the problem. Exploring the dynamics involved in this situation in family counseling may help the adult son or daughter develop differentiated autonomy and the confidence to leave the parents' home both physically and psychologically. Family therapy also provides assistance to the parents as they learn effective behaviors that calm their anxiety and support the departure of the adult child.

A related situation is the *boomerang* adult child. In this situation, the individual has successfully differentiated and "left the nest" but for some reason—usually divorce or a financial setback—returns to the parents' home. This often gives rise to problems concerning authority and responsibility in the home. Family treatment can be beneficial when these problems are not resolved adequately.

In another increasingly common contemporary situation, grandparents assume parental responsibilities for their grandchildren. Many older individuals who have already raised one family are providing care and financial support for their grandchildren because of the irresponsibility or unfortunate setbacks of their own children. While this situation often is understandable, it can lead to unexpressed feelings of abandonment in the child, guilt in the parents, and resentment in the grandparents. Family therapy involving all three generations can help identify a plan for responding to the dilemma and can help family members communicate more effectively about their plans and expectations concerning this parenting arrangement and its impact on the child, parents, and grandparents.

Care of Elderly Parents

As life expectancy lengthens, many couples are finding themselves responsible for the care and support of their aging parents. As one partner finds his interactions with the elderly parents consuming more and more time, the other may feel unimportant or ignored in the relationship. One individual may feel that she is playing "second fiddle" to the other partner's parents while the partner with parents in need of assistance wants to help but also understands the costs of devoting so much time to the older generation to the relationship. Thus, this person is in a no-win situation and feels guilty no matter what course of action is taken. These situations can place extreme stress on the relationship and on each partner (Montalvo & Thompson, 1988). This stress is exacerbated when the demands from aging parents coincide with problems the couple may be having with their grown children leaving home or with issues in their own relationship.

Assisting the couple in working through the issues related to the support of elderly parents may help to resolve tensions in the relationship created by this demand. Including the elderly parents in some of the sessions is a powerful systems intervention and is important in gaining their perspective on the current situation and their ideas about what they need and want from their adult children and what they do not. Often, to avoid hurt feelings, elderly parents do not tell their adult children that some of the help provided is not needed. Putting all the cards on the table is one of the most significant strengths of family therapy. When all the members of the system, elderly parents, the couple, and other involved family members are aware of one another's concerns and desires, workable solutions are possible. When the family interacts with each other based on unfounded assumptions and their accompanying emotions, problems in relationships result. Family therapy can bring the generations together to deal with the problems of aging parents, often clarifying issues and improving relationships to everyone's delight.

Alzheimer's Disease and Other Cognitive Impairments

One of the most devastating problems confronting families with elderly members is Alzheimer's disease. This form of incurable dementia has predictable effects on family members. Initially, they hope it is memory loss resulting from the normal effects of aging and that memory loss will progress slowly. When that hope is dashed, family members, including sons and daughters, may react by denying the severity of the problems and withdrawing from the affected family member and caregivers.

Of course, this behavior is not helpful to the primary caregiver, who may be living the *Thirty Six Hour Day* (Mace & Rabins, 2001). This title refers to the tremendous stress felt by the caregiver (usually the partner) of an Alzheimer's patient. Providing care for the Alzheimer's patient is important. However, even more important is providing care for the primary caregiver of that patient. The caregiver is frequently elderly and is adamant about not placing the patient in institutional care, even when the requirements of caring for an Alzheimer's patient becomes more than the caregiver is physically able to manage. It is not uncommon for the caregiver to be hospitalized with an illness precipitated by a weakening of the body's defenses resulting from the tremendous effort required to care for an Alzheimer's patient, particularly one in the later stages of the disease. Thus, other family members and friends must be constantly on the alert for signs that the caregiver may not be taking adequate care of herself. A family therapy consultation including friends and other members of the caregiver's support system is important to help family members decide how each can best contribute to the care of both the Alzheimer's patient and the primary caregiver.

Family Therapy in Rural Communities

Rural families present unique challenges for the counselor. Most family therapy training programs prepare therapists to work with clients in urban locations. Training is also needed to prepare therapists to work in rural settings. Clients in rural areas differ from those in urban areas in significant ways (Fenell, Hovestadt, & Cochran, 1985; Hovestadt, Fenell, & Canfield, 2002). Therapists must be aware of and be comfortable responding to these three specific aspects of workings with families in rural communities:

1. Rural settings lack confidentiality.
2. Traditional sex roles are often accepted in a rural community.
3. Much of rural America subscribes to traditional religious values.

Counselors who are not comfortable in the situations described will have a difficult time gaining acceptance in rural communities, and without acceptance it will be extremely difficult to help rural families deal with their problems (Fenell, Hovestadt, & Cochran, 1985; Hovestadt, Fenell, & Canfield, 2002).

Family therapists working in rural settings often encounter their clients while running errands and must be comfortable in these situations. Clients will want to strike up a conversation with the off-duty therapist and make friendly small talk like they would with any other member of the rural community. Moreover, clients are not usually secretive about being in treatment, as other community members usually know what is taking place. Many members of the community are likely aware of the family's issues. These community members may try to engage the therapist in discussions about the family in a caring rather than nosey way. The family therapist must tactfully handle these situations by acknowledging the caring of the community members while at the same time not breaking confidentiality. At times, with certain community-based problems, it is helpful to include extended family and relevant community members in treatment. This meeting of the extended "community family" could be helpful in developing a community-based system to support the changes resulting from therapy.

Therapists trained in urban settings who are comfortable with more egalitarian sex roles may have difficulty accepting and empathizing with client families who maintain a different perspective. Therapists do not impose their personal values while helping the family resolve its issues. This can be a daunting challenge when the therapist's value system is quite different from the rural family's and rural community's values.

Another situation that can be challenging for family therapists working in rural setting is the strong religious convictions that are held by many families in rural settings. It would not be unusual for a couple working on their marriage to want to know what the therapist believes about religious aspects of the union. The therapist needs to be tactful while also being honest in responding to the question posed.

Families with Chronic Health Problems

When a person develops a serious medical problem, its impact reverberates throughout the family. The demands of the illness frequently require family members to reorganize their activities in response. A growing body of evidence suggests that family dynamics can affect many illnesses for better or worse (Campbell & Patterson, 1995). Disruption to the family caused by the onset of the illness can lead to emotional problems for the sick individual and other members of the family (Nichols, 2009).

Medical family therapists work in conjunction with the family and the healthcare system to help families experiencing serious medical problems maintain as normal a lifestyle as possible. If the illness is likely to exacerbate in the near future, the therapist can help the family prepare for this. If it is already present, the therapist can help family members identify negative impacts of the disease and make changes that are appropriate.

Illness interacts with the family dynamics, structure, life-cycle stage, and belief about the course of the illness (Nichols, 2009). By increasing the family's awareness of these characteristics, the therapist assists the family in utilizing its resources to best respond to the realities of the disease. Goldenberg and Goldenberg (2008) identified two additional ways in which family therapy may complement medical treatment. The first is responding to noncompliance with medical advice. Individuals who are noncompliant are often helped through family interventions, as other members are enlisted to monitor and support the patient in following medical orders.

The second concern relates to overutilization of medical services, which may occur when individuals are overstressed by family problems and develop physical symptoms in response. They hope that the doctor will "fix" them, when in reality the stress associated with the family problems are the source of the symptoms. These patients often overutilize medical services and underutilize family therapy. The savvy treating physician often prescribes family therapy for these patients to help break the overutilization cycle.

Summary

Numerous avenues to the resolution of family-related problems are available when working with families that may not be possible when working with individual clients. While it is clear that therapy with individuals has a definite place in the delivery of mental health services, family treatment ought to be the treatment of choice for many problem situations such as those described in this chapter and others presented later in this book. The challenge for counselors and psychotherapists is to know when to engage in family systems work and when individual treatment may be more appropriate. This book is designed to introduce the developing family therapist to the knowledge base and fundamental skills necessary to respond to the myriad problems that occur in the family. This will help the aspiring family therapist develop the ability to conceptualize the family from a systems perspective and implement systemic interventions in family treatment.

Recommended Reading

Gladding, S. T. (2011). *Family therapy: History, theory and practice.* Upper Saddle River, NJ: Merrill.

Goldenberg, I., & Goldenberg, H. (2008). *Family therapy: An overview.* Belmont, CA: Brooks Cole.

Nichols, M. P. (2009). *Family therapy: Concepts and methods.* Boston: Allyn & Bacon.

The Emergence and Evolution of Marriage, Couple, and Family Therapy

This chapter provides an overview of the profession of family therapy. Family systems therapy began to appear in the early 1950s. This contextual approach to treatment was a radical departure from mainstream psychoanalysis, the treatment model that was in vogue in the first half of the 20th century. To fully understand and appreciate the theories and techniques associated with family therapy, it is important for the counselor to be aware of the events that were taking place prompting a few rebellious and, some would say, radical psychoanalysts to violate the cardinal principles of analysis and begin treating couples and families. These early pioneers introduced a new and revolutionary treatment paradigm.

This chapter describes the events leading to the development of cybernetic, feedback-based family therapy treatment models. In addition, 21st century feminist and postmodern critiques of the traditional systems-based treatment models developed by the family therapy pioneers will be discussed.

Key Concepts

- ○ Child guidance movement
- ○ Conjoint marital therapy
- ○ Concurrent marital therapy
- ○ Constructivism
- ○ Cybernetics
- ○ Deconstruction
- ○ Double bind
- ○ Family system
- ○ Group dynamics
- ○ Postmoderninsm
- ○ Schizophrenogenic mother

Questions For Discussion

1. As you review the events that led up to the family therapy movement, which do you think were most significant? Why?
2. Do you believe family therapy is truly a revolutionary approach to mental health treatment? Why or why not?
3. In what ways are small groups similar to families and in what ways are they different?
4. Should marriage and couple counseling be part of the family therapy profession or a separate treatment modality? Defend your answer.
5. What is your reaction to the postmodern position that absolute truth can never be known? Do you agree? Why or why not?
6. In what ways have the feminist and constructivist critiques affected the family therapy movement for better and for worse?
7. Do you think the pioneering family therapy theories inappropriately stereotyped women? If so, what are the consequences of this tendency?

amily therapy is a young profession that developed in the 1950s as a rebellious and revolutionary challenge to classical psychoanalysis and individual psychotherapy treatment models. Family therapy was revolutionary because it challenged the long-held notion that mental health treatment should be a private consultation between a therapist and a single client. Rebellious family therapists began including other family members in treatment and ultimately insisted through their writings and conference presentations that including the entire family as a unit in treatment was a more effective way of identifying and dealing with the patterns of behavior in the family that created and supported the symptoms of one or more of the family members.

Overview of the Evolution of Family Therapy

In the 1950s and 1960s, family therapy emerged as a profession in the making. In the 1970s and 1980s, family systems therapy solidified its position as a unique and powerful treatment paradigm as colorful, brilliant, and iconoclastic leaders of the field, such as Gregory Bateson, Don Jackson, Jay Haley, Salvador Minuchin, Murray Bowen, Carl Whitaker, James Framo, and Virginia Satir popularized their systemic approaches to the family change process. These pioneers took family therapy to the members of the psychotherapy profession with their prolific writings and popular lectures and by providing live demonstrations of the rapid and observable changes that effective family system interventions could produce.

Family therapy took on a more mature and less aggressive position within the mental health community in the late 1980s that continues today. The powerful and respected pioneering family therapy theorists were, in turn, challenged in ways that paralleled the challenge they themselves made to the psychiatry profession in the 1950s. A movement toward postmodern and constructivist approaches to family therapy emerged in the late 1980s. Young therapists, freshly trained in the newly developed family therapy training programs throughout the nation, began to criticize the pioneers for developing theories that were often highly directive, seemed to stereotype gender roles, and had not paid sufficient attention to racial and gender diversity. Moreover, the critics believed the move away from a biological understanding of problem formation and problem resolution by the family therapy pioneers was too extreme. In the 1990s and throughout the first decade of the 21st century, these challenges continue to be addressed by the profession.

The postmodernists and constructivists presented the notion that multiple versions of reality can be constructed based on the experiences of the individual. They believed that the old ways of doing family therapy were too directive, giving *privilege*, or emphasis, to the therapists' version of the cause of the problems and the best ways to bring about change. The postmodernists believed that therapy should be a process of coconstructing, with the clients, an understanding of the causes of the problems and the best ways to bring about change. This is a more collaborative process than the approaches used by most of the early pioneers, as will be demonstrated in the sections of this book that present these specific family therapy theories.

In the 1970s, family therapy began the process of becoming an acknowledged mental health profession. The American Association for Marriage and Family Therapy (AAMFT), the internationally recognized professional association for practitioners interested in family therapy, experienced tremendous growth, prompted by the widespread interest in family therapy by mental health professionals across the nation. The *Journal of Marriage and Family Therapy* became the primary vehicle for communicating theory, research, and practice for the profession. Several governmental agencies established formal relationships with AAMFT and recognized family therapy as a profession. Family therapy training programs, specializing in family systems interventions, were developed to prepare both masters and doctoral level professionals. The Commission on Accreditation for Marriage and Family Therapy Education (COAMFTE), a national accrediting body, was developed to ensure the quality of the increasing number of family therapist training programs. All of these important developments were essential in the emergence of family therapy as a profession alongside psychology, counseling, and social work.

Family Therapy: Setting the Stage

Prior to the early1950s, most psychological theories were based upon the psychodynamic idea that psychological problems were *intrapsychic,* that is, problems are caused by an individual's internal dynamics and exist *within* the individual's mind. About this time, maverick psychiatrists and psychologists began exploring the notion that psychological problems could have their origins in dysfunctional interactions between persons rather than by internal psychological dynamics or by some individual character flaw or other personality defect. To better understand the conditions that led these pioneers in family therapy to develop new theories of problem formation and problem resolution based on dysfunctional interaction patterns, an understanding of the history of the family therapy movement is necessary.

Sigmund Freud is the acknowledged father of psychotherapy. All therapies have their origins in psychoanalytic theory. Although his therapy was predominantly with individual patients, Freud was one of the first to recognize the importance of the family in the development of sound psychological health. He believed that successful passage through a series of developmental stages between birth and late adolescence was necessary for development of a sound personality.

According to Freud, difficulties could arise at any of the stages to create psychological problems in the individual. He believed that resolution of the Oedipal and Electra stages of development are especially critical to sound development, because it is here that healthy relationships with parents and persons of the opposite sex are established. In the widely quoted case of Little Hans, Freud (1909) actually treated a father in order to help his son overcome his fear of horses. This case is one of the earliest examples in the psychology literature of a family intervention.

Alfred Adler was one of Freud's colleagues and followers. He broke from Freud, however, by emphasizing the importance of the individual's *perception* of early life events rather than the *actual* events themselves as critical in the development of mental health problems. Adler's theory set the stage for the interpersonal, humanistic, postmodern, constructivist, and narrative approaches to family therapy that have emerged in recent years. Adler believed that individuals make early decisions about themselves based on these perceptions and that awareness of these choices allows individuals to make new and more effective life decisions.

Adler, like Freud, emphasized the importance of family interactions in the formation of personality and developed a theory based on the effects of birth order on behavior. He is also recognized as the founder of the first child guidance clinic. The child guidance movement and its impact on the development of family therapy will be described in more detail later in this chapter. Adler emphasized the social nature of humans and believed that all have a basic drive to be socially productive. Further, he viewed all behavior as purposeful—an idea that many family therapists have adopted. Adler's belief that an individual's perception of events is more important than the actual events themselves is an idea adopted most recently by narrative family therapists as well as social constructivists (Corey, 2009; Gladding, 2011; Nichols, 2009).

Contributions of the Group Therapy Movement

The group therapy movement had a profound effect on the evolution of the family therapy profession. Groups were designed to create a more accurate social reality where clients would play out their behaviors in reaction to other members, much like a family. Many of the interactional dynamics present in a small group were also present in the group members' families. After all, a family is a type of group with certain significant characteristics, such as history and blood relationships that differentiate it from a therapy group.

As early as 1920, social psychologists studied the behavior of members in small groups. These researchers discovered that effective working groups attempted to create structure, interpersonal boundaries, and rules that allowed for individual growth, autonomy, and differentiation to occur. They also found that successful groups were perceived as supportive and significant in the minds of its members.

Kurt Lewin, (1951) in his work with small groups, developed the concept of "field theory." His observation of group behavior led to the concept of the group being more than the sum of its parts. By this he meant that individual members of groups could behave in certain ways and express distinct points of view but that a unique dynamic, something distinctly different than the combination of the individuals' behaviors, was taking place in the group. While group members might express the desire to make personal changes, a dynamic often occurred in the group that made these changes difficult or impossible. This inability to change was often the result of group members recreating family dynamics in the group and thus being stuck or frozen in old behavior patterns. To get the group unstuck, Lewin believed that something had to occur to disrupt the pattern of resistance in the group, allowing group members to recognize and accept their roles in the group. Once the role shift occurs, change becomes possible. Families, like groups, are stuck in repetitive patterns of behavior. Effective family therapy needs to employ interventions to help the family get unstuck and become open to change.

Group therapists also identified the role behavior of members in groups. Once a role was assumed (often unconsciously) by a group member, it was often difficult to change that role. For example, group members might take the role of leader, challenger, withdrawn one, clown, analytic one, and assistant therapist. Family members also take on persistent roles in their relationships to one another. Pioneering family therapist Virginia Satir (1988) identified the family roles of the distracter, the super-reasonable one, the placator, and the blamer. As family and group members came to understand and accept their roles in the system, they were more able to make changes in their behaviors.

Furthermore, group therapists emphasized the importance of identifying process and content in group dynamics. That is, the therapist needs to be able to follow the interactional patterns that occur in the group and determine the result or content produced by the interactional process. Early group researchers discovered that there were often differences between what members said they wanted from the group and what their behaviors demonstrated they wanted. Thus, communication was identified as a critical component of group process. Recognizing and responding to communication inconsistencies is also a critical skill for family therapists.

Despite the distinct similarities between group therapy and family therapy, there are also significant differences, as shown in Figure 3.1. Nichols (2009) considered the differences so significant that he believed the group therapy model has limited applicability for family treatment. For example, families have a long history together while groups are usually brief and time limited. Families have a future together and groups do not. Because of families' history and future together, the atmosphere of trust and acceptance created in groups is often impossible to create in family therapy. The honest disclosure that occurs in groups may not occur in families because the family will be going home together after the session and will be responding to the events that take place in the session. Group therapy offers its members a respite from the stress of everyday life while, in family therapy, the family's stress is brought in to the sessions. Moreover, in group therapy an egalitarian system is created in which all members are equal. In family therapy, the family's hierarchical structure is brought to the session. Each family member has a differing ability to access power and control. Furthermore, in family therapy, one member is usually identified as the "problem." This is not true in groups, where all members have problems and are working on resolving their personal issues.

Contributions of Marriage Counseling, the Child Guidance Movement, and Social Work

In the 1930s and 1940s, marriage counseling emerged on the mental health scene, Child Guidance Centers were established in major cities throughout the United States, and the social work movement was active in providing support to families. Each of these developments was significant in the emergence of the family therapy profession.

- Families have a history together—groups do not
- Families have a future together—groups do not
- Disclosure is often limited in family therapy—groups can afford to be more open
- Families, a permanent social system, bring their anxiety to the therapy session—groups, a temporary social system, provide a time to get away from the anxieties of daily living
- Power among members is not equal in family therapy—groups are more egalitarian, even though groups over time may develop a working hierarchy
- One member of the family is the patient—group members are all patients

Figure 3.1   Differences between Group and Family Therapy

Marriage Counseling

Psychoanalysts have always treated individual patients with marital problems; however, the treatment focused on the psychodynamics and neuroses of the individual patient, not the relationship problems. Rarely were the spouses treated together in a single session. Classic Freudian analysts believed the important transference relationship between the therapist and patient would be contaminated by a third person in treatment. Analysts believed that when the individual issues were resolved, the patient would make the necessary adjustments to the marriage.

During the 1930s, the first centers for the treatment of marriage difficulties were established in Los Angeles, New York, and Philadelphia. Early marriage counselors began a significant shift in treatment goals by directing their treatment to what was wrong in the marriage rather than what was wrong with the individual. Pioneers in the marriage counseling movement were Paul Popenoe, Abraham and Hannah Stone, and Emily Mudd (Broderick & Schraeder, 1991).

At about the same time, and perhaps as a result of the marriage counseling movement, a few psychoanalysts began to experiment with marital counseling. These analysts would treat the couple in sessions together, known as *conjoint therapy,* or treat both spouses separately during the same time frame, know as *concurrent therapy.* Clarence Oberdorff (1938) hypothesized that married couples created neurotic interactions in their marriages and that these neuroses could best be treated by working with the couple together.

In the 1940s, analyst Bela Mittleman (1948, 1956) further hypothesized that individual neuroses would often flourish in the marital relationship, creating irrational dynamics. He believed that treating both spouses conjointly provided important clues in helping complete the analysis successfully. He also posited that actual behaviors exhibited in marriages based on object relations were just as important as intrapsychic dynamics. Also during the 1940s, communications researchers Jay Haley and Don Jackson wrote about communication patterns in marriages. They found that communication difficulties were almost always present in problematic marriages (Nichols, 2009).

Child Guidance Movement

The child guidance movement also helped form the foundation for family therapy. Adler started the first Child Guidance Center in Vienna in the early 20th century (Corey, 2009). In the 1930s, a number of centers were established in major American cities. The child guidance model was an early precursor to family therapy. It did not take long for therapists to recognize that problems experienced by the children treated at the centers were intimately connected to the home environment and parental behaviors. Thus, families were encouraged to participate in treatment. Treatment was generally provided to the child by a psychiatrist, and family members were seen by a collaborating social worker. In the 1940s, those in the child guidance movement began to theorize that the problems experienced by children were caused by overprotective mothers and fathers who were too impotent to correct this situation. The tendency to blame parents for their children's problems continues to be a misapplication of family systems theory today. Eventually, the child guidance movement began to consider all members of the family as interconnected pieces in a repetitive pattern of behaviors. Psychopathology did not reside in the patient, and psychopathology was not the result of poor parenting but a result of the interaction between and among family members (Nichols, 2009).

In the late 1930s, psychiatrist Nathan Ackerman, considered by many as the first family therapist, advocated conceptualizing the entire family as the *unit of treatment* when there was a problem with *any* of the members of the family. He believed that to appropriately diagnose the problem in an individual family member, it was necessary to meet and evaluate the entire family. Based on this theory, he began treating families in his psychoanalytic practice.

The Social Work Influence

The social work movement also played a major role in the development of the family therapy profession. Social workers have traditionally focused their efforts on supporting families within the greater context of society. Thus, social workers have always recognized the impact of the social environment on individual families. It was only natural that social workers would narrow their lens and recognize the impact of the family social unit on the behaviors of individual family members. As the family therapy movement gathered momentum in the 1950s and 1960s, social workers, including Virginia Satir, Monica McGoldrick, and others, provided leadership and made significant contributions to the profession (Nichols 2009).

Professional Associations

Another major milestone in the development of the profession of family therapy was the establishment of the American Association of Marriage Counselors (AAMC) in 1945. This organization has evolved into the American Association for Marriage and Family Therapy (AAMFT), the most widely recognized and established professional organization for marriage and family therapists. AAMFT advocates nationally in legislatures in support of the interests of marriage and family therapists. Moreover, AAMFT has established credentialing criteria for family therapists; publishes an excellent journal, the *Journal of Marital and Family Therapy;* and annually sponsors the largest professional conference for marriage and family therapists.

Family Therapy: An Emerging Profession

In the 1950s, family therapy began to gain recognition and created controversy as it challenged traditional models of individual and group treatment. John Elderkin Bell, one of the few psychologists involved in the early years of family therapy, began treating families using a model based on the stages of group therapy. He believed that family change, like group change, occurred as a developmental progression through predictable stages. He called his approach family group therapy. Bell and Ackerman are contenders for the title of first family therapists. Bestowing such a title is difficult, because several individuals were adopting a family systems perspective during this period (Broderick & Schraeder, 1991).

Nathan Ackerman

Nathan Ackerman, a psychiatrist, was a key figure in the child guidance movement in the 1930s. Because of his work with children and their parents, he came to recognize the significance of the family unit as a context for developing and maintaining the psychological problems of an individual family member. He came to believe that the family was the basic unit for psychological treatment. Ackerman, along with Don Jackson, founded the first family therapy journal, *Family Process,* in 1957. This journal is still one of the most respected family therapy publications.

One of the most significant breakthroughs in the development of the field of marriage and family therapy resulted from the work of therapists in the early 1950s who studied schizophrenia. These researchers began to recognize that patients' symptoms improved when they were hospitalized but deteriorated when they were in direct contact with significant family members (Bodin, 1981).

Gregory Bateson

Gregory Bateson and his colleagues at the Mental Research Institute in Palo Alto, California, were awarded a federal grant to investigate the role of communication in schizophrenia. Their discovery that a patient's psychological symptoms might worsen when in contact with a significant family member encouraged these researchers to more carefully examine the communication patterns between schizophrenic patients and members of their families. From this research emerged the *double-bind hypothesis* of dysfunctional communication (Bateson, Jackson, Haley, & Weakland, 1956, 1971). According to this hypothesis, parents send confusing and contradictory messages to the schizophrenic patient. No matter how the patient responds to the message, the patient's answer or response is inevitably incorrect, inappropriate, and unacceptable. Thus, the patient is in a "no win" situation because no rational response is acceptable. For example, a parent, frequently the mother in this research project, might say to her child, "You never tell me you love me." Then the child responds and tells the mother that she is loved. The double-binding parent responds, "You only tell me that because I made you— you don't really love me at all." Thus, the child is in an untenable situation and in a captive environment, one that offers no escape. Thus, the child escapes from this painful reality through a retreat into mental illness (Bodin, 1981).

It was believed that schizophrenic patients retreat into psychoses to avoid dealing with the repeated and inescapable double-bind messages and the untenable position in which these messages place them. The mother of the schizophrenic patient was often detected as the person communicating the double-bind messages. Frieda Fromm-Reich, a psychiatrist, coined the term *schizophrenogenic mother,* indicating that the mother's double-binding communication caused the patient's symptoms. During the first decade of the family therapy movement, Fromm-Reich's classification was frequently misapplied. Its use undermined the family therapy axiom that *all* family members are part of an interconnected system and each plays a role in, and contributes to, conditions within the family system that support and maintain symptoms of an individual family member. It is important to remember that an individual's symptoms are not *caused* by a mother or any other family member, but are in response to the pattern of behavior maintained by the family system comprised of the actions and interactions of all family members (Bodin, 1981).

Accordingly, fathers of schizophrenic offspring also play a role in the family's communication family pattern. While mothers were often observed as overinvolved with the schizophrenic patient, fathers were observed as disconnected from and uninvolved with other family members and unable or unwilling to confront the interactional behaviors of mother and child. The main reason mothers were most frequently detected in double-bind relationships with the schizophrenic offspring was that the mothers had more intense and frequent contact with the patient than the withdrawn and uninvolved fathers did. Thus, the mothers' opportunities for engaging in dysfunctional interactions with the schizophrenic child were much greater than the father's. The key finding was that one parent would create the double-bind and the other would *collaborate* by withdrawing and not identifying and confronting the spouse's and the offspring's dysfunctional behaviors. Ultimately, no family member is able to step back and recognize the entire systemic interactional pattern and make changes to it. Therefore the pattern continues (Fenell & Weinhold, 2003).

The double-bind research conducted by Gregory Bateson, Don Jackson, Jay Haley, and John Weakland (1956, 1971) had a tremendous impact on the mental health field. Therapists began to realize that the dysfunctional communication patterns in schizophrenic families also exist in less intense forms in most other families. The member of the family who exhibited symptoms was recognized in the family therapy literature as the identified patient (IP) and symptom bearer of a dysfunctional family unit. As a result of this research, implications of the double-bind communication theory extended well beyond families with a schizophrenic member.

The researchers believed that dysfunctional communication patterns are at the root of many family problems and that family therapy could focus on identifying and correcting the inauthentic and incongruent communication patterns between and among all family members rather than focusing solely on the behaviors exhibited by the IP. When the problems in communication between family members were corrected, the symptoms of the IP were frequently found to diminish or disappear. Writing about the numerous significant contributions of the Mental Research Institute to family therapy, Bodin (1981) stated that the double-bind theory "stands as perhaps the most definitive landmark in the revolutionary shift from an individual to systems focus in concepts of psychopathogenesis" (p. 281).

Virginia Satir

Virginia Satir (1983, 1988) was another pioneer in the family therapy field. Satir worked with Bateson and his family communications research group at the Mental Research Institute (MRI) in Palo Alto. After several years of research with the Bateson group, Satir left the because of her disagreements with the impersonal approach advocated by the MRI therapists. She developed her own unique style of family therapy, combining both humanistic and systemic characteristics. The contrast between Satir's approach and that of the MRI will be highlighted in subsequent chapters describing family therapy theories

Two of the earliest family therapy publications were *The Psychodynamics of Family Life* by Nathan Ackerman (1958) and John Bell's 1961 monograph, *Family Group Therapy*. These books began to popularize family therapy and systems theory, and they prompted discussions of systems theory in mental health treatment centers, colleges, and universities (Broderick & Schraeder, 1991).

Lyman Wynn

Another early contributor to the family therapy movement was Lyman Wynne (1923–2000), whose early research focused on dysfunctional communication within families with schizophrenic members. Wynne coined the term *pseudomutuality* to describe families that appear to be open, caring, and clear in their relationships and communication patterns when this is really not the case. Pseudomutual families develop elaborate patterns of relating that often are superficial and disguise underlying relationship problems. Offspring from pseudomutual families often grow up doubting themselves and their perceptions of reality (Wynne, Ryckoff, Day, & Hirsch, 1958). Wynne's later work includes an extensive overview of family therapy research (Wynne, 1988) and expands the definition and functions of family therapists to "family consultants" and "systems consultants." Consultants would focus more on assessing system dynamics and strengths attending to the agenda of the client (Wynne, McDaniel, & Weber, 1987).

Murray Bowen

Another psychiatrist and first-generation family therapist, Murray Bowen (1913–1990) also conducted research with schizophrenic families in the 1950s. Under Bowen's care, the mothers and fathers of patients lived in the hospital with the patient to facilitate family treatment (Bowen, 1960, 1961, 1976, 1978).

Carl Whitaker

Carl Whitaker (1912–1995), also a psychiatrist, began experimenting with treatments that included spouses and, eventually, children in therapy as early as 1944 (Whitaker, 1976; Whitaker & Keith, 1981). Both Bowen and Whitaker developed family therapy theories that will be reviewed in later chapters.

Salvador Minuchin

Salvador Minuchin also had a tremendous impact on the family therapy field. He developed structural family therapy theory. Beginning family therapists often adopt this model as they are becoming comfortable with treating families because it is simple, straightforward, and quite powerful in facilitating family change (Fenell & Weinhold, 2003).

Emerging from the structural model was strategic family therapy. Several variations of strategic therapy took hold under the direction of well-known leaders in the profession, including Jay Haley (1923-2007), the Palo Alto group, the Milan group, and others. These therapies introduced techniques that, while powerful, were considered by some counselors as too directive and not respectful of the client family's thoughts and feelings. This issue was not fully addressed until the feminist critique of the family therapy movement began (Nichols, 2009).

Family Therapy: The Postmodern Era

The well-established schools of family therapy briefly described above had their heyday in the 1960s through the 1980s. However, in the 1980s, the winds of change were blowing in the family therapy community. Just as pioneering leaders of the family therapy movement challenged the orthodoxy of psychoanalytic therapy, now young family therapists were challenging the orthodoxy of the established schools of family therapy. The cybernetic model adopted by the pioneering "first generation" family therapists understood the family as a single cohesive system of individuals engaged in patterns of predictable interactions. The job of the therapist was to intervene in the system until it developed new and less disturbing patterns of behaving and communicating. The critics found these approaches to be too mechanistic and too reliant on the power of the therapist. They further argued that these theories were too directive and did not sufficiently include the family members in the therapeutic decision-making process. The family therapy theories of Salvador Minuchin, Murray Bowen, Virginia Satir, James Framo, and others were now under attack (Kuehl, 2008).

The founders of the family therapy profession had developed competing theories and had popularized these theories through their writings, conference presentations, and live demonstrations of family therapy with actual clients. They were able to demonstrate the ability of the approaches to bring about therapeutic change. These theories were developed from a positivist and modernist perspective using the *scientific method*, which states that reality can be known and that families behave based on a set of basic laws that, when known, can be applied to bring about healthy change for the families. This model regarded the family therapist as the expert in leading the family through the change process and to better and less problematic relationships.

The *postmodern* and *constructivist* critique of family therapy and many of the nation's other widely accepted institutions emerged at the forefront of much of American society in the late 1980s. The postmodernists believed that knowledge was not fixed but was created based on a person's experiences and was culturally and contextually dependent. Thus, the "truth" of the laws of cybernetics that undergirded systems theory was called in to question. Family therapy theories were deconstructed. That means the theories were taken apart piece by piece and the assumptions that supported each piece of the theories were highlighted. The deconstruction of the traditional family therapy theories demonstrated that these theories were based upon certain assumptions about family behavior that perpetuated stereotypes of male and female behavior, social class, sexual orientation, spirituality, and religion, among others. The critics believed that the stereotypical assumptions made about families could lead to certain outcomes in treatment that may not be in the best interests of client families.

Feminist Critique

The attacks came first from the women's movement. The feminist critique of family therapy, coupled with the postmodern and constructivist family therapy movements, began to challenge the approaches of many of the most established family therapy theories. The feminist critique indicts the original theories of family therapy as serving to keep women in stereotypical roles. For example, early studies of family dynamics pinpointed the overinvolved mother in a pivotal role in the genesis of dysfunctional communications with children, the distancing of the husband from the family, and subsequent problem development in the family. The innovation of the systemic view of problem formation was the emphasis on all members' equal involvement in the family's problems. The feminists argued that the problem was not in how each family member performed his or her role but inherent within the roles and their relations to one another. They maintained that women's behavior was the product of millenia of unexamined tradition. They further emphasized that the culturally and socially expected behaviors reinforced by therapeutic interventions served to isolate women, keep them dependent on men, and maintain their role as the primary caregiver of children in the family.

The feminist critics insisted that these conditions needed to be addressed in therapy and that simply helping the mother and wife become less involved with the children and the husband and father more involved in family functioning was not sufficient. Feminists advocated for theories of therapy that advanced women's issues and women's privilege, ensuring a more egalitarian approach to the family change process (Nichols, 2009). The feminist critique was successful in changing views about gender in the family and was embraced by many family therapists. The critique was expanded to consider diversity in a broader context within the field as family therapy challenged itself examine assumptions about multiculturalism, race, sexual orientation, spirituality, and religion.

Constructivist and Postmodern Critique

The constructivist and postmodern critique of traditional family therapy approaches deconstructed family therapy theories by examining their component elements. This critique expanded on the feminist critique: It stated that many of the family therapy theories in vogue were not respectful of the family members' realities and attempted to impose solutions rather than engage the families in a process of finding their own solutions (Anderson & Gehart, 2007; Anderson & Goolishian, 1992). Moreover, some of the frequently used family therapy techniques such as paradox—often known as reverse psychology—and symptom prescription were viewed as manipulative, ungenuine, and serving to create distance in the important relationship between therapist and family (Duncan, 2010).

Because of these critiques, traditional family therapy interventions became less directive and more collaborative, and they engaged family members in discovering their own solutions to their problems. Moreover, new approaches to family change were introduced. Narrative therapy (White & Epston, 1990) and social constructivist approaches emerged during this time period, along with internal family systems theory (Schwartz, 2001) and emotionally focused couple's therapy (Greenburg & Johnson, 1988). Relationship-based, individually-oriented approaches to treatment, such as Carl Rogers' (1961) person-centered therapy, were often dismissed by the pioneers of the family therapy movement. However, the second wave of collaborative family therapy theories began to give Rogers and other relationship therapists the credit they so richly deserved. The relationship theories and the skills associated with these theories were especially effective in establishing collaborative working relationships with all family members. A body of research demonstrated that establishing collaborative relationships with clients predicts the potential for positive outcome in treatment (Duncan, 2010). Professional counselors and other mental health professionals who are trained extensively in the use of relationship skills have a tremendous advantage when moving to a family therapy approach. Through the effective use of these relationship skills, coupled with effective use of family systems theory and techniques, therapists can maximize the assistance they provide to the families they serve.

The postmodern critique has challenged the traditional models of family therapy and prompted the development of new approaches. The reader should remember that the traditional approaches are still widely employed in family treatment; however, they are typically applied in a more collaborative and family centered manner.

Summary

The family therapy movement has evolved through early challenges to the individual model of psychotherapy, coupled with the emergence of the child guidance movement, the group therapy movement, and the marriage counseling movement, which set the stage for a new systems-based model that recognized that individual psychological problems occur in relationship to other family members. Moreover, the problems of individual family members are often maintained and supported by the family's behavior patterns. Several pioneers who provided leadership in the evolution of the family therapy profession have been briefly introduced. Finally, the feminist and postmodern critiques of the family therapy movement challenged traditional models of the family therapy movement, resulting in the development of several new and more collaborative models of family intervention.

The next chapter describes how the profession of family therapy has organized itself to train, license, and support the profession and members of the profession.

Suggested Readings

Anderson, H., & Geheart, D. (2007). *Collaborative therapy: Relationships and conversations that make a difference.* New York: Brunner/Routledge.

Broderick, C. B., & Schraeder, S. S. (1991). The history of the profession of marriage and family therapy. In A. S. Gurman & D. P. Kniskern (Eds.), *Handbook of Family Therapy* (Vol. II, pp. 3–40). New York: Brunner/ Mazel.

Duncan, B. L. (2010). *On becoming a better therapist.* Washington, DC: American Psychological Association.

Kuehl, B. (2008, September/October). Legacy of the family therapy pioneers. *Family Therapy Magazine, 7*(5), 12–49.

Current Issues, Ethics, and Trends in Marriage, Couple, and Family Therapy

This chapter introduces the reader to the issues, ethics, trends, and challenges that face the family therapy profession today. I will identify the obstacles facing family therapy in maintaining and solidifying its position as a distinct mental health profession along with professional counseling, psychiatry, psychology, and social work. Then I will describe the status of family therapy in relation to other mental health professions, types of accredited training programs available to students who want to become family therapists, ways of becoming a family therapist, and licensure.

Next, two important and competing schools of thought concerning the best way to provide family therapy to our clients will be presented: the *evidence-based practice* model and the *common factors* approach to clinical treatment. These two schools of thought have stimulated a lively debate in the family therapy profession. I will then describe the key features of this book and how it can assist counselors in developing the abilities to provide effective marriage and family therapy to our client families. Finally, I will present legal, ethical, and training issues in family therapy.

Key Concepts

- ○ Characteristics of a mental health profession
- ○ Accreditation of marriage and family therapist preparation programs
- ○ Evidence-supported therapies
- ○ Common factors approach to MCFT treatment
- ○ Ethical and legal issues unique to family therapy

Questions for Discussion

1. How do you distinguish between a mental health profession and specialty area?
2. Do you believe that marriage, couple, and family therapy is a distinct profession or a specialty area existing within another mental health profession?
3. Fenell and Hovestadt (1986) described four distinct options for providing MCFT education. Which option is most like your training program? Which option seems the most beneficial to you?
4. Which of the characteristics of a mental health profession seem most important to you? Why are these characteristics the most important?
5. What are the differences between accreditation of marriage and family training programs by the Commission on Accreditation of Marriage and Family Therapy Education (COAMFTE) and the Council for Accreditation of Counseling and Related Educational Professions (CACREP)?
6. How do you plan to implement confidentiality in your family therapy practice?
7. Go to the library and review recent editions of *Journal of Marital and Family Therapy*, the *Family Journal*, and the *Family Psychologist*. How are these publications similar and distinct?

Family systems therapy was developed by clinicians from the established professions of psychiatry, social work, communication, anthropology, and psychology, emerging in the 1950s as a new and controversial paradigm for treating human problems. The systems approach to providing therapy to couples and families was at first not well received by the dominant mental health professions of the era, psychiatry, psychology, and social work. Psychiatry was focused on treatment using a psychoanalytic model. Clinical social workers provided support to the psychiatrists in the treatment of their hospitalized patients. Psychology was focused on clinical assessment and behavior therapy. At that point in time, none of the recognized professions acknowledged family systems therapy as a valid form of treatment.

Characteristics of the Family Therapy Profession

The lack of acceptance of family therapy, in the early years, caused the originators of the family therapy movement to develop their clinical approaches and interventions in isolation. Even so, these mavericks discovered each other through their publications and conference presentations. They recognized that their treatment models were similar in that they viewed the family as the focus of treatment rather than the intrapsychic conflicts of the individual patient. These family therapy pioneers formed loose associations and many became members of the American Association for Marriage Counselors (AAMC), which has evolved in to the American Association for Marriage and Family Therapy (AAMFT), the largest and most influential professional association for couple and family therapists today.

All this is a preamble to the fact that family therapy did not have a professional home. The established professions of psychiatry, counseling, social work, and psychology did not recognize family therapy and the systems approach as effective or appropriate for treating individual neurosis and learned behavioral problems. Thus, in the early years, family systems therapists were not well represented within the mental health professions.

Initially, only a few therapists were curious about family therapy. These professionals often elected to become members of the AAMC, a group of diverse sociologists, clergy, and psychologists who focused their work on helping families through the treatment of marital problems. Later family therapists allied with the marriage counselors, leading to the renaming of the AAMC as the American Association for Marriage and Family Counselors (AAMFC) in 1970. The association was renamed once again as the American Association for Marriage and Family Therapists (AAMFT) in 1978 (Broderick & Schrader, 1991).

Interest in family systems therapy exploded during the 1960s, and aspiring family therapists sought university-based training opportunities. In response, a few departments of child development and family studies in universities across the nation instituted programs to train family therapists at the masters degree level. These programs were highly successful, and other universities responded by establishing family therapy training programs of their own. Later, doctoral programs in marriage and family therapy were established at a few universities. These doctoral-level academic training programs gave family therapy the credibility it needed to make the claim that it was a distinct approach to the human change process and a profession in its own right, clearly distinguished from psychology, social work, professional counseling, and psychiatry. Of course, this claim was rejected by most of the aforementioned professions, who countered that marriage and family therapy was only a subspecialty of psychiatry, psychology, professional counseling, and social work. Even though marriage, couple, and family therapy is a licensed profession in all 50 states, tension between the profession of family therapy and the other mental health professions continues today (AAMFT, 2007).

The AAMFT was instrumental in organizing the support of concerned politicians, marriage and family therapists working in private practice, government agency leaders, and the university training programs in a systematic effort to establish the profession. The following criteria distinguish marriage and family therapy as a discrete and independent mental health profession.

The profession of marriage and family therapy had to demonstrate that it was a clearly defined occupation that provides an essential service to society. This was accomplished by providing information about MCFT services and the unique training required to become a family therapist to both public and professional audiences.

- *Service to society.* The profession clearly articulated to the public its function in service to society for the treatment of problems experienced in families, marriages, and other close relationships.
- *Unique body of knowledge, theories, and practices.* The profession and members of the profession had to demonstrate that a *body of knowledge* differentiated MCFT from other professions, that a set of theories and practices distinguished MCFT from other mental health professions, and that this body of knowledge and set of theories and practices are not possessed by the nonprofessional or by other mental health disciplines. The creation of professional journals specific to family therapy was crucial is meeting this criteria.
- *Code of ethical conduct.* Ethical codes developed by the AAMFT and the International Association of Marriage and Family Therapists (IAMFC) guide the practice of MCFT professionals. Ethical conduct as a family therapist is discussed later in this chapter.
- *Autonomous decision making.* Members of the profession are involved in independent decision making in the service of their clients.
- *Professional associations.* The family therapy profession has three major professional associations: AAMFT, IAMFC, and the Society for Family Psychology (SFP). AAMFT is the largest of the three organizations and is the only one that recognizes MCFT as a stand-alone profession. IAMFC views MCFT as part of the broader counseling profession, and SFP recognizes MCFT as part of the profession of psychology. These competing views of family therapy have created tensions in among the three organizations and delayed the licensure of family therapists in several states (AAMFT, 2007).
- *Professional research and publication.* Treatment of clients using family systems interventions is supported by a body of published research that supports the efficacy of family therapy theories and techniques in the service of the public. The *Journal of Marital and Family Therapy* is the research and practice publication of AAMFT. The *Family Journal* is the publication of IAMFC, and the *Family Psychologist* is the publication of the SFP.
- *Performance standards and training programs.* The family therapy profession has developed agreed-upon performance standards for

admission to the profession and for continuance within it. AAMFT developed rigorous *clinical membership* requirements that were incorporated into most academic preparation programs. Moreover, preparation for and induction into the family therapy profession is provided through a protracted preparation, usually in a professional school on a college or university campus. The profession developed rigorous academic therapist training programs and supervised clinical practice requirements that must be met in order to become certified as a clinical member of AAMFT and licensed as an MCFT in one of the 50 states. Clinical member standards were important before licensure became ubiquitous in the United States. However, clinical membership standards have now been superseded by state licensure laws because licensure laws for marriage and family therapists have now been ratified in all 50 states.

- *Doctoral programs.* The family therapy profession has more than 20 accredited doctoral programs that prepare MCFT researchers, advanced supervisors, and practitioners for the profession.
- *Recognized professional journals.* Numerous professional journals, including those mentioned above, disseminate information about MCFT research and practice and are provided to academic libraries throughout the world.
- *Public trust and confidence.* The profession's demonstrated capacity to provide service markedly beyond that which would otherwise be available has established a high level of public trust and confidence in the profession as a whole and in the quality of individual practitioners. The Commission on Accreditation for Marriage and Family Therapy Education (COAMFTE) is a nationally recognized accrediting body that ascertains the quality of family therapy preparation programs throughout the United States and Canada. The Council for Accreditation of Counseling and Related Programs (CACREP) also accredits couple and family training programs within counselor education programs (AAMFT, 2007).

All mental health professions should be able to demonstrate these qualities. The mental health professions have significant overlap in terms or their role in society and their role with clients. Members of psychology, social work, professional counseling, and psychiatry treat couples and families, in addition to individuals and groups. This overlap has created conflicts between professionals who view family therapy as a stand-alone profession and other mental health professionals who view family treatment as only one part of their mission. With MCFT licensure in all 50 states, numerous accredited masters and doctoral degree programs in the United States and Canada, and the growing body of research and the recognition of the effectiveness of MCFT treatment by the general public, a strong case can be made for family therapy being an independent profession along with psychology, social work, professional counseling, and psychiatry. This recognition paves the way for the next step in the maturation of MCFT, universal recognition by third-party payers, including commercial insurance providers and government insurance programs such as the Department of Veterans Affairs (VA), TRICARE, and Medicare (AAMFT, 2007; Barstow, 2010).

Preparation of Family Therapists

Marriage, couple, and family therapists are prepared in a variety of different ways. The most common sources of preparation are family therapy training programs housed in colleges and universities throughout the United States and Canada. Many of these academic training programs are accredited by COAMFTE, the accrediting arm of professional marriage and family therapy, or by CACREP, the accrediting arm of professional counseling. Graduates of COAMFTE accredited programs most often seek state licensure as marriage and family therapists (LMFT). Graduates of CACREP accredited marriage and family therapy training programs generally seek licensure as professional counselors (LPC), although some graduates may have the necessary coursework and clinical experience to seek dual licensure as an LPC and LMFT. A listing of the accredited university-based marriage and family therapy academic programs is provided in Table 4.1. Doctoral preparation as a marriage, couple, and family therapist takes place in 22 COAMFTE accredited training programs. Approximately 100 colleges and universities in the United States and Canada offer masters degree preparation as a family therapist in COAMFTE or CACREP accredited training programs (www.aamft.org; www.cacrep.org).

Postgraduate degree training programs have been established in several major cities in North America. These free-standing institutes were created as family therapy clinics to provide marriage, couple, and family therapy services to the public. In addition to providing family therapy

Table 4.1   Accredited University-Based MCFT Academic Programs

Program	Masters	Doctoral	COAMFTE	CACREP
Auburn University–AL	X		X	
California State–Fresno	X			X
California State–Northridge	X			X
California State Sacramento	X			X
Loma Linda University–CA	X	X	X	
Hope International University–CA	X		X	
Alliant International University–CA	X	X	X	
San Diego State University–CA	X		X	
San Francisco State University–CA	X			X
Bethel Seminary–CA	X		X	
University of San Diego–CA	X		X	
Chapman University–CA	X			X
Colorado State University	X		X	
University of Colorado–Denver	X			X
University of Northern Colorado	X			X
University of Connecticut	X	X	X	
Southern Connecticut State U.	X		X	
St. Joseph's College–CT	X		X	
Central Connecticut State U.	X		X	
Fairfield University–CT	X		X	
Barry University–Miami Shores–FL	X			X
Florida State University		X	X	
Nova Southeastern University–FL	X	X	X	
Stetson University–FL	X			X
University of Florida	X			X
Mercer University–GA	X		X	
University of Georgia		X	X	
Valdosta State University–GA	X		X	
Idaho State University	X			X
Northwest Nazarene U.–ID	X			X
Northwestern University–IL	X		X	
Governor's State University–IL	X			X
Northeastern Illinois University	X			X
Northern Illinois University	X		X	
Southern Illinois University	X			X
Christian Theological Seminary–IN	X		X	
Indiana Wesleyan University	X			X
Purdue University–Calumet	X		X	
Iowa State University	X	X	X	

Table 4.1   (continued)

Program	Masters	Doctoral	COAMFTE	CACREP
Friend's University	X		X	
Kansas State University	X	X	X	
Louisville Presbyterian Seminary–KY	X		X	
University of Kentucky	X		X	
University of Louisville	X		X	
Western Kentucky University	X			X
Our Lady of Holy Cross–LA	X			X
Southeastern Louisiana University	X			X
University of Louisiana–Monroe	X	X	X	X
University of Maryland	X		X	
Boston University–MA	X		X	
Michigan State University	X	X	X	
Capella University–MN	X			X
University of Minnesota		X	X	
St. Cloud State–MN	X		X	
St. Mary's University of MN	X		X	
Mississippi College	X			X
Reformed Theological Seminary–MS	X		X	
Southern Mississippi University	X		X	
St. Louis University–MO		X	X	
Forrest Institute–MO	X		X	
Montana State University	X			X
University of Nebraska	X		X	
University of Nevada–Las Vegas	X		X	
University of Nevada–Reno	X			X
Antioch U. New England–NH	X	X	X	
University of New Hampshire	X		X	
Seton Hall University–NJ	X		X	
Syracuse University–NY	X	X	X	
University of Rochester–NY	X		X	
Iona College–NY	X		X	
Appalachian State University–NC	X		X	
East Carolina State University	X	X	X	
U. of North Carolina–Greensboro	X			X
North Dakota State University	X		X	
Ohio State University		X	X	
University of Akron–OH	X	X	X	X
Oklahoma State University	X		X	
Lewis and Clark College	X		X	
University of Oregon	X		X	

Table 4.1   (continued)

Program	Masters	Doctoral	COAMFTE	CACREP
Drexel University–PA	X		X	
Duquesne University–PA	X			X
Geneva College–PA	X			X
LaSalle University–PA	X		X	
Seton Hill University–PA	X			X
University of Rhode Island	X		X	
Converse College–SC	X		X	
University of South Carolina	X			X
Abilene Christian University–TX	X		X	
St. Mary's University	X	X	X	
Texas A&M–Corpus Christi	X			X
Texas State University	X			X
Texas Tech University		X	X	
Brigham Young University	X	X	X	
Utah State University	X		X	
College of William & Mary–VA	X			X
Virginia Tech–Blacksburg	X	X	X	
Virginia Tech–Falls Church	X		X	
Antioch University–WA	X		X	
Pacific Lutheran University–WA	X			X
Seattle Pacific University–WA	X		X	
Edgewood College–WI	X		X	
University of Winnipeg–Canada	X		X	
University of Guelph–Canada		X	X	
University of Houston-Clear Lake–TX	X		X	
University of Wisconsin-Stout	X		X	
Geneva College–PA	X			X
University of Montevallo–AL	X			X
University of Central Florida	X			X
University of Illinois Springfield	X			X
Portland State–OR	X			X
Mid-American Nazarene University–KS	X			X

services, free-standing institutes provide COAMFTE accredited MCFT training to individuals who have mental health degrees in fields other than family therapy and who seek to augment those degrees with appropriate coursework and supervised clinical experience in order to become licensed as an LMFT. A list of COAMFTE accredited free-standing training institutes is provided at Table 4.2. A few universities and colleges provide postgraduate as well as graduate training in MCFT. These programs usually incorporate postgraduate students in their family therapist training program with modifications to the plan of study based on the student's recent academic and clinical experiences.

While specific marriage, couple, and family therapy training is provided by accredited programs housed in colleges, universities, and free-standing institutes, MCFT preparation also occurs in other settings. Traditional mental health training programs in professional counseling, psychology, social work, and psychiatry may offer one or more courses in MCFT to their students. These programs are not accredited specifically to provide family therapist preparation; however, the programs are important because mental health professionals trained in all disciplines are likely to be selected by clients seeking assistance with relationship problems. Thus therapists from all professions must be prepared to provide basic services to couples and families in their practices or know how to make appropriate referrals (Fenell & Hovestadt, 1986).

Table 4.2   COAMFTE Accredited Free-Standing Training Institutes

Institute Name	COAMFTE Accreditation
Colorado School for Family Therapy	X
Denver Family Institutes	X
University of Louisville	X
St. Cloud State–MN	X
St. Mary's University of MN	X
Forrest Institute–MO	X
University of Rochester–NY	X
Blanton-Peale Institute–NY	X
Philadelphia Child & Family Training Center–PA	X
Council for Relationships–PA	X
Drexel University–PA	X
WestGate Training & Consult–SC	X
Aurora Family Therapy Training Institute–WI	X
Calgary Health Region	X
Interfaith Institute–Ontario	X
Jewish General Hospital–Montreal	X
Argyle Institute–Quebec	

Family Therapy Training Models

In an effort to understand the various approaches employed by family therapy training programs, Fenell and Hovestadt (1986) proposed a model that described the status of marriage and family therapy training in colleges and universities. We described four different approaches to MCFT training, based on whether the academic program recognized marriage and family therapy as a stand-alone profession, like professional counseling, psychology, or social work; as a specialty that is part of another mental health profession; or as an area of elective study providing one or MCFT two courses within another professional training program. Our model, presented in Figure 4.1, conceptualizes family therapy training as existing on a continuum with family therapy viewed as an independent profession at one extreme and family therapy viewed as simply an area of elective study within another mental health profession at the other end.

In quadrant A of the model, family therapy is shown as a *separate profession*. MCFT is a stand-alone profession that is the equal of other mental health professions like psychology, social work or professional counseling. Quadrant A programs are almost universally accredited by COAMFTE. All COAMFTE accredited doctoral programs would fall within Quadrant A. Moreover, most COAMFTE accredited masters degree programs would fall within quadrant A.

In quadrant B, family therapy is shown as an overlapping independent profession with another mental health profession such as social work, psychology, or counselor education. In such programs, family therapy and the other overlapping profession are recognized as a coequal professions. In this academic situation, family therapy and the other profession typically "share" coursework that is appropriate for both professions, such as courses in basic counseling skills training, assessment, research, and human development. As students advance in their respective overlapping programs, the training for the two coequal professions separates with "MCFT specific" coursework provided to students as required for state licensure. The two distinct professions in dual track programs are frequently accredited by different accrediting agencies. For example, the family therapy masters degree training program within the academic unit may be accredited by COAMFTE while the counselor education or counseling psychology doctorial programs may be accredited by CACREP or the accrediting arm of the American Psychological Association (APA).

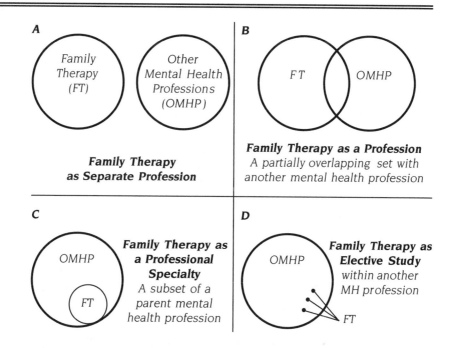

Figure 4.1   Relationship of Family Therapy to Other Mental Health Professions

In quadrant C, family therapy is recognized as a specialty area or a subset of a parent mental health profession (not MCFT). In training programs like this, the academic unit is not accredited by COAMFTE: Coursework and clinical preparation are not sufficient to meet their standards because the emphasis of the training is on the "parent" mental health profession, psychology for example. However, this model does include a planned and sequential series of courses in family therapy training that is an integral part of the academic program. Students who complete the family therapy specialty course sequence usually seek licensure in the parent profession, for example professional counseling, rather than as an MCFT. The level of MCFT training in quadrant C typically does not approach the breadth or depth of training provided in quadrants A and B and usually does not meet requirements for MCFT licensure in most states.

In quadrant D, family therapy is recognized as an area of elective study within a mental health profession such as professional counseling, psychology, or social work. Students in programs based on the model depicted in quadrant D may learn about and become familiar with family therapy through *course modules of instruction* in courses like counseling theories. Or students may take a course or two in family therapy designed to broaden training in the parent profession of professional counseling, psychology, or social work. Some masters degree students with quadrant C or D preparation will seek advanced training in MCFT at free-standing institutes or seek doctoral preparation specifically in family therapy (Fenell & Hovestadt, 1986).

Each of the training models described has implications for the professionalization of marriage, couple, and family therapy. To the extent that family thrapy is recognized as a distinct mental health profession like psychology, social work, and professional counseling, it becomes increasingly likely that family therapy will gain recognition by third-party payers including health insurance companies, government sponsored insurers such as the VA, TRICARE, and Medicare, and will be recognized with legitimate job descriptions within the federal government including the Department of Defense and the Veteran's Affairs system. To the extent that family therapy is not recognized as a coequal profession, these important accomplishments are more difficult to achieve. Moreover, students who seek academic and clinical training as family therapists would be well advised to research and understand the distinctions among the various mental health professional training institutions and programs and to select a program that meets the student's goals for licensure and professional identity (AAMFT, 2007).

Empirically Supported Family Therapy Treatments

Over the last decade, a great deal of the research in family therapy and the broader field of psychotherapy in general has been focused on identifying empirically supported models of treatment (Sexton, Ridley, & Kleiner, 2004). This research has been driven by the mandate that clinicians conduct research to determine which treatment models are most effective in resolving specific client problems such as anxiety, depression, family problems, marital difficulties, and other behavioral health concerns. Health insurance companies that pay the bills for much of the mental health treatment provided in the United States have a vested interest in ensuring that the treatments the companies pay for and clients receive are more likely than not to help clients resolve their presenting problems. Most health insurance companies now require that psychotherapy treatments be validated by outcome research. Thus, the increased focus on empirically supported treatment is driven by (1) the therapists' desire to use the best methods available to help clients resolve their problems and (2) the requirement that therapists demonstrate that the treatments provided to clients have been validated by solid clinical outcome research in order to receive payment from health insurance companies.

The terminology surrounding empirically validated treatment in individual, group, marital, couple, and family psychotherapy can be confusing. In 1995, the Society of Clinical Psychology (Division 12 of the APA) developed criteria for identifying *Empirically Validated Treatments* (EVTs). Empirically validated treatments were later renamed *Empirically Supported Treatments* (ESTs) as the term *supported treatments* was considered to more accurately describe the outcomes of the research studies conducted in the evaluations of various models of therapy. In 2006, the terminology broadened even further with the identification of *Evidence-Based Practice in Psychology* (EBPP) by the APA. This new distinction in terminology was developed because ESTs were often considered too restrictive and limited in their application to the full range of client problems and their sociocultural context. Evidence-based practice in psychology was designed to incorporate evidence-based treatments whenever possible. The objective of EBPP is to (La Roche & Christopher, 2009):

- promote effective psychological practice;
- apply empirically supported principals in assessment and case conceptualization;
- apply empirically supported principals in establishing effective therapeutic relationships and clinical interventions; and
- improve treatment by considering the full range of evidence, including empirically supported treatments (ESTs), in identifying the most effective treatment for each client.

Empirically supported research is based on the scientific method. Therefore, effective practices are based on outcome research that requires a sound experimental design with the researchers taking steps to control all conditions in the experiment except for the comparison being made between the treatment model of interest and other treatment models or a control group.

For example, a study could be conducted that is designed to determine whether cognitive–behavioral marital therapy (CBMT) is more effective than no treatment for couples experiencing conflict concerning their child rearing approaches. The researchers would design and conduct an experiment with couples having conflict with child rearing practices. The research controls would attempt to keep all factors in the study consistent except that one group of couples would receive CBMT while the other group would receive no treatment. After the experiment is concluded, the researchers analyze their data and publish the results of the comparison in peer reviewed professional journals. If the research demonstrates empirical support for the efficacy of the cognitive–behavioral marital therapy in this study (and hopefully several other studies), the treatment model is likely to be recognized by mental health service providers, the behavioral health professions, and managed care insurance providers as an empirically supported approach to treating the specific problem of helping couples resolve child rearing conflicts. Of course, a limitation to this type of research is that it focuses on only one specific problem and the results cannot be generalized to other presenting problems, such as an inability of couple to agree on financial issues or their sexual relationship. New controlled research studies would need to be conducted to provide empirical support for the treatment of other specific presenting problems.

When a treatment model is approved by managed care insurance companies, it means that therapists know that if they use this model in the manner prescribed by the research, they will most likely be reimbursed for their work. If therapists do not describe the use of EST models in their treatment plan, some insurance companies may not reimburse for the therapy provided. It is understandable that insurance companies want therapists to apply ESTs to the treatment of their client families. However, this approach by insurance companies can be frustrating to therapists who may wonder whether they will be reimbursed for providing therapy that is helping their clients while using a treatment model that has not been empirically validated.

Investigations designed to provide empirical support for a specific treatment model must clearly identify the condition or problem that will be treated. Moreover, the *application of the treatment* must be standardized as well. To this end, researchers attempt to ensure that the treatments provided to all clients by all therapists in a research study are identical. This is usually accomplished by developing a *treatment manual* that describes a standardized format for the application of the therapeutic treatment to a specific and well-defined client population and presenting problem. Treatment manuals specify as clearly as possible:

- *what* the therapist *does* in therapy,
- *how* the interventions are applied, and
- *when* the interventions are implemented.

To further strengthen the controls of the research study, therapists involved in providing the treatment are given specific training and practice on implementation of the treatment model with clients based on the information provided in the treatment manual. This training is to further ensure that the treatment provided to each client or family by all therapists participating in the study is as consistent as possible. Several authors (Gehart, 2010; Chambless & Hollon, 1998) have identified the characteristics required for psychotherapy approaches to be recognized as EST:

- Participants must be assigned randomly to treatment groups.
- Either a no-treatment, alternate treatment, or placebo treatment group must be used for comparison.
- Results must show the treatment is significantly more effective than the no-treatment control group and as least as effective as comparison treatment groups.
- Treatment is based on a specific, written treatment manual with criteria for identification of appropriate clients for the study.
- A clearly identified population with *specific* presenting problems is treated in the research.
- Reliable and valid treatment outcome assessment instruments are employed, and statistical techniques used are appropriate for the experimental design.

Higher order recognition than ESTs occurs when two additional conditions are met:

- The treatment must have undergone *at least two* independent investigations.

- The treatment must be *superior* to alternative treatments in at least two independent studies.

Empirically supported treatment is based on the medical model. When your physician prescribes a medicine for a specific illness, the medicine either leads to improvement or does not (we hope it does not make you worse). The personal and professional qualities that the physician possesses have no impact on the *effects* the medicine has on curing your illness. With empirically supported treatments, the therapy treatment model is analogous to the medicine in this example. The researchers work diligently to ensure that the therapists who provide the treatments for the study are equivalent to one another, provide nearly identical treatment to the clients in the study, and treat equivalent client problems. These experimental controls are designed to ensure that any improvement in the client is the *result of the treatment model*, not of the skill, personality, gender, or race of the therapist (Blow, Sprenkle, & Davis, 2007) and not the result of differing levels of the severity of the problems being treated.

In the following chapters of this book, I will present several family treatment models. The marital, couple, and family therapists who have developed these models may have a vested interest in conducting research that demonstrates the efficacy of their approaches. Criticism has been leveled at these model developers, suggesting that, despite using controlled studies, they and their followers, who often serve as therapists in the research, have an unintentional bias toward finding therapeutic effectiveness. This is called the *allegiance effect*. A second criticism of ESTs is that the treatment is focused on narrowly defined problems. It is rare for a client to enter therapy with just one specific issue or concern. Usually the client presents a constellation of interrelated concerns that require intervention (Sprenkle & Blow, 2004).

Therapists need information about therapy model effectiveness so that they can determine the best treatment to use with various presenting problems or to refer the client if the therapist is not qualified in the treatment model needed to resolve the problem presented. Legal and ethical concerns also emerge. For example, if a therapist did not use an identified EST model and a client became worse, would the therapist be subject to a legal action for not using the empirically supported approach?

The general public has a need to know and understand which treatment models have been demonstrated to be effective with various types of presenting problems to aid in identifying an appropriately trained therapist for their therapy. And, as previously stated, managed care insurance companies have a vested interested in knowing which treatment models are empirically supported in order to authorize treatment and payment to therapists.

Empirically Supported Psychotropic Medications

An important outcome of the empirical studies conducted to determine effective treatments of various psychological problems is that psychopharmacological treatment for 20 disorders, including schizophrenia and major depressive disorder, are supported by the research. For 19 of the disorders, *psychotherapy* was identified as an empirically supported treatment (Nathan & Gorman, 2007). Employing psychotropic medicine in conjunction with psychotherapy remains a controversial issue for many therapists who believe the drugs mask symptoms and can hinder treatment. However, much of the current research demonstrates that when psychotropic medicine and psychotherapy complement one another, with just the right amount of each used, treatment may move more quickly and positive behavioral changes accompany changes in affect as the medications help the client begin to feel better while the therapy helps the client do better.

Empirically Supported MCFT Treatments

Sexton et al. (2004) conducted a review of the literature of a wide range of studies that demonstrated empirical support for marriage, couple, and family therapy treatment models. Their review concluded that couple and family interventions (p. 133):

- are effective for a wide range of individual, relationship, and family problems;
- are effective with a diverse array of family types; and
- facilitate changes in treatment that appear to continue over time.

They reported that research evidence suggests that functional family therapy (Sexton & Alexander, 2002), parent management training (Feldman & Kazdin, 1995), and multisystemic therapy (Curtis, Ronan, &

Borduin, 2004) were effective in treating adolescent externalizing behavior disorders. Two family treatment models were effective in treating adolescent drug use and abuse problems: multidimensional family therapy (Liddle & Dakof, 1995) and brief strategic family therapy (Robbins & Szapocznik, 2005). Moreover, Sexton and Alexander reported that certain marriage and family therapy models were more effective in addressing several specific clinical problems. These effective models are behavioral marital therapy, emotionally focused couple therapy, multisystemic family therapy, and functional family therapy.

Sexton et al. (2004) asserted that controlled clinical trials will continue to produce evidence that supports the efficacy of *specific* family therapy treatment models. These researchers wanted to build on the substantial body of research that suggests that, in the broadest sense, MCFT is effective. The challenge now is for researchers to conduct clinical trials to determine what specific mechanisms and processes of the treatment models make the therapy effective. In this era of managed care and accountability in therapeutic service delivery, the objective for the family therapy profession is to identify "an adequate explanation of the process and mechanisms of the bigger and more complex change process" (p.138).

Other authors have identified the need to broaden the standards for ESTs. Woody, Weisz, and McLean (2005) reported that ESTs are being taught in the classroom but are declining in use in clinical work. Reasons for this decline in clinical training and practice are:

● uncertainty about how to implement the manual-based treatments,
● lack of time,
● few appropriately trained supervisors,
● inappropriateness of the ESTs for the problems treated, and
● philosophical opposition to the EST movement.

While acknowledging that evidence-based treatment has become the gold standard for mental health care, Dattilio (2006) warned that many practitioners are becoming too mechanical in their adherence to treatment manuals and protocols following a step-by-step formula in treating clients. Dattilio encourages the use of evidence-based treatment but with the caveat that therapists not lose their common sense approach, unique style, sense of humor, and spontaneous interaction with their clients.

Evidence-Based Practice

Evidence-Based Practice (EBP) should not be confused with Empirically Supported Treatment (EST) or Evidence-Based Treatment (EBT). While ESTs and EBTs are based on highly controlled empirical studies, *evidence-based practice* is a method that consults published research to inform clinical practice (Gehart, 2010; Patterson, Miller, Carnes, & Wilson, 2004). Widely employed in medical settings, EBP is based on the following process:

- Develop a specific question to be answered. For example, what is the best treatment for resolving conflict in the marriages of returning military veterans?
- Search the research literature for empirically supported methods of treatment that answer the question.
- Evaluate the quality of the research to determine whether it was conducted effectively and whether the findings are based on sound statistical methods that are appropriate to answer to the question posed.
- Determine whether the research findings are appropriate for the current problem situation and assess the potential gain and risk involved in applying the interventions recommended.
- Implement and evaluate the effects of the EBP on the outcome of the problem posed. Did the problem get better, stay the same, or worsen?
- Based on the answer to the question posed above, begin the process again with a new or revised question.

EBP as described above is useful in identifying potentially effective approaches for the treatment of individual, couple, and family problems. The review of the research might discover ESTs that have been identified for the question to be answered. However, in the absence of an EST, the therapist must be aware that the process used in EBP may be very helpful but is not as scientifically rigorous as the empirical research process used to identify effective treatments for specific problems. As described previously, the EST based treatment approach is more rigorous than EBP describe here. The evidence-based treatment model is very important in identifying which psychotherapy treatments have been recognized by the profession as effective for specific presenting problems under specific clinical conditions (Patterson et al., 2004).

Common Factors in Marriage and Family Therapy Research

In their book, *The Benefits of Psychotherapy,* Smith, Glass, and Miller (1980) analyzed the effects of several well-recognized psychotherapy treatment approaches and concluded that psychotherapy in a general sense is effective in bringing about client change. However, these authors reported that despite the very distinct ways that the various theoretical treatment models approached the change process, the differences in the outcomes of the various and distinct treatments was slight. They made the following statement: "We did not expect that the demonstrable benefits of quite different types of psychotherapy would be so little different" (p. 185). So while these researchers found therapy to be effective, they determined that one approach was about as effective as any other approach. This discovery prompted other investigators to attempt to determine whether there were any *common elements* involved in the very different therapy models investigated that might result in positive changes made by the clients in the studies considered. This research set in motion the hypothesis that common therapeutic factors that are present in all psychotherapy treatments were the elements that produced change rather than unique and distinguishing factors present within the various models. This idea came to be known as the *common factors* approach to understanding change that occurs in psychotherapy.

In a well-designed meta-analytic study of the current psychotherapy research literature, Wampold (2001) came to a similar conclusion: Reporting that the outcomes produced by the unique qualities of the various psychotherapy treatment models that he studied varied only slightly. A meta-analysis is a statistical technique that combines the results of a number of previous and similar outcome studies. The purpose of the meta-analysis is to determine the effectiveness of the various treatment models included in the analysis and to determine whether there is an overall effectiveness of all treatment models combined.

These researchers did conclude that therapy, in the general sense, was quite effective. Wampold's (2001) meta-analysis found that the average client who receives counseling is better off than 79% of people with similar problems who did not receive counseling. However, in the meta-analysis, the differences in the outcomes produced *by the different models* evaluated in the study were small. In other words, once again, any single theoretical approach to treatment seemed about as effective as any other approach. The conclusion reached by Lambert and Ogles (2004) in the *Handbook of Psychotherapy and Behavior Change* that also holds true for individual psychotherapy as well as couple and family therapy is that the elements that make one treatment model effective are *common* to other effective treatment models. Further support for the common factors model was reported by Shadish and Baldwin (2003), who reported that the MCFT approaches analyzed demonstrate clear indications of overall effectiveness. However, their review found little or no difference between the effectiveness of any of the specific models of treatment. Thus, the *common factors approach* emphasizes the importance of characteristics that appear in and are common to all therapeutic treatment models (Davis & Piercy, 2007).

The common factors approach to therapy outcome stands in contrast to the comprehensive model-based change process (Sexton et al., 2004). Evidence-based research reports, such as those cited in the previous section of this chapter, describe theoretical models that have specific elements within them that are hypothesized to bring about therapeutic change. For example, in structural family therapy, the therapist identifies and takes specific steps to develop cooperation in the relationship between the husband and wife. This is a model-specific therapeutic intervention known as *strengthening the spousal subsystem.* This is one specific intervention indicated by the structural family theoretical model to help create a more functional family organization. The strengthening of the spousal subsystem would be a specific element of the treatment; in other words, it is a factor that is *specific* to the structural family therapy model of behavior change. If research on the structural family therapy model demonstrated that the intervention of strengthening the spousal subsystem was effective in producing change, the conclusion would be drawn that this specific factor of the model was change producing.

The structural family therapist also ensures that a solid relationship is formed with each family member through the technique called *joining.* While this might seem like a specific factor in structural family therapy, it is actually a *common factor.* The reason joining is a common factor is that all effective family therapy treatment approaches require an effective, collaborative, and supportive relationship between the therapist and family members for a successful outcome to occur. Therefore, joining, or establishing an effective working relationship, would be considered a common factor that is necessary to positive treatment outcome in all treatment models.

Sprenkle and Blow (2004) and Blow et al. (2007) reviewed several meta-analyses that demonstrated that MCFT is effective in producing change in a general sense. Additionally, these reviews, once again, found no identifiable difference between the therapeutic outcomes produced by one model of treatment over any other model. In summary, several respected researchers conducted well-designed MCFT meta-analytic studies over the past 40 years and have concluded that MCFT is effective overall but that no single treatment model is more effective than any other model.

In their review of the literature of psychotherapy and family therapy research, Sprenkle and Blow (2004) identified the components of the common factors approach. The factors common to all individual and family psychotherapy are:

- characteristics of the client,
- characteristics of the therapist,
- the therapeutic relationship,
- expectation for outcome of therapy, and
- nonspecific treatment variables.

Sprenkle and Blow acknowledged that these categories are not discrete and there may be overlap among them. For example *establishing a therapeutic relationship* is clearly a *therapist quality*. However, the client's expectation that the relationship with the therapist will be good (or bad) overlaps with and impacts the ability to establish an effective relationship.

The Client as a Common Factor

Beutler, Bongar, and Shurkin (1998) studied important factors in therapy outcome and concluded that the key to effective outcome was the client's motivation, awareness, expectations, and preparation for therapy. Duncan (2010) asserted that the therapy is useless unless it activates the natural healing processes unique to each client. Tallman and Bohart (1999) suggested that, in successful treatment, the client possesses the ability to take almost any therapeutic intervention delivered by the therapist and modify it in a way that provides help to the client in problem resolution. Research by Beutler, Harwood, Alimohamed, and Malik (2002) suggested that clients who are introspective and introverted are likely to benefit from insight-oriented therapy. Active and impulsive clients do better with a directive, skills-building approach that focuses on symptom removal. The authors cited above would concur that the client is the prime factor in determining the positive or negative outcome in psychotherapy.

Therapist Effects as a Common Factor

Therapists possess personal characteristics that are independent of any theoretical model but that contribute to therapeutic outcome. For example, several therapists in a community might work from the same theoretical model. However, effectiveness research may show that some of these therapists are more effective in helping clients than others, even though their treatment models are similar. Common factors proponents assert that the difference can be attributed to qualities of the therapists, not the treatment models. Despite intense speculation about what makes an effective therapist different from an ineffective one, not much solid research specifically identifies these qualities except for the therapeutic alliance, to be discussed later. While gender, race, and other personal characteristics might seem important, research does not bear out this hypothesis if other effective therapist skills are present. Research by Beutler et al. (2002) suggested that therapists who have an activity level—being active and directive or reflective—consistent with a client's expectations may produce more effective outcomes. Effective therapists are able to recognize clients' expectations and preferences and then interact in a way that is consistent with them. Additionally these researchers thought that therapists who produce better outcomes are personally well integrated and are creative problem solvers who are able to effectively suggest alternative ways for clients to approach problematic situations.

The Therapeutic Relationship as a Common Factor

Counselor training has historically been based on the acquisition of specific necessary relationship-building skills including empathy, respect, genuineness, and unconditional positive regard (Rogers, 1957). These therapist skills are common factors, employed by all effective therapists.

More recent research has been devoted to the interactive relationship components within the therapist–client relationship. Research concerning congruence between therapist and client perceptions of the therapeutic relationships suggests that therapist and client evaluations of the relationship are often different, with the client's evaluation being considerably more predictive of therapeutic outcome (Bachelor & Horvath, 1999). Lambert (1992) conducted research that assessed factors that lead to therapeutic change. Based on this research, he estimated that 30% of the outcome of psychotherapy is related to the therapeutic relationship. Bodin (1979) identified three elements that compose the therapeutic relationship:

1. bonds,
2. tasks, and
3. goals.

Bonds contribute to the relationship when trust, caring, and involvement are communicated between therapist and client. The use of basic skills such as empathy, reflection of feelings and content, genuineness, communication, and unconditional positive regard (Rogers, 1957) contribute to this factor. *Tasks* contribute to the relationship when the activities and interventions introduced in therapy are deemed credible and helpful by the client. *Goals* contribute to the therapeutic relationship when the therapy is directed toward outcomes that are compatible for both client and therapist. Thus, it is important that the therapist and client work toward the same outcome. If the therapist is trying to help the client change in ways that are not consistent with the client's goals, it is easy to imagine how this could damage the relationship and negatively impact the therapy.

Sprenkle and Blow (2004) asserted that therapeutic relationship skills are necessary but not sufficient for positive therapeutic outcome. The relationship is important but must be accompanied by other common therapeutic factors for successful outcome to occur. This contrasts to Carl Rogers's (1957) position that if the therapist provided the necessary core conditions, the relationship alone would be sufficient to bring about therapeutic change in the client. Sprenkle and Blow (2004) identified three empirically supported MCFT treatment models that emphasize the importance of developing of a strong therapeutic alliance in producing client change. These theoretical models are emotionally focused therapy (Johnson, 2003), functional family therapy (Sexton & Alexander, 2003), and multisystemic family therapy (Sheidow, Henggeler & Schoenwald, 2003).

Expectancy as a Common Factor

Improvement in therapy that is based on the client's belief that the treatment will be effective is also recognized as the placebo effect. Placebo effects may be based on a conscious belief in treatment or on subconscious associations between recovery and the experience of being treated. Research by Lambert (1992) suggested that approximately 15% of the client's improvement in psychotherapy is related to the client's awareness that he or she is in treatment accompanied by hopeful feelings that may occur as a result and a belief that the treatment will be effective (Sprenkle & Blow, 2004). While very few studies specifically focused on the effects of hope and expectancy in the marriage and family therapy literature, Johnson and Talitman (1997) reported that successful outcome is more likely when the therapist presents the treatment model in a way that is congruent with the client's expectations.

Nonspecific Treatment Variables as a Common Factor

The Sprenkle and Blow (2004) review of the literature on common factors suggested that three global nonspecific variables are common factors in psychotherapy outcome (Karasu, 1986):

1. *Behavioral regulation,* also referred to as *changing the doing,* occurs when the therapist helps the clients learn new skills, such as showing support to one another, communicating openly, establishing more effective boundaries, and learning new child discipline techniques.
2. *Cognitive mastery,* also referred to as *changing the viewing,* occurs when the therapist helps the client think differently about the interactions that take place within the family relationships. This occurs when the therapist identifies a family pattern, provides new information to the family, offers interpretations concerning behavioral sequences, and reframes difficult interactions in ways that are understandable and acceptable to the family members.
3. *Emotional experiencing* occurs when the therapist helps each family member get in touch with and identify feelings that occur in their

relationships. Moreover, family members are helped to recognize and acknowledge the feelings of other family members. Emotional experiencing helps family members identify the pain and joys felt by themselves and all other family members and, as a result, think differently, feel differently and ultimately behave differently and more compassionately towards one another.

The factors described above are common to all types of psychotherapy: individual, group, marital, couple, and family. Sprenkle and Blow (2004) identified three common factors that they asserted are unique to MCFT and that are the mechanisms through which the common factors already described are delivered to family systems:

1. *Relational conceptualization.* Marriage, couple, and family therapists think about individual problems in a larger social or family context. For example, if a family enters therapy describing the problem as a child who is misbehaving in school, the therapist views the child's acting out in relation to the family's dynamics at home, potential relationship issues and other disagreements between the child's parents, and the child's interactions with teachers and other students at the child's school. In other words, the child is not viewed as a dysfunctional individual in isolation but as a person exhibiting behaviors that are consistent with the relational dynamics within the family, school, and larger social context.

2. *The expanded treatment system.* Marriage, couple, and family therapists believe that problems presented by individuals exist within a larger family and social contest. Therefore, in order to be able to identify the elements of behavior in the family and social system that support the behaviors of the symptom bearer, the family therapist seeks to expand the treatment system by bringing other family members and other involved persons outside the family into the treatment process. This permits the family therapist to observe first-hand the interactional and communications patterns that exist within the family and that may serve to maintain or support the undesired behavior in the symptom bearer. Actual observation of the family system in action in the therapy room or setting where the client, family, and others interact is contrasted with relying on the client's perceptions and verbal report of the behaviors of family members. Engaging as many key members of the system as possi-

ble in treatment is important because the verbal report of the client obtained in an individual counseling session would reflect reality for the client, but may not accurately portray the actual feelings, motives, and behaviors of other family members.

3. *The expanded therapeutic alliance.* Common factors research emphasizes the importance of the therapeutic alliance in positive therapy outcome. MCFT is unique in that effective therapists work with an expanded treatment system and must be skilled at establishing a therapeutic alliance with each individual in the family and, when necessary, individuals in the broader system. Moreover, the family therapist must also be able to identify key family subsystems, such as the parental subsystem or sibling subsystem, and establish therapeutic relationships with these key subsystems as well as forming a therapeutic relationship with the family system as a whole.

Critiques of the Common Factors Approach

Sexton et al. (2004) acknowledged that the basic assumptions of the common factors approach are probably correct. They acknowledged that important common factors cut across what appear to be very different theoretical positions. They also recognized the solid body of literature that supports this position. They further suggested that this approach is useful in that it simplifies the important lessons that must be taught to developing family therapists.

Sexton and Kleiner (2004) also raised a number of issues about the common factors approach. They stated that most of the common factors research cited in the current debate is dated and based on meta-analytic studies of predominantly individual psychotherapy approaches. They argued that current systemic approaches are quite distinct from the older approaches and are likely to have specific theory-based effects. They suggested that more studies must be conducted that assess the unique effects of current models of systems-based psychotherapy before the model-based change mechanisms are discounted in favor of a common factors approach.

As an example, Sexton, Ridley, and Kleiner (2004) referred to the problems of acting-out adolescents. Recent research has demonstrated that family-based approaches are superior to individual and group approaches for these problems. Moreover, they emphasized that the way in which the problems are addressed in family-based therapy are significantly different from the way other approaches address them. The family-based approaches target the relational systems that are impacting the identified client. Thus, these researchers continue to hypothesize that it is primarily the specific effects of the treatment models, perhaps supported by common factors influences, that make family-based treatments effective. The authors cautioned that the common factors proponents may inadvertently be leading the field away from conducting important research designed to identify significant family systems model–based change mechanisms.

Both sides of the debate agree that preparing family therapists with relationship-building skills is critical. Moreover, they agree that therapists who can develop effective therapeutic relationships will be better able to create and deliver change-producing interventions in treatment. However, the common factors proponents are not convinced that differing models of treatment have intrinsic, theory-based change-producing properties (other than the common factors that exist in all models). Davis and Piercy (2007) conducted a series of studies and found common ground. They identified common factors that cut across all of the therapy models they examined and also common factors that are model dependent. Sprenkle and Blow (2004) also attempted to bridge the gap while maintaining their common factors position by stating that theoretic models are the *vehicles by which the common factors are delivered* in providing help to families in treatment.

Ethical and Legal Issues in MCFT

The ethical guidelines developed by the American Counseling Association (ACA) and the American Psychological Association (APA) primarily address the therapeutic relationships between one client or group and one therapist. These ethical guidelines do not directly address many of the issues encountered by the marriage, couple, and family therapist. The marriage, couple, and family therapist encounters specific legal and ethical issues surrounding confidentiality, child custody, and divorce. To communicate effectively with clients who are dealing with legal issues in the family, family therapists must be very familiar with the laws in their state governing professional practice (Margolin, 1982).

Ethical Considerations

Margolin (1982) identified six areas of specific ethical concern to the marriage and family therapist:

1. Therapist responsibility
2. Confidentiality
3. Client privilege
4. Informed consent and right to refuse treatment
5. Therapist values
6. Training and supervision

These areas of concern will be discussed briefly, with suggestions for how the family therapist might respond to each.

Therapist Responsibility

Therapists who counsel individuals are responsible for the client's welfare. In family therapy, this issue becomes more complex. Who is the client when more than one person is present in the therapy room? Is it each of the individuals involved in treatment, or is it the family system? What may be in the best interests of one family member may not be in the best interests of another.

Consider the following example. Mr. North has decided he wants to leave the marriage. He is unwavering in this decision yet has agreed to join his wife in marriage counseling to see whether something can change his mind. Mrs. North is a homemaker with no career and is terrified of going it alone. She pleads with the therapist to help restore the marriage. Over the course of several sessions, the scenario does not change. Mr. North still plans to leave the marriage. What is the ethical responsibility of the therapist, and to whom does the therapist owe allegiance? Should the therapist:

- provided support for Mrs. North during the divorce process,
- provide support for Mr. North as he extricates himself from the marriage he no longer wants,
- continue to treat the couple and hope to salvage the marriage, or
- refer each spouse to an individual therapist?

What is good for one family member is not always good for another. The therapist strives to help the family system change in some manner that is reasonably satisfactory for all concerned. The therapist must balance the responsibility of helping each individual, while also working to help the family system adjust to a more satisfactory condition—an often difficult position to reach. Ultimately, in this situation, the therapist must assist both clients in the transition that will take place as the husband leaves the marriage. It is likely that Mrs. North will require more therapeutic support. If Mrs. North is unhappy with the therapy because the marriage was not repaired, referral to another therapist might be required.

Confidentiality

The confidentiality of the relationship between client and counselor has long been an ethical hallmark of psychotherapy. Except in cases of child abuse, potential physical harm to the client, or potential physical harm to others by the client, the therapist is bound to maintain client confidentiality. Maintaining confidentiality may become a problem for the family therapist when individuals share secrets with the therapist. For example, suppose a couple is in therapy to attempt to rebuild the marriage because the wife has had an affair. The husband agrees to remain in the marriage if they enter couple therapy, and the wife agrees to stop her affair. In a private call to the therapist, the wife reveals that she is still involved in the affair and does not want to end it, but that she does not want her husband to know. How should the ethical marriage and family therapist respond to this situation?

Helping family members learn to communicate openly is one of the typical goals of therapy. A serious problem arises in therapy when the therapist is triangulated into an alliance with one of the members through the revelation of a secret that must be kept. When this happens, a family member divulges a secret to the therapist and creates a situation that does not allow the therapist to communicate openly with all family members without revealing the secret and betraying the person who revealed the secret. The problem for the therapist becomes even more complex when the other members need the information contained in the secret to make responsible decisions.

Some family therapists attempt to prevent the revelation of secrets by informing the family members before beginning therapy through the use of the professional disclosure statement that the therapist will not keep secrets. This policy has a potential down side. If it is implemented, it may prevent a family member from divulging information that could be essential to the therapy. Unfortunately, therapists who agree too readily to maintain confidentiality by keeping secrets often find themselves unable to intervene in a productive manner.

A potentially productive middle ground for the therapist is to clearly articulate a position to the family at the beginning of therapy stating that, in the interest of helping to resolve presenting issues, the therapist may use any information provided by a client. If information received in a private conversation would be helpful to the therapy, the therapist has the freedom to bring the information into the therapy process.

Whatever course of action the therapist takes regarding confidentiality, the family members must clearly understand the policy from the beginning of treatment. In addition to being a legal requirement in many states, a professional disclosure statement signed by the clients and therapist that describes the therapist and the therapy process, including information concerning confidentiality, is an invaluable way to communicate critical information about family therapy to clients.

Some family therapists find a one-way mirror useful in family treatment. Therapists who use the mirror as an adjunct to therapy place a team of one or more colleagues behind the mirror to observe the session and provide suggestions to the therapist and family during and after the session (Fenell, Hovestadt, & Harvey, 1986). In addition to the observation team, sessions can be videotaped for later review by the therapist, the team, and, in some cases, the family.

Involvement of an observing team and supervisor in the therapy process also creates issues of confidentiality. Family members should be fully informed about the mirror, video recorder, and observation team. Again, a disclosure statement signed by the clients will ensure that clients are informed and agree to the process. Family members must be told how the therapy process works with the amount of detail they care to know. Furthermore, members of the observation team and family members alike should be reminded of the need for confidentiality regarding information revealed in the session.

Client Privilege

Closely related to the issue of client confidentiality is the issue of privileged communication. Privileged communication protects the client from a situation in which confidences from therapy are revealed on the witness stand in court. Privilege belongs to the client, but when the therapist treats a family or couple, who is the client? When one family member asks a therapist to testify regarding another family member, courts have typically recognized that the client privilege belongs to each family member; thus, therapists have not been required to testify. This is not always the case, though. Herrington (1979) reported a case in Virginia in which the judge ruled that when a husband and wife are in therapy together, there is no privilege because the statements were not made in private to a professional counselor but in the presence of a third party.

Marriage, couple, and family therapists may be able to convince a judge that it is not ethical to provide this type of testimony by arguing that the unit of treatment is the entire family rather than any single individual. Thus, as Gumper and Sprenkle (1981) suggested, testimony about any part of the family system would violate the *privilege of the family*. Nonetheless, courts still may order therapists to testify regarding information obtained in multiperson therapy sessions. Therapists are advised to determine and advise their clients about what the laws of their own states require concerning client privilege in marriage and family therapy situations.

Informed Consent and Right to Refuse Treatment

In today's legalistic society, it is important that clients be clearly informed concerning their rights and responsibilities in therapy, as well as the therapist's responsibilities. All psychotherapists are required to present their professional disclosure statements to their clients. When clients read and sign the disclosure statement, they acknowledge that they have been informed about the treatment that will be provided and that they consent to participating in therapy. The disclosure statement also advises clients of their right to refuse treatment at any point in the therapy process. Before families agree to participate in therapy, counselors must fully inform them about the nature of therapy and important aspects of the process. Most states now have laws requiring therapists to use disclosure statements. Gill (1982) delineated important elements of consumer information that should be included in the professional disclosure statement:

● Describe the purpose of psychotherapy.
● Describe what leads people to enjoy more satisfying lives.
● Describe what clients should expect as a result of therapy.
● Describe the responsibilities of clients in therapy.

- Describe the primary therapeutic approach employed and the techniques that support this approach.
- Describe the types of problems that have been successfully resolved using this approach.
- Describe the conditions that might precipitate referral to another therapist or agency.
- Describe the limits of confidentiality in the therapeutic relationship and how emails and other electronic communications will be handled.
- Inform clients that they may refuse treatment at any point in the therapy process.
- Ask clients to sign the disclosure indicating that they have been fully informed and consent to treatment.

The family therapist will want to ensure that all family members have agreed to participate in therapy and that all have signed the informed consent form. Clients engaging in MCFT should be informed of possible negative outcomes of therapy. When working with multiperson systems such as families, the outcome of therapy may be viewed as undesirable by one or more of the family members (Gurman & Kniskern, 1978b, 1981a; Wilcoxon & Fenell, 1983, 1986).

Finally, therapists who provide treatment only to the entire family should be prepared to refer families who refuse to bring all members into treatment. The therapist should refer these families to other therapists who do not have this restriction on treatment (Margolin, 1982; Napier & Whitaker, 1979).

Therapist's Values

One of the most critical ethical issues confronting marriage, couple, and family therapists concerns their core values and beliefs. With the remarkable plurality of family styles, some therapists may find their value systems challenged. Therapists must carefully examine their core beliefs and ensure that their values do not adversely affect their ability to help the client family reach its goals for treatment. When counselors encounter family values in certain clients that are opposed to their own beliefs, biases may form against these clients, or the therapist may intentionally or unintentionally impose her values on the family. This rarely leads to successful outcome. According to Margolin (1982), specific values that may cause problems for the therapist include attitudes toward divorce, infidelity, sex roles, and same-sex relationships.

Attitudes toward Divorce.   Because it is almost a certainty that family counselors will work with couples who are divorcing or will decide to divorce based on what they learn in therapy, it is critical that counselors examine and acknowledge their values concerning divorce. Divorce is a painful option, but at times it may be in the best interests of family members to sever the marital relationship. Counselors must be certain that they are not pushing couples either to stay together or to divorce based on their own family-of-origin experiences and the values that have emerged from these experiences. The therapist's role is to help the couple identify issues in the marriage to be resolved and provide help to the couple in resolving these issues. If the relationship does not improve with treatment, the therapist can help the couple come to a joint decision about whether to stay in the marriage or to divorce. When couples ask a counselor about his biases regarding marriage and divorce, the counselor should be honest with his clients. If clients are not comfortable with the counselor's values, the counselor should offer referrals.

Attitudes toward Infidelity.   The counselor's attitude toward infidelity can hinder therapy when it conflicts with the attitudes of one or both partners. If the therapist believes that affairs are acceptable and one or both of the relationship partners disagree, clients may perceive the counselor as advocating behaviors that are destructive to a relationship in need of help. If the counselor believes that affairs are harmful to the relationship, she must be careful not to side too heavily with the partner who was faithful and attack the unfaithful partner. This attitude could create the perception that the problems are entirely the fault of the person who had the affair. This is a nonsystemic conceptualization of the problem created by both partners. A counselor who employs systems theory will seek to discover how each partner engaged in behaviors that created the problems and how those relationship problems resulted in the affair. While not condoning the affair, it is most beneficial for the couple to discover how each shares responsibility for the problems and how each will need to make changes in any effort to restore the relationship.

Attitudes toward Sex Roles.   Some family systems therapists, with strong beliefs about traditional marriage, have stereotyped women's roles and have encouraged women to stay in unsatisfactory and, at times, abusive relationships. Therapists should be careful not to pay less attention to a woman's career, perpetuate the notion that children's problems are the result of poor mothering, exhibit a double standard that views the woman's affairs more severely than the man's, or places more emphasis on the man's needs in a relationship. When a counselor has certain values that may have a significant impact on the therapy, the therapist should inform the clients so they can make a responsible choice concerning the appropriateness of treatment with the therapist (Corey, Corey, & Callahan, 2006).

Same-Sex Relationships.   Much controversy swirls around the issue of gay marriages. Regardless of the outcome of that debate, same-sex couples will be together and some will have relationship problems. These couples will seek the help of a competent family therapist. The skills needed to help a same-sex couple are the same as those required for working with a heterosexual couple. However, therapists with uncomfortable feelings about homosexuality and same-sex relationships may not be able to effectively provide the help needed. In the ideal world, all therapists would be prepared to help all clients in need and would not allow their personal biases to interfere. However, in the real world, this ideal is still an aspiration. Therapists who are uncomfortable with gay couples, divorce, infidelity, or egalitarian sex roles in relationships are encouraged to refer the clients to other helpers who are comfortable with diverse clients and their problems and are skilled in providing effective treatment. Moreover, the ethical therapist should consider seeking supervision to remove the blocks that prevent serving certain clientele.

Training and Supervision

Marital, couple, and family problems are widespread. Therefore, most mental health practitioners have frequent opportunities to treat these problems. But not all therapists are adequately trained to treat marital, couple, and family problems. Gurman and Kniskern (1981b) suggested that, if treatment is to be successful, family therapists might need to use more directive intervention methods than therapists who work only with individuals. Furthermore, Margolin (1982) reported that adequate preparation in MCFT is the exception rather than the rule among mental health service providers. Thus, therapists who work with couples and families must be careful not to exceed the bounds of their competence.

Fenell and Hovestadt (1986) developed a three-level model of clinical training for family therapists and suggested that therapists should evaluate their ability level and limit their practice to marital, couple, and family problems they are appropriately prepared to handle. Therapists must have access to clinical supervision by skilled family systems therapists for assistance in evaluating couples and families who may need referral to a professional with more training and experience in systemic therapy.

Ethical Standards for MCFT

Most professional organizations have ethical standards for practitioners. The American Association for Marriage and Family Therapy (AAMFT, 2001) has developed a revised set of standards specifically for marriage and family therapists. This set of standards, entitled the *AAMFT Code of Ethics,* addresses the following major points:

- *Responsibility to clients.* Marriage, couple, and family therapists advance the welfare of families and individuals. They respect the rights of those persons seeking their assistance and make reasonable efforts to ensure that their services are used appropriately.
- *Confidentiality.* Marriage, couple, and family therapists have unique confidentiality concerns because the client in a therapeutic relationship may be more than one person. Therapists respect and guard the confidences of each individual client.
- *Professional competence and integrity.* Marriage, couple, and family therapists maintain high standards of professional competence and integrity.
- *Responsibility to students and supervisees.* Marriage, couple, and family therapists do not exploit the trust and dependency of students and supervisees.
- *Responsibility to research participants.* Investigators respect the dignity and protect the welfare of research participants and are aware of applicable laws and regulations and professional standards governing the conduct of research.
- *Responsibility to the profession.* Marriage, couple, and family therapists must respect the rights and responsibilities of professional colleagues and participate in activities that advance the goals of the profession.
- *Financial arrangements.* Marriage, couple, and family therapists make financial arrangements with clients, third-party payors, and supervisees that are reasonably understandable and conform to accepted professional practices.
- *Advertising.* Marriage, couple, and family therapists engage in appropriate informational activities, including those that enable the public, referral sources, or others to choose professional services on an informed basis.

The complete *AAMFT Code of Ethical Principles for Marriage and Family Therapists* is presented in Appendix A.

When a violation of the AAMFT code is suspected, the AAMFT Ethics Committee is contacted, and procedures are set in motion to determine whether the complaint is against an AAMFT member, to determine whether the complaint has validity, and to determine action by the Ethics Committee and the association. A thorough appeals process is provided for members who believe the process has been managed improperly.

Understanding the ethical principles for marriage and family therapists is critical in providing ethical services to clients and in maintaining a solid reputation for integrity in the profession.

The IAMFC, a Division of the ACA, has also developed ethical standards identified as the *Ethical Code for the International Association of Marriage and Family Counselors* (2011). These standards cover the following key points:

- Client well-being
- Confidentiality
- Competence
- Assessment
- Private practice
- Research and publications
- Supervision
- Advertising and other public statements

The entire IAMFC ethical code is presented in Appendix B. The reader will note the similarities between the IAMFC code and the AAMCFT code.

Family Therapy Training

Family therapy claims to be more than another set of techniques for helping families change. Experienced practitioners believe that family therapy is a different way of thinking about problems that people encounter in their daily living. Because of the distinctions between the practice of individual and family therapy, training approaches have evolved for family therapists that differ from typical approaches used in training individual therapists (Fenell & Hovestadt, 1986; Fenell, Hovestadt, & Harvey, 1986; Liddle, 1991).

Academic Preparation

Professionals who identify themselves as marriage and family therapists come from a wide range of academic training programs. Family therapy, for example, is taught in graduate departments of counselor education, family studies, psychiatry, psychology, social work, nursing, and pastoral counseling (Fenell & Hovestadt, 1986; Hovestadt, Fenell, & Piercy, 1983). Many graduates of these programs seek clinical membership in the AAMFT. The following is a summary of the requirements necessary for clinical membership under the evaluative track.

1. Masters or doctoral degree in MCFT or related mental health field from a regionally accredited institution.
2. Must successfully complete the 11 required courses outlined in the AAMFT curriculum guidelines, either during the graduate program or in a postdegree training program accepted by the AAMFT.
3. Supervised clinical practicum must be completed during graduate program. The practicum consists of a minimum of 1 year and 300 hours of supervised direct client contact with individuals, couples, and families.
4. Minimum 2 years, 1,000 hours of clinical work experience in MCFT, completed concurrently with 200 hours of supervision. At least 100 of the 200 hours must be individual supervision. Supervision must be completed with an AAMFT approved supervisor or supervisor candidate. An alternate supervisor may be approved by the AAMFT on a case-by-case basis (AAMFT, 2011).

COAMFTE accredited academic institutions providing appropriate graduate preparation were listed in a previous section of this chapter.

Clinical Training and Supervision

One of the features of MCFT that sets it apart from most treatment approaches for individuals is the focus on the family as a system. This emphasis is taught in the academic portion of the therapist's training program and is practiced in supervised clinical experience. Many family therapy training programs have on-campus clinics where graduate students practice therapy under supervision. In most of these clinics, a one-way mirror allows the therapist to be observed working with the couple or family. Often, a supervisor and a team of the trainee's colleagues will observe the therapist working in the session. This observation permits the supervisor to obtain an accurate impression of the work the therapist is doing and to offer immediate feedback to the student regarding the session.

Family therapy supervisors and trainees generally have an understanding that when the supervisor identifies ways the therapist in training could be more effective, the session may be interrupted to inform the therapist of the possible interventions that could be used. Because family therapists can easily become emotionally engaged with the family system, having a supervisor and team of observers behind the mirror offers a unique opportunity for feedback on what may be going on in a session that is outside the therapist's awareness. Initially, trainees may believe they are being judged and become defensive to in-session suggestions. Over time and through their own participation in observing other trainees, however, they come to value the meta-perspective of the supervisory team and learn to use the feedback effectively to improve their family therapy skills.

Although much has been written about family therapy supervision (Fenell & Hovestadt, 1986; Liddle, 1991; Liddle & Halpin, 1978), little research has been attempted to demonstrate the effectiveness of family therapy supervision over traditional case-presentation supervision (Kniskern & Gurman, 1979). One study using a small sample compared family therapy supervision with traditional supervision. The results showed no correlation between the acquisition of family therapy skills and the supervision method used (Fenell, Hovestadt, & Harvey, 1986). Liddle, Davidson, and Barrett (1988) discovered that live supervision could lead to excessive dependence on the supervisor, especially early in the training process. All the researchers suggested that assumptions regarding effective family therapy clinical training should be examined and evaluated for effectiveness.

The AAMFT established the COAMFTE as the agency for accreditation of clinical training programs in MCFT at the masters, doctoral, and postgraduate levels. COAMFTE accreditation is recognized by the US Department of Education and the Council for Higher Education Accreditation (CHEA, formerly CORPA) and is a requirement for obtaining eligibility for participation in federal programs. Further information on specific standards for accreditation candidacy and a complete listing of COAMFTE training programs and addresses are available (COAMFTE, 2011) online at http://www.aamft.org/.

Summary

This chapter focused the reader on the current issues, ethics, and trends in the family therapy profession. First, the required characteristics of a profession were described with a summary about how family therapy met those professional requirements. Next the preparation of family therapist was addressed. Four ways of designing family therapist preparation programs range from training programs that require intense, focused graduate work specifically in family therapy to training programs that offer one or two elective courses in family therapy, and the chapter includes a listing of accredited family therapy training programs. These programs will serve the aspiring family therapist well if future educational endeavors are being considered. Evidence-based models of family treatment are crucial to provide treatment based upon recognized empirically supported models and to satisfy the requirements for reimbursement of many managed care insurance companies. Following this, the ongoing debate between proponents of the common factors approach and the model specific approach to the therapeutic change process in family therapy was presented. Finally the reader was presented with information about ethical issues in family therapy practice and training.

In the next chapter, specific family systems concepts will be introduced. These concepts are critical in the understanding of the family systems intervention process.

Suggested Readings

American Association for Marriage and Family Therapists (AAMFT). (2007). The making of the MFT profession. *Family Therapy Magazine, 6*(4), 12–19.

Broderick, C. B., & Schraeder S. S. (1991). The history of professional marriage and family therapy. In A. S. Gurman & D. P. Kniskern (Eds.) *Handbook of family therapy* (Vol. 2). New York: Brunner/Mazel.

Duncan, B. L. (2010). *On becoming a better therapist.* Washington, DC, American Psychological Association.

The Family as a
Living System:
Essential Concepts

This chapter presents basic and essential information concerning family therapy. To be effective in working with couples and families, the counselor has to understand the concepts and language unique to family therapy and be able to conceptualize family problems systemically. This means that the counselor has to recognize the family as a functioning organism connected by its relationships, history, and shared experiences. Further, the effective family counselor must be able to conceptualize the family system, not a specific individual, as the client and as the focus of treatment. This is a challenging shift in thinking for many counselors. In addition, the counselor must develop the relationship skills necessary to connect with each family member and develop interventions that impact the entire family system.

This chapter provides the reader with specific information about family system functioning. Key topics covered in this chapter are the fundamentals of family functioning, including family health, family dysfunction, family assessment, and family development.

Key Concepts

○ Double-bind hypothesis
○ Identified patient
○ Schizophrenia and the family
○ Family as a living system
○ Family subsystems
○ Paradigm shift
○ Circular causality
○ Family homeostasis
○ Subsystem boundaries
○ Adaptability and cohesion
○ Disengaged families
○ Enmeshed families
○ Family life cycle
○ The circumplex model

Questions for Discussion

1. How can family systems theory be helpful to the counselor in professional practice?
2. What are the major differences between systems theory and individual theory?
3. Which terms and concepts introduced in this chapter describe your own family? How are they appropriate for your family?
4. How can the circumplex model be used in understanding and assessing family functioning?
5. What are key characteristics of effective communication? Why is communication essential to effective relationships?
6. How is knowledge about family life cycle development helpful in family therapy?

This chapter introduces key family therapy terms and concepts. The counselor in training must understand these terms and concepts thoroughly to appreciate the family therapy theories presented later in this book. Most of the theories employed with individual psychotherapy are based on the assumption that psychological problems reside within the individual. Therefore, if the therapist can help resolve issues that are internally disturbing to the individual, therapeutic cure has occurred. The notion that the locus of pathology resides within the individual is deeply rooted in contemporary American culture, which rewards and highly prizes individual achievement. When a person is successful, she is viewed as having *made it as an individual*; the belief is that the individual possesses the characteristics that made the success possible.

Personal failure and psychological problems are viewed as deficits that also reside and are maintained within an individual. If a person is unable to succeed or has psychological problems, the overwhelming preponderance of social opinion suggests that the person has some character deficit or flaw. Given the importance of individuality in this society, it is not difficult to understand why psychological problems are primarily viewed as existing within the individual, and this ideology further explains why treatment of psychological problems focuses on helping the individual. In this text, an alternative systems-based view to this traditional understanding of psychological problem formation is considered.

Developing a Family Systems Perspective

To understand family systems and to practice counseling from a systemic approach, therapists must understand that systems exist at many levels. One of the easiest ways to understand the concept of living systems is to consider the human body. The human is a living system composed of subsystems, which in turn are composed of other subsystems. The biological human is composed of a nervous system, a digestive system, a circulatory system, a skeletal system, a respiratory system, and a reproductive system. Each of these systems is a subsystem of the total human system. Furthermore, each of these subsystems is composed of other subsystems. The circulatory system, for example, consists of the veins, arteries, and heart. Each of these subsystems is composed of other subsystems. The heart, for example, is composed of cells, and the cells are composed of cellular subsystems, and so on. For the body to be healthy, all subsystems must function effectively and cooperatively. If the heart were not functioning properly, the other subsystems (and the body as a whole) would be radically affected.

Just as humans are living systems composed of subsystems, each individual lives in a subsystem of a larger living system, as shown in Figure 5.1. Understanding this point is essential to develop the skills required to provide effective therapy for families. A person is known as the *individual subsystem* and is a part of a larger living system called the family. The family is part of a living system called the extended family, which is part of a larger system called the community. The community is part of a larger system, perhaps known as the state, which is also

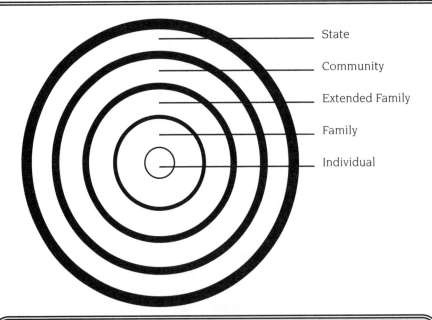

Figure 5.1   Levels of Systems

part of a larger system, the nation, which is part of the international community which is part of the planet, solar system, and so on.

Because of these interrelationships among systems and their subsystems, if a problem arises in one of the subsystems of a biological or social organization, that problem may affect other subsystems or the larger systems of the organization. This concept is most important when a therapist treats a family in which the problem seems to reside in only one of the members. Systems therapists recognize that, although an individual exhibits the presenting problem, the symptoms may be maintained by behaviors of other family members. Furthermore, the systems therapist recognizes that the problem behavior affects the behavior of every other member of the family system in some way or another.

The family theorists and researchers introduced in Chapter 3 were initially schooled in models of psychotherapy that emphasized treatment of the individual. These models focused on problems of an intrapsychic nature—problems that resided within the mind of an individual. Each of these family therapy pioneers sought to understand the nature of problem formation in a more inclusive way than had been accepted without question in the past. These visionaries, rather than viewing the client's problem as intrapsychic in nature, came to view the psychological problem as a symptom of dysfunctional patterns (Minuchin, 1974) in the identified patient's (IP) family system. Thus, a new way of conceptualizing psychological problem formation was born. This new way of looking at problem formation resulted in new models and strategies for problem resolution.

Family Subsystems

Salvador Minuchin (1974) described family systems in a helpful and understandable manner. He thought of the family system as composed of smaller units called subsystems. Among the subsystems that may exist within the family are the spousal subsystem, composed of the husband and wife or the couple, the sibling (children's) subsystem, the females' subsystem, the males' subsystem, and individual subsystems composed of each individual in the larger family system. In addition to these basic units, other subsystem configurations may exist, such as mother–son and father–daughter subsystems. In some families today, the grandparent–grandchild subsystems are particularly powerful elements. Each family system has a *set of rules* that governs the behaviors of the family members, and each member has certain predictable *roles* to play in the family. These rules and roles are an important key to understanding the functions of the family's subsystems. According to Minuchin, the therapist's responsibility is to identify and work to change the key family subsystems involved in maintaining the presenting problems while strengthening functional subsystems and adding new developmentally appropriate and functional subsystems to the family.

Paradigm Shift

The movement from an individual perspective to a systems perspective of problem formation and problem resolution is called the *paradigm shift* (Haley, 1971), a term frequently used in the family therapy literature. To most effectively employ systems-based counseling interventions, therapists must make this paradigm shift, developing the ability to understand how an individual's symptoms are one aspect of the family's interactive sequences of behavior and how those symptoms may serve to stabilize and maintain the current family system.

A classic example of this concept is the case of a child whose symptoms divert the concern of the parents from their marital problems and thoughts about divorce to the problems of the child. By manifesting psychological symptoms, the child has preserved, at least temporarily, the unity of the family through the symptomatic behavior. The parents rarely dwell on their marital problems when they are needed to help their child. The result of the child's symptomatic behavior is the preservation of the larger system, the family. Thus, the symptoms of the child signify a larger problem with the marital relationship within the family system.

Linear and Circular Causality

Therapists who make the paradigm shift can differentiate between linear causality and circular causality in the formation of family problems. Linear causality refers to the concept of *cause and effect*. One person's action causes another person's predictable reaction. The figure below demonstrates an example of *linear causality* in a family in which the husband and wife are arguing about the husband's drinking behaviors. If the wife is asked about the problem she might say, "He drinks too much when he comes home from work and when he does I get angry and complain." This pattern could be diagramed in the following way:

cause   *effect*

husband drinks ⟶ wife complains

In this linear model, according to the wife, the husband's drinking *causes* her to complain to him. This explanation is perfectly acceptable and understandable from an individual counseling theoretical perspective, but it may not be a complete explanation of the situation. If we were to ask the husband to explain his drinking, he might report, "When I come home from work my wife's complaining gets to me, and I have a couple of beers to calm down."

cause   *effect*

wife complaining ⟶ husband drinks

Again we have an acceptable linear and understandable cause-and-effect explanation for the behavior. The husband drinks because he cannot tolerate his wife's complaining, and the drinking dulls his anger toward her. This may not be a complete explanation either.

Circular causality considers both explanations and incorporates them in a more complete systemic conceptualization of the problem. The wife complains to stop her husband from drinking, and the husband continues to drink because it helps him tolerate his wife's complaining. This understanding of the problem is known as circular causality.

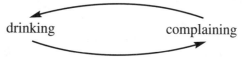

drinking   complaining

A counselor working with this couple would understand the problem more completely by thinking about it using the circular causality model. According to this view, the behavior of *both* persons maintains the problem behavior. The couple's problem may not necessarily be either the drinking or the complaining but, rather, their inability to resolve the power struggle concerning who will control the relationship or something else such as serving as a distraction from other more fundamental marital problems.

Understanding Family Health and Dysfunction

One of the most striking characteristics of family systems theory is the unique ways in which systems therapists define the presenting problem and identify the location of the problem. In most counseling theories, the focus of treatment is the individual because the problem is believed to reside within the person. Family therapists base their work on the concept of systems theory suggested by Ludwig von Bertalanffy (1968). He proposed that systems are composed of interrelated parts and that the organization of the interrelated parts constitutes a higher level system.

A family, composed of its individual members and all their relationships, is one such higher level system. Family systems therapists choose to describe the family as the unit to be treated in therapy rather than to identify one family member of the system for treatment, as is common among individual therapists. Systems therapists recognize that dysfunctional behavior exhibited by the symptomatic individual in the family is usually a manifestation of other problems within the larger family system.

For many family therapists, the whole family system, rather than a single individual in the family, is recruited for treatment. The symptoms that one family member exhibits are viewed as a part of the dysfunctional interactional patterns of the family rather than as a character or personality flaw residing solely within the individual. Another way of stating this is that the IP, or symptom bearer, may be signaling, with his symptoms, a more encompassing problem within the family's relationships and organization.

It is important for the novice family therapist to recognize that just because she is thinking systemically about the family problem does not mean that the family is thinking the same way. In the beginning of treatment, the family thinks therapy is exclusively for the purpose of changing the behaviors of the symptom bearer. The therapist must work to establish a solid working relationship with the family and gradually expand the family's definition of the problem through skillful interventions.

Typically, the IP in a family system is one of the children. When the child's symptoms become disturbing to parents or teachers, individual therapy for the child is usually recommended. If individual treatment is successful, the child's behavior changes, and the change is maintained, the problem was most likely an individual issue with the child and not a manifestation of a more complex family problem. But, if the treatment is not successful; change is not forthcoming; and the frustration of the child, parents, and school officials continues, the parents and school officials may seek a different kind of therapy. This is when family therapy may be considered as an option.

When a family seeks family therapy, it is not necessarily because the members understand that the problem is systemic in nature. In truth, a family rarely is aware of the interactional nature of the IP's symptoms prior to entering family therapy. Instead, the family is there because other forms of treatment have not been successful and the family members desperately want help. The family may come to understand the systemic nature of the symptoms as representative of a problem with the family's interactions through the learning that often takes place in the later phases of family therapy.

Homeostasis

When all family members abide by the family's rules and act in ways consistent with the rules and their roles, family homeostasis (Minuchin, 1974), or balance, is achieved. *Homeostasis* is the tendency of living systems to desire to be at rest or in balance. Living systems, including families, attempt to achieve and maintain homeostasis. When a family member deviates from established family rules or roles, the homeostasis of the family system is threatened. At this point, the other family members begin to engage in corrective behaviors, providing negative (corrective) feedback to the deviating member, in an attempt to return the member and the system to accepted ways of acting, thereby restoring the family homeostasis.

An example of homeostasis is demonstrated by the human body's ability to maintain its temperature of 98.6° on a hot day. Negative feedback is provided and perspiration begins as the body overheats. It evaporates on the body to cool it to the appropriate temperature and maintain homeostasis. When the proper body temperature is restored, positive (stabilizing) feedback is provided that signals the body to stop perspiring. A related example is that of a thermostat. The thermostat senses the temperature of the air in a room and, if the temperature is too low, provides for heat. If the thermostat senses that the temperature is too hot, it shuts down heat production until heat is needed again. Thus, the thermostat regulates a consistent temperature and maintains homeostasis.

Families also exhibit homeostatic mechanisms. For example, a family rule might be that teenage children will be home by 9 o'clock on school nights. The parents allow for some fluctuations in the arrival time of the teenager, but when she returns home more than an hour late, the parents become upset. If this becomes a recurring pattern, the parents begin rule-enforcing measures to bring the system back into balance. As long as the daughter maintained her behavior within an acceptable range and was no more than a few minutes late, this minor deviation from the norm did not upset the family homeostasis, and she had no problems with her parents. But, when she regularly returned home more than an hour late, clearly disregarding a family rule, the parents' tolerance level and family home-ostasis were challenged, and the parents took measures, implementing a restriction policy to reestablish the family system homeostasis.

As long as the daughter followed the family rule, homeostasis is maintained and relationships are fine. If she does not follow the rule and is disciplined, additional problems, such as hostility and resentment, may emerge and further negatively affect relationships between the daughter and her parents and further upset the family's homeostasis. When the parents agree that the problems with their daughter cannot be solved by their restriction policy, they might seek individual therapy for the daughter's defiant, acting-out behavior. If the family has an extremely rigid family structure and the daughter is challenging this dynamic, individual treatment is not likely to be effective in the long run. If the individual therapy is not helpful, the family might chose to try family therapy in a further response to their daughter's defiance and acting out. Family ther-apy would examine the parents' rules, rigid structure, and behaviors along with the daughter's rebelliousness. This broader contextual ap-proach is likely to produce cooperation in rule setting and lead to more positive and long-lasting results than individual treatment. It might help the family restore a revised homeostasis with a set of more functional rules. For example, homeostasis might be restored by the parents' recog-nition of their daughter's need for more autonomy, and in therapy the family might negotiate new rules concerning the curfew.

Boundaries

The flow of information from one family subsystem to another is con-trolled and regulated by the *boundaries* between the subsystems. Boundaries are created primarily by the rules the family establishes for regulating information flow between and among members. Families that are extremely private and do not share many of their thoughts and feelings have *rigid boundaries*. These families do not share very much personal information with one another and especially not with outsiders. They often live in homes where closed bedroom doors are the norm in order to ensure privacy and distance from one another.

Families composed of subsytems that share almost all information with one another as well as many outsiders have *diffuse boundaries*. These families often live in homes where closed bedroom doors are not allowed and family members have detailed information about one another. They are typically very empathic and feel one another's emotions. For example, when a child has been humiliated by another and is in tears, it is not uncommon for the parents or other siblings to cry along with the child.

To understand the effects of boundaries on the family, consider the following example. In a certain type of family, a husband and wife may have a relatively impermeable boundary around their spousal subsystem. This boundary serves to minimize participation or interference by the children in their spousal interactions. To some, this seems harsh and unloving. However, another explanation is possible. The husband and wife also serve in the roles of mother and father to their children. When performing parental functions, they exist in the *parental subsystem*. When the couple is in the *spousal subsystem*, participation of the children is discouraged by family rules. When the couple is in the *parental subsystem*, the subsystem boundaries are permeable, and inclusion and appropriate participation by the children are encouraged. The family as a whole system may have a *permeable boundary* that readily includes members outside the family unit, or it may have a *rigid boundary* that makes inclusion of "outsiders" difficult. To recap the main point here, the nature of the boundaries of the family determines the ease or difficulty of the flow of information within the family and the inclusion or exclusion of participants in the family system and subsystems.

During the first few family therapy sessions, the therapist is engaged in an assessment of the family's characteristics. This assessment process attempts to identify the type of boundaries between family subsystems and between the family and the outside world. If the therapist and family conclude that the boundary functions are impeding healthy family interactions, by either restricting the flow of clear communication or by exacerbating the flow of too much irrelevant and confusing information, the therapist will intervene to assist the family in changing the boundaries and the rules that define those boundaries and the interactions among family members.

The Circumplex Model of Marital and Family Systems

Olson, Russell, and Sprenkle (1989) developed the circumplex model of family functioning to assess families on the dimensions of adaptability and cohesion. Later, they added the third dimension of communication. Shown in Figure 5.2, this model has been widely used in assessing family health and dysfunction.

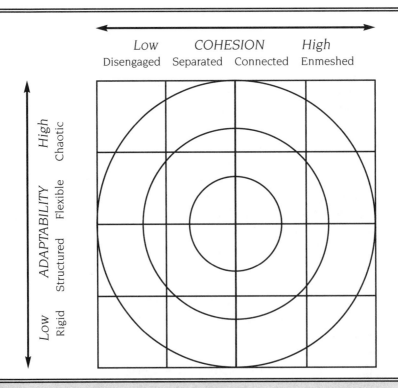

Figure 5.2 Circumplex Model of Family Functioning

Adaptability and Cohesion

Three additional characteristics are used for diagnostic purposes. These are family adaptability, family cohesion, and family communication. Referring to the figure, the constructs of adaptability and cohesion each have four levels. Thus, this 4 × 4 model offers the possibility of identifying 16 types of families. *Adaptability,* (also described as *flexibility*), refers to the family's leadership style; organization; and ability to negotiate and modify its rules, roles, and structure in response to the pressures and conflicts of family life. *Chaotic* families are at the extreme end of the adaptability continuum. These families have little structure for dealing with the problems of family life: Rules are unclear and frequently are not enforced. Clear lines of authority and predictable structure is absent. *Flexible* families are receptive to change and have the ability to resolve problems through negotiations and appropriate changes in rules and roles. *Structured* families are less able than flexible families to modify rules and roles; however, these families are able to adapt and change when necessary. *Rigid* families are at the other extreme. These families are organized to resist change: They are reluctant to change rules and roles and tend to maintain the status quo at all costs.

Cohesion refers to the level of emotional bonding and togetherness in the family and the amount of individual autonomy granted to family members. *Disengaged* families are at one extreme of the dimension. Members are afforded maximum autonomy and may not identify significantly with their family. *Separated* families value individual autonomy, but they have a sense of family unity and identity. *Connected* families value closeness and may prefer it; however, connected families also recognize and support development of autonomy in their members. *Enmeshed* families are at the other extreme of the dimension. These families value closeness above all. In enmeshed families, to sacrifice togetherness for independence is considered a major violation of family rules. The 16 types of families possible in the circumplex model are identified by the level of adaptability (high, mid-range, or low) and the level of cohesion (high, mid-range, or low) present in the family. The therapist can assess the characteristics of the family using the constructs of the circumplex model to understand the family and expedite the family change process. The concepts are easily understood by families and may readily serve as basis for discussion with the family about how they are presently and how they would like to be at the end of therapy (Olson, 2011).

Families in the midrange of the circumplex model have moderate scores on the adaptability and cohesion scales. According to Olson et al. (1989) families with moderate scores are more likely to exhibit characteristics of family health. Families at the extremes (rigid, chaotic, disengaged, or enmeshed) of the two dimensions are more likely to exhibit characteristics of family dysfunction. Olson and his colleagues cautioned, however, that not all families with extreme scores are necessarily dysfunctional and that some mid-range families experience family problems. In general, however, the mid-range families tend toward healthier functioning.

A summary of the characteristics of healthy and dysfunctional families is provided in Table 5.1. Counselors who plan to work with families have to be able to understand and diagnose family functioning and be able to classify families based on the characteristics they exhibit during the therapy sessions. The information provided in Table 5.1 should help the family counselor understand and classify significant family behaviors.

Family Communication

In later revisions of the circumplex model, Olson and his colleagues added *family communication* as a third dimension that should be assessed in the early stages of therapy. Research by Bateson, Jackson, Haley, and Weakland (1956) hypothesized that the double-bind communication style described earlier in this book contributed to the development of schizophrenic symptoms in vulnerable family members. While this hypothesis was not supported by the research, smilar dysfunctional communication patterns were shown to be a feature of other family systems with less severe presenting problems such as impulsivity, anxiety, or depression. Thus, one important objective for effective family therapy is to help clients recognize and modify dysfunctional patterns of communication. Moderate improvement by family members toward more clear and direct communication is often sufficient to ease the severity of other symptoms and paves the way for additional therapeutic gains. Clear, concise, and open communication skills are hallmarks of effective family functioning.

Communication is vital to healthy family functioning because members have to be able to express their thoughts, feelings, and desires to others (Satir, 1983). When family members are unable to express themselves

Table 5.1   Characteristics of Healthy and Dysfunctional Families

Family Health	Family Dysfunction
Subsystem boundaries are clear and may be altered as family requires.	Subsystem boundaries are rigid or diffuse and are not subject to change.
Family rules are clear and fairly enforced. Rules may change as family conditions change.	Rules are unchanging and rigidly enforced, or family has no rules or methods of organizing behavior.
Family members have a clear understanding of their roles and may seek changes in their roles as conditions change.	Roles are rigid and may not be modified, or roles are not clearly defined and members are unsure what is required to meet expectations.
Individual autonomy is encouraged, and a sense of family unity is maintained.	Individual autonomy is sacrificed for family togetherness, or autonomy is required because of lack of family unity.
Communication is clear and direct without being coercive.	Communication is vague and indirect or coercive and authoritarian.

clearly and honestly, problems may develop in one or more family members. For example, when communication is vague and indirect (Satir, 1983), family members are prone to misinterpret the desires and intentions of other members. In these families, conflict and chaotic relationships are likely.

Alexander and Parsons (1982) maintained that an effective negotiation style is an important general goal for all families because negotiation is the key to resolving the myriad differences that arise in families. These authors described the following characteristics of effective family communication:

● *Brevity.* Communication must be short and to the point. This avoids confusing the listener with too much information.

- *Source responsibility.* Wants and needs are expressed most effectively in "I statements." These allow the sender of the message to take responsibility for the wants, thoughts, or feelings expressed. By maintaining source responsibility, the sender avoids making accusations to the listener and keeps the communication flow on a positive level.

- *Directness.* When it is necessary to identify behaviors in others that have been problematic, the communicator should identify the person and the behavior directly. Directness avoids the problem of not clearly identifying what is needed for change to occur. An indirect statement would be, "No one in this family ever helps me in the kitchen." A more effective statement would be, "I need more help from you in the kitchen."

- *Presentation of alternatives.* Effective communicators are not overly demanding; they present alternatives to solving a problem. In addition, they are open to alternative solutions suggested by the listener. For example, a husband may say to a wife, "I cannot get all the rooms painted by the time your parents come. Would you like me to start on the first floor or upstairs?"

- *Congruence.* Effective communicators present messages that are consistent or congruent at all levels. The verbal message is consistent with the nonverbal message, and the message is appropriate for the context of the conversation. If a husband needs more affection from his wife, he should ask for this in a pleasant manner with congruent body language rather than asking for this with a critical tone and demanding scowl on his face.

- *Concreteness and behavioral specificity.* Effective communicators specify clearly what behavior is needed from the listener. Rather than saying, "You complain too much," the effective communicator would say, "I become angry when I hear you complain about my not helping in the kitchen." This level of specificity permits the communicators to know exactly what they need to work on.

- *Feedback.* Effective communicators seek clarification from all parties in a way that does not interrupt the purpose of the interaction or change the topic of discussion. For example, when a wife tells her husband that his "long work hours are creating distance in the relationship," she could seek feedback by asking him what he understood her to say. Possibly, the husband heard criticism from his wife when she wanted him to hear that she was lonely. This feedback technique is an important way for couples to be sure their communication is clear.

Improving dysfunctional communication is usually an important goal of family therapy. Family therapists can help families identify and modify their dysfunctional communication patterns by educating clients about the components of effective communication and by allowing clients to practice these skills during counseling sessions where feedback can be provided by the family members and the therapist. This "in session" practice and immediate feedback involving all family members with therapist supervision is one of the features that sets family therapy apart from individual treatment.

Family Life Cycle

Professional counselors and other psychotherapy practitioners must be able to design therapeutic interventions that are appropriate for the developmental stage of the individual receiving treatment. In the same vein, family therapists who treat couple and family difficulties must be able to design systemic interventions that are appropriate for the developmental stage of the family. Just as individuals move through predictable stages in their development, families pass through predictable stages of development as well.

Carter and McGoldrick (1980, 2005) suggested that families move through stages of development in the process of marriage or uniting as a couple in a committed relationship, childrearing, and preparing for life as a couple with grown children. Typically, three generations of the family are involved in the life cycle process. Carter and McGoldrick delineated specific developmental tasks that must be accomplished at each of the developmental stages of the family, as described in the following list. The family life cycle may be entered at any point. We enter at the stage in which the individual has left the family of origin and may be seeking a life partner.

● *The unattached young adult.* During this stage, parents and child come to accept the separation that has developed between the generations. The offspring begins to develop intimate peer relationships and establish a career pattern.

- *The joining of two families.* During this stage, the young adult commits fully to establishing a new family system through marriage or permanent commitment. Critical events are the realignment of relationships with extended family and peers to meet the requirements of the newly formed union.
- *The family with young children.* During this stage, the couple must change the family system to make room for children. The parents must increase their role responsibilities to include parenting, and they must adjust their relationships with each other and with the older generation. The members of the older generation now move into new roles as they assume new responsibilities as grandparents.
- *The family with adolescents.* During this often stormy stage, parents must allow more autonomy for adolescents. Adolescents begin to move out of the family system and seriously seek autonomy. Parents deal with mid-life career and relationship issues and begin preparing to assume responsibilities of caring for the older generation.
- *Launching children and preparing for life without children.* During this stage, the parents help the children leave the family to establish their own lives. In addition, the partners begin to renegotiate their relationship as a two-person system. During this stage, the couple may adopt the new roles of in-laws and grandparents. Finally, they must deal with the declining health and death of their own parents.
- *The family in later life.* During this stage, the couple deals with passing the torch to the next generation. Specifically, the two of them must maintain their own interests in the face of declining health, support a more central role for their children (middle generation) in the family, and create a place for themselves in the family system without trying to control the middle and youngest generations. Ultimately, each partner must prepare for and perhaps deal with loss of their partner and prepare for their own death.

Counselors may best use the family life cycle by understanding that specific issues emerge for family members at each of the stages. Knowledge of these stages and the most frequent issues that emerge prepares counselors to identify effective interventions to help their client families deal with these significant issues in acceptable ways. This knowledge also enables counselors to engender hope by reassuring family members that events that are currently creating stress for the family may be normal aspects of family development and can be handled as such rather than as psychological dysfunction. This intervention can provide tremendous relief for many families and pave the way for rapid resolution of family problems.

For example, parents frequently become overly critical of their teenager when their son begins the normal process of establishing independence from his parents. Parents often diagnose their adolescent as having emotional or psychological problems such as depression because of the withdrawal that takes place during this stage. More often than not, the teenager is not behaving abnormally. He is actually engaging in rebellion and withdrawal from parents that is part of the normal life cycle process of differentiating from the family of origin. Although differentiation is often painful for the parents and children alike, it is not necessarily a sign that the adolescent has psychological problems. When the counselor reassures the parents and the adolescent that what is happening in the family is a normal aspect of family development, the stress and anxiety that had been present are often significantly reduced, and healthy family functioning is enhanced.

The family therapist, while normalizing certain predictable developmental issues, may reassure the family that normal process are unfolding and that there are more effective ways to deal with the issues that have emerged. The family systems therapy approach, which engages all family members in the solution of the problem, is extremely useful in helping families respond effectively to their life cycle development issues. A caveat: family therapists should be very careful when normalizing family developmental issues. If normalization is not done effectively and with sensitivity, family members may believe that their problems are being discounted and may terminate therapy prematurely.

The family life cycle development model is based on the rules and roles of the traditional family composed of three generations and two parents. Although many of the developmental tasks described are appropriate for nontraditional family systems, such as remarried families, single-parent families, and other minority and alternative family types, they frequently have additional tasks to accomplish. Specific issues of nontraditional families will be treated in Part Three of this book.

The Sandwich Generation

This term describes couples who have children, perhaps in college or graduate school, who are still dependent on them for support and have elderly parents who may be experiencing medical problems and need help as well. The couple is sandwiched in between their own children and their parents. This is a very stressful position for the middle-aged couple. The competing tugs of the older and younger generations can cause the couple to lose focus on their own relationship. It can be a time when the couple grows distant from each other, and they may experience marital problems of their own as they try to sort out competing demands on their time, emotions, and financial resources.

This problem can be exacerbated when grown children "fail to launch" and return home. In the worst situations, this occurs when the oldest generation may need to be considering a retirement facility. "Boomerang children" are offspring who have been launched into the world and have not been economically or socially successful so have returned to the family home. Family therapists frequently work with these families, and it may seem that failure to launch is widespread. However, this is not the case. Michael Rosenfeld (2010), a sociologist, has analyzed this phenomenon. He reported an upturn in young unmarried Americans under the age of 30 who live with their parents since 2000. In 2009 approximately 40% of women lived with their parents compared to 35% in 2000. For men, 45% lived with parents in 2009 compared with 42% in 2000. This is a role reversal from previous decades when men were more autonomous and more likely to live away from their parents than women. While the recent trend suggests more men and women are living with their parents today, Rosenfeld (2010) reminded us that the number of unmarried adult children living with parents is at a historical low. In 1960, 55% of men and women lived with parents and in 1940 approximately 70% lived with parents. So, contrary to popular media presentations, "failure to launch" adult children is not as big a problem as many believe.

Summary

This chapter has provided a brief description of important concepts required to understand the family as a living system and the appropriate focus of treatment in family therapy. Readers have been introduced to several key family therapy concepts such as homeostasis, circular causality, subsystems, boundaries, cohesion, flexibility, and communication. The family has been described as being composed of several subsystems, and intervention strategies have been identified. The circumplex, communications, and family life cycle models were presented to help therapists in training to understand and assess normal and abnormal family functioning.

Suggested Readings

Carter, B., & McGoldrick, M., (Eds.). (2005). *The expanded family life cycle: Individual, family and social perspectives.* Boston: Pearson.

Minuchin, S. (1974). *Families and family therapy.* Cambridge, MA: Harvard University Press.

Olson, D. H., Russell, C. S., & Sprenkle, D. H. (1989). *Circumplex model: Systemic assessment and treatment of families.* New York: Haworth Press.

Rosenfeld, M. J. (2010). The independence of young adults in historical perspective. *Family Therapy Magazine, 9*(3[E2]), 16–19.

Making the Paradigm Shift: Building Bridges from Individual to Family Systems Theory

This chapter provides information about the similarities and differences between individual and systems theories. Too often the differences between individual and systems theories have been emphasized without sufficient consideration of their similarities. Effective therapists use both individual and systems theories in clinical practice. In order to understand when and how to select an individual or systems approach to treatment, the therapist must be aware of the strengths and limitations of each. This chapter also presents a five-step treatment procedure that may be used by therapists with experience in individual counseling but less experience applying family systems theories. Then the core competencies necessary for the effective practice of family therapy are presented. Finally the classification scheme used to organize the individual and systems theories presented in Part Two of this book is described.

Key Concepts

- ○ Locus of pathology
- ○ System as client
- ○ Joining
- ○ Systems therapist as expert
- ○ Expanding the definition of the problem
- ○ Paradigm shift
- ○ Brief family therapy

Questions for Discussion

1. What are the major *similarities* between individual and systems theory approaches to counseling?
2. What are the major *differences* between individual and systems theory approaches to counseling?
3. What can the counselor do to expand the definition of the presenting problem in family therapy? Why is this important?
4. Why is it important to join with each family member in family counseling?
5. What basic counseling techniques may be used in the joining process?
6. Why do family systems counselors consider it important to treat the whole family as the client?
7. Which of the major domains of the AAMFT core competencies seem most important to you? Which seem less important? Defend your choices with sound reasoning.

During the formative years of the family therapy profession, considerable emphasis was placed on the differences between individual counseling approaches and family therapy. As Gurman and Kniskern (1981b, p. xii) stated, transactional analysis (TA), client-centered, rational–emotive, Adlerian, cognitive, and Gestalt therapies have been the primary influences in individual and group therapy, but they do not employ systems concepts. Although Gurman and Kniskern acknowledged that some family therapists have adopted aspects of these individual theories in their work with couples and families, they emphasized that these theories have not exerted a significant influence on the family therapy field.

In part, theories that were developed to help individual clients have not been very influential in family therapy because of a perceived dichotomy between the practice of individual and group therapy and family therapy. This dichotomy is based on the idea that individual and group theories conceptualize problems as existing within individuals and that these problems are maintained by the actions of the individual or by past thoughts, feelings, and experiences. Family therapy, on the other hand, based on systems concepts, assumes that psychological problems in an individual are conspicuous elements of a more encompassing problem that involves the individual as well as the interpersonal system. Most often, the interpersonal system is composed of the members of the identified patient's family.

This dichotomy between individual and group theories and systems-based theories obscures the fact that many of the skills that individual therapists possess can be used effectively to help couples and families change. Effective therapists should be able to conceptualize problem formation in clients from both individually-oriented models and systems-based models. Many counselors believe they are in some way being disloyal to their theoretical position if they do not adhere to the concepts in exactly the same way as the founder of the theory. This observation applies to counselors who adhere to individual as well as systems-based theories. I have found that the most effective therapists are those who have identified a theoretical approach that is consistent with their own value system and who are open to modifying their approach in response to client needs, new information, and evidence from the research literature.

The purpose of this book is to help counselors with experience working with individual theories build bridges linking their current way of conceptualizing problem formation to a model of helping that is systems based. To begin this process, it is important for readers to understand the similarities and differences between individual and family systems therapies.

Similarities between Individual and Systems Theories

For counselors to comfortably cross the bridge from individual to systems-based treatment, they need to reaffirm their awareness that the ultimate goal of all counseling theories, including individual and systems theories, is to help alleviate human suffering. Once the counselor recognizes that the goal of therapy is the same for all approaches, the question becomes: What is the best way to incorporate theory and technique to alleviate this human suffering? While research confirms that most theoretical approaches to therapy are effective (Duncan, 2010), I believe that counselors who do not incorporate systems-based family therapy in their skill repertoire may not be as well-equipped to help their clients as a therapist who is able to conceptualize and treat from both individual and systems-based theoretical orientations as the client's needs dictate.

A second similarity between individual and systems-based theories is that each respects the dignity of the client. The client seeks the services of the therapist. The therapist, in turn, attempts to help the client resolve the difficulties that are affecting the client's life. To be successful in helping the client, the therapist must clearly communicate that he respects the attempts, however ineffective, the client has made to resolve the current problems. Moreover, the therapist communicates, through *respect*, that the client possesses the resources necessary to make significant life changes (Rogers, 1957, 1961).

If counselors accept that both individual and systems theory treatments seek to alleviate human suffering and respect the dignity of their clients, it will become easier to adopt a systems perspective when this approach is in the best interests of the client. It is critical that counselors who operate from an individual counseling theoretical orientation recognize that they need not reject their current knowledge and unlearn their skills. Moreover, they are not asked to surrender their belief in the dignity of the client. These characteristics are shared by individual and systems theorists alike.

Differences between the Theories

I have identified four specific differences between individual treatment theories and systems-based family therapy theories. These differences are based on the ways that individual and systems therapists *think about* psychological problem formation and problem resolution. Understanding this fundamental difference is the key in making the shift from individual to family systems treatment.

1. Location of the Problem

Traditionally, therapists serving individual clients believe that the locus of pathology (or the location of the problem) is within the person's psyche. According to this model, problems occur because the client has not resolved certain issues in her current or past experiences. The therapist's goal is to help the client examine and resolve these internal psychological issues and conflicts. The client gains insight into the sources of the problems and uses the insight to make behavioral changes.

The systems therapist does not discount this model. However, the systems therapist considers an alternative hypothesis of problem formation and locus of pathology. Although an individual's problem may lie within the his psyche, systems theorists assume that the client's concerns occur as a result of problematic interaction patterns between and among significant persons within his social context. This social context is most often the client's family. Thus, for the systems theorist, the the problem is with the client's social system or family. From a systems perspective, the problems experienced by one family member are believed to be conspicuous elements of a family pattern in which *all* members play a role in the creation and maintenance of the problems.

2. Focus of Treatment Interventions

From an individual theorist's perspective, the focus of treatment is generally on the individual client. The therapist concentrates on helping the client explore her past and present world and discover what could be changed to make life more satisfying. When employing individual counseling methods, the therapist gathers information based primarily on the *client's perceptions* of what has occurred in the past and what is occurring presently in her life. For example, if the client is having problems relating to a member of her family system, the individual therapist will facilitate discovery of ways to change thoughts, behaviors, and feelings to respond more effectively to other family members. In other words, the client herself makes all the changes.

The family therapist considers the family unit, not the individual with symptoms, to be the client. Therefore, the focus of treatment is on *all the members* of the family system of the client. The family member who has the symptoms and is designated as *the problem* is referred to as the identified patient (IP). When possible, the family systems therapist will treat the IP's entire family and will assist each family member develop new and more effective ways to relate to each other and to the IP. When the therapy is successful, all family members have changed their patterns of interaction and improved in ways they had not imagined at the beginning of treatment. Moreover, the symptoms of the IP usually decrease in intensity and duration and may eventually disappear. In family therapy, the therapist identifies and modifies interaction patterns and family structure. In addition, the therapist must respond effectively to the perceptions of all the family members, just as in individual treatment. Moreover, the therapist is responsible for observing and helping the family modify their actual behaviors, thoughts, feelings, and interactions. Recognizing and validating each family member's perceptions is vital in establishing trust and is an important step in helping each family member become ready to accept the challenge of examining and modifying their behaviors.

The individual psychotherapist usually speaks only to the client and must trust the client's perceptions and reports concerning his behavior in relation to the other members of the family. This, of course, can present a skewed picture of what is actually happening when the family interacts at home. In contrast, the family therapist can directly observe the behaviors of the IP and each of the other family members during the sessions. This is a *major strength* of family therapy. No longer must the therapist rely on the perceptions of an individual client. The therapist can now form an opinion about the family problems based on actual observation of the family interacting around real and immediate issues during family therapy sessions. Based on observations of family interaction patterns, the systems therapist helps each member of the family adjust his or her behavior to a more satisfying state for all concerned. In family work, everyone has the opportunity to change—not just the IP. Systems therapists believe that lasting change is more likely to occur when all members of the system are participating in the change process and invested in maintaining it.

3. Unit of Treatment

The individually-oriented therapist treats an individual client in therapy. This approach makes perfect sense based on the theoretical assumption that the problems reside within the psyche of the individual. It may be the treatment of choice for certain types of presenting problems.

Family therapists want to treat the entire family or, at a minimum, involve the most motivated members of the family, the ones who are feeling most concern about the family's issues. The therapist's ability to help is increased when several members are present in treatment. Rather than focusing on one client and attempting to help that person change, the family therapist can engage all the family members in discussions about how the problem emerged and what the family might do to resolve it. Several heads working together under professional leadership are better than one! This feature greatly increases the possibilities for change and contributes to a more rapid resolution of the presenting problems. Because systems therapists believe that individual problems are symptoms of broader problems within the family, they believe that that appropriate unit of treatment is the entire family system or, if this not possible, engaging as many members of the family in treatment as is possible.

4. Duration of Treatment

Traditional therapists serving individual clients want to help them resolve internal conflicts that may have roots imbedded deeply in the past. Thus, treatment may continue until the client has not only fully worked through problems that occurred in the past but is also functioning effectively in the present. This type of treatment may be quite lengthy, depending on the specific presenting problem and the theoretical orientation of the therapist. Such treatment, in addition to being expensive and lengthy, also has the disadvantage of potentially creating client dependence on the counselor over the long duration of the counseling.

Family systems theorists attempt to provide brief treatment for the resolution of family-related problems. Systems theorist wants to help families alter their current patterns of dysfunctional behavior and then terminate the therapy as quickly as possible. Family members learn to depend on each other, rather than on the therapist, in the resolution of their difficulties. Once termination of family therapy occurs, client families are encouraged to return to therapy only if further difficulties occur at a later date. The therapist trusts the power of the family system to sustain the changes made in treatment. Although the length of treatment varies widely, family therapy tends to be briefer than most forms of individual psychotherapy, often lasting from as few as one to as many as 24 sessions. The systems therapist is not trying to help family members resolve longstanding internal conflicts. Rather, the family therapist expects to help the family resolve only its immediate crisis through alteration of the current pattern of dysfunctional interaction among the members. She then encourages the family to terminate treatment and implement the systemic changes in the home environment.

Applying Individual Counseling Theories and Techniques to Family Treatment

Counselors trained in individual and group theories often believe that they are not adequately trained to work with families because they lack expertise in systems theory. However, counselors with training and experience in individual and group therapy can begin to work effectively under supervision with couples and families, using core counseling skills they have already developed (Fenell & Hovestadt, 1986). Moreover, the individual counseling theories emphasized in most counselor training programs can be employed in working with couples and families, as will be demonstrated in subsequent chapters in Part Two of this book. Core counseling skills may be used to accomplish a series of five steps that are important in both individual and family systems therapy.

1. Establish Effective Relationships with Family Members

To help an individual or a family change through psychotherapy and to develop a productive counseling relationship, the first step for the therapist is to establish an effective relationship with each individual involved in the treatment. The skills counselors develop in their training programs (e.g., empathy, respect, genuineness) that enable the therapist to establish a therapeutic relationship with clients are the same skills the family therapist needs to develop a working relationship with the members of a family system (Duncan, 2010; Rogers, 1961). In family therapy, establishing an effective working relationship with each family member and the family system is known as *joining* (Minuchin, 1974). Joining with each family member is an important prerequisite to further productive work in therapy.

2. Establish Therapist as Expert

Establishing the therapist as an expert who can help the family change is a step that some counselors may find inconsistent with effective therapy. Many counselors trained in group and individual psychotherapy have learned to implement person-centered therapy techniques (Rogers, 1961). Roger's approach is based on the assumption that the *client is the expert* concerning the problem and that the client will resolve his own problems if the therapist can provide an effective, nonjudgmental relationship with the client. Even though the theory postulates that the client is expert, the counselor is also an expert in helping the client activate the potential to be self-directed and to change behaviors. Thus, nondirective therapists establish themselves as experts in helping their clients, although they accomplish this through empathy, warmth, and genuineness rather than through more readily observable and directive therapeutic interventions that are more common in family systems approaches.

Establishing the therapist as an expert in helping the family change may be accomplished directly or indirectly. In the direct approach, the counselor may give specific suggestions to family members to help the family change dysfunctional behavioral patterns. For example, the directive therapist may share perceptions with the family concerning the family's repetitive patterns and then describe ways that needed change might occur. Direct leadership may also be asserted by referring to experts in the field or citing research relevant to the presenting problem. For example, a therapist may assist a couple using direct leadership by citing a research study on characteristics of long-term marriages that might be helpful to them (Fenell, 1993a).

If expert leadership is established indirectly, the counselor becomes a significant source of self-esteem for the members of the family through demonstrating genuine caring, respect, and understanding of each family member. Basic relationship skills taught in virtually all counseling programs, such as empathy, respect, warmth, and genuineness, are particularly effective in establishing expert leadership indirectly.

3. Expand the Definition of the Problem

To work most effectively with a family, the counselor has to redefine the presenting problem as one that exists and is maintained within the family system. The family's definition of the problem, which must be expanded by the therapist, is that the problem exists entirely because of the behaviors of the IP. They believe that the family would be just fine if only the IP would change.

To expand the definition of the problem, the therapist must acknowledge and demonstrate respect for the family's current explanation of the problem while concurrently pointing out specific words and actions that show that other members are involved in supporting and exacerbating the problems of the IP. Expanding the definition of the problem in a way that is embraced by the family is essential in implementing a systems-based intervention plan (Haley, 1983). If the family continues to believe the problem is solely the responsibility of the IP, the members are less likely to make their own changes in support of new behaviors by the IP, changes that could positively affect the outcome of treatment.

The counselor can help the family expand the definition of the problem by applying basic counseling skills. For example, the counselor is already trained to identify problem behaviors exhibited by an individual client and to communicate to the client how the behaviors maintain the undesired symptoms. In the same manner, the counselor may observe and identify behaviors or communication styles in other family members that directly or indirectly affect the IP's problems. By using effective relationship skills learned in most counselor training programs, the therapist can empathically and concretely help other family members discover how their behaviors play a role in the maintenance of the presenting problems and identify steps each family member might take to institute change.

A classic example of expanding the definition of the problem occurs when a family comes to therapy seeking help with a misbehaving daughter. The therapist may quickly discover that the parents hold quite different opinions about how to best deal with the child's behavior. In fact, their disagreement on this point may be quite problematic in itself. The family therapist will use all the information presented by the IP and the parents to expand the definition of the problem to include the parents and the IP. The therapist will help the parents recognize that they send contradictory and confusing messages to their daughter and that the parents' behavior places the child in a bind that may precipitate the acting-out behavior. Moreover, resolving the disagreement between the parents concerning their expectations for their daughter and helping them learn to send direct and congruent messages to her will be an additional focus of therapy. As mentioned previously, the therapist must develop excellent observational skills to detect important family patterns. Excellent relationship and communication skills are needed to present this information effectively to the family in a way that will allow them to accept the expanded definition of the problem.

It is critical that the therapist accurately describe the *actual behaviors* of the family members in the expanded definition of the problem. By using actual family behavioral data in the expanded definition, the therapist increases the likelihood that the family will accept the expanded definition, as the members come to acknowledge their actions and recognize how they fit in to an overall pattern in the family. Furthermore, by joining with the family members using effective relationship-building, communication, and observational skills, the therapist will establish himself as an expert concerning family behaviors. The therapist can then exert effective leadership in helping the family recognize their interactional patterns and how these patterns serve to the maintain the presenting problem. After accomplishing this, it follows that the new and expanded definition of the problem will be accepted by the family system.

Expanding the definition of the problem is important in family treatment. If the family's definition of the problem is maintained, the family remains the expert concerning the problem. If the family is the expert, they will continue to do what they have done in the past by employing different variations of the same ineffective solutions they have previously attempted. Increased frustration and intensified symptoms in the IP are likely. When a new and expanded definition of the problem is presented and accepted by the family, the therapist becomes the expert on the problem and its resolution. Thus, problem resolution will be expedited as the family turns to therapist for leadership in the change process. When the therapist becomes the expert on the problem, the family will defer to the therapist and more enthusiastically try new behaviors and more creative solutions to their problem.

4. Engage All Members in Solving the Problem

After the counselor has successfully expanded the definition of the problem to include other family members, it is important to engage the family members in solving the problem. This step can be accomplished during a session by asking two family members to discuss how the newly defined problem can be resolved. Some members may be reluctant to participate at first; however, if the therapist has established herself a caring and empathic expert, she can successfully encourage the less verbal family members to participate. This is particularly important because the reluctant participants usually have excellent new insights into the family and are able to suggest ways that the family could behave in more effective ways. Thus, it is critical to the success of therapy that the therapist be certain *all members* are included in the process of problem resolution.

Remember that all family members are likely to participate willingly, suggesting new and more effective ways to deal with thier problems once the problem and the context have been redefined as a family, rather than an individual, concern. After accepting the redefinition, family members are no longer faced with the same insoluble situation that brought them to therapy. Rather, they are dealing with a new and expanded version of the problem, which may lend itself to new and creative solutions involving all members of the family system.

5. Make a Paradigm Shift

The last and possibly most difficult step in the process of working effectively with family systems is developing the ability to make the paradigm shift to systems thinking. Counselors are well trained and prepared to accept new ideas and to implement them when they are in the best interest of their clients. Systems therapy offers avenues for therapeutic change that cannot be easily achieved from other theoretical orientations. Thus, the competent counselor will want to be able to use systems therapy when it is in the best interests of the client family.

Each of the five steps listed above can be accomplished by any competently prepared therapist. However, these steps will be nothing more than a set of techniques to be routinely followed if they are not supported by consistent systems-based theoretical assumptions and actions. Therefore, counselors who work with family systems need to make the paradigm shift from conceptualizing problems as existing within the individual to thinking about problems as conspicuous aspects of a dysfunctional family system. The living family system is the client, not the individual family member identified by the family as the problem.

Too often counselors adopt a way of helping and adhere to the tenets of the theory as if it were a religion to be followed faithfully. Counseling theories are not religions; they are models developed to help clients make life changes. If one model for helping does not work, effective therapists will try other models. Systems theory offers a powerful alternative helping paradigm that counselors can employ with their clients. However, this model cannot be effectively implemented if the counselor is unable to conceptualize the family as a living system and as the focus of treatment, in other words: *making the paradigm shift.*

Competencies Required to Become an Effective Family Therapist

As the profession of marriage, couple, and family therapy has matured, training standards identifying the core competencies required of effective therapists have been developed. Both the American Association for Marriage and Family Therapy (AAMFT) and the Council for Accreditation of Counseling and Related Educational Programs (CACREP) have developed such competencies. The core competencies identified by the AAMFT are briefly described here. The AAMFT competencies are focused on specific behaviors that effective therapists should possess, while the CACREP standards attend to specific family counselor learning experiences and competencies that graduate programs must provide to their students.

The AAMFT Core Competencies

In response to pressures from graduate training programs, managed care insurance companies, and state licensing boards, the AAMFT commissioned a task force to identify the core competencies needed to define the knowledge, skill level, and other characteristics of proficient marriage and family therapists. In 2004, the Task Force released its findings by presenting 128 specific competencies that were necessary to perform successfully as an independent marriage and family therapist. The AAMFT Core Competencies are used by the government and many managed care companies to evaluate the qualifications of practicing family therapists and to determine those who qualify for third-party payments.

The Marriage and Family Core competencies are composed of six broad domains:

1. *Admission to treatment.* This domain covers competencies needed to get therapy started and build a working alliance with family members.
2. *Clinical assessment and diagnosis.* This domain describes the competencies required to identify the family's structure, patterns of functioning, and most significant problems.
3. *Treatment planning and case management.* This domain identifies the competencies required to develop a plan to provide effective treatment to the family and to carry the plan to completion or revise it as client circumstances warrant.
4. *Therapeutic interventions.* This domain is concerned with the therapist's ability to comprehend and implement a variety of effective evidence-based, individually-oriented approaches as well as systemic, evidence-based therapeutic approaches to assist their client families.
5. *Legal issues, ethics, and standards.* This domain specifies that competent family therapists must be familiar with all pertinent laws, regulations, and professional ethical standards that apply to the practice of marriage, couple, and family therapy.
6. *Research and program evaluation.* This domain requires that therapist be familiar with the professional literature and outcome research that pertains to the delivery of marriage, couple, and family therapy services. Moreover, practitioners are expected to understand research methodologies and be able to evaluate the effects of their interventions on the families they treat.

To more precisely specify the competencies needed for effective delivery of marriage and family therapy services, each of the six major domains of the marriage and family therapy core competencies described above are divided in to five subordinate domains.

1. *Conceptual.*This subordinate domain emphasizes the importance of knowledge about family therapy theory and techniques and the ability to think clearly about the treatment process.
2. *Perceptual.* This subordinate domain emphasizes the therapist's abilities to clearly view what is happening with the family in the therapy session. It is the ability to "know what is going on" with your clients at any given moment in the treatment process.
3. *Executive.* This subordinate domain emphasizes the ability of the therapist to effectively implement family therapy interventions based on conceptual and perceptual skills.
4. *Evaluative.* This subordinate domain focuses on the therapist's ability to evaluate his or her own effectiveness in the therapy process and to evaluate the impact of the interventions made during the therapy process.
5. *Professional.* This subordinate domain requires that family therapists provide professional treatment in accordance with appropriate legal and ethical standards.

The core competencies just described provide the reader with a sense of the magnitude of the learning process required to become ethically prepared to deliver professional marriage and family therapy service to clients. A complete listing of the AAMFT Core Competencies is provided in Appendix D for readers interested in a more thorough review of the abilities required to an effective marriage and family therapist.

Classification of Theories in This Book

The theories in this book have been organized into three categories to aid readers in understanding the material presented. The categories are psychodynamic, cognitive–behavioral and interpersonal theories. The classification scheme builds on the work of Levant (1984), who developed a multilevel classification system for family therapy theories.

The present classification system is unique in that it describes how theories developed to treat individual problems can be used in working with couples and families. Further, several major family therapy theories are presented that may be incorporated by counselors and psychotherapists after appropriate training and supervision.

Each of the theories will be presented in the same organizational format for the purposes of comparison and to develop the bridge between individual and systems theories. First, I will present the background for each theory and clarify why and how each theory was developed. Second, I will present the philosophical tenets of each theory and discuss the assumptions underlying each theory. It is of critical importance that counselors understand the assumptions underlying their method of providing therapeutic assistance to clients. Third, I will describe the major techniques associated with each theory, including the major interventions used to bring about therapeutic change. In addition to describing these three areas for each individual and systems theory, I include case examples demonstrating the actual use of each theory. Finally, I will present the strengths and limitations of each theory.

As you study each of the theories in this book, it is important to note that certain theories will make more sense to you and be more acceptable and relevant than others. This is as it should be. Each theory is based on certain assumptions and philosophical tenets. Counselors are most comfortable with theories that are based on philosophical tenets similar to their own beliefs about the development of psychological problems and the alleviation of these problems. I suggest that you initially become familiar with the theories that seem most relevant to you and seem most promising for the client and client family. As you begin your work as a family therapist, use these relevant theories in your practice. Then, after becoming grounded in one or more theories, carefully consider and implement theories that are less comfortable, when in the best interests of your client or family. When you are thoroughly grounded and very comfortable with a familiar theory, you will have the ability to move from that theory to study other theories carefully. A return to the familiar is always possible if the study of the new theories becomes too uncomfortable. I believe that having a strong theoretical home base permits the family therapist in training to engage in a more thorough exploration of other more personally challenging theories.

This book describes the major individual and systems theories that can be employed in family counseling. Several of these theories may serve as a comfortable home base as the counselor studies other systems models developed for treating families.

Summary

This chapter has introduced the aspiring family therapist to several basic concepts that are needed to begin successful treatment of couples and families. The similarities and differences between family therapy and individual therapy were presented. A five-step process to guide the work of beginning family therapists was identified. Next, the AAMFT core competencies were described. These competencies can guide the developing family therapist in attaining the conceptual, perceptual, executive, evaluative, and professional skills expected of a well prepared family therapist was descried using the AAMFT. Finally, the structural framework for presenting the theories to be studied in Part Two of this book was described. It is recommended that developing competencies in the delivery of a core therapeutic approach supported by expertise in a variety of other methods in order to be equipped to meet the needs of a wide range of client needs.

Suggested Readings

Horne, A., & Ohlsen, M. (Eds.). (1982). *Family counseling and therapy.* Itasca, IL: Peacock.

Gehart, D. (2010). *Mastering competencies in family therapy.* Brooks/Cole–Cengage Learning.

Levant, R. (1984). *Family therapy: A comprehensive overview.* Englewood Cliffs, NJ: Prentice Hall.

Minuchin, S., & Fishman, C. (1981). *Family therapy techniques.* Cambridge, MA: Harvard University Press.

Using Core Counseling Skills in Marriage, Couple, and Family Therapy

This chapter describes 12 core counseling skills taught in counselor preparation programs. Each of the 12 skills is identified, and recommendations are made concerning how the skills may be applied in individual, group, and family therapy.

Key Concepts

- Rapport building
- Joining
- Information gathering
- Minimal encouragers
- Genogram
- Structuring
- Information giving
- Reflecting content
- Reflecting feelings
- Feeling cross
- Summarizing
- Self-disclosure
- Confrontation
- Interpretation
- Reframing
- Behavior change
- Closure and termination

Questions for Discussion

1. Why is rapport building important in individual, group, and family counseling?
2. What steps should the family counselor take when joining with a family?
3. What is a genogram, and how is it useful in family counseling?
4. How is reflection of content different from reflection of feeling, and why is each skill important in counseling?
5. What is reframing, and why is it important in counseling?
6. What are the components of behavior change skills, and how are these used in individual, group, and family counseling?
7. Which skills described in this chapter do you believe are most important in the helping process?
8. Describe a situation where use of the feeling cross would be helpful.

The five fundamental steps described in the previous chapter suggest a framework for counselors trained in individual therapy to begin working with couples and families. Counselors in training who begin to work with couples and families are trained in the use of specific core therapeutic skills and should have qualified supervision available. This chapter describes 12 core counseling skills that may be used in individual, group, and family counseling. Each of the following sections will demonstrate how these core skills, which are already in the repertoire of most counselors, may be used as a bridge from individual and group counseling to marriage, family, and couple counseling.

Core Skill 1: Rapport Building

When counseling individual clients, rapport building involves behaving in an attentive manner toward the client both verbally and nonverbally. Examples of good nonverbal attention include sitting attentively and facing the client, maintaining good eye contact, and being relaxed. Verbal attention would include staying with the topic the client is discussing and not changing the subject.

In group counseling sessions, rapport building is more difficult because of the number of people involved. The basic premise is the same, however, as with the individual. The goal in group therapy is to let the group members know you are "with them" and that you accept them rather than approve or disapprove of them. It is also useful to pay close attention to the language the clients use, which will indicate their favorite way of accessing information (visual, auditory, or kinesthetic). Research has shown that matching a client's way of accessing information is an effective way to build rapport. If a client says, "I am clear [visual] that it wasn't my fault," you might match that by saying, "You don't see why people are blaming you." The key is to let the client know you are attentive and tracking by matching his verbal and nonverbal behavior (Dilts & Green, 1982).

In marriage, couple, and family therapy, rapport building with clients is called joining (Minuchin, 1974). Working with a couple or family requires establishing rapport with each individual in the family. The effective therapist must join with each member of the family system and also identify and join with the significant subsystems of the family.

Joining with Each Family Member

Each person in a family has a story to tell. Each individual needs to tell her story and to know that she has been heard, understood, and validated by the counselor. Thus, excellent listening skills and effective verbal and nonverbal communication skills are essential for the counselor to let the individual know that she has been understood. If rapport building, or joining, is successful, the counselor will become a significant source of self-esteem for each family member (Minuchin & Fishman, 1981). When the family members look to the counselor to meet self-esteem needs in the therapy session, the counselor's ability to influence and to intervene effectively with the family will increase.

Unlike group counseling, in family therapy the story that each family member tells will be related to the story of every other member. The effective counselor is nonjudgmental and will hear and understand each version of the story without favoring any of the versions. This skill takes practice, as the counselor's own values frequently support one family member's position over the others. If the counselor's values do become obvious, the ability to intervene in creative and effective ways becomes limited as the counselor is "sucked" into the family system, becoming a member of the problematic family interactions while losing therapeutic objectivity. This happens to most therapists at least once in their careers and is an important lesson about the family's power to induct the therapist in to its dysfunctional pattern. When this occurs, the therapist is advised to seek effective supervision immediately to understand what in his own family background was triggered by the client family and his role in the family's problem and to develop steps to become disengaged from the power of the client family system and regain therapeutic objectivity.

Joining with the Family

In addition to successfully joining with each individual, the counselor must be able to join with the entire family system and the significant subsystems within the family. The counselor must identify important patterns of behavior that the family exhibits and respect these patterns. Moreover, the counselor must be able to identify family rules early in the treatment to ensure that she does not violate these rules unintentionally.

Finally, each family contains significant subsystems, such as the husband–wife or couple, parental, and sibling subsystems. The counselor must identify and join with these subsystems. If the counselor does not join the significant (powerful) subsystems, these controlling units can hinder the therapy process. Just as individuals need to feel valued, so do family systems and subsystems. If the counselor is successful at rapport building, the prognosis for assisting the family is greatly enhanced.

Core Skill 2: Information Gathering

In individual counseling, open-ended questions help the counselor gather more information than closed questions. An open-ended question allows the client to respond in several ways; a closed question lends itself to yes–no responses. An example of an open-ended question would be: "Tell me about your relationship with your partner." A closed question would be: "Do you get along with your partner?" Minimal encouragers also aid in information gathering. A minimal encourager prompts the client to provide additional information, as, for example, "Tell me more," or, "Give me an example of that."

In group counseling, the same techniques can be employed. The use of open-ended questions and minimal encouragement statements can have a modeling effect when used in a group. Group members may begin to use this technique with each other if it is effectively modeled by the counselor.

In marriage, couple, and family therapy, the counselor must obtain information from several persons, as in group counseling. However, the information obtained in family counseling will have a *central theme* and will be related to issues the family is confronting. In family counseling, the therapist needs an additional skill: *blocking information* provided by a family member who is not being addressed or who is attempting to control the flow of information in the family interview.

For example, the identified patient (IP) may be providing information to the counselor about the family situation when the mother interrupts with, "Be sure to tell him about how rude you were to your father yesterday." At this point, the counselor must block the mother's attempt to control the son's responses. The counselor can accomplish this by saying, "Thanks for your concern, Mrs. Smith; however, at this point I'm interested in Tom's thoughts about the situation. If you will be patient with me for a few minutes, I will get to you and find out what you are thinking and feeling about the situation." The family counselor must begin to use blocking techniques early in the therapy to prevent more powerful family members and subsystems from controlling and limiting the flow of information provided by less powerful members of the family. If powerful individuals control the information flow, identifying the less obvious family patterns and problems will become more difficult. It may be necessary for the family therapist to gently identify the attempts by powerful family members to guide the discussion in order to give less powerful members the confidence to share their perceptions of the family situation. Identifying this pattern may make the therapist more effective in identifying and helping resolve other less obvious problematic patterns.

Another helpful information gathering tool used primarily in family counseling is the genogram. The genogram is a visual depiction of the family tree that frequently covers three generations of the family. Important family information is reported on the genogram, such as names of family members, their ages, marital status, divorces, significant life events, and years of deaths. The genogram is a useful aid that frequently helps the counselor elicit important information concerning the family members, the problems in the family, and the emotional reactivity in the family to various members and events. The genogram also demonstrates how family characteristics and values, as well as family problems, are transmitted from one generation to the next (Carter & McGoldrick, 2005). An example of a four-generation genogram that identifies gender, date of birth, date of marriage, date of death, military service, and graduate education of the family members is shown an in Figure 7.1.

Core Skill 3: Structuring

Individual counseling sessions require the therapist to have skills in structuring the nature, limits, and goals of the session. This ability can help the client make better use of the session. It lets the client discover

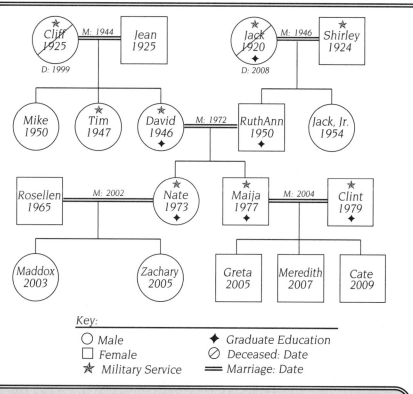

Figure 7.1 Four Generation Genogram

how she responds to the therapist, what the interactional style of the therapist will be, whether the counselor can help resolve the problems, and what the goals and expectations the client and therapist have for the therapy process. Structuring also clarifies the following:

- *Time limits.* Example: "We have agreed to a one-hour appointment today."
- *Role limits.* Example: "I see my role as helping you explore your problems and concerns and helping you find solutions that are personally satisfying."
- *Process limits.* Example: "I will help you by pointing out obstacles that I believe are getting in your way and preventing you from solving your problems."

- *Action limits.* Example: "I will ask you to try out new ideas outside the session and report back to me."

The counselor should involve the client in the structuring process by asking open-ended questions such as, "What motivated you to come see me?" and, "How may I be of most help to you?"

In group counseling, the skill is practiced in a similar way. The main difference is that, in a group, more time has to be devoted to structuring so all members have an equal opportunity to become involved. The time spent structuring the purpose and goals of the group is often time well spent because it helps the group members use the group time more effectively, helps encourage reluctant members to participate, and limits the participation of dominant group members (Gladding, 2008).

In family therapy, structuring is of critical importance. When a couple or family enters therapy, the clients are frequently locked in a mutually reinforcing pattern of problematic behavior. Despite the pain the family experiences, each person continues to repeat the same behavior patterns because those patterns are reinforced by the complementary behavior patterns of other family members. A family can quickly overwhelm a therapist with dysfunctional sequences of behavior if the therapist does not manage the session from the outset. In family therapy, this structuring begins with the initial telephone contact. Often, the person contacting the therapist will have already decided who needs treatment and why that person needs it. This family spokesperson is already active in setting up therapy and in determining who should be present for treatment. The therapist must recognize that this family member's attempts to control treatment, no matter how well intentioned, may have the effect of maintaining the family's problems. The spokesperson, if allowed, is likely to structure the participation in therapy in a way that maintains the present ineffective patterns of behavior. Helping the family engage in new behavior sequences can be accomplished most effectively when the therapist is able to structure the therapy without seeming authoritarian to the family members. For example, the mother may call to set up a therapy appointment and tell the therapist that everyone can attend except her husband, who is too busy with his work. The therapist must respond in a way that acknowledges the mother's concern for her husband's schedule but that also includes him in the therapy, as his presence is important to the treatment.

Core Skill 4: Information Giving

Individual counseling is designed to help clients decide what they might do to make their lives more effective and happy. However, frequently, the therapist is called upon to provide specific information to the client rather than helping the client explore options. At these times, called teachable moments, facts or data about experiences the client is having may expand the meaning or learning for the client. The three main purposes of information giving are to

1. identify alternatives,
2. evaluate alternatives, and
3. correct erroneous information.

To be most helpful to the client, the information must be accurate and revealed gradually and only when the client is ready for and needs it.

In a group counseling session, this skill may be utilized in much the same way as in a session with an individual. There are many opportunities to teach group members concepts that will help them function more effectively in the group and outside the group.

In marriage, couple, and family therapy, information giving takes on an increased importance for two reasons:

1. As couple and family therapy tends to be brief, clients need information to begin making changes relatively quickly in the therapy.
2. To alter dysfunctional patterns, the family or couple needs to understand what these patterns are. Accurate and timely information must be provided for this to occur.

To ensure that therapy is brief, effective, and focused, the therapist identifies the dysfunctional patterns and provides the information the family needs to understand the pattern and change it. The information provided by the therapist should meet the following criteria:

- The information is understood and accepted by the family.
- The information does not overwhelm the family.
- The information is accurate and based upon actual behaviors exhibited by the family in therapy.
- The information is provided at the appropriate time.

Without giving accurate and helpful information, the counselor's ability to help the family change their currently dysfunctional patterns of behavior is greatly reduced.

Core Skill 5: Reflecting Content

Individual psychotherapists use the skill of accurately reflecting content to communicate to clients that they are heard and understood. Moreover, by hearing their words reflected back to them in a concise manner, clients are able to crystallize their thoughts and feelings. Finally, the counselor is able to validate his perceptions, ensuring they are consistent with what the client is trying to convey by asking whether the reflection of content is accurate. Although the focus is on content, the counselor also recognizes the client's feelings. For example, if a client says, "I don't know about him—one moment he is as nice as can be and the next he is a real jerk," the counselor might say, "He seems like a pretty inconsistent guy who is hard for you to be with. His erratic behavior keeps you pretty confused." Thus the counselor acknowledges both the content and affect associated with the client's message.

As a group counseling skill, the reflection of content simply changes from a focus on individual information to a focus on information that is spoken by group members. Whenever group members seem to ignore, avoid, or deny some important content, the group therapist should intervene and draw out, identify, and ask about what is not being acknowledged. Three specific skills are involved (Gladding, 2008):

1. *Eliciting group content* means asking open-ended questions and making statements that draw out the content. For example, the counselor may say: "Sammy, I noticed you avoid looking at other people when you talk to them. What is going on with you? What do other members notice about this?"

2. *Identifying group content* means helping group members identify issues that they have overlooked. For example, the counselor may say: "Most of you seem to have trouble with certain subjects. I noticed that when Bill mentioned having trouble with his mother, everyone got quiet, and Jim changed the subject. What have others noticed about this?"

3. *Reflecting group content* means restating or clarifying some issue in your own words. For example, the counselor may say: "It seems to me that several of you are saying that you have problems in dealing with people in authority. Will you give me feedback on my perceptions?"

Reflecting content is an important skill for the marriage, couple, and family therapist. For the counselor to provide information to clients about their current patterns of behavior, the counselor must be able to assess current interaction patterns. When the counselor notices a certain repetitive behavioral sequence that may require modification, she reflects the observation of that behavior to the family. For example, the counselor may say to the family, "I notice that whenever Bill seems to have trouble gathering his thoughts, dad jumps in to help him." At this point, the counselor should check out this observation with those directly involved as well as with other family members. It is essential that the therapist get "buy in" from the family on the observation and reflection. If the therapist does not get buy in, she should back off and return to the issue at a later time when the pattern appears again … and in family therapy, you can count on the patterns reappearing! Family patterns are repetitive. If the therapist attempts to force the observation and reflection on the family, they may become defensive, and that could damage the therapeutic relationship, perhaps leading to the family withdrawing from treatment.

In addition, reflecting content is critical in the joining process in the early stages of family therapy. If each member of the family feels heard and understood, the family is more likely to place trust in the therapist, which improves the prognosis for therapy. One of the most effective ways to ensure that family members feel heard and understood is to accurately reflect the content of each family member's communications in therapy.

Core Skill 6: Reflecting Feelings

This skill is used to help individual clients move toward more complete self-awareness, self-understanding, and ultimately towards enhanced adaptability and behavior change. In reflection of feeling, the counselor expresses the central concern the client is feeling. This skill had three aspects:

1. Listening for feeling
2. Timing
3. Reflecting the feeling

In listening for feelings, the therapist listens for what is not being said as much as for what is being said. The counselor also observes nonverbal behaviors carefully, such as a person's breathing, a sigh, a blush, a stammer, or a swallow, as clues to feelings. Verbal clues include the use of feeling words and tone of voice. Good timing requires that the counselor wait for an appropriate moment before reflecting, being careful not to move too quickly into sensitive areas or to interrupt the client's feeling process. It is also important not to lag behind the client. Reflecting feelings requires the use of a feeling word when the client may not have said one. If a client says, "I wish I could talk to my dad like this," the counselor might say, "You have been a little afraid to be open with your dad." The counselor's reflection adds the client's unspoken experiencing of being afraid to the reflection.

In the early stage of group counseling, feelings are often overlooked or not dealt with. Most people have been conditioned not to express feelings in public. Therefore, a group counselor must help elicit, label, clarify, and reflect individual and group feelings. A group member might say, "It is hard to bring up things like that." The therapist replies, "You seem scared to talk about your problems in a group. Do any other group members share this feeling?" Thus the group counselor brings the individual's feelings to the group and encourages the group members to respond to those feelings by expressing their own affect.

According to several marriage, couple, and family therapy theories (Fisch, Weakland, & Segal, 1982; Haley, 1971; Minuchin, 1974), reflection of feeling is viewed as important in the joining process, when intense feelings about the family situation are often expressed. The counselor must accurately hear and reflect the feelings.

The views of many family therapists toward client feelings are different from those of individual or group therapists. Family therapists recognize that family problems may evoke a great deal of affect. However, because family therapy tends to be brief, affect is dealt with only to the extent necessary to allow the client to move on to aspects of therapy that are viewed as being more helpful in changing dysfunctional interaction patterns of all family members. A notable exception to this rule of thumb is emotionally focused couple and family therapy (Johnson, 2004). This approach will be described later in this book.

Because emotional catharsis is not usually encouraged by many family therapy theories, feelings expressed in therapy are not deepened and are not pursued unless their expression is critical to establishing more effective family patterns. However, the therapist must be careful not to discount the client's feelings even though their expression may not be directly contributing to problem resolution. In such a situation, the counselor would want to hear, understand, empathize, and reflect the feeling. When the time is appropriate, the counselor should ask if the client is ready to move to another issue. This technique contrasts with many individual counseling theories, which teach the therapist to help the client stay with the feelings, deepen them, and work through them fully before moving to other issues.

The Feeling Cross Technique

Counselors working with individuals, groups, couples, or families regularly encounter clients who are not skilled at recognizing and reporting their feelings. The following pattern often occurs in marriage and couple counseling. A couple enters therapy with the wife complaining that her husband does not understand her feelings about their difficulties. He complains that she will not listen to his ideas about how to improve the marriage. They are at an impasse. When the counselor asks the husband to report his feelings, the husband automatically shifts into a cognitive, rather than affective, response. The communication sequence might go like this:

Counselor: Your wife is telling us that you do not recognize her feelings about the situation and that you have even less awareness about your own feelings. Can you tell your wife and me how you *feel* about the marital difficulties you two are currently experiencing?

Husband: I know she says I don't have feelings, but I do. I *think* she is so down on me that no matter what I do I am wrong.

Counselor: How does it *feel* to be wrong no matter what you do?

Husband: I've always *thought* she was frustrated with me.

Counselor: Yes, but tell us how you *feel*.
Husband: I *think* I'm not being appreciated.

This sequence of the counselor asking for feelings and the client reporting thoughts could continue for a while. In fact, it often mirrors the ineffective communication sequence that the couple uses.

One good way to interrupt a dysfunctional sequence is to use the feeling cross technique developed by Fenell (1990). In this technique, the counselor draws a cross on a chalkboard or piece of paper (see Figure 7.2) and in each quadrant writes the feeling word: happy, sad, angry, and scared.
Then the session continues as follows:

Counselor: I've just drawn a feeling cross with the four major feelings listed, one in each quadrant. Can you read each feeling for me?
Husband: Sure, that's easy—happy, sad, angry, and scared.
Counselor: Great! Now, when you say that you feel that you are wrong no matter what you do, that your wife is frustrated with you and that you are not appreciated, you have a feeling or feelings about this. Please touch the word on the feeling cross that comes closest to how you feel now.
Husband: Well, there is anger for sure, but mainly I feel sad because the marriage that I want so badly seems to be out of my reach, and I'm scared I won't be able to make it better.
Counselor: So you feel sad and scared. Can you tell your wife how you feel like you told me just now?

Happy	Sad
Angry	Scared

Figure 7.2   The Feeling Cross

The husband tells his wife, thereby demonstrating that he does feel and care about the situation, and the couple begins a new sequence of communication behaviors. The feeling cross can be given to the couple to display on the refrigerator for reference when needed to enhance interactions at home.

When using this technique, a couple of additional points should be considered. First, men usually have more difficulty with feelings than women, but not always. This technique can be applied to anybody, including young children and surly adolescents. Second, when the client points only to angry and does not mention sad or scared, the therapist explains to the client that anger is a *surface feeling*. Below that surface feeling of anger is a deeper one—sadness, fear, or both. The counselor then asks, "As you feel your anger, tell me what other feelings you experience." The client will almost always will recognize one or both of the more vulnerable feelings of sadness or fear and report this to the counselor and, more importantly, to the partner. Once deeper feelings are introduced into the communication between partners, the intensity of the anger in the relationship dissipates almost immediately, providing hope for the couple that the relationship might improve.

Core Skill 7: Summarizing Content and Feelings

At times in individual therapy, the counselor wants to recapitulate, condense, or crystallize the essence of what the client said and felt. Although this skill resembles reflection of content and feeling, it is more comprehensive and covers more of the details concerning what the client said and felt. Summarization can be used at the beginning of a session to review aspects of the previous session or at the end of a session to review what has happened. This technique can also be used when a client rambles, is unclear, is at the end of a discussion on a particular topic, or is in conflict.

Summarization can be used in similar ways in group counseling, except the emphasis is on summarizing the collective content and feeling from the members of group as a whole. In a group as well as with individuals, themes or processes should be summarized from time to time to help clients stay focused.

In marriage, couple, and family therapy, summarization pulls together critical aspects of the session for the family. As in group therapy, counselors must be certain that summarizations include the thoughts and feelings of as many family members as possible. If the summarization of content and feeling focuses on only one member, the family (and perhaps the therapist as well) may have lost sight of the problem as a family system problem and been "sucked in" to the family's description of the problem being isolated only with the IP. This situation will happen to any therapist who works with families long enough and is almost always a major clinical error. The effective family therapist will always keep the family context of the problem in mind and recognize that the problem is a maintained by the interactional patterns of all members. As noted previously, the family therapist will generally use summarization of content more frequently than summarization of feeling.

Core Skill 8: Self-Disclosure

Unless counselors and therapists understand themselves, they will find it difficult to understand others. With individual psychotherapy, there are times when counselors will want to share personal thoughts, feelings, and experiences that relate to a client's situation. At a basic level, self-disclosure involves listening to the client, reflecting content and feelings, and explaining to the client the therapist's own reactions, thoughts, and feelings to what the client presented. Carkhuff (1969a) described this skill as counselor *immediacy*, which is giving an immediate personal reaction to the client in the here-and-now moment of the therapy session. Another type of self-disclosure that is less appropriate occurs when the counselor attempts to describe a personal experience that is similar to the client's reported experience in an attempt to establish rapport and credibility. This type of self-disclosure can be problematic, as it takes the focus off the client and puts it on the therapist. Moreover, an experience that the therapist perceives similar to a client's experience may not be similar at all in the client's view.

In group counseling, self-disclosure can be a very useful way to give group members feedback on how their behavior affects others. For example, a group member may be critical and judgmental about his brother. The group counselor says, "You seem so angry that I feel afraid of you when you talk that way about your brother. I get angry myself and want to tell you to shut you up. Can you respond to my feelings of anger, John? What do other group members feel about my reaction or John's anger?" Group members may then comment on their perceptions of John's and the counselor's behaviors. Significant progress can be made in group counseling when group members establish a trust level that permits them to honestly and openly self-disclose to one another.

In marriage, couple, and family therapy, the use of self-disclosure is sometimes appropriate. When family members are not genuinely reacting to each other, for example, the therapist may share her reactions about the behavior with a member who is particularly receptive to the therapist and aware of the family's withholding information. For example, the therapist may say, "You know Sarah, I'm sensing there is more to your parent's description of their feelings toward you than they are expressing. What is your sense of this?" If the counselor is on target with the self-disclosure, frequently one or more members of the family will feel more comfortable sharing the their perceptions and confronting other family members about the situation.

Family therapists must be careful not to use self-disclosure inappropriately. Frequently, counselors think self-disclosure means to share or describe a situation they experienced that was similar to the one the family is experiencing. Because family problems are widespread and therapists are not immune to family problems of their own, it is possible that the family's behaviors or interactions will remind the therapist of a similar situation in his own life. The therapist should rarely discuss the similar situation with the family, because it takes the focus off the family and puts it on the therapist. In general, therapists should not share this kind of personal information unless they are certain it will be therapeutic for the family by normalizing the problem or putting the family more at ease.

Core Skill 9: Confrontation

In an individual counseling session, the counselor may notice a discrepancy between what the client is saying and how she is behaving—for example, if she is talking about a sad subject and laughs. Such discrepancies almost always have some significance. It may indicate a conflict in feelings or an attempt to avoid or deny facing feelings. When the counselor confronts these discrepancies by pointing them out, this helps the client gain deeper insight into the problem or brings the problem out into the open so the client might choose to deal with it. Confrontation is most effective when done from a caring position that shows respect for the client and validates her as a worthwhile individual. The counselor's tone of voice, posture, and gestures all contribute to the success of the confrontation. Harsh confrontation or challenges to clients are rarely effective, and, when effective, are almost always delivered by a highly skilled therapist in a critical moment in the therapeutic process.

In a group counseling situation, confrontation takes on even greater importance. Interaction within a group often reveals patterns of behavior more quickly than sessions with individuals. Within a group, members assume roles that parallel the ones they fill as members of their families or in other significant relationships outside the group. Through effective confrontation, the counselor gently challenges group members to look introspectively at their behaviors in the group and, with the help and support of other group members, relate their actions to relationships outside the group.

Confrontation in marriage, couple, and family therapy is similar to confrontation in group counseling. However, in group counseling, the client comes to recognize a pattern of behavior in the group that is similar to his behavior outside the group. The client must then leave the group to try new behaviors in the social setting. Furthermore, the people in the client's social setting will not be participating in the treatment and may not be prepared to reinforce the client's new behaviors. In family therapy, not only are all members experiencing their roles in the therapy, but they are also each in a position to change their roles with the awareness, support, and reinforcement of other family members both inside and outside the therapy session. Thus, the change is more likely to be maintained, because all family members are participating in that change in therapy and at home.

Confrontation in marriage and family therapy serves the same function as in individual and group therapies. It helps the family recognize that what is expressed by an individual may not be congruent with the expressed desires for change. Confrontation helps the family members clarify what they want and encourages movement toward that goal (Corey, 2009).

Core Skill 10: Interpretation

Interpretation in an individual counseling session occurs when the counselor presents the client with a new frame of reference through which the client can view the problems and better understand the situation. This advanced skill relies on the counselor's mastery of reflection of content and of feelings, because the interpretation will be imbedded in the information gained through the therapist's accurate and effective reflections. The accuracy of the interpretation and the client's readiness to receive it determine whether the client can utilize the information provided in the interpretation. Effective interpretations occur when the counselor synthesizes the essence of what the client has said, summarizing it for the client, and adds appropriate new information for the client to consider. The following example illustrates this. A client with a record of absenteeism states, "I really feel bad about missing so much work." The therapist could respond with an interpretation, "You are worried about your absenteeism. You know how the company views absenteeism, and you are probably afraid your job may be in jeopardy." The counselor understands what the client reports and adds to this substantially with the interpretation.

In group counseling, interpretation may include some aspect of the group process or the interaction of several group members. For example, a group member continually rescues other members whenever there is even a mild confrontation. The therapist may offer the following interpretation to the rescuer: "I have noticed that you jump in and try to protect when someone in the group is challenged. You seem to have a real need to take care of other people. Sometimes people who have a need to protect others feel pretty scared and insecure themselves. Could that be true for you?" In this situation, the data for the interpretation included the behavior of the client in the group context as well as the counselor's experience with other clients.

In marriage, couple, and family therapy, effective interpretation is often crucial to helping the family change. When family members come into therapy, they are stuck in behavior patterns that seem appropriate to them, given the actions of the identified patient. For example, parents may feel that harsh restrictions are exactly what is needed when a son defies curfew. They continue this punishment even though their son continues to sneak out at night and defy the family's rules. To help the family change, the therapist needs to understand the current behaviors of family members and recognize that these represent their best, though ineffective, attempts to resolve the problems they are facing. One of the therapist's first interpretations is to acknowledge the family's genuine attempts to resolve the problem and to suggest that current methods are not working. In fact, these efforts to change the identified patient may even make the problem worse. Family members usually appreciate this interpretation because it shows that the therapist is proficient enough to recognize thir genuine attempts and also to recognize that the family's efforts to change have not been effective in solving the problem. Furthermore, this interpretation *engenders hope* in the family that through therapy other ways to solve the problem may be possible.

Another interpretation critical to helping the family resolve its problems occurs when the therapist presents a new understanding or explanation for the family's problem. This new explanation, or definition of the problem, must be based on actual statements and patterns of behaviors exhibited by family members in the session yet present the information in a new and creative way that offers the possibility for change.

So long as the family's initial definition of the problem is used in the therapy, the family remains the expert on the problem and may disqualify many of the therapist's suggestions for alternative behavior. Typically, a family spokesperson will say, "We have tried that, and it didn't work." This type of response greatly reduces the therapist's ability to intervene effectively.

To avoid this situation, the therapist interprets the problem situation in a new way and offers the family a new understanding of the situation. This type of interpretation is called redefining the problem, or *reframing*, and it presents the family with a new problem to solve based on the information provided to the therapist in the sessions. Because it is a *new problem* that is introduced by the therapist, the family is no longer the expert and turns to the therapist as the expert for help in resolving the new problem.

A very simple example of redefining the problem through interpretation can be demonstrated by considering a couple beginning marital therapy. The couple is frequently in much turmoil and experiencing a great deal of anger. The wife needs confirmation that she is loved and the withdrawn husband would like to reengage in the relationship. The couple defines their problem as a demanding wife married to a withdrawn husband. All their behaviors are based on this definition of the problem, and as a result pain and distance are increasing yet positive change is not occurring.

Once the therapist determines that the couple is serious about wanting to improve the relationship, the wife's "demanding that the husband express his feelings" may be redefined as her "need to hear that she is loved and valued by him." In the same manner, the husband's "withdrawal" may be redefined as "his feeling bad that he is unable to meet his wife's needs." In this case, the redefinition of the problem changes the problem from one of blaming each other to one of each spouse asking for what is needed to feel better in the marriage. This form of interpretation must be done carefully and with appropriate timing. If the therapist attempts to redefine the problem when the partners are venting their anger toward each other or are not able to accept the redefinition, this could cause the clients to feel misunderstood and feel uncertain about continuing in family therapy.

Core Skill 11: Behavior Change

During individual counseling sessions, implementing behavior change is an advanced skill and employs all the preceding skills. Each of the four stages of the behavior change process employ different skills:

1. *Identifying and clarifying the problem* involves use of rapport building, information gathering, structuring, reflection of content, and reflection of feeling.
2. *Establishing workable goals* requires the use of information gathering, information giving, summarization, and self-disclosure.
3. *Establishing criteria for effectiveness of the action plan* may require the use of confrontation and interpretation as well as reflection skills so both client and counselor will know when the objectives of therapy have been achieved.
4. *Implementation* involves summary skills, reflection skills, confrontation, interpretation, and closure skills—in short, the skills needed to help the client make desired changes.

In group counseling, these same skills would be useful with the additional advantage that other group members are involved in supporting the changes individual members are making. The support provided to members in group therapy is one of the major strengths of the group approach to treatment (Gladding, 2008).

In marriage, couple, and family therapy, changing the behavior of family members is critical to system change, which is the ultimate goal of treatment. The steps described above are appropriate for family therapy. As the family therapist and family members work toward behavior change, they must remember that problem identification and clarification, establishing workable goals, identifying criteria to evaluate change, and implementing interventions can only effectively support systems change when the difficulties are understood as problems of the family system, not of one individual within that family. Therefore, all family members should be recognized as important in both the definition and the resolution of the problems.

Establishing workable goals is important in family therapy. Determining those goals *with the family* based on an effective redefinition of the presenting problem increases the probability of successful interventions.

The family therapist, like any other therapist, must establish criteria to evaluate the effectiveness of the treatment. In family therapy, the most basic way to evaluate effectiveness is to look for change in the IP. Change in the IP, however, is not the only way to evaluate the effectiveness of the therapy. Successful family therapy outcomes may be evaluated by changes made by family members surrounding the IP. When this type of change occurs, the behaviors of the IP no longer have the power and influence over other family members that they had prior to treatment. The behaviors of the IP may be relatively unchanged, but the ability of the other family members to accept or deal with the behaviors may be greatly improved. Family therapists also view this type of change as a successful family therapy outcome and a therapeutic success.

Systems therapy offers the therapist multiple criteria for evaluating effectiveness. A major strength of the family systems approach to therapy is that several therapeutic outcomes may be perceived as effective by the family members. The therapist should be aware that system changes often occur in ways quite different from what might be expected. Such unplanned changes are every bit as effective as changes produced by well-designed treatment plans.

Behavior change in marriage and family therapy is most likely to occur when the therapist has:

- successfully joined with each family member and the family system,
- established herself as an expert who is highly qualified to help the family solve the problem it confronts,
- expanded the definition of the problem to include the entire family and demonstrated how several family members are maintaining the problem through their own behaviors,
- engaged all significant family members in the solution to the problem, and
- conceptualized treatment and provided interventions from a family systems orientation.

Core Skill 12: Closure and Termination

One of the most common concerns for individual psychotherapists is the termination and closure process. Inexperienced counselors report that termination is a difficult time in the counseling process. Closure skills enable the counselor and the client to accomplish the following:

- Bring a particular issue or problem to some resolution
- Bring a session to an end
- Terminate work with a client

In the first instance, it is sometimes necessary for the therapist to ask, "Have we gone as far as we can on this problem? Is resolution complete?" If the therapist has made a specific contract with the client, it is easier to reach a mutual decision about whether resolution is complete in terms of meeting the goals of the contract. Without a contract, the counselor should summarize what has been covered, ask probing questions, and reflect content and feelings to complete the closure. Some counselors are timid and avoid closure, and others may be too aggressive and close a topic prematurely. Summarizing skills are useful in closing a session. It is usually helpful to ask the client to summarize what he got out of the session and to reevaluate the structure of therapy in light of the contract you have with the client.

Final termination may require several sessions to complete and usually involves self-disclosure and interpretation of the current status of the client as well as a thorough review and summary of the therapeutic contract. Some therapists write a formal evaluation of the treatment so that if the client returns to therapy or goes to another therapist a comparison can be made with the present level of functioning.

In group counseling sessions, closure of an issue being dealt with by one group member has to be complete before the emphasis can shift to another group member. The therapist must tactfully ensure that it is appropriate to move on to another issue so the client does not feel cut off or discounted. Closure of a group session provides a transition for all the group members and gives them a chance to either complete unfinished business or contract to complete it outside or in a future session of the group. In the final termination of a group, it is important to review the life of the group and take care of any unfinished business group members may have with each other. Some time should be spent on closure when an individual terminates from the group unexpectedly.

Closure in marriage and family therapy generally follows one of two patterns. In brief forms of family therapy, closure of the therapy occurs as soon as possible after the family has begun more functional behavior patterns. To keep the family in therapy after it has made basic family system changes would imply that the changes are not real or may not last. Family systems theorists believe that changes made by a family will be self-reinforcing and foster even greater change outside of therapy. Therefore, clients should be encouraged to end treatment as soon as possible and be invited to return for more sessions if and when other problems develop. The therapist needs the skill to identify when system change has occurred and must ensure that the family understands that its work, not the actions of the therapist, is responsible for the changes that have occurred. Moreover, the therapist helps the family feel confident that it is capable of maintaining the change after termination. For the family members to maintain their change, they must believe that they, not the therapist, are responsible for the good things that occurred in treatment. If the family believes the therapist is responsible for the change, it is less likely to be maintained.

A second form of closure in family therapy may take place after the family has made desired family system changes. At this point, the therapist may offer the choice of termination or the opportunity to remain in therapy for a few more sessions to process the experience and to learn how the changes took place and how to bring about similar changes without therapy in the future. This psychoeducational approach (Johnson, 1987) supports the idea of teaching families what it takes to bring about family system change. After this teaching stage of the therapy, termination occurs.

In family therapy, intense personal relationships that are frequently established in group and individual counseling may not develop. Therefore, many of the dependency issues that occur in the termination of individual and group treatment may not occur when effective family therapy ends.

Summary

This chapter demonstrates how 12 core counseling skills used in individual and group counseling may be effectively used in the treatment of couples and families. However, it is important to remember that systems therapy applies the basic core skills in unique ways. To most effectively help couples and families, counselors should seek additional supervision of their work to receive feedback on their counseling skills in their work in practicum and internship experiences with marital and family system problems (Gladding, Burgraff, & Fenell, 1987).

In Part Two of this text, I will present counseling treatment models that are already familiar to most counselors. Moreover, I will describe how these theories may be employed in work with couples and families. Next I will introduce several of the most important systems theories that are closely related to the familiar treatment models already understood by most counselors in training.

Suggested Readings

Alexander, J., & Parsons, B. V. (1982). *Functional family therapy*. Pacific Grove, CA: Brooks/Cole.

Carkhuff, R. (1969). *Helping and human relations: Selection and training*. New York: Holt, Rinehart, & Winston.

Carkhuff, R., & Anthony, W. A. (1979). *The skills of helping: An introduction to counseling*. Amherst, MA: Human Resources Development Press.

Gladding, S. T. (2008). *Group work: A counseling specialty* (5th ed.). Upper Saddle River, NJ: Prentice Hall.

Ivey, A., & Authier, I. (1978). *Microcounseling: Innovations in interviewing, counseling, psychotherapy and psychoeducation* (2nd ed.). Springfield, IL: Thomas.

Ivey, A., & Gluckstern, N. (1984). *Basic influencing skills* (2nd ed.). Amherst, MA: Microtraining.

Ivey, A., & Matthews, W. J. (1984). A meta-model for structuring the clinical interview." *Journal of Counseling and Development, 65,* 237–243.

Johnson, S. (2004). *The practice of emotionally focused marital therapy: Creating connections* (2nd ed.). New York: Guilford

Part Two

Helping Couples Change with Individual and Systems Theories

Chapters

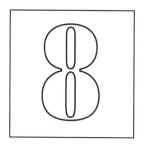

Helping Families
Using Psychodynamic
Individual Theories

This chapter demonstrates how psychoanalytic approaches can be adapted to family therapy. The work of Sigmund Freud is presented as the first theory that recognizes the power of family dynamics. Next, Adlerian approaches to family therapy are presented. Rudolf Dreikurs, Raymond Lowe, and John Carlson are three students of Adler who have developed applications of this theory for work with families. Finally, the transactional analysis (TA) approach to family therapy is discussed. Building on the work of Eric Berne, TA-oriented family therapy provides beginning family therapists with an easily understood model for initiating family treatment.

Key Concepts

- Psychosexual stages
- Object constancy
- Symbiotic relationships
- Individuation
- Inferiority complex
- Ego states
- Strokes
- Narcissistic needs
- Intrapsychic conflict
- Transference
- Phenomenological orientation
- Natural and logical consequences
- Injunctions

Questions for Discussion

1. What are the unique aspects of psychodynamic family theories?
2. With what kinds of family problems would these approaches work best? Why?
3. Which psychodynamic therapy *techniques* can be used most effectively in working with families?
4. How might a psychodynamic family therapist handle the resistance to therapy of a family member?
5. What information would an Adlerian family therapist need to help the family change? What methods would the therapist use to collect this information?
6. How would a TA-oriented family therapist work with a family that had a domineering father, passive mother, and acting-out children?
7. How would you use the parent–adult child model of TA with a family or couple?

The term psychodynamic is generally used more broadly than the term psychoanalytic. *Psychoanalytic* theories refer to classical Freudian principles, such as resistance, repression, narcissism, transference, libido, id, ego, and superego, as well as to Freudian techniques, such as free association and dream interpretation (Freud, 1949). *Psychodynamic* theorists attempt to understand the dynamic interplay of the conflicting components and experiences of the mind. They may or may not use Freudian principles or techniques. According to this definition, if a psychodynamic theory uses Freudian principles or techniques, it can be called psychoanalytic; if it does not, it is called psychodynamic. Using this definition, Henry Stack Sullivan, Alfred Adler, Carl Jung, and some of the TA theorists are classified as psychodynamic but not psychoanalytic. This chapter will cover traditional psychoanalytic theory as well as two psychodynamic approaches, the Adlerian and TA theories.

Goals of Psychodynamic Approaches

With psychodynamic family therapy, the therapist develops insight into the family as a social unit and discovers how family members' intrapsychic development—their internal thoughts, feelings, and goals—is affected by their relationships. Using such an approach, the therapist can help each family member become aware of her projections about the motives for other family members' attitudes and behaviors and take responsibility for these projections. Therapy requires each family member to develop an observing ego to understand and integrate her awareness with the knowledge gained from the interactions with all other family members. The psychodynamic family therapist also helps family members set appropriate and functional ego boundaries between themselves and other family members. A clear understanding of *self* and *other* and the boundaries that exist between the two is crucial to effective therapy outcome. Often, family members believe they are functioning for the self, when in reality they are unconsciously directed by the desires of others. This pattern leads to feelings of incongruence and self-deprecation, which contribute to family dysfunction.

One of the goals of this approach is to strengthen and preserve the family as a social unit without interfering with the functional autonomy of each individual family member. The importance given to the functional autonomy of the *individual* in this approach is the reason it is included in this chapter covering individual theories. The intimate and intense family relationships discovered in family therapy are excellent vehicles to help promote completion of unresolved parent–child conflicts left over from early childhood. Therapy is used to facilitate this completion process. Therapy attempts to help family members neutralize and integrate primitive urges from the id, which only wants self-gratification, so that their behavior is motivated more in the service of the ego, which seeks enlightened self-interest and effective relationships.

The Process of Psychodynamic Approaches

In general, psychodynamic family therapy involves a four-stage process:

1. *The therapy contract.* The contract includes all the administrative details of therapy, such as fees, vacations, appointment times, and so forth. The ability of clients to keep agreements made in the therapy contract and to successfully negotiate changes as needed is seen as a clear indication of their functional level.
2. *The initial phase of treatment.* In this phase, the couple or family members gain insight into the communication patterns of the family unit. The psychodynamic family therapist is primarily interested in the historical pattern of relationships and the dysfunction and conflict that has been caused by these relationships. Tools for effective conflict resolution are taught, and therapeutic alliances are established with each family member.
3. *The working-through stage.* The therapist actively attempts to help a couple or family members strengthen alliances with each other by helping them to reveal previously unexpressed feelings, share secrets, and develop more trust and empathy. Identifying and analyzing transference is an important aspect of treatment. Transference is the client projecting onto the therapist qualities that are not truly

there but that may be wished for in family relationships. This work helps to bring out unconscious patterns of communication, rooted in the past, that are deeper than those brought out in the initial phase of treatment. These patterns often show up as resistances, an unwillingness to consider integrating the unconscious motivations that emerge through the interactions with family members in therapy. The therapist must be skillful in confronting resistance and in helping the family member recognize and work through this difficult process.

4. *Termination.* When a termination date is set, conflicts and new defenses often emerge. These conflicts signal the need for the couple or the family to identify and work through anxiety about the impending loss. The therapist must help clients review and identify the therapeutic gains they made during therapy to overcome their unconscious dependence on therapy and the therapist. Family members must be able to recognize and acknowledge *their own roles* in the growth process that has occurred in order for therapy to be truly over.

The goal of this phase is to help each family member reduce anxiety and ambivalence about separation, to reinforce the therapeutic gains that were made, and to develop usable tools for continued growth. It is important that each person accept and understand the uniqueness and role played by every other family member. Family members must be able to resolve conflicts with a minimum of psychic injury to themselves or others. Some couples or families attempt to prolong therapy rather than deal with their feelings of loss. In such situations, the therapist might consider a gradual tapering off of sessions with periodic follow-up sessions. However, the therapist must not unconsciously transmit the message to the family that they cannot make it without the help of the therapist, a common mistake of beginning therapists. The therapist must communicate without hesitation that the tapering off is the family's desire, not that of the therapist, who is convinced the family will do well even without the follow-up.

Advantages and Disadvantages of Psychodynamic Approaches

Psychodynamic family therapy provides the therapist with both a conceptual framework for understanding conscious and unconscious behavior in the context of marital and family relationships as well as a developmental framework for behavior. Freud's psychosexual stages of development, when combined with Erikson's psychosocial stages of development, provide a comprehensive model for understanding behavior at every age. The model helps to bridge the gap between inner experience and outer, social behavior.

The psychodynamic approaches offer conflicted families and couples an opportunity to achieve cognitive and affective mastery of some conscious and unconscious causes of human suffering. These approaches also provide an opportunity to learn effective interpersonal communication skills and to correct misperceptions and distortions of early childhood experience that other approaches ignore. The therapeutic relationship can be used as a tool for change. Many people enter therapy because of poor relationships. These approaches center on using the intensity and honesty of the therapist–client relationship as a model for teaching new relationship skills to all family members.

But psychodynamic approaches also have disadvantages. These approaches offer few easily operationalized techniques, so techniques from other approaches often have to be employed. The focus on the past and the history of relationships may lead the therapist to overlook present causes of dysfunctional family behaviors. These approaches tend to overemphasize pathology and unconscious determinism rather than wellness. Moreover, the transference relationship between each person and the therapist can dilute the powerful transference relationships between husband and wife or mother and child. Because the focus is often on individual behavior change rather than changes in the family structure, structural problems can be overlooked, which may cause families to maintain dysfunctional aspects despite individual changes. Finally and most importantly, there is a tendency for the therapist who is not clear on his or her own intrapsychic conflicts and problems in past relationships to create an overprotective and domineering paternal or maternal relationship with clients that fosters dependency and inhibits their growth and autonomy.

Classical and Neoclassical Psychoanalytic Approaches

Freud (1949) did not do family therapy as we now think of it. His major contributions to family therapy came from his theory on the cause of dysfunctional behavior in families. Freud contributed to an understanding of the important influences of the family matrix on the development of the personality of the individual. His theory identifying the psychosexual stages of development helps us begin to chart the course of early childhood development and shows the importance of the early parent–child relationship for the subsequent personality development of the individual. In Freud's (1963) classical case histories, such as the case of Dora and the case of the Wolf-Man, we can see Freud's analysis of the role of family dynamics in shaping the personality and the possible psychopathology of the individual.

Colleagues of Freud also studied the influence of the family on child development (Flugel, 1921; Spitz, 1965), but psychoanalysts did not begin treating the whole family until the early 1950s, when child analysts began to treat the mother and child together (Paolino & McCrady, 1978). However, development of analytic forms of family therapy had to wait for the theoretical work of Harry Stack Sullivan (1947, 1953, 1954), Erich Fromm (1941, 1947), and Erik Erikson (1946, 1950, 1959) to provide the psychosocial focus.

Sullivan, the most family-oriented of all the American analysts, saw the growth and development of the child as a response to the social environment of the family. In addition, he was the first to demonstrate that schizophrenia could be treated by psychotherapy. He was more interested in the clinical application of his work than in the theory itself. A number of early leaders of family therapy were heavily influenced by the work of Sullivan, including Don Jackson, Virginia Satir, and Murray Bowen.

Philosophical Tenets

Freud was influenced by scientific realism and logical positivism, which placed emphasis on the objective knowledge of subjective experience. According to this view, the process of knowing requires an external interpreter, the therapist, to understand the preexisting structure of the personality. There is a deterministic essence, or preexisting human nature, that controls and governs behavior. The instinctual drives of the individual are what control human behavior.

Psychoanalytic theory assumes that human behavior is determined by past experience. Humans are not aware of their unconscious drives and how these affect the process and content of their reality. They are enslaved by their past until the unconscious parts of their behavior can be brought into consciousness, typically through psychoanalysis. In addition, Freud believed that the ultimate basis of morality is conscious reasoning based on scientific principles that have to be understood and integrated into one's life.

Theoretical Constructs: Theory of Cause

The works of Freud, Sullivan, and, more recently, Margaret Mahler (1968; Mahler, Pine, & Bergman, 1975) showed that the human infant begins life in a symbiotic relationship with a significant mothering figure and during the first 2 or 3 years of life goes through a set of developmental stages that enables the individual to achieve an independent and relatively autonomous emotional separateness from this parental figure. The successful completion of this developmental sequence enables the person to establish a coherent sense of self, which allows her to develop object constancy, or a constant sense of who she really is. Mahler calls this development the *psychological birth* of the individual.

Failure to complete this developmental process forces the individual to remain trapped in dependent relationships, never quite able to "go it alone," and to have difficulties in differentiating between self and others. These individuals remain stuck in infancy until they can learn to achieve some degree of separateness. They adopt a false sense of self that is acceptable to those upon whom they feel they are dependent, and they gradually lose sight of their true selves. As adults, these people often have a hard time developing values or beliefs that are clearly their own. Frequently, they become excessively involved in causes, beliefs, leaders, and ideologies that they hope will provide them with the sense of stability and direction they cannot provide for themselves. If they find very few ways to establish their own identity and their lack of differentiation is severe, they may become psychotic.

Neurotic behavior comes from the same source. Such people constantly need praise and cannot tolerate criticism. They look to others to build up their fragile sense of self-esteem, and they take any criticism as rejection or hostile assault. Families with a number of such individuals exhibit constant emotional upheaval over the competition for praise and reassurance. These overwhelming needs distort reality. Projections abound, usually derived from repressed or split-off aspects of the individual who does not have enough self-esteem or ego strength to own or integrate the repressed or split-off material.

In couples, the symbiotic process is recapitulated when each partner fills in a missing part for the other to make up one complete person. This process leads to a survival orientation and a dependency relationship based on control. If either partner tries to break out of this dependency and assert his own needs in the face of the demands of the other or attempts to establish his own self-identity, he can expect the partner to pull out all the stops and use every form of manipulation, exploitation, pressure, rejection, and force to maintain the dependency.

In families, one member is sometimes singled out as the family scapegoat or "whipping boy" to help all the others maintain their dependent patterns. Even in this individually-oriented psychoanalytic approach, the interrelationship of all family members is recognized. The mobilization of one family member in the direction of autonomy and individuation will likely be seen as a threat to the security of the other family members. Therefore, some psychoanalytically-oriented family therapists will insist on seeing all family members in family therapy. Others may combine individual therapy with each family member with occasional family therapy sessions.

Psychoanalytic approaches emphasize close couple relationships and those between parent and child. Individuals come to their committed adult romantic relationships with unresolved narcissistic needs, and they seek to have these needs met in the relationship. When they are not met and their efforts are frustrated, the couple often has children and hopes the children will meet these needs. The child then becomes an object to fulfill the unmet needs of the parents; as such, the child cannot meet her own needs to develop a separate self. Thus, the cycle starts all over again with the next generation. As the child grows up in that family, this battle of wills is constantly played out until the child leaves home to start a family in an effort to get the needs met in the adult romantic relationship that went unfulfilled in childhood.

Main Therapeutic Interventions: Theory of Change

Psychoanalytic literature gives much more attention to a theory of cause than to a theory of cure. The recovery of the true self and the resolution of childhood intrapsychic conflicts seem to be the important goals of psychoanalytic theory. Freud (1949) defined healthy functioning as the ability to work productively and to love and be close to other people. This goal, of course, requires neutralization and integration of aggressive impulses and childhood complexes so people can behave toward themselves and others more in service of their ego and less by impulse and intrapsychic conflict.

According to psychoanalytic theory, cure comes when the patient brings his intrapsychic and unconscious conflicts into conscious awareness and then works through these conflicts in the context of a safe therapeutic relationship. The fundamental belief in psychoanalytic theory is that the client's full expression of repressed or suppressed emotions and thoughts has more value than any therapeutic act on the part of the therapist. The cure for these conflicts or complexes is for the client to become aware of them and express formerly unconscious material in the therapy session as the therapist listens without judgment.

Psychoanalytically-oriented family therapists maintain that insight must come first and then appropriate behavioral changes will follow. Behavioral techniques may be employed only to achieve immediate symptomatic relief, but these techniques are seen as deterrents to reaching and solving deep intrapsychic conflict. Clients are reassured that they have nothing to fear from any thought or feeling, no matter how irrational or threatening it might seem.

As clients feel safe and secure in the therapeutic setting, the transference neurosis develops, which then provides the vehicle for clients to work through and resolve the conflicts. Transference is a phenomenon by which unconscious childhood conflicts are brought to the surface and projected onto the therapist. By utilizing the therapeutic alliance and by reexperiencing these conflicts with the therapist within the transference situation, the patient is able to apply his more adult modes of thinking and reality testing to the problem. Because the client is now an adult and has a stronger ego, he usually has more options available to resolve the conflict than as a child. The therapist has to be less intimidating or threatening than the patient's parents were for the transference to be worked through and the childhood conflicts resolved.

In the initial stages of therapy, the therapist attempts to:

- determine the ego strengths and weaknesses of each family member,
- determine their motivation for therapy,
- define the goals of therapy, and
- establish a therapeutic alliance.

CASE EXAMPLE

Psychodynamic Family Therapy

Mr. and Mrs. Smith had been married for three years when they entered therapy. The reason they gave for seeking therapy was that Mrs. Smith, age 27, was interested in having children, while Mr. Smith, age 36, was not. When they married, each assumed that the other shared common values and goals about a future family.

In the initial phase of therapy, both discussed rather openly their disappointments about the lack of common values on this issue. Mrs. Smith idolized her father and performed to meet his standards but believed she always fell short. She behaved toward her husband much the same way and felt that she was "bad" for holding an opinion different from his. Mr. Smith, the only boy in his family, was adored and pampered by his mother and sisters. His father was cold, distant, and demanding. He expected the same adoration and pampering from his wife and looked to her to support the correctness of his views.

In the middle stage of therapy, Mrs. Smith began to understand the father transference aspects of her relationship with her husband, and she developed more autonomy and self-esteem. She became more involved in her career and more certain about her wishes to have children. The therapist supported her growth. At the same time, Mr. Smith grew more fearful of parenthood. He was able to separate his feelings about his wife from his feelings about his mother, but he still wanted to express his creativity in his career and not in his family. He saw the therapist as being similar to his father and complained of the therapist's "cold, analytical style."

Videotape was used to help resolve the transference neurosis between Mr. Smith and the therapist. Mr. Smith began to understand what was happening in his relationships and gradually worked through his anger and sadness about the poor relationship with his father. He recognized that his fear of having children was related to a fear that if he became a father, he would be just like his father. With this awareness, he approached his wife and suggested they start their family. Mrs. Smith was delighted with his initiative. The couple continued in marital therapy during this time, and both were able to resolve their intrapsychic conflicts and became effective parents and loving partners in their relationship.

Once the therapeutic alliance is established with each family member, the therapist can begin to interpret the unconscious material imbedded in the conscious statements of the clients as well as interpret the resistance and maladaptive ego defenses of the clients. Done repeatedly over time, this technique leads clients to acquire new and adaptive defense mechanisms. Through interpretation, the therapist attempts not to extinguish or encourage aggressive expression but to understand the unconscious source of the aggression and its effects on others in the family.

Video playback can also be used as an adjunct to therapy. Sessions are recorded on video and then played back and analyzed by the therapist and the clients. This helps each family member develop an observing ego and become more aware of nonverbal messages and unconscious material present in the session. Video is useful when clients are denying or resisting threatening information or interpretation. When family members observe their actions on the video, resistance often dissolves.

Adlerian Approaches to Family Therapy

Adlerian family therapy has its beginnings in child guidance centers founded by Alfred Adler in Vienna during the first quarter of the 20th century. Adler's therapy focused primarily on relationship problems between parents and children.

Alfred Adler was a student and colleague of Freud but broke away from him in 1912. Adler stated that the personality was unified and not broken into id, ego, and superego, as Freud hypothesized. Adler's social views were shaped by the writings of Charles Darwin and David Lamarck. He formulated the theory that humans have an innate social interest that enables them to contribute to the welfare of others without thought of reward (Adler, 1927; Murdock, 2009). This view has been incorporated in many of the more recent humanistic counseling theories. It is a comment on the innate goodness of humans and their desire to form a more perfect society.

Although Adler visited the United States frequently from 1926 to 1937, it was one of his students, Rudolf Dreikurs, who firmly established Adlerian family therapy in this country. Dreikurs established a family counseling center in Chicago in 1939, which remains one of the centers of Adlerian work even today. Jon Carlson, also from the Chicago area, has extended the work of Adler and Dreikers in the United States and is one of the foremost Adlerian family therapy theorists and practitioners today (Carlson, Watts, & Maniacci, 2005).

Philosophical Tenets and Theoretical Constructs

Adlerian psychotherapy, also referenced as *individual psychology,* was perhaps the first theory to take a phenomenological orientation toward therapy. Adlerians focus on the subjective reality of the client and how their worldview or lifestyle determines how they organize their behavior. Adlerians adopt a concept of *indeterminism,* which means they believe that neither heredity nor environment determines one's behavior; rather, the individual's creative power determines what a person will or will not do.

Adlerians tend to focus more on operational day-to-day reality than on ultimate reality, which they agree can never be known completely. They take the stance that what is good is determined by prevailing social values. The family is seen as a social instrument to teach sound values and help people live effectively in a democratic society. All behavior is seen as purposeful and goal-oriented; Adlerian psychotherapy's teleological view distinguishes it from the Freudian deterministic view. The focus is more on the present and future than on the past (Corey, 2007; Mosak, 2005; Carlson, Watts, & Maniacci, 2005; Murdock; 2009).

Theory of Cause

Adler saw all behavior disturbances as:

- a failure to develop appropriate social interest,
- a faulty lifestyle, and
- a mistaken goal of success.

Adler said that clients do not suffer from a disease but from a failure to solve the normal problems of daily living. Therefore, Adlerian family counseling is an educational model of therapy. Adler postulated that a child's personality characteristics are directly influenced by birth order and the way the child is treated by parents and siblings in the family constellation.

Disturbances can result from either permissive or authoritarian parenting methods. In either case, children grow up with distorted views of how to get along with others. Permissive methods give children the impression that they have no social responsibility for their behavior, and authoritarian methods teach them to fear authority and, ultimately, to rebel against it. In either case, a child can develop inferior feelings or an inferiority complex. People often compensate for these feelings of inferiority by attempting to master their environment or strive toward superiority. As such, inferiority feelings are strong motivators for purposeful, goal-oriented actions (Corey, 2007; Mosak, 2005; Carlson et al., 2005; Murdock; 2009).

Theory of Change

To alter disturbed behavior in Adler's framework requires the use of democratic parenting methods that enable the child to recognize and establish effective limits and participate successfully in the decisions that affect the child within the family, the school, and the larger community. To help shape the behavior along socially acceptable lines, Adlerians use the concepts of natural and logical consequences for behavior. A *natural consequence* is one that occurs naturally as a result of some action, such as the pain that results from touching a hot skillet. These natural consequences provide a way for humans to learn to modify their own behavior. *Logical consequences* refer to reasonable, agreed-upon outcomes of behavior. For example, a child who repeatedly interferes with another person by not coming to dinner on time is told how the behavior affects the parents and that if the behavior continues she will not be scolded but will have to fix her own dinner. Depending on the age of the child, this intervention could be a consequence or a punishment. Consequences should enable the child to assume responsibility for her behavior; punishment requires others to assume responsibility. Because the behavior of parents has to change before the behavior of children can change, more responsibility is placed on the parents, who are presumably more mature and able to change. Adler was thinking systemically years ahead of his time.

Main Therapeutic Interventions

The main goal of Adlerian family counseling is to facilitate improvement of parent–child relationships by helping family members identify and change faulty lifestyle patterns and selfish goals so all members can become successful in accomplishing their life tasks (Murdock, 2009).

Therapy sessions are geared toward teaching family members the skills and knowledge they need to achieve and maintain effective relationships so that they can relate to the family, neighborhood, nation, and the world.

To accomplish this goal, the therapist attempts to help parents understand the dynamics that contribute to poor relationships and then to teach them constructive alternatives. The essential techniques therapists use include the following (Lowe, 1982):

- *The initial interview*. This stage is an important part of Adlerian family therapy. A structured interview form is usually used and includes (1) information on the members of the family constellation, (2) presenting problems, (3) working hypotheses by the therapist, (4) a description of a typical day in the family, (5) a children's interview, and (6) teachers' reports and recommendations. This information is used to diagnose children's goals, to assess the parents' discipline methods, to understand the family atmosphere, and to develop a plan of action.

- *Role playing*. The therapist attempts to have family members act out how they perceive their situation. This technique is accomplished by identifying a current family issue and encouraging the family to resolve it as best they can while the therapist observes. Information gained from this process helps the therapist better understand the family and teach new responses and new communication skills.

- *Recognition reflex*. The therapist watches the responses of the children to specific events. The responses are usually nonverbal, such as a slight smile or a twinkle in the eye.

- *Disclosure and interpretation*. Adlerians use interpretation and disclosure of their own observations as a way to teach parents and children new responses.

- *Action-oriented techniques*. Adlerians may use homework and other similar ways to promote effective practice of skills. Family meetings are also recommended so that family members can practice their newly acquired skills.

- *Information giving and teaching*. Part of the session may be devoted to teaching and giving information necessary for new learning to occur.

- *Limit setting*. The therapist models and teaches parents how to set effective limits.

- *Minimizing mistakes*. The therapist emphasizes what can be done that will help the family improve rather than what was done that was wrong.
- *Encouraging family fun*. The therapist encourages family members to plan fun activities together as a way to strengthen their work in therapy.

Adler's theory had a profound influence on the theories that followed. His belief in social interest and the goodness inherent in humankind is a

---

CASE EXAMPLE

Adlerian Family Therapy

The Thompson family entered therapy with an Adlerian family therapist. The parents were concerned because their 10-year-old daughter was acting out at home and school. The therapist met with the couple alone and also met with the daughter alone for two sessions. The therapist identified the mistaken goals of each family member. Dad felt his role was only to provide financially for the family and was very distant. He said that Mrs. Thompson spoiled their daughter. The mother saw her role as nurturing their gifted daughter, receiving accolades for her daughter's talents, and complained that her husband was not connected to the rest of the family. The daughter saw her role as creating mischief so that her parents would pay more attention to her. The therapist also identified a pattern among all family members that focused on selfishness rather than on developing a healthy social interest and providing support for others, both within and outside the family. This pattern contributed to a mistaken goal of what it meant for the Thompsons to be a successful family.

When these roles were identified and explored in a session with all family members present, each recognized and acknowledged the roles and patterns the therapist identified. The family collaborated and decided upon a family-based goal that included autonomy for each family member as well as specific times when the family would engage in activities together. They further discussed ways to become more connected to their community and to share their talents with others. Through this collaborative process, the relationships among all family members improved, the daughter's acting out decreased, and the family developed a healthy social interest through their participation in community service.

major contributor to the humanistic approaches. His focus on basic mistakes in life was later modified and included in cognitive theory. His examination of family dynamics, the effects of birth order, and the establishment of the first child guidance clinic also exerted tremendous influence of the evolution of family therapy. Most important, Adler broke from the deterministic traditions of Freud's classic psychoanalytic theory (Murdock, 2009).

Limitations of Adlerian Family Therapy

This theory, like the all psychoanalytic approaches, tends to try to explain much of human behavior. This is laudable, but the concepts are difficult to measure in controlled research studies. Thus, little research has been done to date on Adlerian family therapy. This theory seems to be most useful when the family problems are not severe. It is limited in that the approach is very information-oriented and does not place as much emphasis on the value of the therapeutic relationship as do other humanistic theories. Moreover, family members can overadapt to the authority of the therapist and learn only enough to please the therapist rather than making lasting changes in the family system.

Transactional Analysis Approaches to Family Therapy

Transactional analysis (TA) seems to have fallen out of favor during the past two decades. Few of the most commonly recommended individual counseling theory textbooks include this approach to treating individual, couple, and family problems. Corey (2007) and Gladding (2008) discuss TA in their group counseling textbooks but not in their individual counseling volumes. This trend may suggest that contemporary models of TA are more appropriate for work with groups and families than with individuals.

Building on the theoretical work of Eric Berne (1961), the founder of TA, many practitioners have applied TA to family therapy. TA is an interactional therapy based on the assumption that current behavior is based on past experiences and that these past experiences cause us to make decisions about who we are and what we are like, who other people are and what they are like, and what the world is like. For example:

- Am I a good person or not so good?
- Are other people good and trustworthy or not?
- Is the world a threatening or safe place for me and my family members?

The answers to these questions lead us to make decisions that form our *life script*, which we can only change with increased self-awareness, adaptability, and life skills. Because TA was developed primarily as a group approach, it was relatively easy for practitioners to apply it to marital and family therapy. However, TA still emphasizes the dynamics of the individual, and the basic goal of TA family therapy centers on the contract each person makes with the therapist to change current family relationships. TA therapists approach work with family members by addressing the way they think, feel, and behave toward each other. Each client must recognize the impact of these three dimensions to make necessary family changes (Corey, 2007).

Philosophical Tenets and Theoretical Constructs

TA is a philosophically diverse theory because its practitioners often use techniques drawn from other theories, such as Gestalt, behavior therapy, and psychoanalytic therapy. As a psychodynamic theory, TA therapists still hold to the theory of an essential human nature, but they disagree over what the essence of human nature is. Harris (1967) postulated an essential "not-OK-ness," sort of like original sin, while James and Jongeward (1971) disagreed and saw humanity as basically OK.

TA has a strong phenomenological emphasis as well. The meaning people give to their experiences, rather than the experiences themselves, determines how they act. TA stresses the importance of the subjective reality of the client, but this reality can be understood through a set of objective laws and principles. Finally, most TA therapists, like other psychodynamic practitioners, hold that the client must gain insight about his behavior for change to take place.

Theory of Cause

According to Berne (1961), the interplay of three ego states—parent, adult, and child—determines an individual's personality. These ego states parallel in certain ways the structure of the personality in psychoanalytic theory. The child from TA and id from psychoanalysis, parent and superego, and adult and ego exercise many similar functions in both approaches. Thus, TA is included in this chapter among the psychodynamic theories. The pattern of strokes people receive determines how they view themselves and others. *Strokes* are verbal and nonverbal signs of acceptance and recognition, and they can be positive or negative, conditional or unconditional.

The most damaging are negative strokes, which often come from parents and other adults in the form of injunctions (e.g., "Don't be close," or "Don't be you") and counterinjunctions (e.g., "Be perfect," or "Try harder"). These injunctions and counterinjunctions cause people to make decisions about themselves and others such as, "I can't be who I really am" or "I am stupid." Berne (1972) saw people as victims of their injunctions and the decisions based upon them.

Mary and Robert Goulding (1979) disagreed with Berne, seeing people as making conscious choices and decisions that are adaptive and changing them when they cease to be adaptive. The Gouldings insisted that many decisions children make are not the result of parental injunctions but of faulty thinking and fantasies on the part of the child.

Berne (1961) discussed two types of problems that affect the structure of the personality: exclusion and contamination. *Exclusion* means that a person is stuck in stereotyped or rigid responses. The person is conditioned to respond from only one ego state, such as the parent ego state, perhaps in critical and controlling ways, or the child ego state, by communicating a lack of seriousness or seeming to be uncaring or ineffective. The individual would then exclude the other two ego states. *Contamination* means that material from one ego state overlaps with another, causing a double message. A person may try to respond from the adult ego state while using parental and controlling gestures, for example.

TA pays attention to strokes people receive, *games* people play in their communication patterns, injunctions received as children and adults, and the decisions each made in developing a *life position*. People adopt four basic life positions:

1. I'm OK—You're OK
2. I'm OK—You're not OK
3. I'm not OK—You're OK
4. I'm not OK—You're not OK

TA practitioners believe that once a life position is chosen, it remains fixed until some intervention, such as therapy, occurs to help people change their stroking patterns, injunctions, and decisions. The life position was seen by Berne (1972) as representing a basic existential decision that colors all the perceptions of our transactions with all other people, in the world, including family members. The life script tells us how to act out our basic life position and as such determines the patterns of our thinking, feeling, and behaving (Corey, 2007; Gladding 2008).

Theory of Change

To change a decision, a script, or a basic life position, TA therapists believe that people have to take responsibility for their own behavior and stop blaming their problems on other people. For most clients, this is the most important and often the most difficult step in changing. Clients are seen as having the power to change their own lives. In order to take on that responsibility and challenge, some clients have to reexperience aspects of their past; others can take this step in the present without much reference to the past. The effective therapist, in consultation with the client, will need to decide whether exploring the past will be necessary to change the present and the future.

Although TA is designed to help clients develop both emotional and cognitive awareness, the focus is clearly on the cognitive aspects. Understanding and insight into the functions of the parent, adult, and child ego states and the life script are necessary for lasting behavior change to take place. Those who combine Gestalt techniques with TA theory place less emphasis on insight and cognitive understanding than on decisive action. More traditional TA approaches, however, rely on cognitive teaching methods to instruct the client about how to better understand and manage behavior. In either case, when therapy is effective, the client develops tools to solve pressing personal problems. The autonomy of the client in deciding what will be done and what will not is seen as an important part of the process of change.

Main Therapeutic Interventions

The primary techniques used in a TA approach to family therapy vary with the stages of the treatment process. McClendon (1977) proposed three main stages in a TA approach to family therapy: determining the family dynamics, therapy with each family member, and developing a functional family.

Stage One: Determining Family Dynamics

The therapist looks for the patterns of communication among all family members, remembering not to focus attention on the problem member. The intention is to identify each person's role in the dynamics of the family's problem. The therapist might use open-ended questions with each member, asking about his role in the family. While doing this, the therapist watches how the other family members behave. For example, when the father talks, the mother looks away and the oldest boy starts playing with a pencil. These observations are shared with the family to increase their awareness of family dynamics and to determine whether any changes are desired.

Interpretation of family dynamics is also employed in TA with families. The therapist may use a story or metaphor to illustrate a point that is designed to give family members permission to do or say things they seem reluctant to do or say under normal family circumstances. The therapist may confront family members on discrepancies between their perceptions and their behavior in sessions. Therapists may also confront statements that reinforce injunctions or problematic life script messages and provide information about healthier responses. For example the therapist may suggest changing the statement "I can't do this homework" to "I won't do this homework" so the client will take responsibility for the decision to either do it or choose not to do it.

Stage Two: Therapy with Each Individual

The focus of this stage of therapy is on individual psychodynamics and life script analysis. Clients become aware of the preferred ego state, parent, adult, or child, that they employ when interacting with others. Once aware of their dominant ego state, clients may then choose to employ other ego states that are more functional in a given situation. This intervention may require the therapist to see family members in individual therapy, work on individual issues within a family therapy framework, or work conjointly with the couple and not the family. All configurations of family and individual subsystems can be the focus of treatment in TA. Techniques such as video recording, feedback from family members, or encouragement from the therapist may be employed to help individual family members identify and change their script decisions.

Stage Three: Developing a Functional Family

Reintegration aimed at developing a functional family structure (Minuchin, 1974) is the focus of this stage. A functional family structure is one in which each family member can meet basic needs. The structure is designed to support the optimal emotional and psychological growth of each family member. During this stage, the therapist employs psychoeducational techniques by teaching family members strategies to negotiate and get what they want and need. Homework assignments may be given to reinforce learning and behavior changes and to assess the effectiveness of the family structure. In this stage,

---

CASE EXAMPLE

Transactional Analysis Family Therapy

The White family was referred for therapy by a school counselor who had worked with the daughter, Sandy. Sandy was doing poorly in school and creating problems at home. The family consisted of the father Jim, age 38; the mother Susan, age 34; and two children Sandy and John, ages 9 and 4. The Whites had been married for 12 years.

The initial session consisted of the family members introducing themselves and telling what they thought the problem was and why they had come to family therapy. Jim was on the offensive, saying that he thought the problem was his wife's inability to handle the children. He said he resented that Susan called him at work to complain about the children. Susan complained about the lack of emotional support she got from Jim, who, she said, was always working late. Sandy told the therapist that she didn't know what the problem was or why they were in family therapy; things were just fine. John said that Sandy sometimes picked on him and teased him. The therapist worked alone with Sandy to get her to open up about her problem. She reported that no one liked her at school and that her mother picked on her at home. The therapist brought the family together in a conjoint session, teaching ego states by helping each family member identify when he or she was acting parental, childlike, or in the adult mode. The therapist also helped the family members identify how they provided

---

(continued)

family members actively ask for what they want while also giving freely to support others.

Limitations of TA Approaches

Little research has been done comparing this approach with other approaches. One limitation of TA is that it offers a cognitive approach to understanding behavior but offers very few techniques for changing behavior. Moreover, the cognitive focus may keep the clients in their head and short-circuit attempts to explore feelings. TA is often combined with other techniques such as Gestalt and psychodrama, making it difficult

---

Transactional Analysis Family Therapy *(continued)*

strokes or reinforcers effectively and ineffectively to other family members. In the second phase of therapy, Susan identified her pattern of moving into a critical parent role with her daughter. She worked on managing her anger by focusing on her role as a loving parent and by engaging Sandy in an adult manner. This helped their relationship tremendously. When Sandy was approached in a loving or adult manner, her acting-out behaviors ceased. Sandy was also able to identify when she was acting in the role of a defiant child and was able to modify her role. Sandy also developed the ability to communicate from an adult ego state and was able to express her needs and wants directly to Jim and Susan.

Susan began relating to her husband from the adult ego state and told Jim that she wanted more contact with him and more freedom to develop her own interests outside the home. As the result of script analysis, Jim learned that his life script included a pattern of working hard and keeping distant from the family. Jim saw that he was modeling his life after his father and decided to change his earlier script decision and spend more time with his family. He also learned to speak from the adult ego state and was able to stop using his critical parent ego state to communicate with his family.

The final phase of therapy centered on couple work with Jim and Susan to restabilize the family. Sandy's problems at school subsided, and her teachers reported that she was more attentive and was relating better to her peers.

to teach the approach to counselors in training. Finally practitioners can use the structure and vocabulary of TA to distance themselves from intimate and genuine contact with clients. Clients who are taught jargon may believe that change is taking place when in reality they are only using new words to describe their continuing problems (Corey, 2007).

Summary

This chapter reviewed the psychodynamic theories that have been adapted for use in marriage and family therapy. Representative psychoanalytic, psychodynamic, Adlerian, and transactional analysis theories were described. Psychodynamic theories pay close attention to the experiences encountered in the early childhood of the family members, the unconscious motivations of each person, and the creation healthy self–other boundaries. Adler was the first psychotherapist to view truth from a subjective perspective, acknowledging that the reality of the client must be recognized and validated for therapy to be effective. TA builds upon the Freudian ego states and develops a contemporary model that recognizes the life choices people make about themselves, others, and the world. It helps clients change their life choices in more effective directions. These theories are the first of several we will study that build bridges from individual therapy to family systems therapy.

In the next chapter, I will describe the major psychodynamically-oriented systems theories that have been used in marriage and family therapy. The skills and techniques of these systems theories will be presented, and I will illustrate how they can be used in family therapy.

Suggested Readings

Erskine, R. G. (1982). "Transactional analysis and family therapy." In A. M. Horne & M. M. Ohlsen (Eds.), *Family counseling and therapy*. Itasca, IL: Peacock.

Carlson, J., Watts, R. E., & Maniacci, M. (2005). *Adlerian therapy: Theory and practice*. Washington, DC: American Psychological Association.

Corey, G. (2007). *Theory and practice of group counseling* (7th ed.). Belmont, CA: Thomson-Brooks/Cole.

Gladding, S. T. (2007). *Groups: A counseling specialty* (5th ed.). Upper Saddle River, NJ: Merrill.

Lowe, R. N. (1982). Adlerian/Dreikursian family counseling. In A. M. Horne & M. M. Ohlsen (Eds.), *Family counseling and therapy.* Itasca, IL: Peacock.

Mosak, H. H. (2005). Adlerian psychotherapy. In R. J. Corsinsi & D. Wedding (Eds.), *Current psychotherapies* (7th ed.). Belmont, CA: Books/Cole-Thomson Learning.

Murdock, N. L. (2009). *Theories of counseling and psychotherapy: A case approach.* Upper Saddle River, NJ: Merrill.

Nadelson, C. C., & Paolino, T. J. (1978). "Marital therapy from a psychoanalytic perspective." In T. J. Paolino & B. S. McCrady (Eds.), *Marriage and marital therapy.* New York: Brunner/Mazel.

Sager, C. J. (1981). Couples therapy and marriage contracts. In A. S. Gurman & D. P. Kniskern (Eds.), *Handbook of family therapy.* New York: Brunner/Mazel.

Helping Families Using Psychodynamic Systems Theories

This chapter introduces the reader to three major family systems theories with psychodynamic roots. The systems theories of Murray Bowen, James Framo, and Richard Schwartz were selected for presentation here because each links intrapsychic processes with systems thinking. Both the Bowen and the Framo theories have been used for more than 30 years, have been reported widely in the literature, and are practiced by many family therapists. Moreover, both of these theories emphasize the effect of family-of-origin experiences during childhood on later functioning as an adult, a parent, and a spouse or partner. Schwartz's theory is relatively new and looks at the individual's conceptualization and feelings about her internal intrapsychic system. It holds promise for expanding the use of systems concepts with individual clients. Each of the theories presented in this chapter has a systems base and underlying assumptions that examine recollections about the family's past and is thus are included in this chapter describing psychodynamic systems theories.

Key Concepts

- Emotional illness
- Family of origin
- Family-of-origin sessions
- Differentiation of self
- Family projection process
- Fusion
- Internal Family Systems (IFS)
- IFS exile
- IFS manager
- IFS firefighter
- Multigenerational transmission process
- Emotional cutoff
- Triangulation
- Couples group therapy

Questions for Discussion

1. What are the major goals of Bowen's family systems therapy?
2. How would you use the differentiation-of-self scale in family therapy?
3. What are four ways that fused families dissipate anxiety?
4. What do you think makes sessions with one's family of origin so effective?
5. Describe Framo's three-phase approach to family therapy.
6. What are the specific goals of Framo's family-of-origin session?
7. What are some of the issues in your own family of origin that have been highlighted in this chapter?
8. Do you think family-of-origin therapy would help with these issues? Why or why not?
9. Do you consider internal family systems (IFS) theory a systems or individual theory? Defend your answer.
10. What is the goal of IFS?
11. What is the role of the IFS therapist?
12. What are the manager, exile, and firefighter in IFS? How do they function?

The three systems theories selected for discussion in this chapter are rooted in psychodynamic theory. Both Bowen's family systems therapy (1961, 1978) and Framo's family-of-origin therapy (1982) have been prominent family therapy approaches for several decades. Schwartz's internal family systems therapy is a relatively new approach, gaining a dedicated following of therapists with the publication of *Internal Family System Therapy* in 1995. Bowen's pioneering work in family systems theory will be presented first, followed by Framo's refinements incorporated in family-of-origin therapy. Finally, Schwartz's internal systems therapy will be introduced and described.

Bowen's Family Systems Theory

Murray Bowen (1913–1990) was the leading proponent and developer of family systems theory. His shift to the family systems movement began in the early 1950s when family therapy was in its infancy. Bowen was trained as a psychiatrist. Much of his early theoretical formulations came from his work at Menninger's Clinic with schizophrenic patients and their families. During this time, Bowen developed the concept of mother–patient symbiosis, which was based on the premise that the mother and the infant could form an intense bond that was so powerful it would not permit the mother to differentiate herself from the self of the child (Bowen, 1960, 1961). This intense emotional bond could make it difficult for the mother to allow the child to grow up and differentiate from the her as he matured. Other classic psychodynamic symptoms, such as maternal deprivation, hostility, rejection, and castration anxiety, were seen as secondary and less important features of the intense attachment. Based on these findings, Bowen hypothesized that schizophrenia developed as a result of this emotional stuck-togetherness of the mother and child (Kerr, 1981).

Later, Bowen modified his initial theory to include the whole family constellation, not just the mother and offspring, in his understanding of the etiology of schizophrenia in a patient. He came to recognize that a reorientation of his psychodynamic thinking would be required to work effectively with families. In his early work with patients with schizophrenia, Bowen began hospitalizing entire families. He stopped treating his patients with individual psychotherapy as he began to focus on family group treatment. Bowen later recognized that the characteristic interaction patterns and other behaviors that a schizophrenic family exhibits are similar to interaction patterns and behaviors in other families with less severe symptoms in the identified patient (IP). Bowen then expanded his theory, reporting that the concepts of family systems theory can be employed with a wide range of family problems (Kerr & Bowen, 1988).

Philosophical Tenets and Key Theoretical Constructs

To understand the key concepts of family systems theory fully, it is important to understand that Bowen hypothesized that individuals encounter problems in their families and in other systems when they are *emotionally impaired.* By emotionally impaired, Bowen meant that the individual was not able to "distinguish between the subjective feeling process and the intellectual thinking process" (Bowen, 1971). When this impairment occurs, the individual cannot establish an *I position.* This means that the individual has extreme difficulty in taking a stand that is in opposition to another person, especially someone close to her. Rather, the emotionally impaired person strives to achieve togetherness and agreement at the expense of self. The inability to distinguish between feelings and thoughts coupled with an intense desire to avoid conflict and disagreement discourages individuality and differentiation and leads to the development of psychological symptoms.

Bowen described the inability to differentiate the feeling and thinking processes as emotional illness. He viewed emotional illness not as a disorder of the mind but as a disorder of relationships. Bowen discontinued his use of the term mental illness in favor of the term emotional illness to describe what occurs in family relationships to cause emotional impairment of one or more members (Friedman, 1991).

Emotional Triangle

Bowen considered a three-person emotional triangle to be the basic element of any emotional system. Bowen's emphasis on the importance of triangles within families is widely used by many other family therapists today. He observed that a two-person system was unstable, especially during conflict, and always would pull in a third person to create stability. These emotional triangles tend to have two stable sides and one side that is in conflict. For example, two children might be in conflict. To attempt to resolve the disagreement, they attempt to include another sibling, parent, or friend to lend support to one or the other's position. The third person is usually not in conflict with either party in the argument. Thus the third party is *triangulated* into the argument, perhaps taking a side and perhaps not. According to Bowen, the mere presence of the third person adds stability to the conflict in the two-person system. In marital and couple therapy, it is the counselor who becomes triangulated into the unstable couple system, lending stability and support to the couple through the therapy provided. This creates the emotional triangle, which, according to Bowen, is fundamental to all family systems.

Differentiation of Self from Family of Origin

Differentiation involves an individual's ability to develop a strong sense of self and to choose behaviors independent of the influences of others. Bowen (1978) described the level of differentiation as the degree to which one's self fuses or merges with another person in a close emotional relationship. Bowen developed a conceptual scale to describe levels of differentiation, with a score of zero indicating little or no differentiation from others and a high level of fusion. A score of 100 represents maximum differentiation of self from family and suggests a high level of autonomy. Of course most people lie between these extremes, able to demonstrate both differentiation and fusion depending on their childhood experiences within the family of origin.

The level of differentiation is believed to be established in childhood and is a reflection of how adequately the child is able to establish a sense of self separate from her parents. If a child has parents who are quite fused and undifferentiated, the child is unlikely to be able to establish a high level of differentiation of self during childhood. Undifferentiated parents have difficulty encouraging the autonomy of their offspring.

The level of differentiation established in childhood is thought to be stable throughout life unless specific actions such as family therapy are taken to change it. Those who are less differentiated from their family of origin have a more difficult time separating thoughts from feelings and are often controlled by their emotional system. Fenell (1993b) described an effective intervention technique that employs Bowen's differentiation-of-self scale (Figure 9.1) in helping couples renegotiate the rules of their relationship and separate emotions from reason in their communication process.

Bowen postulated two levels of self. The *solid self*, on the one hand, is the part of the self that develops slowly and from within. It develops firmly held convictions that may be changed from within through rational processes but never through coercion by others. The *pseudo-self*, on the other hand, is made up of the beliefs, values, and opinions held by others that are uncritically accepted. Emotional health is likely to be found in persons whose solid self is in control of their behaviors.

Individuals with low levels of differentiation of self live in a world dominated by emotions. They are not readily able to distinguish facts from feelings. Their rational processes are frequently clouded by their emotional experiences. Much of their energy goes into seeking love and approval or punishing others for not providing that approval. Thus, they have little energy left for engaging in productive, goal-directed activities. These people have a greater incidence of emotional and physical concerns.

People with low differentiation of self must receive tremendous amounts of validation and recognition from others in order to feel satisfied. Individuals who are lower on the differentiation-of-self scale may be reluctant to express their opinions if they are concerned that their ideas would not meet the approval of significant others. They are unable

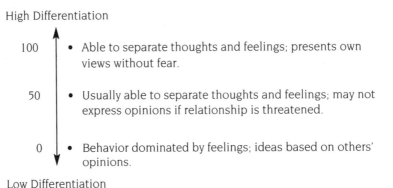

High Differentiation

100 • Able to separate thoughts and feelings; presents own views without fear.

50 • Usually able to separate thoughts and feelings; may not express opinions if relationship is threatened.

0 • Behavior dominated by feelings; ideas based on others' opinions.

Low Differentiation

Figure 9.1   Differentiation-of-Self Scale

to provide self-approval, relying on the approval of others to validate their self-worth. They are driven by their emotions.

Those with higher levels of differentiation of self are aware of the differences between thoughts and feelings, and they are able to experience both. They are able to acknowledge feelings without allowing their feelings to dominate their rational thought process. These people are able to state their positions on issues clearly and are open to modification of their positions based on new information and internal choice. Differentiated individuals recognize and acknowledge their feelings as a source of information to be used with other facts in making rational decisions

Family Projection Process

The family projection process is related to the emotional triangle because it describes how parental problems can be projected onto a child. Family projection occurs when one parent is more emotionally focused on the child than the other parent is. Because of traditional gender roles, the mother is more often the emotionally enmeshed parent. The father is typically disengaged, demonstrating another example of lack of differentiation. The father senses the mother's anxiety about the child and supports her in her emotional overinvolvement. The child feels the mother's anxiety and may begin to behave in ways that confirm the mother's need to be overinvolved and overprotective. The father supports this behavior pattern either by backing the mother or by withdrawing from, but not confronting, the situation when he disagrees with her. With the father's support, the mother focuses her energy on relieving the child's anxiety *rather than on dealing with her own.* This pattern of behavior gradually leads to increased emotional impairment for the child, and significant behavior problems may develop in adolescence. Eventually, if problems become severe, another party (frequently a counselor) will be triangulated in to help stabilize the emotional system.

Nuclear Family Emotional System

The concept of the *nuclear family emotional system* is a logical extension of the family projection process. Bowen and other family systems theorists postulate that the family system seeks to attain *homeostasis,* or balance and stability. However, Bowen observed that the family's attempt to balance the system might be at the expense of a vulnerable family member. According to Bowen, there is no such thing as a perfectly differentiated individual or family. All families maintain some level of fusion, defined as the act of losing one's sense of individuality in a relationship. Those who experience fusion to a greater degree are driven by their emotions and are less able to employ their intellectual processes in resolving personal and family difficulties. Families with high levels of fusion are also highly anxious, trying desperately to minimize conflict and please others. This style of interacting often leads to a variety of family problems. Bowen indentified four dysfunctional patterns families adopt in order to dissipate their anxiety. It is important that the therapist be able to recognize these attempts to reduce anxiety and be capable of helping the family identify and resolve their anxiety in more effective ways.

1. *Establishing emotional distance.* When family members are emotionally reactive to each other and are unsuccessful at managing their reactivity, they tend to create distance between themselves and others (Kerr, 1981). This distancing may not be a conscious choice but, instead, a means to avoid the nuclear family emotional process. The distance is created so the family members avoid fusion by creating an illusion of agreement when in fact agreement is not present. When distancing occurs in families, togetherness needs may be met in other relationships and infidelity can occur.

2. *Marital conflict.* Through marital conflict (or conflict between partners in committed relationships), individuals can meet their needs for emotional closeness and distance. These needs, however, are not met through choice but, rather, through a cycle of intense anger and conflict over an issue that involves withdrawing from the partner during conflict (emotional distance) and making up and forgiving (emotional closeness). Marital and couple conflict is one of the key processes used by individuals in relationships that prevents them from examining their own lack of autonomy. On the one hand, through the conflict, the couple is able to convince themselves that they are autonomous. On the other hand, they know that they will make up without ever having to resolve the basic disagreements that are present in the relationship, thus reestablishing an undifferentiated homeostasis. Therapist should recognize that marital and couple conflict in itself may not harm the children unless they are somehow made to feel guilty, involved in, or responsible for the conflict.

3. *Dysfunction of one spouse or partner.* Another way to lessen the anxiety created by the nuclear family emotional system is through the dysfunction of one spouse or partner. In this situation, one partner becomes submissive and the other becomes dominant. In this type of relationship, each person believes that he or she is adapting to the other, yet they rarely discuss this belief with each other. The partner who adapts the most becomes a *no-self* (Bowen, 1971) and is susceptible to physical illness, emotional illness, or social dysfunction such as alcoholism. These dysfunctions tend to become chronic and may be difficult to reverse. The therapist must be aware that the couple will usually come to couples therapy if individual work with the "sick one" has been ineffective. The couple will present to the family therapist with a healthy partner and a partner who is the IP and the one with problems. The systems therapist must acknowledge the presenting problem as described by the couple in the early phase of therapy, while at the same time employing a systemic conceptualization that assumes that the problem is the result of a dysfunctional relationship of undifferentiated partners rather than the behaviors of the IP. The therapist will then treat the couple accordingly through exploration of the lack of differentiation in their relationship.

4. *Projection onto children.* Projection occurs through the family projection process previously discussed. Children become impaired when the fusion or lack of differentiation of one or both of the parents is projected onto the child or children through intense focus on physical problems or detecting the smallest flaw in the child's behavior and overreacting to it. Typically, because of traditional family roles, the most intense fusion may occur between the mother and a vulnerable child. The fusion, however, can be between the father and the child in certain circumstances. When the child is impaired, the parents are able to focus their attention on the child and ignore their personal anxiety concerning their own lack of differentiation from their families of origin and from each other, which, according to Bowen, is the source of the problems. The family therapist will want to identify this pattern and stabilize the child's symptoms, then remove the child from therapy while focusing work on the lack of differentiation of the couple. This will allow the therapist to help the adults identify problems in their own relationship and their lack of differentiation, thus reducing the projection on the child. The

result of this intervention is that the child becomes better as the parents recognize and deal with their lack of differentiation while simultaneously encouraging the child's autonomy and differentiation from them.

Multigenerational Transmission Process

Bowen conceptualized the development of emotional illness as a multigenerational process in which undifferentiation or fusion is projected onto one or more of the children *over a series of generations*, leading to increased emotional illness with each succeeding generation. This concept, more than any other, links Bowen's systems theory with psychodynamic processes and places it among the natural systems of the universe (Friedman, 1991), as it describes the historical development of symptoms over several generations. Bowen asserted that people marry partners with similar levels of differentiation of self. When these couples produce children through a random genetic process, one or more of the children is the most vulnerable and possesses a lower level of differentiation of self than the parents or other children. Bowen also hypothesized that other children are likely to have a higher level of differentiation than the parents or have similar levels of differentiation.

The child with the lower level of differentiation often becomes the vulnerable one in the family. This child becomes an adult and then marries at his level of differentiation and produces a child who has a lower level of differentiation. This child marries at her level, and the multigenerational transmission process continues with each succeeding generation, producing a less differentiated child who is increasingly prone to emotional illness. Bowen hypothesized that over the course of 10 or more generations, this process could produce a severely impaired offspring. The impairment might be schizophrenia, Bowen's initial area of expertise, or one of many other significant problems such as serious antisocial behavior, severe chemical dependency, or severe psychosomatic physical disability (Kerr, 1981). Use of the genogram (Carter & McGoldrick, 2005) in therapy with families is a useful technique in reconstructing the history of emotional impairment over the generations to gain clarity concerning the generational transmission of emotional illness.

The multigenerational transmission process may be slowed by favorable life circumstances that calm the anxieties of one generation. If a generation severs itself from the emotional intensity of another generation, this *emotional cutoff* may slow the multigenerational transmission process. Although emotional cutoff is commonly thought to solve the problem of emotional fusion between the generations, it actually only slows the process. It does not stop the recurring dynamics that maintain the multigenerational transmission process. Frequently, couples say that their problems with the older generation were solved by moving away. Bowen would suggest that the problems may have been forestalled temporarily but would have to be dealt with through one of the four mechanisms of the nuclear family emotional system described earlier or else treated and resolved in family therapy (Anonymous, 1972).

Bowen built upon Adler's work and believed that the birth order of the children can serve as a predictor of adult behavior. Toman's (1961) study of birth order gives 10 profiles of sibling positions. The most common are seen in the oldest and youngest children. Typically, the oldest child assumes an overfunctioning role and believes that she has the ability to control family events. The youngest child is often taken care of by older siblings. Because of this, he tends to be more reluctant to take initiative and may wait for others to take the lead in activities. These patterns are adaptive and functional for some, but when there is emotional illness characterized by intense fusion and lack of differentiation of self, the birth order patterns are likely to be dysfunctional to the individual in marriage and other close relationships.

Main Therapeutic Interventions

Bowenian family therapy is like most other systems based approaches because families request therapy when they want help in resolving problems in only one of the family members, the IP. Bowen did not consider that the IP is the source of the family's difficulties. He conceptualized the problem as arising from unrecognized emotional fusion within the family. This emotional fusion leads to emotional responses to problematic situations that intensify the already charged emotional environment. Thus, the therapist's first task is to defuse the emotionally charged situation in the family, neutralizing it as much as possible.

A differentiated therapist is the key to neutralizing the emotional system in the family. The therapist must be able to remain outside the emotional forces that are in play within the family. The emotional forces active within the family have the power to pull undifferentiated therapists into the fray, thus neutralizing them and their ability to be of help to the family. To remain outside the emotional field, therapists must be reasonably differentiated and must have done their own family-of-origin work. Bowen required that therapists training with him at the Georgetown Family Institute work on issues of differentiation of self from family of origin to prepare them to support their client families in doing the same. The method Bowen used for his own differentiation process is enlightening and is recommended reading for all family therapists (Anonymous, 1972).

The therapist neutralizes the family's emotional system by using *reason* to respond to each of the emotionally charged issues the family members raise. Some critics contend that Bowen discounts the feeling process. Others disagree and argue Bowen's therapy focuses on the *effects of emotions* on the family members more fully than any of the other systems approaches. Early in the treatment process, the therapist gradually introduces the family to a Bowenian systemic understanding of the problem and how the problem and differentiation are inextricably linked. The therapist must have gained the family's trust and had success in neutralizing the emotionally charged atmosphere within the family. When this initial process has been accomplished, the family will be better able to engage their intellect in understanding the reasons for their difficulties and in considering healthy alternatives to current dysfunctional behaviors. At this stage of treatment, the therapist will be able to discuss with the families the fours patterns (described previously) that families employ to reduce anxiety and to explore which of these attempted solutions the family is using.

Bowen (1971) attempted to resolve the problems of symptomatic children through work with the adults in the family. For the purposes of treatment, he defined the family as the two most responsible family members. The unit of treatment, according to Bowen, is almost always the parents of the children in the family. Prior to 1960, Bowen included the children in therapy. He considered his results less than satisfactory because the parents terminated the therapy when the child's symptoms were sufficiently reduced without resolving issues of the parents' (and child's) differentiation from their families of origin. After 1960, Bowen instructed the parents to enter therapy without the symptomatic child and explained to them in the initial session that problems are a result of the parents' problematic relationship and that changes in the child's symptoms will occur *automatically* when the parents are able to redefine and modify their relationship. Bowen thought that his approach allowed the parents to focus on their relationships, the issues regarding their own differentiation of selves from their families of origin, and the way their lack of differentiation may be affecting the child.

Bowen (1978) viewed the therapist as having four main functions in assisting the family (pp. 247–252):

1. Defining and clarifying the relationship between the partners
2. Remaining detriangulated from the family emotional system
3. Teaching the functioning of emotional systems
4. Demonstrating differentiation by taking an I position during the course of therapy

In therapy, Bowen would direct the couple not to speak directly to each other about subjects that created anxiety for either of them. Instead, Bowen instructed the them to talk directly to him in the most objective and low-key manner possible about anxiety-producing issues of concern. This technique of having each person speak to the therapist, rather than to each other, prevented the couple from engaging in a well-established emotionally reactive pattern and permitted each to hear more accurately what the other is communicating. Because the partners were speaking to the therapist rather than to each other, they were not emotionally connected and were therefore able to more clearly hear and understand what the partner was revealing. Later in therapy, when the partners were better able to separate their emotions and their thoughts, Bowen would encourage the partners to speak directly to each other rather than through him.

If, when speaking directly to each other, one partner's comment created an emotional overreaction in the other, Bowen suggested that the therapist quickly turn the communication flow back to discussion between the therapist and client by asking questions of one partner rather than escalating the emotional reactivity emerging between the couple. As the reactivity subsided, Bowen would ask each partner to describe to him what had taken place and how that reactivity might be handled better in the future. The therapist helps the couple discuss their thoughts, feelings, and reactions with the therapist rather than act out these feelings and reactions with each other.

This phase of therapy is critical. When each partner is talking to and through the therapist, they are more able to really understand what the other is thinking and feeling, perhaps for the first time in the relationship. When one spouse speaks directly to therapist, the other is able to listen from a new differentiated and objective position. The fact that each is removed from the emotional relationship system increases the under-standing of each partner because the emotional reactivity that is usually present in the communication process is removed. As each partner speaks to the therapist, the other is hearing the content in a new and more rational way.

If therapy is to proceed effectively, the therapist must remain detri-angulated from the family's emotional system. To successfully maintain detriangulation, the therapist has to be sufficiently differentiated from his own family emotional system and must be able to stay outside of the couple's emotional system. The therapist has to understand the na-ture of relationships and the way two-person relationships always sta-bilize by involving a third party to form triangles. Initially each client will want the therapist to support her positions in disagreements. The therapist must be capable of remaining detriangulated and not ally with one partner over the other. The therapist should focus on the process of what is happening in the session without becoming emotionally in-volved in the content. When therapists begin to feel themselves becom-ing emotionally engaged in what is happening in the session, they are probably being inducted in to the family's emotional system because of their own lack of differentiation. Supervision with a trusted colleague is essential when this occurs.

The quality of differentiation of the family therapist is critical in Bowenian therapy. For therapists to be able to help families change, they must be reasonably well differentiated. The key assumption of Bowen's family systems theory is that "the emotional problem between two peo-ple will resolve automatically if they remain in contact with a third per-son who can remain free of the emotional field between them, while relating to each" (Bowen, 1971). Remaining free of the emotional field as another way of saying *differentiated from family of origin*. A good way for therapists to gauge whether they are outside the emotional force of the relationship is to attempt to demonstrate to each client that some of the couple's most cherished assumptions concerning the relationship have alternative interpretations. When therapists are unable to respond with alternative conceptualizations for the situation, they are probably emotionally caught in the triangle.

Another technique used in family systems therapy is to teach the family the functioning of emotional systems. This process begins by the therapist's use of *I messages*, which communicate the differentiated po-sition of the therapist and model effective behavior for the couple.

Through the use of I messages, the therapist can communicate knowledge concerning emotional systems without expecting clients to necessarily accept the concept.

Later, this teaching may be accomplished through parables, metaphors, and descriptions of the resolution of other family situations. Much later in therapy, when the emotional reactivity and anxiety are quite low, this teaching can be didactic. When couples understand the functioning of emotional systems and are able to relate to each other, their children, and their parents in a differentiated way, therapy has been concluded successfully.

Strengths and Limitations of the Family Systems Approach

Like all theories of psychotherapy, Bowen's family systems theory has strengths and limitations. The major strengths of the approach are the following:

- It conceptualizes problem formation from a systems perspective. Symptoms are viewed as the result of interactions between and among family members over several generations.
- It does not diagnose and label an individual as having mental illness. Rather, it conceptualizes *emotional illness* as a systems-based phenomenon without labeling any single member of the system.
- It conceptualizes emotional illness as resulting from a multigenerational transmission process and recognizes the importance of assisting clients in differentiating from their families of origin.
- It recognizes the importance of neutralizing the emotional process that occurs in families to permit the couple to progress to more advanced stages of therapy.

The following are limitations of this approach:

- Because the focus of treatment is on the parental dyad, the effects of children on the system may not be fully considered.
- Concepts such as the differentiation-of-self scale are not fully developed and have little empirical validation.
- The approach may overemphasize past experiences at the expense of current functioning.

- The approach may not give enough emphasis to the importance of affect in problem resolution.
- The approach frequently requires a longer time commitment to therapy than some other systems approaches.

Bowen's family systems theory is a good example of a systems theory with psychodynamic roots. The theory relies on understanding past experiences in the development of the family emotional system. The importance placed on family-of-origin experiences and differentiation of self places Bowen's family systems theory in the category of psychodynamic family systems theories.

CASE EXAMPLE

Bowen's Family Systems Therapy

Mrs. Brown contacted a family systems therapist because of problems with their son, who has been getting into trouble at school and ignoring his homework. The therapist suggested that the best way to approach the problem is for Mr. and Mrs. Brown to come into therapy without their son to discover how they might best help him.

When the Browns began therapy, the therapist helped the couple define and clarify the nature of their own relationship by remaining detriangulated from his clients' emotional system. He had the couple speak through him, not to each other. This intervention helped the couple reduce their anxiety regarding their son's behavior. The therapist then helped the couple recognize that there was considerable emotional reactivity in their own marriage relationship.

The therapist assisted the couple in identifying the anxiety they felt in their own families of origin, how that anxiety is with them today, and how it affects their marital relationship. Moreover, the therapist helped the couple understand how their own anxiety is projected onto their son, contributing to his problematic behaviors. The therapist then helped the couple recognize how their behavior has been based on emotional reactivity. He then guided the partners as they identified ways to include their emotions as one element of information in rational decisions

(continued)

Framo's Family-of-Origin Theory

James Framo (1922–2001) trained as a clinical psychologist with a deep interest in family process. He developed a family therapy theory emphasizing the importance of recognizing and resolving the issues that emerge in a person's interactions with the family of origin. Although Framo's theory is presented in this chapter on systems theories with psychodynamic roots, it would be safe to say that Framo himself may not have classified his theory in this way. Framo seemed to believe that Foley's (1974) classification of his theory as integrating a number of family

---

Bowen's Family Systems Therapy *(continued)*

about their behavioral choices toward their son and toward each other. During this portion of the therapy, the counselor described the functioning of emotional systems to help the spouses gain insight into what happened to them as children in their families of origin and what has to happen in the future to establish differentiated selves in their current families.

Through this process of therapy, Mr. and Mrs. Brown began to react less emotionally to their son, and gradually his problems at school began to decrease. They began to react as differentiated selves within the family and respond to family problems through intellect rather than emotion. Specifically, the couple recognized the following changes through therapy:

1. They developed a more realistic understanding of the influences of their families of origin on their concerns about their son.
2. They developed the ability to recognize that their current anxiety was related to their previous family-of-origin experiences, and this awareness provided the ability to minimize projection of that anxiety onto their son and onto each other.
3. They developed an ability to remain in sustained intimate contact based on rational choice rather than neurotic emotional dependency.
4. They developed an ability to allow autonomous functioning of their children and each other without fear that this is harmful to the family.

theories more accurately described what he tried to accomplish. Furthermore, Framo winced when he found himself categorized as a psychoanalytic family therapist, even though his approach relies heavily on assumptions taken from the psychodynamic concept of object relations theory (Framo, 1981). I agree that Framo was not a psychoanalytic family therapist in the classical sense, but he was indeed one of the most widely recognized practicing systems theorists emphasizing the historical importance of childhood relationships within the family of origin as critical in adult functioning. While there is no doubt that Framo was a systems thinker, there is also no doubt that many of his assumptions about therapeutic change had psychodynamic roots; thus, his inclusion in this chapter.

Framo began treating couples and families in 1958. He continually revised and modified his therapeutic approach to meet the needs of families in distress. James Framo died unexpectedly on August 22, 2001. He was 79 years of age.

Philosophical Tenets and Key Theoretical Constructs

Framo's work was based heavily on the concepts of object relations theory as developed by Fairbairn (1954). Framo theorized that families can best be treated by depth therapy and that marital, couple, and family problems result from individuals failing to resolve issues that existed in their families of origin. These unresolved issues become an introjected part of the individual's personality. An example of *introjection* occurs when a child develops representational images of his parents into himself, simultaneously fusing them with his own personality. Thus, the individual may treat persons in close interpersonal relationships, such as spouse or partner and children, in a manner that is based on the experiences from relationships in the family of origin rather than on actual behaviors of the family members. Therefore, past experiences may dictate how a person will interact when under pressure in a meaningful present relationship.

Furthermore, Framo asserted that when individuals respond to these issues from the past in therapy *with members of their families of origin actually present*, issues that are problematic in both the current and past family relationships can be resolved. Framo argued that one session with the family of origin may be more powerful in resolving current problems than several individual, marital, couple, or family sessions (Framo,

1981). The specific tenets of Framo's theory are the following (Framo, 1981, 1982):

- Human behavior is motivated by the drive to establish a successful relationship with another person.
- In the early years of childhood, parent–child relationships create frustrating experiences that the child cannot change. These negative experiences are incorporated in the child's personality to surface in important relationships later in life.
- The individual grows to adulthood forming committed relationships, usually through marriage, and by having children. These adult relationships recreate the frustrations experienced in the family of origin during childhood.
- Problems emerging in families have their roots in the unresolved conflicts experienced in the adults' families of origin.
- People select life partners who will recreate unresolved family-of-origin conflicts within the committed relationship.
- Unresolved issues from the family of origin are often projected onto the children rather than acted out in the relationship. When this occurs, the children may develop symptoms.
- Problems may be best resolved by returning to their source with adult children entering therapy with their families of origin.
- When individuals explore the past to resolve issues with their families of origin, they are better able to understand their current marital difficulties and are able to relate to their own partner and children as they actually are rather than as symbols of unresolved conflict in the family of origin.

Main Therapeutic Interventions

Framo is most widely recognized for his work with his clients and their families of origin (Framo, 1981). While he has pioneered other ways of working with individuals and families, his family-of-origin work is the approach that will be addressed here. When problems arise in a family through symptoms in one of the children or through relationship conflict, the therapist meets the family for a few sessions to deal with the crisis that has brought the family or couple into treatment. Once the crisis is under control, the couple may profit from continued work that will explore and perhaps correct the underlying circumstances that created the situation that brought the family to treatment.

Specifically, Framo developed a three-phase treatment process that has provided successful therapy for the families he counsels. The phases of the treatment program are (1) therapy with the couple, (2) couples group therapy, and (3) family-of-origin therapy.

Therapy with the Couple

Each stage of Framo's treatment approach has specific goals and techniques. During the first stage, the therapist meets with the couple with the primary goal of establishing a solid working relationship with each partner, based on mutual trust. This goal is accomplished through the use of the relationship skills of the therapist, who develops an understanding of both partners as individuals and develops an accurate understanding of the relationship system. The therapist spends the first several sessions learning about the couple and developing trust without deliberate attempts to intervene (Framo, 1982). During this stage of the therapy, Framo seeks diagnostic information by asking relevant questions in several areas, including:

● information about the referral source,
● basic demographic information about each client,
● a brief statement about the problems from each client,
● duration of marriage or relationship and age of children,
● previous therapy and results,
● reasons for mate selection,
● prior marriages or significant relationships,
● family's reaction to mate,
● conflict styles,
● whether the couple love each other,
● commitment to the marriage or relationship,
● characteristics of the marriage or relationship,
● quality and quantity of sexual relationship, and
● motivation of each for therapy.

Once each partner has had the opportunity to discuss these issues, the therapist has a much better sense of the quality of the relationship and the problems that are present. This initial phase of the therapy provides the therapist and the couple ample opportunity to develop a trusting relationship before beginning the intervention stage of couples therapy.

After a trusting relationship with each individual has been established, the therapist must focus on the remaining therapeutic goals of treatment: The therapist must specifically identify the goals of each partner and with this information determine the therapist's goals. Framo believed that for treatment to be successful, the family therapist must conduct therapy in a manner that meets the expectations of both partners and the therapist. If the goals of the couple are not met, one or both of them are likely to drop out of treatment. If the therapist is not able to meet his goals, the therapy will likely lack coherent direction and be unsuccessful. In all phases of treatment, including couples therapy, couples group therapy, and family-of-origin therapy, the therapist must be aware of the clients' changing goals and expectations and work to meet these goals in the context of the therapist's own treatment goals (Framo, 1981).

When the therapist has joined with each individual and a solid, trusting relationship has been established, the process of defusing intense conflicts within the relationship may be initiated. This goal is accomplished through basic interventions, such as communication skills training and negotiation training, and by emphasizing the positive characteristics of the relationship that have been discovered by the therapist. After any immediate crisis issues are defused, the therapist educates the couple about object relations theory. The focus is on how issues that have long remained unresolved in the family of origin may be responsible for the present difficulties in the relationship and the family.

In this stage, Framo gently introduced his desire to have the couple talk directly with their families of origin in therapy at some later date. Framo recognized that the notion of interacting directly with the family of origin causes extreme anxiety for most clients. He assures them that they will be adequately prepared to meet their families and most likely will benefit from the encounter.

Couples Group Therapy

To best prepare couples to meet with their families of origin, Framo found that the couples group therapy format is most advantageous. The couples group format is suggested as a step toward the family-of-origin work for numerous reasons:

- It is reassuring for each person to know that other couples have similar fears and anxieties about dealing with their families of origin in therapy.

- By participating in a couples group, the individuals come to recognize the universality of problems that they have with their families of origin. Thus, couples feel more normal and self-accepting.
- Couples in a successful group come to trust each other and share information that might not emerge in the marital/relationship therapy stage. Furthermore, group members may be open to feedback and support from other couples that may be more effective than interventions provided by the therapist.
- The genuine caring the couples feel for each other is therapeutic.
- Through feedback from group members, the couples usually come to modify their goals in productive ways.
- Through feedback and modeling by other couples, the partners come to recognize their unrealistic expectations of their mate.
- The effective leadership by the therapist helps the group members explore the genesis of their unrealistic expectations of their partner. This process returns the focus of couples group therapy to the importance of resolving issues with the family of origin.
- Despite each person's fear of interacting with his family of origin in therapy, members of the group are supportive of other members who are about to initiate their family-of-origin sessions. This group support is instrumental in helping members develop the courage and resolve to invite their parents to family-of-origin sessions.

The couples group is usually composed of three pairs of clients. Ideally, these couples are at various stages of their preparation for the family-of-origin sessions—one couple graduating, one couple in the middle of couples group work, and one couple joining the group after stage one couples therapy sessions have just been completed. Framo always employed the couples group format unless some compelling reason precludes placing a couple in the group. He found that the groups are most successful when the couples are at a similar family development stage, such as a family with young children, a family with adolescents, couples who have contemplated divorce, or couples who are similar in other significant ways.

In summary, the couples group helps the partners further understand their own relationships and improve them. It creates a sense of community in which the couples support each other in their attempts to recognize and confront unresolved issues from their families of origin that are affecting their current relationships. Moreover, it provides support for the members inviting their parents to join them in therapy and a place to debrief after the family-of-origin sessions.

Family-of-Origin Therapy

As individuals become ready to meet with their families of origin, preparations begin to convene the family-of-origin session. Needless to say, each partner does not necessarily become ready for these sessions at the same time, and this is not required. When an individual returns to the couples group after meeting with the family of origin, the encouraging effect on the partner and the other group members is a significant factor in motivating the others to arrange their own family-of-origin sessions.

Prior to having the family-of-origin session, the client and therapist are thoroughly prepared for what to expect in the meetings. The family of origin is also prepared for the meeting to the extent possible by communications with their offspring and the therapist. While the client is usually nervous about the meeting, the family of origin is doubly nervous, because they do not know with any certainty what to expect and fear that they will be blamed for their offspring's difficulties.

Normally, Framo would meet the family of origin on a single day with 4 hours devoted to the session (Framo, 1981). Later, other formats were introduced including a 2-day process with a 3-hour session held on each day. Framo found that the family took advantage of their evening together to process the initial encounter. The family's evening together identified new concerns that were introduced at the 2nd day's meeting.

Despite the initial reasons most clients give for why the family-of-origin sessions would be impossible, the success rate of engaging the family in therapy is quite high. Framo found that when clients truly recognized the importance of the meeting for their development, they would communicate without ambiguity that importance to members of the family of origin and gain their willing participation. Framo's position has been supported by decades of experience in the practice of family-of-origin therapy.

The most important goal of the family-of-origin session is for the client to make contact with the family and have a *corrective experience* with the family (Framo, 1981). The family-of-origin session is held without the spouse or partner present in the sessions. Framo observed that having the partner present could easily detract from the purpose of correcting the perceived problems between the generations and between or among siblings. If the partner were present, much of the attention could be placed on that individual and the couple's relationship, and the main goals of the family-of-origin work would be missed. The specific goals for the family-of-origin session are as follows:

- The client makes contact with the family of origin, parents and siblings, in a way that is based on adult (rather than child) interactions.
- The client and therapist may discover which of the client's attitudes developed in the family of origin are being projected onto the client's spouse or partner and children in present-day encounters.
- The client may increase differentiation (Bowen, 1971) from the family of origin, which will lead to enhanced relationships with members of the family of origin as well as with the current family.
- The meeting sets the stage for getting to know the parents as real people and sharing important thoughts and feelings with them. It is also a time for the parents to be honest and real with their adult child.
- The meeting provides the client with an opportunity to forgive the parents for their mistakes, real and perceived, and to tell the parents that they are loved. The importance of this goal cannot be overstated because Framo said that no one wants to hate her parents. Because if you hate your parents, you hate yourself—because your parents are in your head and in your heart.

Framo found that the family-of-origin sessions were usually positive for all participants. Normally, the couple's relationship is improved and relationships with parents and siblings are better. Occasionally, however, some issues emerge that may increase tensions between the family of origin and the client. Thus, the immediate effects of the session may not be positive. Clients are prepared for this possibility and are encouraged to use the group for support if this is the outcome. Moreover, the family of origin is provided with referral sources in their home community if they need or request further therapy.

In some cases, when individuals complete their family-of-origin work, they recognize that their marriage or relationship is based on projections and unfinished business with the family of origin rather than on love and respect for the partner. In these cases, the couple may decide not to work on correcting the projections in therapy, and the result may be divorce. Although these negative outcomes are uncommon, clients should be made aware of this possibility. Framo viewed family-of-origin work as the *major surgery of family therapy* and cautioned that this therapy, like all therapy approaches, is not without its risks (Framo, 1981).

Framo's family-of-origin therapy is an active and directive approach to resolving issues affecting the family that have their roots in the family of origin. He considered working with an opposite-gender cotherapist to be the most effective way to provide treatment. The composition of the cotherapy team allows the therapists to relate to both the same-gender and opposite-gender clients, providing multiple sources of information to them. It alleviates the clients' fears that alliances by gender may occur. Further, the cotherapy team, through effective collaboration, is much better able to respond to the myriad of issues that emerge in therapy. One therapist may become extremely involved in the content and affect of the situation presented, while the other may remain more detached and objective, observing the process rather than content of the interactions. Cotherapy teams make it possible to more effectively meet the needs of the clients. Other important techniques used in this approach are as follows:

- Framo did not meet with one spouse or partner alone. He set appointments when both would be present. If this was not possible, he referred the couple to a colleague who treated members of a relationship separately.
- The couple is prepared for family-of-origin sessions gradually and without coercion from the therapist. Preparation begins early in the individual couple sessions and continues more vigorously during couples group sessions.
- Clients are asked specifically about events occurring in their families of origin. If the therapist does not specifically seek this information, couples will not normally view it as relevant to the current problems.
- Individuals in the group who are willing to meet their families of origin help prepare others who are reluctant.
- While a couple prepares together for family-of-origin work, their relationship problems diminish as their support for one another increases.
- Resistance to the family-of-origin sessions is to be expected. The combination of the therapists' interventions and group support emphasizes the importance of the sessions. The therapist does not pressure the individuals, allowing them to become ready at their own pace. One partner may become ready for the family-of-origin session

well before the other. This is not a problem, however, as the one who has had the session can encourage the other who has not.

- The therapists help each client overcome anxiety about the session by developing an agenda of issues to be discussed with the family of origin. This assures the client that the session will have a predictable structure and real purpose. In reality, when the session begins, the agenda often goes "out the window," and the sessions take on a life of their own.
- Spouses or partners are not included in the initial family-of-origin session. These sessions are between the client and his family.
- The partner may be included in a later family-of-origin session if problems exist in the in-law relationship.
- The therapist and the couples group members encourage others to do family-of-origin work.
- As the family-of-origin session nears, nervous calls from family members to the therapist are to be expected. The therapist encourages family-of-origin members to consider any issues they have with their child or sibling and to be prepared to raise them in the session.
- To ensure a productive family-of-origin session, the therapist makes certain that the caring among the family members that is often buried emerges. If it is too focused on negative content, the session may become an unproductive gripe session with a potentially negative outcome.

Strengths and Limitations of Framo's Approach

Family-of-origin therapy has several strengths:

- It is the only therapy that actually has the client deal with issues from the family of origin directly with the family in a session.
- This theory recognizes that problems in the present marriage or relationship may be the result of unfinished business in the family of origin.
- It recognizes the therapeutic power of the couples group and uses that power to help clients develop in their relationships.
- This approach offers the opportunity for individuals to create more meaningful relationships with their families of origin through direct contact about significant issues.

Framo was aware that this approach was not for everyone and acknowledged the limitations of the therapy (Framo, 1981):

CASE EXAMPLE

Framo's Family-of-Origin Therapy

Mr. and Mrs. Taylor were having difficulties with their marriage. She complained that her husband was indecisive and she couldn't rely on him. Mr. Taylor reported that his wife was domineering and unsupportive of any attempts he made to exert leadership. Thus, he had begun to give up on the marriage.

The couple came to therapy for help in making the marriage better. The family-of-origin therapist, working from Framo's model, treated the couple in marital therapy to reduce the tension, anger, and hurt feelings through teaching communication and negotiation skills, establishing trusting relationships with both partners, and understanding each person's experience of the marital difficulties.

During this stage of treatment, the therapist introduced the idea of having family-of-origin sessions so each person might come to understand how some of the present behaviors developed and seek ways to eliminate the problematic behaviors. The therapist engaged both spouses in discussions about their families of origin and the issues that existed within their families. At this point in treatment, they entered couples group therapy because they were ready to begin more advanced work on their marital problems.

In the couples group setting, Mr. and Mrs. Taylor came to feel accepted and cared for by the other two couples in the group. They were working on relationship issues not unlike those of the Taylors. In the couples group, the Taylors, with the support of the other group members, began to recognize that their marital issues might be related to problems that began in their families of origin.

Mr. and Mrs. Edwards, another couple in the group, were in the final stage of preparation for their family-of-origin sessions. Both were excited about the possibilities, yet fearful at the same time. The support the Edwards couple received from the therapist and the group was positive and instrumental in helping each of them have successful meetings with their families of origin. The Edwards' report to the group about their experiences encouraged the Taylors to begin serious preparation for dealing with their own families of origin. The focus on preparing for the encounter with their respective families pulled the two closer together as they supported each other's attempts to prepare for the family-of-origin sessions. Thus, their original marital problems became less of a focus in therapy and at home.

(continued)

Framo's Family-of-Origin Therapy *(continued)*

Several weeks passed before Mrs. Taylor was ready for her family-of-origin session. When the day finally arrived, she was apprehensive. She went into the session armed with a list of issues to discuss with her parents and brother. Although many of the issues were not discussed because of time limitations, several of the most critical issues were covered, and Mrs. Taylor was provided with a wealth of information about herself and her family. Through the family-of-origin session, Mrs. Taylor discovered that her own father was passive and was content to let her mother deal with any problems that emerged. Mrs. Taylor had not accepted this pattern and was angry with both parents because neither tried to change the situation.

Mrs. Taylor had been certain that she would not be domineering like her mother because she would marry a stronger man than her father. But she discovered that she had recreated in her present marriage what she thought she would avoid. Thus, she was faced with the need to deal with her anger toward her parents as well as her anger toward herself for creating a similar situation.

These insights provided Mrs. Taylor with plenty of information, and she was able to forgive her parents and establish more positive relationships with them. Furthermore, she discovered that her brother had similar feelings that he had not expressed before. This revelation opened the door for an improved relationship with her sibling. Finally, and perhaps most significant, she recognized that some of her husband's lack of assertiveness was the result of her need to make him be the way she wanted him to be rather than accepting him as he was. This insight led to immediate marital improvements.

A few weeks later, Mr. Taylor was ready for his family-of-origin session. He discovered that he had never felt adequate in relation to his father. The tasks he was asked to perform were never done quite well enough. Mr. Taylor had grown up feeling that it didn't matter how hard he tried; he would not be adequate. Thus, he married a woman who recreated that feeling.

Through the insights the Taylors achieved in family-of-origin therapy, they were able to establish a more productive marriage and more meaningful ties with their families of origin. Knowing how their behaviors were driven by unresolved family-of-origin issues helped the Taylors move forward both as individuals, as a couple, and as parents to their own children.

- Family-of-origin work is not for couples with relatively minor relationship difficulties that do not require intensive work.
- Some couples do not have access to their families because of death or some other circumstance.
- This approach may highlight the need for individual psychotherapy. If individual therapeutic support is needed after family-of-origin work is completed, Framo encouraged referral to a therapist who understands family-of-origin intervention strategies. If the receiving therapist does not understand the process, problems emerging from the family-of-origin work could be exacerbated rather than resolved.
- This approach relies on the assumption that current problems are a result of past experiences in the family of origin. It is not likely to be effective with clients who do not to accept this assumption.

Internal Family Systems Theory

Richard Schwartz and his colleagues at the Institute for Juvenile Research of Chicago (Nichols & Schwartz, 2001) developed the internal family systems theory because existing models of family therapy were not sufficiently powerful to help their clients with the eating disorders anorexia nervosa and bulimia. This theory "expands systems thinking beyond the boundaries of family into the realm of intrapsychic process" (p. 427). While Schwartz considers this theory to be integrative, his view of personality as a multifaceted construct and his focus on the intrapsychic *internal parts* of the client's personality suggest that this theory fits best within this chapter describing psychodynamic systems theories.

Philosophical Tenets and Key Theoretical Constructs

Schwartz developed the internal family systems (IFS) model out of frustration with limitations of the family therapy approaches that had been used to treat clients with eating disorders. Schwartz theorized that for his clients to get better, they would have to explore the intrapsychic natures of their personalities. He created a unique way to help his clients examine their psychological dynamics by framing their psyche as a "family of inner voices or parts" (Nichols & Schwartz, 2001, p. 427).

Subpersonalities

Like many other individual theorists, Schwartz's notion that the psyche is divided into subpersonalities or parts is not new. Fritz Perls (1969), among others, conceived of the healthy personality as a gestalt, or whole, composed of any number of unrecognized or dominant elements that drive a person's behavior and affect. Moreover, Perls maintained that when the various aspects of the persona are acknowledged, accepted, and integrated, a healthy personality emerges, providing the individual with the power to choose behaviors rather than have behavior driven and controlled by unacknowledged and uncomforted aspects of the self.

Schwartz's definition of the personality is similar to Perls's. Therefore, a critical challenge early in treatment for the therapist is to introduce this framework of internalized personality parts to the client and gain the client's acceptance of the framework. Without client acceptance, this approach has little chance for success. When the client accepts this definition of the psyche as one composed of a number of significant subpersonalities or parts, the therapist is able to help the client identify the struggling parts of the personality and place names on those struggling elements. For example, one part of the psyche may be "timid child" who has felt unloved by another part, "stern father." The therapist would help the client place these parts in the context and consider ways for the timid child to be less timid and the stern father to be more approving.

As another example, a part of the client might want to eat in a healthy way while another part might be afraid of gaining weight and becoming unattractive, wanting to greatly restrict her diet. By using systems principles such as joining and accepting each of the parts of the internal system, Schwartz was able to help the client come to accept herself and begin to sort out the competing drives within the personality. Finally, the therapist supports the client in identifying the healthy and unhealthy parts of the personality. Then the therapist and client work collaboratively to strengthen the healthy parts of the psyche while minimizing the effects of the negative parts.

Internal Client Systems and External Family Systems

Several major assumptions support the internal family systems model:

- Internal systems interact like external family systems. Therefore, change in one part of the internal system must precipitate change in all the other parts of the system as well.

- The parts can be joined with and related to just as if the parts were living members of a family.

- When parts of individual family members are explored in a family therapy setting, other family members come to understand, appreciate, and tolerate one another. Thus, change occurs between and among members of the external family system while the focus of treatment is on the internal system of the client and the internal systems of other family members.

- Key parts of the client's psyche serve as gatekeepers. These key parts must be acknowledged and respected to gain access to the other parts of the internal system. Resistance occurs when key parts are not addressed appropriately and with respect. The model assumes that the individual has a drive toward health and that key parts want the internal system to heal. But the key parts are protectors of the internal system and need assurance that the healing can be done safely by a caring and competent counselor. Schwartz calls these key parts *managers*. They ensure that help will be provided in a safe manner before allowing other vulnerable parts to participate (Nichols & Schwartz, 2001, p. 428).

- Internal systems can function to keep painful thoughts and experiences out of awareness. This assumption is similar to Freud's (1949) concepts of the unconscious and defense mechanisms. The managers may keep these painful parts out of the client's awareness in an effort to protect her. These unconscious parts are called *exiles*.

- When an exiled part is deeply upset, the client will feel great pain or anxiety. The client will behave in ways that are an attempt to quell the pain. Often these behaviors are unhealthy and are viewed as symptoms of psychopathology. The behaviors might include acting out, binge eating, depression, or the excessive use of drugs or alcohol. Acting-out parts are called *firefighters* in this model because the firefighters attempt to put out the fire of pain and anxiety through any means possible—even in ways that are perceived to be highly dysfunctional by observing family members and friends.

- Each individual has a core self that may be difficult to access and is often unrecognized by the client. This core *part* contains the leadership abilites and compassion that may allow the client to deal effectively with the other internal parts and with the members of the client's family. The core self must be differentiated from the other parts in a manner similar to the way Bowen (1978) helped family members differentiate from their families of origin. When the core self is discovered and differentiated, it is able to serve as healer for all aspects of the client's internal and external system problems. A corollary to this assumption is that all people, even those with severe symptoms, possess an inherent wisdom that will direct a healthy transformation of the individual if the correct conditions are present. This assumption by Schwartz parallels Carl Rogers's belief that therapeutic gain in therapy is contingent on a relationship that releases the self-actualizing power residing within each individual.

Main Therapeutic Interventions

The interventions in IFS therapy involve the following elements.

The Relationship with the Client

Internal family systems theory is more than a series of techniques (Schwartz, 1995), but certain techniques are essential for success when employing this model. First, this approach requires a therapist who genuinely values the client and the client family. Of equal importance is the therapist's ability to demonstrate this caring to the client. If the client does not feel valued through the joining process, trust will not develop and exploration of the subpersonalities is unlikely. Thus, improvement will be elusive.

Identification of Parts

After trust has been built, the therapist begins the process of identifying the aspects of the client that are dominant and that exert control over the client's behavior as well as those parts that are less well recognized. This can be accomplished in individual sessions or in family sessions. Family sessions can increase the power of the therapy, as other members often describe strengths in the identified client and in other family members that would not emerge if the client were seen alone. Often the members have not recognized or acknowledged these strengths. Power is further added through family treatment, because the client comes to recognize that other family members are flawed as well, thus diminishing feelings of isolation and self-doubt. This phase of therapy is enhanced by family participation but can be conducted effectively even if other members of the family are not available.

Listening to the Parts

For therapy to progress, the counselor must be able to respond effectively to each part as it emerges. An atmosphere of trust is necessary for the less desirable parts to emerge. Moreover, the client and the parts must feel heard and understood. Rogers (1961) would call this counselor quality *accurate empathic understanding.* This quality can be demonstrated to the client by listening to the deeper messages and feelings conveyed and by communicating, through accurate reflection to the client, the understanding of these deeper messages and feelings.

Empowering the Healthy Parts

During this phase of therapy, the strengths of the individual's subpersonalities are identified and built upon. As the therapist and other family members help the client identify healthy parts, trust among the internal subpersonalities builds. The healthy parts then can be encouraged to exercise more influence over the client's thoughts, actions, and feelings. As the healthy parts take control, problematic behaviors decrease.

Disempowering the Unhealthy Parts

Everyone has strengths and weaknesses. Therefore, treatment will uncover, normalize, and encourage discussions of the negative aspects of the self. It is very important to ensure that the client understands that all behavior makes sense in its context and to understand how the various parts, both good and bad, were useful in providing protection from pain and anxiety. For example, a client who recognizes and seeks to eliminate a heavy drinking pattern will feel validated when the counselor acknowledges that the drinking served to minimize the client's pain and that treatment will identify and implement new and less painful ways to accomplish this goal.

Finding the Core Self

At this point in therapy, the counselor asks the client to have the managers and the firefighters assume less prominent roles in the personality. This intervention is designed to encourage the core self to emerge. As it is emerging, the therapist and other family members, if present, acknowledge and value its emergence. As the client and other family members come to recognize this core self, it is expected that in the future this core will take the leadership in self-regulation and in interactions with other family members. When this occurs, behavior patterns shift away from dysfunction and toward health.

Linking to the External Family System

Linking the core and parts of the individual's internal system with the external family system is possible through individual counseling. However the linking is more powerful and likely to be more enduring when all members identify and report on their prominent parts in conjoint family session. By sharing this self-awareness with other family members, the client and all participating will link with one another and come to understand that all family members have healthy and unhealthy aspects to their psyches. This awareness increases trust and understanding within the family and creates a climate in which they can more fully support each other. Moreover, the family members report on the various strengths they recognize in others. Finally, the family members learn how the therapist is able to listen, trust, and draw out the positive elements of each person, and they are better able to do this with each other in the future.

Strengths and Limitations of the Approach

Internal family systems theory is applicable for use with individuals and families. It unites the concepts of individual therapy and family systems therapy in a clear and usable way. The theory recognizes the importance of respect for the client in therapeutic change and emphasizes the relationship between client and counselor. Finally, it integrates concepts from a wide range of theories and can be used with a wide range of clients and client families. The approach does a nice job of linking the internal intrapsychic system of the individual with the external family system of the larger group.

The main limitations of the approach are the absolute dependence on the client's accepting the definition of the psyche as composed of competing supersonalities with a core self located somewhere in the psyche and the assumption that internal and external systems function similarly. This primary assumption of IFS is treated as an immutable fact rather than one of many helpful ways of conceptualizing problem formation and problem resolution. Moreover, the notion that internal parts respond like members of an external family system, while interesting, requires research support. The concepts of manager, exile, and firefighter may be overly simplistic with little research available to support them or the efficacy of the IFS approach.

Despite the lack of research, the model relies heavily on individual theory concepts and techniques (Rogers, 1961; Perls, 1969) that have

CASE EXAMPLE

Internal Family Systems Therapy

Ted was expelled from school for rowdy behavior in class and disrespect for his teachers. He also was disrespectful at home to his parents and brothers. His mother contacted an internal family therapist for help with Ted's problem.

The counselor met with Ted alone for the first few sessions. She established a relationship built on caring and trust. Gradually Ted began to talk about the parts of himself that were rebellious and disrespectful to others. At the same time, the counselor helped Ted identify the positive parts, which included being a good friend to his buddies, being a good athlete, and being bright and able to do well academically. The therapist asked Ted if he would be willing to bring in his family and discuss the parts of himself that he had discovered. He agreed to invite the family to join him.

In that session, all family members identified healthy and unhealthy parts of themselves and the part that was their core self that moderated and controlled the other parts. The family members were asked to discuss how they could access the core selves in each other when it was important. A process was developed and practiced in the next family session.

Therapy terminated with Ted and all family members feeling better about one another and knowing each other in a way that most families do not achieve. Finally, Ted was much more self-aware and able to call on his core self to deal with issues that emerged at home and at school.

been well established for years. Schwartz's integration of the individual concepts and techniques with family therapy remains an important contribution to the family therapy profession.

Summary

Murray Bowen, James Framo, and Richard Schwartz developed theories of family therapy with psychodynamic roots. Each theory places heavy emphasis on the impact of early intrapsychic, childhood, or family-of-origin experiences on current family functioning. Bowen emphasized the importance of differentiation of self from family of origin. Framo emphasized the importance of bringing members of the family of origin into the therapy room to resolve issues that stem from interactions that occurred in the developmental years of the clients. Schwartz's theory provides a model for working with family systems that exist within the psyche of an individual. This theory applies systems theory to resolving problematic behaviors that are created by the internal processes and conflicts of the individual's psyche.

Suggested Readings

Bowen, M. (1978). *Family therapy in clinical practice*. New York: Aronson.

Framo, J. L. (1982). *Explorations in marital and family therapy*. New York: Springer.

Hovestadt, A. J., & Fine, M. (Eds.) (1987). *Family of origin therapy*. Rockville, MD: Aspen.

Schwartz, R. C. (1995). *Internal family systems therapy*. New York: Guilford Press.

Helping Families Using Cognitive and Behavioral Individual Theories

Four cognitive and behavioral theories widely used in couple and family treatment are presented in this chapter. The application of rational emotive behavior theory (REBT), developed by Albert Ellis, and its evolution into cognitive–behavioral couple and family therapy (CBCFT), championed by Frank Dattilio, will be reviewed. Then the social learning approach developed by Gerald Patterson will be examined as representative of various behavioral approaches to family therapy. Finally, integrative behavioral couple therapy pioneered by Andrew Christensen and Neil Jacobsen will be considered.

Key Concepts

- ○ Modeling
- ○ Cognitive errors
- ○ Irrational beliefs
- ○ ABCDE theory
- ○ Cognitive–behavioral couple and family therapy
- ○ Contingency contracting
- ○ Behavioral assessment
- ○ Reinforcement
- ○ Cognitive restructuring
- ○ Behavioral rehearsal
- ○ IBCT formulation process
- ○ Unified detachment

Questions for Discussion

1. How might the REBT therapist deal with a family member who is making irrational statements to another family member?
2. Do you think the REBT therapist should teach family members a philosophy of life? Do you think there is a way for the therapist to avoid imposing her own values?
3. How would the REBT therapist deal with a family member who starts crying and exclaiming that he feels picked on by the other family members?
4. How would you use the five CBCFT cognitions in treating a couple or family?
5. As a behavioral therapist, how would you respond to aggressive behavior by an older brother toward his younger sister during a family therapy session?
6. What criteria might a behavioral therapist use to determine whether the therapy has been successful?
7. How might a behavioral therapist work with a family in which the mother is an alcoholic?
8. What are the key features of integrative behavioral couple therapy that makes it integrative?
9. Explain the elements of developing emotional acceptance in IBCT.

ognitive and behavioral approaches are often treated separately in the literature, but because they share similar philosophical underpinnings and a common focus on objective behavior, they may be considered together (Baucom & Epstein, 1990; Meichenbaum, 1977). In this chapter, these theories will be presented together as the cognitive–behavioral approach.

Beck (1976) described cognitive therapy as an approach that addresses the formulation of psychological problems in terms of incorrect premises and a proneness to distorted thoughts. These incorrect premises and distorted internal images, also called cognitive errors, lead to incorrect emotional and behavioral responses to external events. Most cognitive therapists attempt to help clients change their thought patterns, beliefs, and attitudes because they think this will lead to lasting behavior change (Ellis, 1991). This theory of problem resolution has been expanded by contemporary cognitive therapists, who have focused their attention and research on an integrative approach to treatment. They have expanded the ways in which cognitive therapy may be employed in family systems. One respected integrative approach is called CBCFT, cognitive–behavioral couple and family therapy (Epstein & Dattilio, 2009; Dattilio, 2010) and is presented later in this chapter.

Behavior therapy, a research-based approach, focuses on changing specific behaviors in predetermined ways through the selective application of reinforcement techniques. Behavioral therapy deals primarily with observable events in the environment that can be objectively identified and measured. One evidence-based approach to behavior therapy is the social learning approach developed at the University of Oregon in the 1970s. This treatment model does not require insight or a change of thinking or attitudes to be effective. The social learning approach is based on the assumption that symptoms are actual problems, and that when counselor helps clients change their behaviors, the clients' thoughts and feelings will also change as a result.

The chief contributors to cognitive therapy are Albert Ellis (1962, 1991, 1993), Aaron Beck (1976, 1991), Donald Meichenbaum (1977) and Frank Dattilio (2010). Important behavioral therapists are John

Krumboltz and Carl Thoreson (1969, 1976), Joseph Wolpe (1958, 1969), Gerald Patterson (1971), Ian Falloon (1991), Richard Stuart (1980), Neil Jacobson (1989), and Arnold Lazarus (1971, 1981). Many contemporary behavioral therapies are based on the theoretical and research efforts of Albert Bandura (1969, 1977).

Consider the following example of the application of the cognitive–behavioral approach with a high school sophomore. He is referred to the school counselor's office because he is not paying attention in class, not following the teacher's instructions, and making jokes that disrupt the classroom. The counselor, using a cognitive approach, first attempts to understand the student's internal logic and help him identify the irrational and self-defeating thoughts with which he indoctrinates himself. For example, the student may believe it is essential that he be the focus of attention at all times. The counselor would help him understand that it is certainly enjoyable to be the center of attention at times, but definitely not essential. As the counselor and student challenge this irrational idea with a more rational one, the student is able to begin to change his acting-out behavior supported by the new and more logical thought. The counselor would attempt to help the student change his self-defeating attitudes and beliefs, expecting that this would improve his classroom behavior. Role playing and rehearsal techniques could augment the challenging of irrational beliefs and be used to reinforce new thought patterns and improved behaviors in the classroom.

A counselor using a behavioral approach would assume that the problem behaviors were the result of prior learning and reinforcement. The behavioral school counselor would try to discover the reinforcement contingencies supporting the undesirable behaviors. In order to help the student change the undesirable behavior, the counselor would remove reinforcers supporting the undesirable behavior and replaced them with reinforcers supporting desired behaviors. The counselor might also involve the classroom teacher in the process by reinforcing the student's more acceptable behaviors with verbal attention or academic credit while at the same time ignoring (to the extent possible) less acceptable behaviors. By ignoring the student's disruptive actions, the teacher would be removing the reinforcing aspect of paying attention to the negative behavior, thus decreasing the likelihood that it would be repeated. By using the behavioral intervention model, the counselor and teacher would provide a reinforcement plan that help the student learn new and more effective classroom behaviors. A critical component of the behavioral approach is the development of a specific method to assess the student's behavior changes. This assessment is frequently quantified; for example, how many times did the student interrupt class discussion during a class period? The behavioral counselor would expect the *frequency, duration,* and *intensity* of the undesirable behavior to decrease over time and the frequency, intensity, and duration and of more desirable behaviors to increase. An effective assessment plan would provide data to confirm or reject the counselor's expectations for change.

Goals of Cognitive Approaches

The two general goals of a cognitive approach are to minimize self-blame and to minimize blaming others. Specific outcomes that result from these two goals include:

- enlightened self-interest that respects the rights of others;
- self-direction, independence, and responsibility;
- tolerance and understanding of human fallibility;
- acceptance of the uncertainty of life;
- flexibility and openness to change;
- commitment to something outside oneself;
- risk taking and a willingness to try new things; and
- self-acceptance.

Goals of Behavioral Approaches

The general goal of behavior therapy is to develop a systematic application of experimentally established principles of learning to change unwanted or dysfunctional behaviors. It also seeks more specific outcomes relating to the problems of the family members, including:

- learning to ask clearly and directly for what one wants;
- learning to give and receive both positive and negative feedback;
- being able to recognize and challenge self-destructive behaviors and thoughts;
- learning to become assertive without becoming aggressive;
- being able to say no without feeling guilty;

- developing positive methods of self-discipline, such as regular exercise, controlling eating patterns, and eliminating stress;
- learning communication and social skills; and
- learning conflict resolution strategies to cope with a variety of family situations.

The Process of Cognitive–Behavioral Approaches

Therapy with couples and families follows a process similar to forming a committed relationship and follows these steps:

- *Initiating the relationship.* In this stage, the therapist assesses the problem and builds rapport. The assessment process might include standardized marital assessment devices or therapist or client ratings of the particular behaviors and irrational thoughts deemed necessary to change. Rapport building and establishing an effective working relationships with each of the family members is necessary to move to the next stage.
- *Strengthening the relationship.* This stage is characterized by a solidification of the therapeutic relationship. The therapist conveys commitment to the couple or family and specifies what the client is expected to contribute to the process. At this stage, they collaborate to determine goals and develop a plan to achieve these goals.
- *Formalized treatment process.* This stage has two important features: (1) enhancement of communication skills between and among family members and (2) developing a written therapy agreement approved by all family members to guide the therapeutic process. An example of the goals that might be included in the therapy agreement are establishing effective communication patterns in the family, developing conflict resolution skills that are helpful in teaching family members how to reduce and clarify misunderstandings, increasing positive verbal interaction among family members, and increasing appropriate expressions of feelings.

  Written marital or family agreements generally involve a commitment by each family member to engage in certain specified behaviors desired by others in the family as well as an agreement about what positive or negative consequences should occur if the specified behaviors are not performed. The therapist and family members assess the goals listed in the agreement regularly to identify the improvement that has occurred through the therapy.

- *Shifting responsibility to the family.* In this stage, responsibility for initiating behavioral interventions gradually shifts from the therapist to the family members. The therapist may encourage members to hold family meetings at home between therapy sessions and to report on the results of those meetings in therapy. Family meetings are important opportunities for family members to describe their new positive behaviors to others and to ask for desired behaviors from others. This phase, when successful, provides the therapist with concrete evidence of the family's ability to solve its own problems and prepares the family for termination.

Advantages and Disadvantages of Cognitive–Behavioral Approaches

One of the main advantages of cognitive–behavioral therapy is that it is based in research. A significant body of research has demonstrated that appropriate reinforcement contingencies can alter problem behaviors. A second advantage is that the therapist is an active participant in the therapy process and can often model effective behavior for the client. By staying with very specific observable behaviors and by using written contracts, clients can easily understand the goals and track the progress of their own therapy. Finally, this approach addresses the self-defeating internal thoughts of clients, challenging these thoughts and replacing them with more effective ones. The combination of cognitive and behavioral interventions provides the client and therapist with two effective research-based intervention strategies to resolve client problems.

Cognitive–behavioral therapies have been particularly effective in the treatment of depression and in stress management (Beck, Rush, Shaw, & Emery, 1979). These approaches are especially effective with clients who tend to be logical and have good reasoning ability. Both cognitive and behavioral approaches tend to be relatively brief treatment modalities.

But cognitive–behavioral therapy approaches also have some disadvantages. Critics have suggested that these treatment models focus too much on symptoms and ignore deeper underlying problems. In addition, the approaches have been described as being too directive and prescriptive for some clients. The possibility that unethical therapists may use these approaches to manipulate clients is another area of concern. The models have also been criticized as having a myriad of techniques with no integrating theory to tie them together. Beck (1991), Patterson (1976) and Dattilio (2010) disagree. They have described the theoretical development of cognitive and behavioral approaches over the past 30 years. All three authors believe that research has supported the theoretical constructs of cognitive and behavioral treatment models. Their beliefs have been validated as cognitive behavioral therapy has been identified as an empirically validated treatment for several behavioral disorders.

Rational Emotive Behavior Therapy

Albert Ellis (1913-2007) first developed rational emotive therapy (RET) in the 1950s. This approach emphasizes the reciprocal interactions among cognition, emotion, and behavior. Ellis later renamed his theory rational emotive behavior therapy (REBT; Corey, 2007; Ellis, 1995). He developed and implemented the ABCDE theory of REBT to systematize his work with individual clients, couples, and families (Ellis, 1989). While the approach has applicability to couples and families, REBT is considered by most practitioners as an approach used with individual clients.

Problem Formation and Resolution

In order to make his approach understandable and relevant to normal everyday clients, Ellis developed a simple, yet effective, way of understanding the process of problem formation and problem resolution in REBT. The ABCDE model describes how client problems develop and the steps that must be taken to eradicate the problems.

- A is the **activating** event.
- B is the irrational **belief** about the activating event.
- C is the **consequences** of the irrational belief about the activating event.
- D is **disputing** the irrational belief and replacing it with a more effective one.
- E is the **effect** of disputing and replacing the irrational belief.

For example, a couple complains that their son is not being as respectful as they would like. The more they insist on respect, the less they receive. The couple is becoming increasingly angry and upset, and this affects their marital relationship and their relationships with their other children.

In this case, the REBT therapist would help the couple identify the ABC of their presenting problem. The activating event (A) is the son's lack of respect. The consequence (C) is that the couple becomes angry, other relationships are affected, and the boy is even less respectful. What this couple is not aware of is their belief (B) about the activating event. In working with this couple, the therapist helps them identify their irrational belief "that it is absolutely essential that their son show respect at all times, and if he does not, they are bad parents and he is a bad son." This belief is considered an irrational belief because of its demanding nature and its lack of acceptance of human imperfections. The therapist helps the couple recognize that it is not their son's lack of respect that causes their anger but their personal beliefs about their son's behavior.

In the next phase of treatment, the counselor helps the couple learn to change, or dispute (D), the irrational belief. Improvement occurs when the couple learns to dispute their irrational belief with a more rational one, such as, "It is preferable to have our son show respect, but it is not crucial. We can still admire the good in him even if he does become difficult at times, and, finally, we do not take responsibility for his actions." As the couple integrates this new, more rational belief, they stop demanding, and gradually their son's behavior toward his parents may improve. Irrespective of the son's changes, the couple's relationship improves, as does their relationship with their other children.

Ellis said that irrational beliefs may be effectively disputed at point D in the model above, by challenging them logically, empirically, and rationally. This rational process causes clients to reevaluate their beliefs and change them to new, more helpful beliefs. This change is the effect (E) of disputing the irrational beliefs. Ellis developed REBT as an individually-oriented therapy but soon saw implications for its use in marital and family therapy situations.

Prior to developing REBT, Ellis practiced classical psychoanalysis. He found that no matter how much insight clients gained or how well they understood how their childhood affected their present behavior, they improved only slightly and often developed new symptoms. He began to realize that the clients constantly reindoctrinated themselves with irrational and childish beliefs about how they should be, how others should be, and how the world should be.

Ellis's concepts differ from the psychoanalytic model, because he believed humans are born as irrational beings. He viewed this irrationality as a normal and natural characteristic and not the result of early childhood relationships with parents. He also considered humans creatures of habit who are lazy and will take simple *preferences* such as a desire for love, approval, success, and pleasure and redefine them as *needs* or *necessities*. While humans are prone to irrational thought, they are capable of rational thinking that leads to a mentally healthy lifestyle. Based on these assumptions, Ellis directly attacked the self-defeating value system and the thoughts of clients. He did not attack clients themselves. He supported the individuals, but strongly attacked their faulty ideas, traits, and performance (Ellis, 1974).

Assumption about Human Behavior

Ellis (1962) believed in an a priori human nature. He believed that humans are born with strong biological predispositions to be socially involved with others. According to Ellis, humans are also naturally predisposed to disturbance and have a tendency to act against their own best interests. Their other innate values are:

- to live,
- to enjoy life,
- to live in a social group and get along with others,
- to work productively, and
- to seek activities that are pleasurable and satisfying.

In line with this philosophical belief, he traced the philosophical roots of his theory back to Epictetus, an early stoic philosopher who wrote that "people are disturbed not by things, but by the view which they take of them." Ellis focused on *objective* thoughts, which he believed must be understood to change *subjective* feelings.

Ellis believed that absolute values corrupt logical and reasonable values, which are more situational. This view put him at odds with many religious groups. He also trusted in external collective values and held that the social nature of humanity dictates that social values, rather than absolute values, are better guides toward rational thoughts and behavior.

Problem Development According to REBT

Ellis emphasized that it is not a person's behavior that has to be changed but rather a person's irrational beliefs. The cause of these beliefs, according to Ellis, is the human condition. He claimed that our basic nature is irrational, and no event or person is to blame for causing these beliefs to develop. Ellis (1993) believed that, because of their nature, humans are easily disturbed and that these disturbances are evident when individuals are alone, in families, or in other groups. The disturbances are the result of individuals constructing strong goals, values, and desires that are initially functional and add to their happiness. These goals, values, and desires later are elevated into grandiose demands: *shoulds, oughts,* and *musts.* When humans create and attempt to behave according to these absolutes, they also construct conditions that lead to their unhappiness and emotional disturbance. He identified several absolutes that lead to emotional difficulties:

- I *must* perform well and be approved of by the important people in my life. If I don't perform well, it is horrible or awful, and I can't stand it. I am a terrible person if I fail to perform well.
- Other people *should* always treat me fairly and be considerate of my needs. It is horrible if people don't treat me the way I want to be treated. They are bad individuals and cannot be trusted.
- Life *must* be the way I want it to be, and if it isn't, I can't stand living in such a world. It is terrible and unacceptable.

Ellis believed that if family members subscribe to one or more of these core absolute beliefs, various forms of emotional disturbance and dysfunctional behavior will result. Referring back to the ABCDE model, problems emerge when an *activating event* occurs and the *belief* about the event is irrational and leads to unpleasant *consequences.*

Resolving Problems Using REBT

For clients to change their beliefs, Ellis said that they have to learn and internalize three basic insights:

1. The causes of the emotional problems of family members are their irrational beliefs, not any external environmental condition.
2. Family members engage in self-conditioning by repeating their irrational beliefs over and over to themselves. Even if they did

originally learn these beliefs from their parents or teachers, they are now responsible for the pain and suffering they are causing themselves.

3. Family members will change their beliefs by being *aware of them* and by working and practicing to think, feel, and act against these irrational beliefs. That is, by following the ABCDE model, change occurs when the client *disputes* the irrational belief. The effect of disputing the irrational belief with a rational one is for the client to *feel* better, to *act* more productively, and to *think* more clearly.

Self-acceptance is also a critical component of the theory of problem resolution in REBT. Ellis believed that this approach teaches clients to fully accept themselves, other people, and the world and thus live happier, more enjoyable lives. He identified several kinds of acceptances that are necessary for therapeutic change (Ellis, 1993):

- Accept human fallibility.
- Accept the human tendency to be demanding.
- Accept that humans may be uncaring and unloving.
- Accept that humans are prone to some degree of disturbance.
- Accept that we are responsible for our own disturbance by turning desires and preferences into absolute and grandiose demands.
- Accept that humans choose their behaviors and that choices need not be absolute or demanded.
- Accept oneself unconditionally.
- Accept others unconditionally.
- Accept that humans experience some unchangeable frustrations.
- Accept that humans may choose not to disturb themselves.

Main Therapeutic Interventions

Three main clusters of therapeutic techniques are used in REBT. They are the cognitive cluster, the emotive clusters, and the behavioral cluster:

1. *Cognitive techniques.* During therapy sessions, the counselor identifies and explores with each family member her irrational beliefs. The therapist confronts the family members about the beliefs that cause their disturbances and gives homework assignments to keep track of their *should* and *must* beliefs. They may be given a self-help report form to fill out to track their irrational and self-disturbing thoughts (Ellis, 1977). The counselor also provides other cognitive tools, such as the Disputing Irrational Beliefs Form (DIB; Ellis, 1974), which offers

new and better alternatives to their present irrational beliefs. The counselor also uses imagery exercises to get clients to imagine themselves making new and more effective responses and may also teach relaxation techniques to help them overcome anxiety and depression.

2. *Emotive techniques.* The counselor attempts to help clients identify their worst fears and to acknowledge the feelings associated with the fears. Role playing helps clients express and work through their feelings of anger, fear, sadness, or unworthiness. Shame attacking exercises identify intense shame and self-deprecating thoughts and then the counselor identifies more productive thoughts to replace the negative ones. The therapist uses humor and paradoxical techniques as effective ways to attack irrational beliefs and the feelings associated with these beliefs. An example of a paradoxical technique is directing the client to intentionally think an irrational thought and, by doing this voluntarily, gain mastery over it. When clients are able to laugh at themselves and recognize the impact of their irrational thoughts, prognosis for improvement is good. Finally, the therapist provides clients unconditional acceptance (Rogers, 1961), which shows that they are acceptable even with their irrational, self-defeating behaviors. Clients may come to realize that if the therapist can accept them fully just as they are, just maybe they can accept themselves that way as well.

3. *Behavioral techniques.* Desensitization is a homework assignment in which clients are asked to deliberately put themselves in an unpleasant marital or family situation until they no longer get upset about it. Behavioral contracts that create specific agreements between family members reinforce cooperative interactions and problem-solving techniques. Skill training, such as assertiveness training, teaches new responses to family conflicts. Flooding, or asking a client to deliberately increase an unpleasant feeling, is used to deal with phobias, compulsions, and obsessions that interfere with family harmony.

Goals of Rational Emotive Behavior Family Therapy

The goals of rational emotive behavior family therapy are as follows:

- To help family members learn not to take too personally what other family members say or do
- To help family members surrender their absolute *shoulds* and *musts* about how they expect themselves and others in the family to think, feel, and act

CASE EXAMPLE

Rational Emotive Behavior Family Therapy

The Robinsons entered rational emotive behavioral family therapy because of chaotic turmoil that was present in their family. The family was composed of a daughter, Emily, age 15; Mary, the mother; and Neal, the father. The therapist did a good job of joining with each family member by hearing and validating the thoughts and feelings of each. When the therapist was certain that a good working alliance was established, she began to challenge the cognitive and behavioral process of each member. While each member was challenged by the therapist, I will limit the description to the challenges of the father. Similar processes were used effectively with Emily and Mary.

The therapist asked Neal to describe an example of one of the most troubling scenarios that played out regularly in the family. He reported that Emily would act out and he would try to correct her. Invariably, Mary would jump into the interaction, defending Emily and accusing Neal of being too aggressive. Emily's behavior was a problem, but Mary's interfering in the interaction was what really made Neal angry.

The therapist implemented the rational emotive ABCDE change model. She asked Neal to describe the activating event (A) that triggered his emotional reactions. Neal responded that it was his wife's interfering in his discipline of Emily. She then asked Neal to describe the consequences (C) of the activating event. Neal said he became very angry and disgusted at his wife and sometimes would withdraw from any interaction with her for a period of time. At this point, the therapist challenged Neal's cognitive process. Neal believed that the actions of his wife caused his anger, disgust, and withdrawal. The therapist advised Neal that it was not the activating event that caused his bad feelings and behaviors but his belief (B) concerning his wife's actions. The therapist then helped Neal identify what his belief (or cognitive thought process) was concerning Mary's behaviors. Neal said he felt diminished and put down, that no loving wife would do this to her husband and this was totally unacceptable.

The therapist worked with Neal to dispute (D) his irrational beliefs and helped him understand that his *belief* that no loving

(continued)

Rational Emotive Behavior Family Therapy *(continued)*

wife would do such a thing and that Mary's behavior was totally unacceptable was the source of his bad feelings and behaviors, not his wife's actions. While it might be nice to be validated and supported at all times, he was in no way diminished by his wife's actions unless he chose to allow himself to be diminished. In fact, by not feeling diminished and angry, he would be in a better position to tell his wife what he wanted from her in similar situations with Emily and improve their relationship at the same time. Neal struggled with this challenge to his belief system at first but gradually came to see how he was giving up his own power by allowing his wife's behavior to affect him so strongly and that, by being angry, he was not in a good position to work with Mary to improve their situation. With practice in therapy and at home, Neal's behavior changed for the better, he was angry less often, and he was better able to communicate with Mary and Emily concerning ways that he would like the family to improve. This changed behavior was the effect (E) of Neal being able to dispute his irrational beliefs and adopt more tolerant and rational ways of handling disappointing situations. Moreover, Neal learned how to use the ABCDE system of change and apply it in other areas of his life.

Mary and Emily participated in a similar process. Family therapy allowed all family members to observe the struggles and changes of others as each went through the ABCDE change process. Witnessing the hard work of other family members seeking positive change also a contributed to a more successful family.

- To encourage family members to feel their feelings and use the energy generated by their feelings to help them think rationally and ask for and get what they want from other family members
- To make family members aware of their irrational beliefs and teach them how to dispute and challenge their own beliefs
- To teach family members a variety of self-therapy techniques for combating their own irrational beliefs
- To teach the family more effective conflict resolution skills that can allow them to be happy and effective at getting what they want
- To teach the family members how to handle whatever happens in their relationships without becoming unduly upset or disturbed.

Strengths and Limitations of Using REBT with Families

REBT has a number of strengths. The ABCDE model of problem formation and problem resolution is easy to understand, and the techniques for helping clients change are clear and understandable. Although REBT is easy to understand, this approach does have its limitations. Lyddon (1990, 1992) suggested that REBT may devalue emotion, may not be humanistic, and may not focus on deeper problems. The confrontive and directive style used by Ellis and some other REBT practitioners may indoctrinate the client into a belief system that rigidly identifies what rational and illogical thinking is. The client may be pressed to develop specific new beliefs, perhaps in a way similar to how the irrational beliefs were first learned. In addition, the therapist may be imposing his value system on the client in a situation where the client may have very little power. Some critics argue that insufficient attention is given to the desires of the client and that the therapist may beat down clients until they accept the premises of REBT (Corey, 2007).

Cognitive–Behavioral Couple and Family Therapy

REBT and other cognitive–behavioral theories are usually considered approaches to counseling that are intended primarily for use with individual clients. Kuehl (2008) conducted an extensive review of the history of family therapy and developed a "family tree" describing the major theoretical influences in the evolution of the family therapy profession. Cognitive–behavioral theories were not included in Kuehl's comprehensive review. Cognitive–behavioral approaches, including REBT, were not considered among the core *systems* theories for several reasons. For example, cognitive–behavioral therapy has been considered a linear, rather than systemic, approach to treatment. The fundamental interventions are designed to identify and change irrational thought processes. Then, as clients develop more effective ways of thinking, the therapist directs the implementation of specific behavior changes, rather than deciding them in collaboration with the family. This is a linear, cause-and-effect approach to the change process, not a systems-based approach.

Other reasons that cognitive–behavioral theory is not included in core systems-based family therapy theories include:

- the approach does not attended to interactional family processes, and
- the approach is focused on the client's thoughts at the expense of her emotional processing (Epstein & Dattilio, 2009).

Epstein and Dattilio (2009) disagreed with this assessment of cognitive–behavioral therapy. They argued that this evidence-based approach has a significant role in the evolution of the family therapy professions. These authors cited studies conducted by Northey (2002) and the *Psychotherapy Networker* (2007) reporting that cognitive–behavioral therapy is used extensively by systemically oriented family therapists, usually in conjunction with other systems approaches. Epstein and Dattilio (2009) also contended that the application of cognitive–behavioral therapy has evolved in recent years and is truly a systemic approach to treatment.

Cognitive–behavioral couple and family (CBCFT) therapy is one of the most recent evolutions of this approach. CBCFT is an *integrative approach* that uses an array of interventions to disrupt rigid, circular patterns of family functioning. Interventions may focus on changing thoughts, behaviors, systemic contextual processes, and recursive patterns of behaviors that affect all family members. It is especially important to note that CBCFT identifies problematic cognitions and behaviors in ways that are similar to past versions of the cognitive approach. However, CBCFT is different in that problematic cognitions and behaviors are considered within the context of the family system. Moreover, the therapists consider the effects of cognitions and behaviors on all family members. In addition, CBCFT identifies the systemic effects of emotional experiences in the family unit and attends to the subjective experiences of family members in the maintenance of effective and problematic family relationships (Epstein & Dattilio 2009).

According to Baucom and Epstein (1990), five types of core cognitions are present in problematic family relationships. While these core cognitions may be held by individual family members, the therapist must ensure that their systemic effects on all other members are identified as a central aspect of treatment. The five core cognitions are the following:

1. *Selective perception:* Family members take note of certain behaviors and ignore others. The therapist must ascertain which behaviors are

selectively identified and what are the implications of this. For example, parents may identify with regularity every time a child misbehaves and react negatively. They may fail to acknowledge the child's many appropriate actions.

2. *Attributions:* Family members are prone to attach reasons for specific behaviors. When a couple is in conflict and one partner does not behave in ways the other desires, a reason such as "she doesn't love me anymore" may be attributed to the behavior. Therapists must identify the attributions, their accuracy, and their effects on all family members.

3. *Expectancies:* Family members are often prone to making predictions about the future behavior of other members. For example, a husband may state to the therapist that if he forgives his wife for a hurtful behavior, she will think that her actions are not problematic and repeat the behaviors. He is thus expecting the behavior to reoccur. Therapists identify and clarify expectancies and their impact on the members of the family system.

4. *Assumptions:* Family members make conjectures about other family members and their relationships. The therapist helps the family identify and clarify these assumptions, identifying the parts that are accurate and the part that are not.

5. *Standards:* Families typically have an array of rules describing how each member *should* think, feel, and behave. These rules may be appropriate, especially for young children. However, they restrict the freedom of choice and may be outdated or inappropriate for the family member's age and developmental stage.

Each of these five relationship-based cognitions can assist the therapist in assessing how the family thinks, feels, and behaves. Moreover, the therapist can identify the systemic interactional patterns of the family members and help each member pinpoint the thoughts, feelings, and behaviors that are associated with those systemic patterns. Finally, Bruce Kuehl (2008), the author of the comprehensive review of the theories that at have most influenced the profession of family therapy, agreed that it was an oversight on his part not to include the CBCFT pioneers in his review of the most significant family therapy theories (Epstein & Dattilio, 2009).

CASE EXAMPLE

Cognitive–Behavioral Couple and Family Therapy

The Garcia family, composed of Evelyn, the mother; Juan, the father; and children Maria, age 16, and Carlos, age 12, entered family counseling because of problems with both children and disagreements in the marriage.

The CBCFT therapist joined effectively with the family members and discussed the problems with the family over several sessions. The therapist structured the interventions around the core cognitions identified as the foundation of the theory. A brief example of each problem related to each core condition will be described. The reader must remember that each of the core cognitions are present in all members and that the cognitions of each member affect and are affected by the behaviors, feelings, and core cognitions of other family members.

The parents identified Maria as their biggest concern. She is academically gifted with the expectation that she would attend a prestigious university upon graduation from high school. The parents reported that Maria was disregarding her studies and reducing her future opportunities. The parents were convinced Maria was depressed because her current actions were so different from her past behavior. Thus the family *attributed* the lack of study to depression. In discussions with Maria, it was learned that she had her first serious boyfriend and was spending time with him or thinking about him. This was affecting her academic performance. She had not told her parents about this. The parents were surprised but encouraged Maria to invite her friend to the house and perhaps they could study together. CBCFT therapists must be able to identify attributions made by family members and determine whether they are accurate.

Juan told the therapist that Evelyn had been constantly critical and distant over the past few months. In discussion with the therapist and his wife, Juan realized that Evelyn had been distant at times, mostly because of her worry about Maria, but that there were actually many times when Evelyn was accessible and close to Juan. The therapist helped Juan recognize that he had implemented the core cognition of *selective perceptions*, noting only

(continued)

Cognitive–Behavioral Couple and Family Therapy *(continued)*

behaviors that he perceived to be negative and ignoring many positive behaviors exhibited by his wife. This awareness had an immediate positive impact on their marriage and lowered the anxiety experienced by the children.

In a similar fashion, the therapist discovered that Carlos had been caught sneaking out of the house one night. Evelyn told the therapist that she was convinced that he was going to continue this rule-breaking pattern. In this case, the mother exemplified three of the core cognitions, *assumptions, expectancies,* and *standards.* In discussion with Carlos, the therapist and family learned that his adventure was a one-time action and that he had no intention of repeating it. He was angry that his mother had this opinion of him. Carlos said if the family rules about him being home by seven every evening were more flexible, he could have asked for permission to stay out later. Mother apologized for her assumption and expectation that her son would continue his disobedient pattern. Juan suggested that the family discuss in therapy ways that family standards might be altered.

Each of these interventions by the CBCFT therapist was based on the systemic effects of the core cognitions that are central to the theory. While the example above is simplified, it gives the reader an illustration of how the CBCFT might be applied to help a family with multiple concerns.

Behavioral Family Therapy

Behavioral theory has been a major force in psychology for more than 40 years, but the application of the theory to family therapy is fairly recent (Liberman, 1970). The increased interest in family applications resulted from various research studies on social learning theory demonstrating its effectiveness with a variety of populations, including families (Falloon, 1991).

It became apparent that the more traditional family therapies were not very effective in cases where family members displayed acting-out and aggressive behaviors. There seemed to be a need for a new theory and new approaches to respond specifically to this kind of behavior problem. In the early 1970s, a group of psychologists at the Oregon Social Learning Center, under the direction of Gerald Patterson and John Reid, developed a behavioral treatment approach based on social learning theory. Initially, they focused on training parents and others in the misbehaving child's environment to act as agents of change. Later, they broadened the approach to work with entire families experiencing parent–child conflicts. They conducted extensive research, mostly on deviant behavior in children and developed a number of effective methods for reducing and managing deviant and disruptive behavior (Patterson, 1976; Patterson, Reid, Jones, & Conger, 1975; Reid & Patterson, 1976). Their later work focused more on systemic family interaction patterns and mitigated the criticism leveled against the approach that it focused too much attention on the identified patient (IP) and not enough on the members of the IP's family, educational, and social context.

Assumptions about Human Behavior

The social learning approach follows the operant conditioning model B. F. Skinner (1971) described in his *New York Times* bestseller, *Beyond Freedom and Dignity*. According to Skinner and other behaviorists, the most important source of knowing (epistemology) is scientific knowledge discovered through rigorous, repeated laboratory research studies. Behavioral theorists view objective knowledge about specific behaviors as the foundation of therapy interventions. Many behaviorists consider verbal reports by clients to be subjective knowledge, and while this provides useful information, it is not as relevant to the change process as observed objective behaviors. The continuum of ways that humans acquire knowledge, according to the behavioral approach, runs the gamut from scientific research, objective findings, scientific facts, and scientific values at the most important extreme— with mental phenomena, phenomenological methods, metaphysical inquiry, subjectivity, and interviewing variables at the less important extreme of the continuum.

Behaviorists consider reality and the nature of being (ontology) to be the external physical or sensory phenomena that can be measured and counted. This principle clearly follows the earlier philosophical tenets of Descartes, Locke, and Hume. The values (axiology) in behaviorism derive from certain truths that emerge as the result of logical and scientific studies. Informed reason based on the best scientific insights available is considered to be the best source of values (Corey, 2009).

This book presents a wide range of treatment models. One of the purposes of this book is to encourage all counselors in training to consider carefully their own epistemology (way of knowing), their own ontology (what is reality and what is the evidence for this), and their own axiology (what is good and of value). Considering these points will be extremely helpful in the development of a consistent and congruent counseling theory and supporting interventions.

As behavioral theory has matured, it has moved from a position that views humans as solely the product of the environment to one that views humans as both producer and product of the environment (Bandura, 1977). Thus, individuals have the potential to create their own destinies rather than being the hapless victims of external reinforcers.

Problem Development According to Behavioral Theory

Current behavioral theories, including the social learning model, examine the reinforcers that are present in a family or other social systems (such as a school classroom). The fundamental question for behavioral practitioners is how these reinforcers affect the behaviors of family members. Social learning theorists believe, as did nonbehaviorists such as Bateson, Jackson, and Haley, that dysfunctional behavior is an understandable and logical response to the reinforcement contingencies of the family system. People and the environments in which they live are seen as reciprocal determinants of each other; thus, the concept of reciprocity, or quid pro quo, in families was developed. It was discovered that an improvement or change in one member's behavior was followed by a change or improvement in another family member's behavior (Patterson, 1971).

Behaviorism, therefore, emphasizes an interactional focus that examines the patterns of behaviors that cause symptoms in family members. Social learning practitioners recognize that it is impossible to assign blame solely to a parent for the dysfunctional behavior of a child. The mother may present cues and reinforcers to the child that contribute to the behavior the child exhibits toward the mother. At the same time, the child is presenting cues and reinforcers to the mother that may influence her interaction with the child. In this way, *each member* of a family influences and is influenced by every other member of the family.

According to this view of behavior in a family system, if the individuals within the family do not developed patterns of positive interactions, problems will inevitably develop. Gottman et al. (1976) described a model of family interactions based on this premise. These authors used the metaphor that family members each have a bank account where they make deposits (or investments) and withdrawals analogous to their interactions with the other family members. In functional families, individuals receive a relatively high rate of exchange on their investments of time and energy with other family members because they experience a long list of positive or equal exchanges. In dysfunctional families, more time and energy is spent "balancing the books" on a regular basis, as each family member attempts to make sure he is not treated unfairly. Gottman's (1993, 1999, 2002) research suggested that healthy families have a ratio of at least five positive exchanges for each negative exchange.

In another important finding for therapists, Patterson, Reid, Jones, and Conger (1975) demonstrated the limited value of coercion in creating desired change in families. An escalation of negative behaviors was more likely to occur when coercion was used to attempt to change behavior in another family member. Thus, behavioral research suggests that family therapists from all theoretical orientations should attempt to decrease coercion while increasing reciprocity of positive behavioral exchanges (Falloon, 1991).

Resolving Problems Using Behavioral Therapy

The primary task of the behavioral therapist is to understand the social reinforcement history of an individual, a couple, or a family and begin to help them develop new reinforcers of healthy behaviors. The therapist has to develop a systematic process for observing the sequence of actions that occur before a target behavior is produced, how the target behavior occurs, and the consequences the target behavior has for each family member. This is a complicated process for the therapist, requiring accurate observational skills and the ability to reflect these observations to the family members in a way that will be understood and accepted. Once this has occurred, the therapist, working in collaboration with family members, identifies reinforcement contingencies that strengthen new and more functional behaviors. Any strategy designed to modify the problematic behavior of one family member must occur concurrently with changes in the behaviors of other key family members. Parents, spouses or partners, siblings, and children are taught to eliminate or decrease the actions that reinforce the IP's negative behaviors. At the same time, family members learn to provide reinforcement to the IP's positive actions (Falloon, 1991).

In developing an understanding of a family's social reinforcement pattern, the therapist must remember a fundamental assumption of system-based family therapy: Current behavior, no matter how dysfunctional it may seem to the counselor, is the family's best attempt to deal with their current situation. Moreover, the dysfunctional behavior makes perfect sense when the context within which it occurs is understood.

Main Therapeutic Interventions

The main tasks of the behavioral family therapist are to analyze the problems, design appropriate interventions, and assess changes in the family. The main core skills a therapist using this approach needs are: (1) attending behavior, (2) rapport building, (3) structuring, (4) summarization, (5) interpretation, and (6) reflection of content. In addition, a therapist has to be skilled in behavioral assessment. Behavioral assessment includes the following:

- Determining which environmental stimulus variables and which behaviors of family members elicit problem behaviors in other members of the family system.
- Discovering the mediating factors present in the family. *Mediating factors* are a person's thoughts and feelings about a problem behavior. Understanding the mediating factors can be helpful in devising a treatment intervention. For example, if the client has mediating feelings of hopelessness about the possibility for change, the therapist will attempt to create a small but positive change in the client's behavior, thus instilling the thought that change *might* be possible.
- Finding out how the individual behaves in response to her thoughts and feelings about the situation. This skill builds upon recognition of the mediating factors discussed above.
- Locating the reinforcers that affect the frequency, duration, and intensity of the problem behavior. To do this, the therapist identifies what happens before, during, and after a problematic behavior is emitted. Then a plan is devised to minimize reinforcers that support negative actions and create reinforces that support positive actions.

An important development in behavioral family therapy is the psychoeducational approach to family treatment. In this approach, the IP and family members are presented with a series of diagnostic-specific interactive educational seminars that describe the nature of the problem and the strategies for managing the problem. This approach has been especially useful for families with a seriously impaired member and is an evidence-based approach to treatment for several specific problems situations, including treatment of schizophrenia in the family (McFarlane, Dixon, Lukens, & Lucksted, 2003).

The behavioral family therapist could also teach family members new communication responses using role playing or behavior rehearsal to correct any inappropriate or ineffective reinforcers. Teaching occurs in two main areas: (1) corrective procedures and (2) reinforcement procedures. Under the heading of *corrective procedures*, the therapist works with the family members to assist them in developing the following skills:

- How to appropriately ignore attention-seeking problem behaviors
- How to make effective use of natural and logical consequences
- How to set up behavioral contingency contracts (e.g., you must do this behavior before you get that reward)
- How to use the principle of *time out* to temporarily remove a young family member from an environment that reinforces negative behavior to an environment where reinforcers are limited or absent
- How to effectively give assigned tasks to family members who do not cooperate
- How to withhold privileges from family members when the other correctional procedures fail

The *reinforcement procedures* used by the behavioral family therapist to assist families include the following:

- How to properly attend to other people by noticing and responding effectively to nonverbal and verbal behaviors
- How to give social praise, including genuine ways of demonstrating approval, appreciation, and satisfaction
- How to give physical attention, such as hugs and touching
- How to structure activities and spend time together
- How to provide equal access to family activities and include children in planning activities that are agreeable to them and their parents

- How parents can use points and other external reward methods to involve children in the process and produce rapid behavior change

Strengths of Behavioral Family Therapy

The behavioral model of family therapy has a number of strengths. It is a clearly presented theory of change, and the reinforcement techniques are well understood and have been demonstrated to be effective through numerous empirical investigations. The approach is concrete and can follow a clearly understood progression of intervention steps. It is based on the scientific method, and therefore the approach lends itself to empirical validation. The theory describes the process of observing and developing intervention strategies to change observable problematic behaviors that occur with individuals, couples, and families. Change is assessed regularly through the use of standardized, systematic evaluations. It is a therapy that is clearly understood by clients, who report at each meeting the frequency, duration, and intensity of unwanted behaviors. Moreover, clients regularly report when desired behaviors have emerged to replace negative ones. Behavioral family therapy is research based, and changes that occur for family members can be measured.

Weaknesses of Behavioral Family Therapy

Critics of behavioral family therapy believe that the method may be manipulative and uses reinforcement contingencies in subtle ways in an attempt to influence and control behavior. Children, for example, who often do not have equal options or resources, must "go along" with the changes they are asked to make. In addition, this theory may reinforce the idea of the IP as the sole source of the family's problems, as family members alter their behaviors specifically to help the IP rather than to achieve the systemic goal of altering the family system for the good of all. Behavioral family therapy frequently focuses on helping parents learn to better control the behavior of their acting-out children or helping struggling couples repair their relationships. Furthermore, the role of the therapist is not always clear. Is the therapist a trusted member of the family social system, or is the therapist an objective person removed from the influence of reciprocal interactions with the family?

CASE EXAMPLE

Behavioral Family Therapy

The following case example was adapted from Horne and Ohlsen (1982, pp. 380–384). Only a portion of that case is presented here to illustrate some of the main interventions of social learning family therapists.

Kevin, a sixth-grade boy, along with his parents, was referred for therapy because of his difficulties in school, which included being expelled for fighting and truancy. In addition, Kevin's two younger siblings attended the sessions. Kevin was described as having a chip on his shoulder; he was often aggressive in his responses to teachers and to other students. The family's reaction was to have the therapist "fix" Kevin, and they did not see why they should be part of the therapy. As each member of the family talked, it became evident that the parents had poor parenting skills and tended to ignore the problem behaviors that resulted from their poor skills until some outside agency like the school intervened. The therapist met first with the parents, Dan and Kim.

Therapist: (summarizing the family situation) Kevin has had problems at school for a long time—pretty much ever since he got started—but you have figured that's the school's problem, that they should be able to handle Kevin.

Dan: Isn't that what they are there for? I was a lot like Kevin, and the teachers certainly handled me.

Therapist: You pretty clearly have a kid who is more than the school can handle—he's a real expert at what he does, which is messing up.

Kim: We can't go to school and sit by him all the time, and we sure can't punish him all the time for coming home in trouble. That hasn't worked.

Therapist: I'm glad you see that. . . . What we do is teach parents how they can work with the school to get the changes that both the school and you want. . . . I think we can do that fairly quickly if you are interested in working with us here, but it does involve some really intensive work for a while and will require that you put in some time on exercises I'll assign you. It won't be easy and, in fact, will be a nuisance a lot of the time.

Dan: Well, maybe Kim should; she's the one that has the problem around the house, not me.

(continued)

Behavioral Family Therapy *(continued)*

Therapist: That's a good point, Dan, and I'm glad you brought that up. You see, dads sometimes have less trouble than moms do. But, as I look at Kim, I see a tired and frustrated woman. She looks like she can use some support, some help. Since you already have pretty good control over how Kevin behaves, would you be willing to work with us to help with the program we have here in order to give Kim the backing she needs, the support she needs? . . . Are you willing to do that?

Dan: Well, I'll help out, but I don't see that I need the help.

Therapist: As I said, we see that all family members are involved in the welfare of the whole family. . . . We're asking for the family to work as a team with us. Okay?

The children were then brought into the session, and during the next part of the session, the parents blamed the children for misbehaving, and the children blamed the parents for being too lax and ignoring conflicts. Then a cotherapist worked separately with the children while the parents completed several inventories.

In the interview with the children, it came out that Kevin was also having problems with his siblings around the house. The data gathered from the parents showed, among other things, that the marriage was on shaky ground. It was decided that in spite of the marriage problems, working on a behavior management contract with Kevin would help both Kevin and the marriage.

The family agreed to a specified number of sessions, and the members of the family were given homework assignments. Kevin's school was contacted and included in the behavior management program. After 3 weeks, the program progressed in the family and at school. The treatment then shifted, and conjoint therapy was done with the couple to work on the marital problems. The course of the family treatment was 4 months. By the end of that time, the home and school conflicts had subsided and more desirable family interactions were occurring. The family required three additional sessions 6 months later when the new school year began and Kevin reverted to some of his previous behaviors. After the three sessions, his behavior changed back to more positive responses at school.

Behavioral theory may be most useful in families with acting-out or disruptive members. It is also useful in marital and couple therapy as partners work to establish mutually satisfactory contingency contracts. Contingency contracts help the couple establish a mutually reinforcing quid pro quo. When one partner does something positive, the other partner reciprocates. This is done in ways that have previously been agreed upon in therapy. It is an educational approach and as such avoids looking closely at underlying causes, dealing primarily with overt symptoms and behaviors. The success of this approach is often predicated on the assumption that couples or families are capable of cooperating in a reciprocal, step-by-step effort to improve their relationships. Couples or families who enter therapy, however, may not possess these capabilities.

Integrative Behavioral Couple Therapy

The work of traditional behavioral therapists, including Gerald Patterson and the social learning theorists, continues to exert a major influence on child and family treatment today. However, more recently, a new approach to behavioral treatment has been developed, incorporating systemic and emotionally evocative concepts with traditional behavioral interventions. Neil Jacobsen (1949–1999), one of the pioneers and leading proponents of behavioral relationship therapy, and his colleague Andrew Christensen expanded and modified the traditional behavioral therapy treatment model by developing the approach they call Integrative Behavioral Couple Therapy (IBCT). The approach is integrative because is merges contemporary systemic relational interventions with classic behavioral treatment strategies (Christensen, 2005). Treatment using the IBCT model is similar to other behavioral approaches in that it employs a consistent and logical sequence of behavioral interventions. It differs from past behavioral models in that IBCT focuses on the goal of acceptance and empathic understanding as a fundamental aspect of the change process.

The Course of Therapy

IBCT follows a methodical progression in assisting couples in resolving their relationship problems. The treatment process has three important features. First, the treatment of the couple is guided by a *case formulation* or treatment plan developed through a *thematic analysis* of the issues and context surrounding the couples' problems. Second, lasting behavioral change depends on the ability of the treatment to assist the couple in developing *emotional acceptance* of one another. Third, treatment employs evocative interventions that help the couple experience their relationship in new ways that offer novel alternatives for understanding and resolving their problems. *Evocative interventions* elicit spontaneous behaviors in the sessions and are contrasted with prescriptive interventions that impose standard behavioral interventions such as teaching communication skills or conflict resolution techniques (Jacobson & Christensen, 1998; Christensen, 2005).

Assessment

The first four sessions of IBCT are designed to provide the therapist with an understanding of the couple's problems, the unique perspectives of each partner, and the context within which the problems exist and are maintained.

The first meeting is a conjoint session attended by both partners. This session allows the therapist to gain an understanding of the couple's presenting problems, relationship history, and interaction patterns. The first session is important, because the therapist learns what attracted the partners to each other during their courtship. This information can be useful later in therapy, as the courtship phase is generally a happy period in the couple's history. Positive feelings between the couple emerge when they recall the reasons for their attraction to each other. These good feelings can generate warmth between the spouses that may serve as a foundation for the remainder of the therapy process. When this intervention is unsuccessful, it is usually because the positives that the couple saw in each other early in their relationship have been overcome by the current relationship difficulties.

Sessions two and three are *individual* meetings with the therapist. The partners are treated separately to gain unique perspectives that might not emerge in conjoint sessions. In these individual meetings, the therapist attempts to understand the problems from the perspective of each partner and to identify the context within which the problems are maintained. The knowledge gained in the individual sessions will be used in future sessions to help the couple express their concerns to each other in new ways that do not elicit anger and defensiveness. The therapist uses all the information gained in the first three sessions to develop a comprehensive formulation of the couple's current situation and a plan for resolution of their problems.

A caution is in order here. Meeting with the partners individually creates a greater risk that the therapist will identify more with the issues and position of one spouse than the other. If this occurs, the therapist should seek supervision from a trusted colleague to ensure that an unconscious alliance is not formed with one of the partners.

In session four, the therapist presents a *formulation* of the problem situation to the couple. In sessions one, two, and three, each of the partners has reveled to the therapist his or her own version of the reasons for the relationship problems. Naturally, these versions will be in conflict, each blaming the other for the relationship difficulties. The therapist's formulation uses elements from each partner's version of the problem and the relationship patterns identified in the previous sessions to creates a new synergistic version of their situation. This new *therapeutic reality* is different from the ones presented by the couple, and it identifies and emphasizes strengths in the relationship without discounting the problems. This new version of the couple's reality creates a new understanding of the relationship dynamics and offers the possibility for change. Of course, the therapist must present the new formulation in a nonblaming way that balances the responsibility for the difficulties, ensuring that both parties share accountability for the good and the bad in the relationship.

Developing the Formulation

The formulation is the cornerstone of the treatment. An effective formulation must include several distinct components identified from the therapist's meetings with the couple during the first conjoint session and sessions two and three, meeting with the each partner individually.

1. In the first component of the formulation, the therapist ensures that the couple feels valued, understood, and reasonably secure in the therapeutic process. When the trusting relationship has been validated, the counselor is able to safely identify differences and incompatibilities in the relationship. A classic example of incompatibility occurs when one partner seeks closeness and intimacy while the other wants privacy and distance. These aspects of the formulation are usually evident to the couple and come as no surprise.

2. The next component of the formulation identifies vulnerabilities in each of the partners. In the example, the partner who seeks intimacy

fears abandonment, and the partner who seeks distance in the relationship fears being controlled and smothered. These vulnerabilities often stem from family-of-origin experiences. If the therapist can link these vulnerabilities to family-of-origin experiences and to the present relationship, it becomes easier for the clients to acknowledge the vulnerabilities. Once the partners acknowledge and accept these vulnerabilities, each person becomes more real to the other, self-responsibility increases, and blaming decreases.

3. The third component of the formulation is the description of the ineffective and effective attempts each partner makes to respond to the difficulties in the relationship. When the therapist describes the ineffective attempts, problems in the relationship may intensify as the clients become defensive about their ineffective efforts. A key role for the therapist is in helping the clients recognize that their ineffective responses to conflict make matters worse while recognizing that each was doing the best he or she could at the time given the situation they were in. Once they grasp this point, the change process becomes smoother. In the example, the partner who seeks autonomy may create distance at a time when the other partner seeks closeness. The one seeking closeness becomes angry and demands attention, which has the effect of pushing the other partner even further away and further damages the already fragile relationship.

4. The fourth component of the formulation identifies the painful emotions that the clients feel when their needs are not being met in the relationship. When the emotions of sadness, fear, and alienation occur, the couple begins to feel hopeless and unable to effect change in the relationship. They begin to say to themselves, "I am powerless in this relationship and the problems we face will never be resolved." When the partners become honest and vulnerable, defenses come down and caring change is possible.

Other concerns, if present, will also be addressed in the formulation including physical or psychological abuse, drug and alcohol dependence, depression, suicidal ideation, or affairs. If any of these issues are present, specific interventions must be incorporated in to the couple's therapy.

In order for the formulation to have its desired effect, it must help the partners begin to create a new narrative or understanding about their relationship. The new narrative must include the possibility of the emergence of new behaviors, lasting change, and the return of love and respect. It is critical to the success of therapy that the clients accept the therapist's formulation. To ensure this occurs, the therapist must present the formulation with empathy and concern for the couple and link each element of the formulation to specific client feelings, thoughts, and behaviors that they clearly recognize (Christensen, 2005; Christensen & Jacobsen, 2000).

Implementing the Change Process

The first four sessions are designed to identify the themes in the relationship and the psychological characteristics and interaction styles of the individuals in the relationship. The four session–assessment process results in a formulation which is presented to the couple and provides a foundation for the treatment. Although the formulation guides treatment, it is not a fixed pronouncement of the couples' situation; rather, the formulation can be expanded as new information emerges in the therapy process.

The key to the change process in IBCT is the ability of the therapist to help the each partner develop *emotional acceptance* of the other. Christensen (2005) identifies three essential interventions that are fundamental to the IBCT approach. These interventions are empathic joining, unified detachment, and tolerance building:

1. *Empathic joining.* This intervention focuses on the very issues that the couple has identified as problematic. Initially, this is a discussion of areas of conflict and disagreement and may raise the clients' defensiveness and anger, leading to blaming the other for the wrongs committed. The therapist must be very skillful in reframing the anger, defensiveness, and blaming as maintaining rather than diminishing the relationship dysfunction. At this point, the therapist introduces the concept that for improvement to occur, true caring must exist in the relationship. The therapist identifies how the defensive interactions hide the softer feelings that exist below the anger and resentments. Through modeling empathic responses to the couple's painful thoughts and feelings, the therapist demonstrates empathic joining. The modeling is followed by gentle coaching, as the therapist helps the clients express the deeper feelings of sadness and fear that hide beneath their anger and defensiveness. As the couple stops

blaming and attacking the each other and begins to reveal their softer feelings, the tone of the interaction changes dramatically. The clients begin to empathize with the feelings of the partner and begin to understand the other's point of view and feelings. This intense focus on client affect and vulnerability in IBCT is a key feature distinguishing it from other behavioral approaches.

2. *Unified detachment.* Empathic joining begins the process of increasing the couple's acceptance of one another by helping them become emotionally connected, decrease blaming, and recognize their vulnerability and painful feelings. In contrast, the intervention of unified detachment helps the clients learn to draw back from emotional situations in their relationship, take an objective view of what is transpiring, and make a rational decision about how to respond. This intervention has both cognitive and behavioral components. The cognitive aspect comes into play as the clients learn to think objectively about the dilemma. The behavioral aspect comes in to play as the clients act upon the rational thought process with effective actions. This intervention is critical as the couple learns what events trigger negative interactions and how to think and act more effectively when such moments occur in their relationship.

3. *Tolerance building.* The third intervention used in developing acceptance in the relationship is tolerance building. The therapist teaches the clients how to increase their tolerance when one partner has a relapse and engages in relationship-damaging behaviors. To increase a partner's ability to tolerate these relapses, the therapist uses the technique of enactment (Minuchin, 1974). *Enactment* encourages the couple to confront moments of conflict in the safety of the therapy session. Situations that have caused problems in the past or a current issue can be introduced in the session to initiate emotionality, blaming, and defensiveness by the partners. As the conflict heightens in the session, the couple will, with the therapist's encouragement if needed, experiment with various emotional joining and unified detachment skills that have been learned in previous sessions to soften the emotions, empathize, think rationally, and choose effective behavioral responses to resolve their conflict in the session. Tolerance-building interventions remind the couple that problematic situations will inevitably develop and that they have the skills to deal with these problems.

CASE EXAMPLE

Integrative Behavioral Couple Therapy

Gina and Eric Olsen entered couple therapy because of severe disagreements concerning the amount of time and emotional energy they should spend in contact with each family of origin. Gina came from a close Italian family where the expectation was that the children would remain close to parents and siblings even after marriage. They expected frequent visits, lots of hugging, and conversation. Eric was of Nordic descent, and his family was quiet, logical, and loving, but not close. The expectation was that after marriage, contact with the family of origin would be at predictable intervals and for special occasions.

Eric was angry because he felt Gina gave more importance to her relationship with her family of origin than to her relationship with him. He even told Gina that he thought she regretted marrying him because he took her away from those she loved the most. He wanted to be the one she loved most and felt he was not. Gina tried to explain that she did love him most, but this only further confirmed his beliefs that she did not. Gina became angry and defensive, blaming Eric for trying to keep her from her parents and siblings in ways that had been traditional in her family for generations. And further, she accused him of being ashamed of her because he didn't bring her to meet with his parents more often. The couple was at an impasse, and they were not sure they wanted to remain married.

The couple decided to try to save their marriage and began marriage counseling with a therapist who used the integrative behavioral couple therapy (IBCT) model. In the first session, the therapist met with the couple and established solid trusting relationships with each partner. The therapist was able to empathize with each spouse without threatening the other person. The therapist learned about the concerns and strengths in the marriage, including when and why they fell in love and what they loved about one another in the good times. In sessions two and three, the meetings were with the partners separately. In these sessions, the therapist was able to identify more clearly the couple's differences, especially those related to interacting with their families of origin and an unspoken but obvious pattern of wanting to be in control exhibited by each spouse. Based on the information obtained in the first three sessions, the therapist developed a *case formulation*, or treatment, plan that validated the concerns and positions taken by each partner while at the same time identifying common ground that the couple shared. For example, they

(continued)

Integrative Behavioral Couple Therapy *(continued)*

both loved their families and were loved by them in return and wanted to maintain contact with them. They also wanted a way to save their marriage while maintaining appropriate contact with their families of origin.

In session four, the therapist shared the formulation with the couple in a conjoint session. The couple's differences were presented and the common ground was identified. Because the therapist's relationship with each spouse was solid, she was able to tactfully introduce the struggle for control and power that was described in the individual sessions. In addition, she introduced the plan for change in this session. She described a goal that took elements of both spouses' positions and melded them into a goal that both spouses could embrace while still allowing both to feel their needs were being met. The new goal was for the couple to discover ways to show that their love for each other was primary, while still respecting each other's unique ways of interacting with their families of origin. Moreover, the therapist suggested they develop strategies for dealing with impasses caused by their competitiveness and need to be in control that might emerge in the future.

During the course of counseling, the therapist ensured that the couple felt valued, heard, and understood and taught them to do this for each other. Then she identified the couple's vulnerabilities and, with the therapist helping, the couple learned to listen to and empathize with the partners' weaknesses. This step helped the couple decrease their need for competition and control. During this phase of the counseling, the therapist also helped the couple reveal the deeper feelings that were present regarding their marriage problems, families of origin, and the feelings associated with their vulnerabilities. As the partners became confortable hearing and supporting each other's feelings, the relationship began to strengthen. Along with these interventions, the therapist coached the couple in identifying their ineffective attempts to make the marriage better so that they would not try these failed procedures in the future. Finally the couple learned *unified detachment*, the IBCT term for managing emotions if the dysfunctional patterns began to emerge, and to then use their newly acquired relationship skills to manage the developing situation.

After several weeks, the Olsons terminated therapy, feeling that each was the primary in the other's life, less competitive and controlling, and able to support each other in interacting comfortably in their own ways with their families of origin.

By implementing IBCT in the manner described above, significant improvement may occur in difficult relationships. In a study of 134 couples with difficult relationship issues, 72% showed clinically significant improvement at the end of ICBT treatment. At the 2-year follow-up, therapeutic gains were maintained by most couples (Christensen, 2005).

Strengths of IBCT

IBCT has several strengths. It is truly integrative and engages clients more fully in the emotional and evocative aspect of therapy than other cognitive or behavioral approaches. A second strength of the approach is that it is systematic without being prescriptive. Thus, therapists in training can learn the fundamentals of the model fairly easily while knowing that they may make modifications to meet the needs of the client. A third strength is that the theory develops a formulation of the problem that incorporates the views of both partners without blaming either one. Finally, the approach teaches effective relationship skills and creates enactments that require the couple to use the skills learned in real in-session conflict. This provides the couple the confidence they need to terminate therapy knowing they have the skills to negotiate problems effectively.

Weaknesses of IBCT

Although the approach stipulates that the focus on emotion is critical, some reviewers have suggested that IBCT remains a cognitive and behavioral theory and that feelings are simply a vehicle to change thoughts and behaviors. Others criticize the use of enactments by the therapist, believing that precipitating conflict between the couple during the session so they can practice and perfect the relationship skills learned in therapy may not be appropriate or ethical.

Summary

This chapter introduced the reader to four important theories for treating individuals, couples, and families. First, Albert Ellis's REBT emphasized the powerful effects of irrational thoughts in producing dysfunctional actions and feelings. He demonstrated how his A-B-C-D-E approach to treatment can guide the therapist in helping clients eliminate irrational thoughts and replace them with more productive ones.

Next, CBCFT expanded the work of Ellis and Beck, applying cognitive and behavioral interventions to couple and family therapy, focusing specifically on the systemic interactions that occur between and among family members.

The behavioral social learning model of therapy as practiced by Gerald Patterson emphasized the important role that behaviors and actions may play in producing painful thoughts and feelings. Behavioral counselors are skilled at presenting effective ways to reinforce positive behaviors and eliminate negative behaviors.

Finally, the contemporary approach of IBCT couples classical cognitive and behavioral change interventions with interventions that focus on developing emotional acceptance in the relationship through increased empathy, the ability to emotionally detach and analyze the emotional situation, and the development of increased tolerance when dealing with relationship differences.

In the next chapter, four widely recognized and empirically validated systems-based cognitive–behavior theories will be presented.

Suggested Readings

Beck, J. S. (1995). *Cognitive therapy: Basics and beyond.* New York: Guilford.

Christensen, A., & Jacobsen, N. S. (2000). *Reconcilable differences.* New York: Guilford.

Dattilio, F. M. (2010). *Cognitive behavioral therapy with couples and families: A comprehensive guide for clinicians.* New York: Guilford.

Ellis, A. (1993). The rational–emotive therapy approach to marriage and family therapy. *The Family Journal, 1,* 292–307.

Jacobson, N. S., & Christensen, A. (1998). *Acceptance and change in couple therapy: A therapist's guide to transforming relationships.* New York: Norton.

Kuehl, B. (2008, September/October). Legacies of the MFT pioneers. *Family Therapy Magazine, 7*(5), 13–49.

Patterson, G. (1976). *Revised families: Applications of social learning in family life.* Champaign, IL: Research Press.

Stuart, R. B. (1980). *Helping Couples Change: A Social Learning Approach to Marital Therapy.* New York: Guilford Press.

Helping Families Using Cognitive and Behavioral Systems Theories

This chapter presents four approaches to family systems therapy that have their roots in cognitive and behavioral theory. These approaches are quite distinct from the systems theories with psychoanalytic roots presented in Chapter 9 and the systems theories with humanistic and experiential roots to be presented later in this book, because they employ directive interventions and focus on the systemic integration of the thoughts and actions of family members in therapy.

The four theories presented in this chapter are structural family therapy, developed by Salvador Minuchin; functional family therapy, developed by Cole Barton, James Alexander, and Bruce Parsons; brief therapy, developed by the staff of the Mental Research Institute (MRI) in Palo Alto, California; and multisystemic therapy with families, developed by Scott Henggeler, Charles Borduin, and Molly Brunk. These four approaches to family treatment have been selected because they are understandable, practical, concrete, and relevant. These approaches are based on easily understandable theoretical concepts and employ intervention techniques that may be implemented by beginning family therapists under appropriate supervision.

Key Concepts

- Subsystems
- Boundaries
- Homeostasis
- Joining
- Tracking
- Accommodation
- Mimesis
- Enactment
- Restructuring
- Symptom focusing
- Empirically validated
- Relabeling the symptom
- Conceptual skills
- Technical skills
- Interpersonal skills
- Paradox
- Brief therapy
- Therapist maneuverability
- 180° solution
- Restraining change
- MST team approach
- Treatment fidelity

Questions for Discussion

1. According to the structural family therapist, what is the relationship between family structure and family function?
2. What are the major steps the structural family therapist would use to help the family change?
3. What is meant by challenging the current family reality? Do you have any concerns about the use of this technique? Explain your answer.
4. What is the functional family therapist's conceptualization of the purpose of symptoms in the family? Do you agree with this conceptualization? Explain your answer.
5. Describe conceptual, technical, and interpersonal skills in functional family therapy. Why are these skills important?
6. How are problems identified and solved according to the brief therapy theory of the Mental Research Institute?
7. What is meant by therapist maneuverability? What is your reaction to this concept?
8. In the MRI approach, what is meant by "the attempted solutions are the problem"?
9. Discuss the process used in multisystemic therapy.
10. What is your opinion of a strict treatment protocol based on an MST Instruction Manual?
11. Who are the clients in MST? Discuss the location, frequency, and purpose of treatment.

tructural family therapy (Minuchin, 1974; Minuchin & Fishman, 1981), functional family therapy (Alexander & Parsons, 1982; Barton & Alexander, 1981), and brief therapy as practiced by the staff of the Mental Research Institute (MRI; Fisch, Weakland, & Segal, 1982; Segal, 1991; Watzlawick, Weakland, & Fisch, 1974;) are theories that have distinct characteristics that distinguish them from other systems theories presented in this book. The characteristics held in common by these theories are:

- the focus is on discovering a practical solution to the problems presented by the family;
- therapy is expected to produce short-term, tangible results;
- therapy is based on taking action to solve the problems rather than talking about them;
- action is emphasized over insight; and
- expression of feeling is viewed as a vehicle to change behavior rather than an end in itself.

In this chapter, the reader will learn about four of the most action-oriented systems theories in practice. Furthermore, specific techniques associated with these theories will offer explicit suggestions for counselors beginning their work as family systems therapists with couples and families.

Structural Family Therapy

Salvador Minuchin was born in Argentina and trained there as a physician with an interest in pediatrics. He immigrated to Israel and served as a physician for the Israeli Army after Israel became a nation in 1948. He immigrated to the United States and received training as a child psychiatrist before returning to Israel to work with displaced children. Returning once again to the United States, Minuchin and his colleagues developed a program for working with delinquent minority children in

New York City. These children frequently came from impoverished and highly disorganized families with few rules for conduct and little structure. Minuchin's work with these delinquent children and their families fostered many of the concepts of structural family therapy. A recounting of Minuchin and his colleagues' work with these families at the Wiltwyck School for Boys can be found in *Families of the Slums* (Minuchin, Montalvo, Guerney, Rosman, & Schumer, 1967). Minuchin is also well known for his work with psychosomatic families with members who have eating disorders or other physical complaints with psychological causes (Minuchin, Rosman, & Baker, 1978).

From 1965 through 1975, Minuchin was the director of the Philadelphia Child Guidance Clinic. Under his leadership, it became one of the most highly acclaimed family therapy service and training institutes in the world. Later in his career, Minuchin worked with psychosomatic families (Minuchin et al., 1978) and has written extensively about structural family therapy. He has also presented numerous training workshops and demonstrations of structural family therapy to professional audiences throughout the world.

Philosophical Tenets and Key Theoretical Constructs

According to Minuchin (1974) the function of the family in society is to support, nurture, control, and socialize its members. A well-functioning family is not defined by the absence of stress and conflicts but by how effectively it handles them in the course of fulfilling its functions" (Colapinto, 1991, p. 422). The ability to handle conflict depends on the structure and adaptability of the family. Structural family therapy, as its name implies, stresses the importance of the structure of the family system. In other words, how a family organizes itself is important to the well-being and effective psychological functioning of the members of the family (Minuchin, 1974).

Structural family therapists assume that a drive toward organization is inherent within individuals, families, and other living systems. The drive toward organization and away from chaos can be seen at various levels of living systems, from the cellular level all the way to the organization of a large corporation or city. Structural family therapists assume that *family function follows structure*. Thus, structural family therapists understand behavior that occurs within a family as a product of the structure and organization of the family. When certain disturbing behaviors occur within the family, the family therapist will try to help the family reorganize its structure in a way that no longer supports or requires the disturbing behaviors and encourages new and more functional interactions. Adaptable families are those that are able to make the changes necessary to develop a new and more functional structure.

Homeostasis and Disequilibrium

Family systems are evolutionary. They are dynamic and constantly changing. The family system passes through periods of homeostasis, where change in the family occurs in rather small and acceptable ways that do not alter the current organization or structure of the unit. These periods of homeostasis are peaceful times; however, in most families the tranquility is eventually interrupted by periods of disequilibrium. Disequilibrium in the family system precipitates changes in the family that challenge the current family structure. Resolving the disequilibrium requires that the family structure be modified to accommodate the changes that are taking place. When the family system struggles to retain its old organization instead of adapting to new circumstances, symptoms may develop in one or more family members. The structural family therapist has the skills to implement intervention strategies to help the family apply the energy it expends in trying to retain its ineffective structure towards a process of reorganization resulting in family growth, development, and change (Minuchin, 1974).

Subsystems

Each family is composed of subsystems that are subunits of the larger family system. An important quality of a family subsystem is that it is both a whole unit and a subunit of a larger system. Minuchin used the term *holon* as a synonym for subsystem (Colapinto, 1991; Minuchin & Fishman, 1981). Each subsystem, like the larger family system, is identified by the boundaries and rules that define who is in and who is out of the subsystem. For example, a subsystem of father and son may exist when the two go hunting. The rules of this subsystem may exclude mother and sister as well as friends of the father and the son. Thus, the boundaries of this subsystem are clearly defined. Yet the father and son subsystem are a part of the larger family system. Four basic subsystems identified by Minuchin are important to a fundamental understanding of structural family therapy (Minuchin, 1974; Minuchin & Fishman, 1981):

1. *The individual subsystem.* Each person in the family is an individual subsystem of the larger unit. However, it is important that the therapist not view the family's problems as being the result of pathology within an individual family member. When families enter treatment, they usually have an identified patient (IP) to blame. The structural family therapist maintains the assumption that problems are the result of the family's poor organization in response to the family's developmental challenges, rather than the behaviors of any single member.

   In families experiencing problems, the various subsystems have an organizational structure that supports dysfunction. The structural family therapist will seek to help the family adopt a more functional organization through treatment. In any event, all subsystems in the family are composed of individuals, and the therapist should not lose sight of this fact. Colapinto (1991) stated, "a change in the system consists of individuals changing each other, and therefore requires the mobilization of untapped *individual* resources" (p. 430). It is important to conceptualize the family systemically and as an organized unit in structural family therapy. However, therapists must never lose sight of the fact that it is individuals within the family who will behave in new ways that promote family health for themselves and in relationships with other family members. Structural family therapists should always remember: *the therapist can never hug a system.*

2. *The executive or spousal subsystem.* The executive subsystem holds the key to effective family change in structural family therapy. The family unit was originally identified by Minuchin as the spousal subsystem. Later he changed the term to executive subsystem to identify the functions of the subsystem rather than the composition of it. The creation of a new family begins when a couple decides to unite and share their lives together. During the time the couple lives together without children, they develop as an executive subsystem. As members of this subsystem, the individuals may support each other in times of crisis and indecision. Furthermore, they may work together to formulate decisions on how the family will be started, nurtured, and regulated. One of the critical functions of the executive subsystem is to develop boundaries that protect the couple from unwanted intrusions from other subsystems, such as their own parents, in-laws, or, eventually, children.

After children are born, a strong, unified, and flexible executive subsystem contributes much to the success of the growing family. Problems frequently occur in families when the couple is more committed to another subsystem, such as the mother–daughter subsystem, than to the executive subsystem. For example, this problem may occur in a marital relationship when the husband is more commited to his work than his spouse or when a wife is overinvolved with her children. The spousal/executive subsystem takes a diminished role while work or motherhood take the most prominent role. When severe problems develop in the executive subsystem and remain unresolved, the effects of the unfulfilling relationship reverberate throughout the whole family. When relationship problems are severe, it is common to find a child with psychological symptoms. This child might be scapegoated as a troublemaker in the family or be brought into an alliance with one of the parents against the other.

An important diagnostic skill of the structural family therapist is to be able to identify a child who is a member of a subsystem of which he should not be a member, such as the executive subsystem. When a child becomes a member of the executive subsystem, the child often becomes allied with one parent against the other. This is a dysfunctional family organizational pattern that is frequently encountered in families that seek therapy.

The spousal/executive subsystem is the subsystem primarily responsible for the regulatory functions of the family. In single-parent families, a mature child may be included in this subsystem to assist the parent in regulatory and support functions. This structural form can be effective and provides needed support for the single parent. However, when ineffective, this family organizational pattern may produce a *parentified* child, one who assumes adult roles too early in life while missing many of the developmental tasks of childhood. It is important to understand that structural family therapy does not prescribe functional or dysfunctional family organizations; rather, this therapy attempts to help families develop new and more adaptive forms to respond to family problems when current structures are not working.

3. *The parental subsystem.* The parental subsystem is composed of the husband and wife or, in a committed unmarried relationship, the adult couple. The couple are members of both the parental subsystem and executive subsystem. However, while operating in the

parental subsystem, the couple are in the role of mother and father. The primary purpose of the parental subsystem is the successful rearing of the children in the family. The parental subsystem is specifically concerned with providing for the needs of their children.

The parental subsystem differs from the executive subsystem in a very significant way. In the parental subsystem, the adults have very flexible roles and boundaries that allow for children to become temporarily parental and for the parents to become temporarily child-like. They are able to switch roles easily and without concern. This ability to spontaneously switch roles allows for the playfulness necessary for successful parenting and also allows children the opportunity to learn how to assume responsible (parental) roles in the family. While in the executive subsystem, in contrast to the parental subsystem, the couple works together to ensure that the children or other well-meaning friends or relatives do not intrude in their family leadership activities. The structural family therapist must quickly assess the functionality of both executive and parental subsystems of the family. Family interventions frequently require the restructuring these subsystems in order to stabilize the family. When families come for therapy, the executive subsystem is frequently weak or nonexistent and must be strengthened as one of the first goals of treatment. Differentiating the roles of the executive and parental systems is critical for successful outcome in structural family therapy. The children are excluded from the executive subsystem but encouraged to enter the parental subsystem. Thus, when the parents change roles and become the family executives, they know what the desires and needs of the children are through interactions with them in the parental subsystem.

4. *The sibling subsystem.* The fourth major subsystem is composed of the children in the family. In healthy families, communication between the members of the sibling subsystem and the parental subsystem is open and clear. As siblings recognize that they are excluded from the executive subsystem, they form a bond in the sibling subsystem that works cohesively to influence the adults in the parental subsystem. Although this cohesiveness in the sibling subsystem is certainly not universal, it is nevertheless often present in healthy families and a diagnostic sign for positive outcome in therapy. Parents are often astounded to hear the therapist say that when their children secretly plot to raid the cookie jar together, it is a sign of a family strength.

Family therapists using the structural approach must be able to rapidly assess the strengths and weaknesses of the subsystems of their client families. The four subsystems identified above are the most common ones noted in structural family therapy literature. It must be remembered, however, that a variety of other subsystems may exist within a family, and the functions of these subsystems may be either helpful or problematic for the family. The structural family therapist should be equipped to identify subsystems and their functioning before proceeding with techniques for making family system changes (Minuchin, 1974).

Why Families Seek Treatment

As previously described, family systems have an inherent drive toward organization and structure that is defined by the boundaries and rules of the subsystems within the family. When the system is relatively stable, the family is in a state of homeostasis or equilibrium. When this homeostasis is altered or challenged, the family system attempts to retain its structure and homeostasis by attempting to restrain the change process. Frequently, the challenges to the family's homeostasis come from natural developmental changes in the family. For example, when a daughter was in her early teens, she was mostly compliant with her parents' rule that she be home by 7:00 each night and had developed a strong subsystem with both parents. However, as she became older, the daughter came to deem this rule childish. She rebelled, did not communicate with her parents in their subsystem as in the past, and came home whenever she pleased. The parents tried everything to get their daughter to be "the wonderful daughter they used to know" and obey the family's rule. In response to their efforts to gain control, however, she escalated her rebellion, the situation became worse, and disequilibrium within the family increased.

This couple became angry and confused regarding their daughter's uncharacteristic behavior and decided to *seek help for her*. The family came to a structural family therapist who helped the parents recognize that the current family structure and the parents' attempt to preserve homeostasis was no longer appropriate for the developmental stage of the daughter and family. The therapist helped the family recognize that the daughter's problem was really a family problem. With the therapist's support, the family established a new structural homeostasis, a new age-appropriate parent–daughter subsystem with new rules and more suitable boundaries (Minuchin & Fishman, 1981). This example demonstrates that families seek therapy when their rules and organization are being severely challenged and all attempts to reestablish homeostasis have failed. They need help because their current way of handling problems within the family no longer works, and they are determined that it should work. The structural therapist helps the family by reconfiguring its organizational structure and subsystems by updating rules and the roles that take into consideration the current developmental stage of the family and its members.

Main Therapeutic Interventions

Structural family therapists assume that family dysfunction occurs because the organization of the family system has been disrupted and the family has been unsuccessful at reestablishing homeostasis or equilibrium. Thus, families come to treatment experiencing a great deal of confusion, anger, and perhaps fear. The confusion arises because they are not able to fix the problem as they have in the past. Anger arises because, typically, one of the family members is identified as the culprit causing the disruption to the family. Fear exists because the family members who come for therapy have little idea of what to expect from the structural family therapist.

Quite naturally, effective therapy will be difficult when members are confused, angry, and afraid. The first task of the structural family therapist is to reduce these affective conditions. This is accomplished by the technique called joining (Minuchin, 1974).

Joining

For family therapy to be effective, the therapist has to establish a solid working relationship with the family members. *Joining* is the process of establishing that relationship with each family member. Joining is an especially critical technique in structural family therapy (and virtually all other counseling approaches) because even though the family members and the therapist share the goal of improving family functioning, the therapist and the family will often differ in their understanding of who has the problem, what causes the problem, and what has to be done to resolve the problem (Minuchin & Fishman, 1981).

As the therapist moves toward identifying the problem as one that is structural and involves all family members rather than as a problem with only one of its members, the therapist challenges the rules of the family. This may cause the family to retreat in an attempt to preserve the ineffective family structure and circumvent the need to change. To avoid this situation, the therapist has to intervene in a way that does not further intimidate the family. They are already under threat by the disequilibrium caused challenges to the current family structure, rules and roles by the IP. They want the therapist to help them to "get things back the way they were," even though the "old ways" are the source of the problems. Under such conditions, gaining the family's permission to help them can be difficult. To accomplish this critical first step in the process, the family therapist must join with each member of the family, engendering trust so they will allow the therapist to use knowledge of structural family therapy to assist them in making needed changes.

If the therapist moves too quickly in making changes before successfully joining with the family, the family may resist the therapist's attempts to help. If the therapist has successfully joined with each family member, the therapist will engender trust and become a significant source of self-esteem and validation for each family member. When family members believe that they have a relationship with the therapist built on trust and acceptance, each will be more likely to welcome the therapist's help and be receptive to the new ideas, suggestions, and challenges presented as part of treatment.

Successful joining requires that the therapist become a significant source of self-esteem and validation for each member of the family. To be in such a position of trust, the family members must experience the therapist as accurately understanding the unique perspectives of *each* individual in the family. The therapist must be able to communicate to all individuals in the family that their unique perspectives are indeed understandable and make sense, given the current behaviors of the other members in the family system. Thus, the therapist validates each person's perceptions of the situation and, more importantly, acknowledges that each is doing the best she can to resolve this family problem while maintaining her personal integrity.

The specific components of joining are tracking, accommodation, and mimesis (Aponte & Van Deusen, 1981; Minuchin, 1974). *Tracking* refers to the therapist's ability to adopt the family's way of thinking about their situation. The more accurately the therapist uses the family's words, symbols, history, values, and style, the more fully understood the family will feel. The therapist uses *accommodation* in the joining process by relating to the family's current rules and roles. In this way, the therapist shows respect for family members as they are. As they understand the therapist's respect for who they are as individuals, they will be more willing to look at ways they could be even more effective. *Mimesis* is the joining technique that refers to the therapist becoming like a family member by adopting the family's style of communication. The therapist adopts similar body language, pace, and other communication behaviors of the family through mimesis.

Techniques for joining will be useless unless the therapist has a genuine interest in the family and is able to provide personal responsiveness to their pain and confusion. Additionally, the therapist will want to ensure that he does not inadvertently become drawn into the family system. If inducted into the family system, the therapist may lose objectivity as the powers of the family's rules will begin to dictate what occurs in the session rather than the expertise of the therapist. Induction is not joining through accommodation. In the joining process, the therapist intentionally adopts the rules of the family. *Induction* occurs when the therapist is inadvertently drawn into the family by its rules and loses therapeutic objectivity (Colapinto, 1991).

Activating Family Transaction Patterns and Structural Assessment

To help families using structural family therapy, the therapist must assess and understand the current family structure and how that organization is failing to meet the family's needs. This process begins during the joining phase of treatment as the therapist notices rules, roles, and subsystems that govern the family's operation. The formal assessment of the family structure begins after the relationship between the therapist and the family has been solidly established. The therapist then learns how the family is structured through the technique of enactment (Minuchin & Fishman, 1981).

Enactment occurs when the family functions in therapy sessions as it does in the home, permitting the therapist to view and understand the family's current structure in action. Enactment may occur spontaneously in family therapy. However, when it does not, the therapist needs to facilitate the enactment. The therapist may direct certain key subsystems to discuss an acknowledged family problem or situation. As the family members engage in the discussion of their problem with one another, they will gradually transition from performing for the therapist to behaving in their accustomed ways. During these conversations about the family problems, familiar patterns and emotions will emerge. This predictable therapeutic phenomenon allows the therapist to discover how the family actually functions and to generate hypotheses about how the family might be able to function more effectively through structural interventions.

Restructuring Family Transaction Patterns

Families initially come to therapy to relieve stress or eliminate symptoms in one of the members. After the structural family therapist has joined with the family, created opportunities for the family to display its current patterns of functioning, and determined how the family functions and how its structure supports this functioning, it is then possible to begin the process of altering the structure in order to improve the functioning of the family.

Structural family therapists have a variety of effective intervention techniques for altering family structure and functioning. Aponte and Van Deusen (1981) identified three major areas of restructuring: system recomposition, symptom focusing, and structural modification.

System Recomposition   Families seeking therapy are often organized rather rigidly into subsystems that may not adequately meet the developmental and emotional needs of the family. When the structural family therapist identifies this as a problem, reconfiguration of the subsystems becomes one method of treatment. Two major interventions may be used to change the composition of the family system. The first is to identify and *create a new subsystem* in the family. For instance, if a teenage daughter was allied with her mother against her father, the therapist may help create (or strengthen) the father–daughter subsystem by prescribing mutually enjoyable activities for them to do together without any of the other family members. The second intervention is to *eliminate subsystems* that are no longer serving a productive function for the family. In the example above, the therapist may seek to eliminate the subsystem of mother and daughter, allied against father, and replace it with a mother-daughter-father subsystem that works jointly on tasks and issues. *Of course most families contain functional subsystems.* The therapist must identify these subsystems, acknowledge their importance, and intervene in ways that strengthen them.

Symptom Focusing   Families usually enter therapy because they want to eliminate a symptom being displayed by one of the family members. It is natural that the family desires to have its members free of painful thoughts, feelings, and behaviors. The family's desire to have the IP's symptoms eliminated presents a clinical problem for the structural family therapist, who understands the presenting problem as a symptom of a dysfunctional family structure rather than a problem within the identified family member. Thus, the therapist needs a variety of techniques for addressing the symptom while encouraging the family to begin thinking about its problems in more systemic ways. These techniques focus on the symptom either more or less intensely: The therapist may *relabel or reframe* the symptom, *alter the affect* of the symptom, *expand* the symptom, *exaggerate* the symptom, *deemphasize* the symptom, or *shift focus* to a new symptom.

A family entering the therapy process has had months or even years of practice at trying to eliminate, while continuing to maintain, its symptoms. If the family therapist attempts to intervene directly to eradicate the symptom, it will be difficult to help the family change because the family itself has already tried most of the reasonable and rational approaches to changing the behaviors. When the therapist suggests ways to resolve the problem, it is likely that the family will have a "yes… but…" response to the therapist's suggestions for change. The family spokesperson will likely comment, "*Yes*, that is a good idea, *but* we have already tried it," or "Yes that is a good idea, but it goes against our family's values." Because the *family is the established expert* on its problem and has been working on the problems for some time, they may disqualify the therapist's attempts to help. Thus, effective interventions must be introduced that permit the therapist, rather than the family members, to be the expert about a *redefined version* of the problem and an expert at the resolution of that problem.

To accomplish this, the therapist has to help the family come to a new understanding of its problem. The blinders that allow the family to comprehend the problem in only one way have to be removed so they may discover new ways of understanding of the problem and its context.

Altering the nature of the symptom redefines the problem. Through this process, the dynamics of the session are altered in a way that empowers the therapist to help the family make structural changes. When the family accepts a new or revised understanding of the problem, the therapist becomes the established expert on the *new problem* and is in a position to assist the family in making changes. The family, because it has no experience dealing with the new problem, will defer to the therapist and rely on the therapist's knowledge about this new problem and about how to resolve it. The family frequently develops a curiosity about how the therapist's knowledge can be helpful in resolving the newly defined problem. The family will no longer be limited by its own extensive knowledge and unsuccessful experience with the problem as they had originally defined it.

Six specific *symptom focusing* techniques that change the meaning and impact of the symptom are the following:

1. *Relabel the symptom.* This technique is one of the most effective ways to alter tension and bad feelings in the family if implemented correctly. It can also be quite ineffective if the therapist has not accurately assessed the family's readiness for a new understanding of the problem. Relabeling or reframing (Minuchin & Fishman, 1981) simply means that the therapist describes the symptomatic behavior in a way that makes it seem understandable and functional, given the current family circumstances. For instance, when a teenage girl has been consistently ignoring her schoolwork despite her parents' orders that she become more responsible, the family identifies her symptoms as rebelliousness. This definition may even be accepted by the daughter. The structural family therapist may reframe the rebelliousness as "the daughter's attempts to establish herself as an autonomous young adult in the family instead of the parents' little girl." If this definition of the problem is accepted, the family has a new and potentially manageable problem that the therapist can help the family resolve. The problem becomes "how can we help our daughter become a responsible young adult" instead of "how can we get rid of her rebelliousness." It is easy to see how the relabeled symptom will require a whole new set of behaviors (rather than the old ineffective behaviors) by the parents and the daughter with the guidance of the therapist.

2. *Alter the affect of the symptom.* This technique is closely related to relabeling except that it involves shifting the *feelings* associated with the symptom rather than the definition of the symptom itself. In the example above, the therapist might reframe the parents' feelings about the daughter's behavior from *anger* at the daughter to feelings

of *sadness* because they had not been successful in transmitting their values of the importance of education to their daughter. As the daughter accepts her parents' feelings of sadness about their own part of the problem, she becomes more inclined to respond more empathetically to them. Once again, acceptance of this new label by the family may open doors leading to the productive resolution of this situation.

3. *Expand the symptom.* Usually, the family will begin therapy with one of its members identified as "the problem," and they will present ample evidence of this person's guilt. With all this supporting evidence presented by the family, how can the problem definition be altered? If the therapist is not able to relabel the symptom or alter the affect of the symptom, the therapist may *expand the symptom* by specifically identifying behaviors other family members engage in to maintain the symptom. As other members recognize their part in the problem, the IP will feel less pressure and may be more likely to change. Furthermore, as other family members begin to understand their roles in maintaining the problem, they may make changes that support change in the IP.

Again, using the example above, the therapist may discover during the enactment portion of therapy that the daughter becomes most rebellious when the mother and father exhibit their disagreement about what would be the best way to get her to study. The therapist could then point out how the parents' disagreement is part of the sequence that could be defined as the symptom. This expansion of the problem takes pressure off the daughter and encourages the parents to examine and alter their roles in the maintenance of the problem.

4. *Exaggerate the symptom.* Paradoxical techniques are those interventions that seem to be opposite of what "reasonable people" think should happen in a given situation. Parents sometimes use *reverse psychology* with their children when other approaches do not work. Paradoxical interventions are like reverse psychology. Exaggerating the symptom, a paradoxical technique, is used when other ways of altering the symptom have not been successful. Using this technique, the therapist places an undue amount of emphasis on the symptom, perhaps focusing on it in a way that makes it more severe than it actually is. The therapist suggests that the family member engage in the symptom more frequently and vigorously because this may be the only way to able to achieve the type of attention needed from the family (Minuchin & Fishman, 1981).

In the case of the teenage daughter described earlier, the therapist would acknowledge that the problem was indeed a severe one. Because the daughter has no other way of obtaining her parents' attention and concern, she should be certain to avoid her studies even more frequently than she has been. The effects of this type of intervention are twofold. First, it normalizes and reframes the behavior as necessary to gain a positive goal of attention from her parents. Second, it puts the *daughter in charge* of not doing homework and takes parental pressure out of the system. This exaggeration sets the stage for later changes, as the daughter could choose to be in charge of *doing* instead of *not doing* homework, and the parents might begin to pay attention to the daughter's positive behaviors rather than her defiance.

5. *Deemphasize the symptom.* This technique is designed to draw the family's energy away from the presenting symptom, as intense focus on the symptom often serves to maintain it. Deemphasizing the symptom is generally accompanied by a move to focus on a new symptom of another family member. In our present example, the therapist might focus on the parents' disagreement about how to handle their daughter's defiance or focus on the lack of attention given to other children because of the parents' preoccupation with the behaviors of the IP. In both of these example, the problem is not the rebellious daughter; rather, the problem becomes the parents' dispute or the inadvertent ignoring of other children. This intervention takes the focus away from the IP and provides a different, yet equally important, problem for the family to address in therapy.

6. *Focus on a new symptom.* To decrease the family's intense preoccupation with the presenting symptom, the therapist will often introduce a new symptom (Minuchin, 1974). Introducing this new symptom can remove tremendous pressure from the IP and place it on other less vulnerable family members. The therapist is often successful with this technique when it is introduced as follows:

> I can certainly understand your concern about your daughter's poor study habits and difficulty in school. It will be important to deal with that issue as soon as possible. First, however, it is going to be necessary for you and your husband to come to some agreement about what are acceptable study habits for your daughter. If you two are not certain what you want, we can't expect your daughter to be able to please you.

This technique allows the therapist to strengthen the spousal sub-system in the family as the couple discusses the issue, while taking pressure off and allowing change to take place in the IP. This technique is effective and often quite reliable in helping families change. However, with this intervention as well as the other presented in this section, the therapist must be certain to first join successfully with the family and ensure that sufficient data has been gathered so the new symptom presented to the family will be recognized and accepted.

Structural Modification   When the therapist joins with the family, she intentionally becomes part of a system that seeks transformation, knowing that the family has developed certain rigid and ineffective ways of managing change. By implementing specific interventions, the therapist begins to assist the family in making structural changes to its current organization. These structural modifications are made through a variety of techniques including challenging the current family reality, creating new subsystems and boundaries, blocking dysfunctional transactional patterns, reinforcing new and adaptive family structures, and educating about family change (Minuchin & Fishman, 1981).

- *Challenge the current family reality.* Families seeking therapy typically have certain rigid cognitive perceptions of the family and of reality in general. The structural family therapist will challenge those realities, not to convince the family that they are wrong but to show them *there are other ways to be right.* For example, a married couple might have agreed at the beginning of their relationship that it is essential in a well functioning family for all members to be home for dinner. When the wife takes a job that does not allow her to be home at dinnertime, she violates the agreement, and her husband may believe she does not value her marriage and family any more.

  An alternative and equally plausible reality drawn out from the wife (or introduced by the therapist) might be that the wife cares so much about her family that she is working difficult hours to help provide the necessities for comfortable living. When family members accept a *different way of thinking* about the situation, family rules can be modified and structural change based on the new understanding becomes more likely.
- *Create new subsystems and boundaries.* This technique is a critical and fundamental aspect of structural family therapy. Structural family

therapists assume that family structure determines family functioning. Therefore, if a family's functioning is problematic, it follows, based on this assumption, that the structure of the family must be altered to support more effective functioning. To alter family structure, the therapist helps the family strengthen subsystems that are functional and appropriate for the family's developmental stage and deemphasizes or attempts to eliminate subsystem relationships that are maintaining the current family problems. Typically, the therapist will make behavioral assignments that create new subsystems and provide less opportunity for dysfunctional subsystems to continue. As family members eliminate subsystems that are no longer needed; strengthen functional subsystems; and develop new, more adaptive subsystems, family structure changes and family functioning is enhanced.

- *Block dysfunctional transaction patterns.* As the therapist works with the family in the enactment stage of treatment, family members will demonstrate dysfunctional interaction patterns. The therapist will note the repetitive and ineffective communication patterns and may intervene to highlight these patterns using the technique of blocking. *Blocking* dysfunctional patterns can be accomplished in several ways. The therapist may simply comment that the previous conversation did not seem to be helpful to the family and ask whether those involved could be of assistance in helping the therapist understanding what was accomplished.

   Once dysfunctional subsystems and communication patterns are identified, the therapist makes assignments that direct other family members to monitor the dysfunctional subsystem and comment when problematic communications occur. This intervention not only alters the dysfunctional communication patterns but also alters the subsystem composition as observers become part of the subsystem with important responsibilities.

- *Reinforce new and adaptive family structure.* When the therapist has helped the family develop more effective subsystems and boundaries, these beneficial changes have to be maintained through reinforcement until they become self-reinforcing. To accomplish this, the therapist will enlist the assistance of family members, extended family, close friends, and colleagues of the family members to report on how well the new subsystems have functioned during the week. In addition, members of the newly established subsystems will be asked to evaluate their own performance. Positive reinforcement of the new behaviors can support and maintain the changes made in the family structure.

● *Educate about family change.* Joining, enactment, and restructuring the family may occur fairly rapidly in structural family therapy. However, after structural changes have been made, behavioral reinforcement may be accompanied by education for the family. At this stage of treatment, often the husband and wife or unmarried couple in a committed relationship will continue in therapy without their children. During the education phase of treatment, the couple will learn the basic principles of structural family therapy and systems theory, including how and why some families are able to change and others have great difficulty. The educational sessions are designed to help the family develop the skills needed to manage their next opportunity for family growth through appropriate structural change without entering family therapy again. Some couples are satisfied and terminate therapy when structural changes have been made and family functioning improves. Others are curious about structural family therapy and elect to remain in therapy for the educational phase of treatment.

Strengths and Limitations of Structural Family Therapy

Structural family therapy has a number of strengths. The theory of change is clearly explained, and the techniques closely follow the theory. The special terminology and concepts, such as subsystems and boundaries, have broad applicability to the family therapy field, not just to this approach. The theory recognizes the IP's symptoms as a manifestation of structural problems in the family. Moreover, the theory focuses on active interventions with the family system to bring about change. An impressive series of studies supports the efficacy of this approach (Aponte & Van Deusen, 1981; Gurman & Kniskern, 1981b; Stanton & Todd, 1979).

Structural family therapy also has limitations. The approach may overlook individual distress in searching for problems in the family structure. It minimizes the role of feelings in problem resolution. In addition, therapist directiveness may take the initiative for change away from the family and foster dependence. Finally, the use of refocusing and relabeling techniques to remove the pressure from the IP may be considered manipulative by some therapists.

CASE EXAMPLE

Minuchin's Structural Family Therapy

A classic example of structural family therapy is provided by reviewing the work of Braulio Montalvo with a family of four at the Philadelphia Child Guidance Clinic. In this example, the presenting problem was a young boy who feared dogs. All of the parents' efforts to help the boy had failed. When Montalvo discovered that the boy's father was a mailman who must have extensive experience dealing with dogs, he took the mother out of the primary role with the son and instructed the father to get the boy a puppy and teach him about dogs. This classic maneuver interrupted the overinvolvement of the mother–son subsystem and established a father–son subsystem, which had previously not existed. Gradually, the boy overcame his fear of dogs. At about the same time, Montalvo discovered that the parents did not have a very solid marriage. The parents were offered the opportunity to look at the marriage in therapy and to strengthen the spousal subsystem. Through the therapy, the parents were able to help their son overcome his fear of dogs and improve their own marriage. The follow-up session confirmed that the changes had been maintained.

Functional Family Therapy

Functional family therapy (FFT) was developed by Cole Barton, James Alexander, and Bruce Parsons and has been comprehensively described in the literature (Alexander & Parsons, 1982; Barton & Alexander, 1981; Sexton & Alexander, 2002). Functional family therapists have considerable expertise in applying behavioral principles when working with families and have conducted important research and published extensively in behavioral family therapy (Alexander & Barton, 1976; Alexander, Barton, Schiavo, & Parsons, 1976; Barton & Alexander, 1977; Parsons & Alexander, 1973; Sexton & Alexander, 2002). As their theoretical propositions became more refined, Barton, Alexander, and Parsons began publishing their research findings and developing a new model of family treatment now know as FFT.

After the principles of FFT were refined for presentation to wider audiences (Barton & Alexander, 1981), the theory was included in Gurman and Kniskern's (1981b) *Handbook of Family Therapy*. FFT was later presented in a textbook (Alexander & Parsons, 1982) for use in family therapist training. Since that time, Tom Sexton has joined the FFT group and has been instrumental in conducting outcome research supporting the efficacy of FFT with at-risk adolescents (Sexton & Alexander, 2002). FFT has been widely accepted as an effective, evidence-based approach to family therapy, largely because of its clear principles and the research that supports the model (Alexander, 1973; Alexander et al., 1976; Alexander & Parsons, 1973; Klein, Alexander, & Parsons, 1977; Parsons & Alexander, 1973; Sexton & Alexander, 2002).

Philosophical Tenets and Key Theoretical Constructs

FFT is understood by its developers as an integration of systems theory and behaviorism. This integration is synergistic. FFT is not simply an eclectic blend of systems concepts and behavioral principles; rather, FFT is viewed as a clinical model that emerges from systems theory and behaviorism but is distinct from each. Barton and Alexander (1981) stated that the theory was developed to have both scientific respectability and clinical usefulness. Research studies have been conducted on the effects of FFT, and a series of clinically useful techniques and instruments have been developed to assist the clinician (Alexander & Parsons, 1982; Sexton & Alexander, 2002).

FFT differs markedly from most behavioral models in that it does not simply attempt to help people change behaviors but is designed to help family members come to understand and change their subjective conceptual and affective states as well as their overt behaviors. FFT not only looks at actual frequencies of behaviors but also attempts to help modify the subjective attitudes family members hold about problem behaviors.

Those who practice FFT adopt a systems perspective and strive to understand how and why the disturbing behaviors of an individual family member make sense, given the actions and attitudes of the other members of the individual's family system. Rather than attempting to determine whether the behaviors are healthy or problematic, the therapist attempts to understand how and why the behaviors exist (the *function* of the behaviors) and how and why the behaviors are supported and maintained by the other family members. Using FFT, the therapist does not judge whether behaviors are good or bad but only understands how they *function* to serve a purpose in the family—thus, the name of the theory, functional family therapy.

Core FFT Assumptions

Two key assumptions regarding FFT emerge from this perspective. The first assumption is that behavior that may be defined as "bad" by the family or society is not so defined in FFT. Rather, the therapist using FFT will be aware that the behavior is serving a function for the individual and family system. The therapist will legitimize as functional the actions of a family member that have been defined by others as bad behavior. The second key assumption is that all behavior is adaptive. That is, behavior is not good or bad. Instead, behavior is simply a process for creating specific outcomes in interpersonal relationships. Thus, the therapist must adopt these two novel assumptions about human behavior to understand and successfully employ FFT in the treatment of family problems.

The functional family therapist needs to understand the behavior of individuals from a broader perspective than the therapist working only with individuals and must be able to determine how client behaviors makes sense in their relational context. Change occurs in FFT when family members:

● are able to *reappraise the meaning* of specific behaviors within the context of the family,
● come to *recognize the function* of the behaviors, and
● recognize *how other family members are supporting* the problematic behaviors.

Another way to think about these concepts is to recognize that all family members are doing the best they can with the resources they have available to achieve their goals.

A brief example of an interaction between marriage partners will highlight these concepts. The pattern described in the example is as valid for unmarried couples as well. Assume that a wife complains about her husband to the point that he leaves the home. Two immediate solutions to the problem that the therapist could consider are that therapy could help the wife reduce her complaining or it could help the husband learn to deal more effectively with the wife's frustration. The functional family therapist would not necessarily move toward either solution. Rather, the therapist would strive to understand the function of the complaining and leaving behaviors. In this case, the function may be to *increase distance* between the spouses. If it is true that the couple needs distance from each other, are there other ways they might be accomplish this function without going to battle? The therapist would believe that the relational outcome of distancing could be accomplished in more effective ways and would help the couple learn to do so.

Main Therapeutic Interventions

To become proficient in functional family therapy and to create conditions for effective intervention, the therapist must develop distinct sets of skills (Alexander & Parsons, 1982):

1. Conceptual skills (how to think about families)
2. Technical skills (what to do with families)
3. Interpersonal skills (how to relate to family members and to apply techniques effectively)

Skillful therapists need to understand the dynamics of the family's interactions to intervene successfully. In applying the principles of FFT, the therapist tries to determine what will motivate the family to agree to use specific change strategies to bring about system change. Moreover, FFT is based on a distinct systemic conceptual orientation that views the family not as a unit harboring a patient but as a system of interacting parts behaving according to certain identifiable principles. Accurately identifying the family's operating principles is one of the key challenges for the therapist.

Skills Needed by the Functional Family Therapist

Technical skills are the basic tools of family therapy used to produce change (Alexander & Parsons, 1982). Techniques are designed and implemented by the therapist to produce change in the following areas of family functioning:

- Perceptions of self and others in family
- Specific overt problem behaviors, such as acting out or defiance
- Specific psychological states, such as depression and anxiety

Communication among family members that maintains these conditions.

Interpersonal Skills

Research completed by Alexander et al. (1976) demonstrated that certain interpersonal skills are necessary to help families change. These skills include

- integrated and congruent affect and behavior,
- nonblaming,
- demonstrating interpersonal warmth,
- alleviating tension with humor, and
- appropriate self-disclosure.

They also discovered that these interpersonal skills have little impact in helping families change unless therapists have a solid conceptual framework and well-developed technical skills (Barton & Alexander, 1981; Sexton & Ridley, 2004). This means that proponents of FFT believe that the relationship skills taught in most counseling programs are necessary but *not* sufficient to bring about change in client families.

The Process of Therapy in FFT

Before the family therapist can begin helping a family change its problematic behaviors, the therapist must understand the function served by the behaviors and specifically what needs to be changed. Thus, the first task of therapy is to complete an effective assessment. In FFT, the focus of the assessment is on identifying the function the problematic behavioral sequences serve. Is the behavior creating distance? Is it creating closeness? Or is it functioning to control and monitor distance and closeness among specific family members? Many functional family therapists view the function of distance regulation that determines relationship intimacy or autonomy between two family members as the primary function of many problematic behaviors.

To determine the function of the behaviors, the therapist gathers information from the family. First, the therapist discovers what the family says is occurring. At the same time, the therapist observes the interactions between and among family members to develop an understanding of how the family works and how their behaviors function to regulate intimacy and autonomy in the family. While the therapist is gathering this information from the family, themes will become evident and important functions of the problematic behaviors can be determined.

Gathering data to make this assessment may present problems for the beginning family therapist if the family is not engaging in its usual behaviors in the session. When the family is not providing the necessary information for an assessment, the therapist may use the following techniques.

- The therapist may reflect back to the family a behavioral sequence that was noted and ask each family member to comment on the sequence. The various perceptions of the family members regarding the sequence may open the door for further data gathering.
- The therapist may use the feelings or thoughts of family members to facilitate discussion. This technique is useful when the therapist is able to pinpoint the feelings of one family member and reflect those feelings back to that member and at the same time observe and comment on the reactions of other family members.
- The therapist may focus on key relationships in the family as a vehicle to gain additional information about the family. In this technique, the therapist deemphasizes the content and affect of what is said and emphasizes the recognized relationship between the parties involved. As the therapist communicates an understanding of the importance of key relationships in the family, the family becomes more trusting and willing to provide more information for the assessment.

Upon completion of the assessment process, the second phase of therapy, the institution of change, is begun. This stage of the treatment is designed to facilitate new behaviors by the members of the family system. Therapy is directed toward developing specific interventions to help the family change thoughts, feelings, and behaviors surrounding key family functions identified in the assessment phase. Alexander and Parsons (1982) suggested specific techniques that may be used in the institution of change phase of therapy:

- Ask questions to clarify relationship dynamics.
- Relate the thoughts, feelings, and behaviors of one family member to the thoughts, feelings, and behaviors of other members.
- Offer interpretations of the function of the behaviors of family members. Ask for feedback from the family members about the interpretations.
- Relabel behavior in a way that removes blame from individual family members.
- Directly discuss the impact that the removal of symptomatic behavior will have on family functioning. If the behavior serves as a stabilizing

function for the family, its removal could precipitate the emergence of a more significant issue. When this occurs, the focus of treatment is on the most significant issue.

- Shift the focus of treatment from the IP to issues present in another family member. This almost always provides new information for the family therapist and other family members. It serves to expand the definition of the problem from the IP alone to the family system.

CASE EXAMPLE

Functional Family Therapy

The Talbot family entered therapy with several concerns. Mr. and Mrs. Talbot were recently married, each for the second time. Mrs. Talbot brought her two children from the previous marriage into the home. During the courtship phase, the children seemed to like Mr. Talbot a great deal. Since the marriage, however, Scott, age 13, has been acting out and is defiant toward Mr. Talbot, who becomes angry and frustrated. When this anger and frustration is generated between Scott and Mr. Talbot, Mrs. Talbot enters the situation to defend her son, which angers Mr. Talbot further.

The therapist gained the family's trust by making an assessment and clearly identifying the sequence of behaviors that was disturbing the family. This accurate assessment was critical for developing a trusting atmosphere for the therapy. In the change phase of treatment, the therapist helped the family understand the functions of the behaviors of the three family members. Mr. Talbot wanted to be a good stepfather, which meant providing discipline. Scott felt that Mr. Talbot's attempts to discipline him were undermining his mother, who had provided effective discipline for the past seven years since the divorce. Mrs. Talbot reacted because she was afraid Mr. Talbot no longer valued her son. Therefore, she sought to defend him. As the family came to recognize the functions the problematic behaviors were serving, tension was reduced. Finally, the family entered the education phase of treatment, and members learned effective communication skills, behavior management principles, and information about issues that typical stepfamilies confront. The family left treatment after 4 months greatly improved and ready to cope more effectively with problems the family situation may present in the future.

Each of these specific techniques can help family members think about the family differently, behave differently, and communicate more effectively.

The third phase of therapy is maintaining change through education. This phase of treatment begins when family hostility is reduced through the techniques presented previously. Education provides the family with the skills to resolve future issues that may arise. Specifically, during this phase of family therapy, members are taught effective communication skills, behavior management and contracting skills, and other team-building techniques. This phase is especially critical because it is here that families learn skills needed to resolve problems that will inevitably arise in the future.

Strengths and Limitations of FFT

FFT is an evidence-based treatment and has a solid base in research supporting its efficacy. The theory's primary distinction is in recognizing that all behaviors serve a function for the family. The approach identifies specific therapist interpersonal qualities that are necessary but not sufficient for effective therapy. Moreover, the approach focuses on specific client behaviors while understanding the behaviors from a systems perspective.

FFT has limitations. It may underestimate the intrapsychic function of affect in favor of a systemic interpretation of behaviors. In addition, it may focus too specifically on overt behavior and not attend sufficiently to cognition and affect. Another danger is that the assessment phase of treatment may distance the family from the therapist. Finally, the approach does not take a stand on the moral value of behaviors such as lying, being disrespectful, or having an affair because all behavior is viewed as being functional in its context.

The MRI Approach to Brief Therapy

In their classic text *The Tactics of Change: Doing Therapy Briefly* Fisch et al. (1982) were careful to define the brief therapy approach of the Mental Research Institute (MRI) of Palo Alto, California, as a theoretically complete model for the treatment of a wide range of human problems. They encourage students not to confuse the MRI approach to treatment with brief crisis intervention or shortened versions of long-term approaches to therapy, made briefer by a lack of time, resources, personnel, or patient finances. MRI brief therapy is an explicit and comprehensive theory that employs innovative techniques for change and focuses treatment on the *main presenting problem*. Gurman and Kniskern (1991) reminded us that "it is essential to understand the distinction between the MRI's Brief Therapy and 'brief therapy' as a much more general reference to a style of practice that includes such diverse forms as brief psychodynamic therapy and brief cognitive therapy" (p. 173).

The history of the MRI is closely linked with the application of *cybernetics*, the study of self-regulation of social systems. Famous names in the history of family therapy played a part in the evolution of brief therapy at the MRI. Gregory Bateson, Don Jackson, Jay Haley, and John Weakland (1971) pioneered the double-bind theory of schizophrenia. Moreover, Haley, Jackson, Virginia Satir, Weakland, and colleagues studied the effects of communication and paradox in families (Segal, 1991). Also participating in the development of the MRI model were Milton Erickson, Richard Fisch, Paul Watzlawick, and Heinz Von Forester. Each of these pioneers "contributed to the understanding of disturbed behavior as a function of an interpersonal system rather than an intrapsychic one, wedding cybernetic epistemology to psychiatry" (Segal, 1991, p. 173).

Philosophical Tenets and Key Theoretical Constraints

The relationship between the theory and practice of brief therapy is critical in that embedded within this theory (and all other theories) are the *views* and *premises* the therapist holds that govern the identification and description of psychological problems. Moreover, theory influences what parts of the information provided by the client will become the focus of attention and what parts if the information will not be the focus. Beginning therapists are usually surprised when they learn that their favorite theory determines what they will *not* attend to as well as what they will attend to in the treatment process. Additionally, theory predicates what actions the therapist will take in the treatment of the client and also determines who will participate in therapy.

The MRI brief therapist views theory as a map to help treat client problems. Theory is designed to help the therapist create a context that provides understanding of the client problems and aids in identifying interventions supporting resolution of the problems. Theory should serve as a guide to treatment, as it may be useful in clarifying obstacles encountered in working with human problems. However, it is important to remember a lesson taught to all trainees by the therapists at the MRI: *theory is only a map, and a map* is not *the territory.* Theory, while quite important, should not become dogma and should never "shortcut" good common sense (Fisch et al., 1982).

Defining the Problem

A clear definition of the problem is critical to successful implementation of brief therapy. According to Segal (1991), a problem is defined in the following ways:

- The client reports experiencing pain and distress.
- The pain or distress is attributed to the behaviors of self or others.
- The client has been trying to change this painful behavior.
- The client has not been successful at changing.

According to the MRI model of brief therapy, the client may be an individual or several members of a family. The treatment approach focuses on problem solving and may involve one or many clients. The brief therapist assumes that *the complaint is the problem* and not the symptom of an underlying pathology. Thus, the goal of brief therapy is to identify and reduce or eliminate the client's pain. The goal may be achieved if the client's behavior changes or if the behavior is no longer troubling to the client. Thus, the therapist is responsible for identifying the goals of therapy. Most frequently, the goals of therapist and client overlap, however, in the MRI approach, it is the therapist who determines what will be useful for the client in bringing about change and in this way the MRI model is one of the most directive family therapy approaches (Segal, 1991). Thus, the therapist is the expert in bringing about change according to the MRI approach to brief therapy.

How Problems Develop and Persist

According to the MRI brief therapy model, problems result from ineffective handling of ordinary life difficulties. The approach is clear on the point that problems result when behavior deviates from what is desired and that repeated attempts to return behavior to its normal state have failed. It is frequently true that misguided client attempts to return behavior to its normal state actually make the problem worse. For example, a parent tells his son to go to sleep so he will be well rested for school. The son refuses to be directed and stays awake. The more the parent attempts to solve the problem by directing him to go to sleep, the more awake the son becomes, and the less sleep he gets. In this situation, trying to force the son to rest actually makes him less sleepy. The parent's attempted solution to the problem has made the problem worse.

Segal (1991) describes four clear patterns of mishandling problems:

1. *Forcing correction when normal life difficulties will self-correct*—for example, when a student has a writing block over a certain assignment. The more she forces herself to write, the more overwhelming the project becomes. Forcing correction causes an ordinary difficulty to become a serious problem.

2. *Seeking a no-risk solution when normal risk is involved*—for example, when a shy man works diligently to perfect his opening remarks to a woman he wants to meet rather than allowing the conversation to develop naturally. The harder he tries to eliminate risk, the more likely he will be to become tongue-tied and interact inappropriately.

3. *Insisting on discussion to resolve a dispute when discussion exacerbates the problem*—for example, when a couple continues to discuss a disagreement past the point of productive communication. It seems logical that they should talk out the disagreement, but the discussion leads to increased hostility and resentment.

4. *Confirming the accuser's suspicion by defending oneself*—for example, when a teenager accuses his parents of meddling in his affairs and separates himself from the family. Without family support, he becomes depressed and withdrawn. Then the concerned parents attempt to be helpful by talking with their child, and this confirms his position that they are meddlesome.

In summary, two key assumptions underlie brief therapy. First, problems persist only if they are maintained by the actions of the client and other members of the client's family system. Second, the problem will be resolved when those behaviors that maintain the problem are changed or eliminated.

Main Therapeutic Interventions

Segal (1991) described the MRI brief therapy model as a series of tasks to be accomplished leading to client improvement. The tasks that must be accomplished are:

- identify the family members who are *motivated for treatment* and arrange for them to attend the initial interview,
- collect specific data about the problem and the ways the family has tried to solve the problem (*what has not worked* in the past),
- set a specific *goal* for therapy,
- develop a *plan* to create change in the presenting problem,
- intervene in ways that *interrupts* the ineffective attempted solutions,
- *assess* outcome of treatment, and
- *terminate*.

In the beginning stages of treatment, the therapist will notice that the family members take positions on such issues such as why the problem exists, which family members are helpful and which are not, why the problem is not being resolved, and, frequently, what the therapist must do to help. The therapist should note these positions and confirm that she understands them clearly. However, it is critical in this approach for the therapist to maintain *therapeutic maneuverability*. The MRI therapist must have the freedom to intervene in ways that are most helpful for the family and that will resolve the presenting problems. The therapist must be careful not to uncritically accept the clients' preferred explanations for their behaviors along with their preferred methods for solving their problems (which have not been helpful in the past). If the therapist thinks about the clients' problems and treats them the way the clients want, the therapist is compromised and will not have the freedom or therapeutic maneuverability to intervene in ways that will be most helpful to the family in achieving the changes they say they want (Fisch et al., 1982; Segal, 1991).

Therapy begins with the first phone contact. The therapist attempts to determine whether the client is a *customer*, who is genuinely seeking help, or a *window shopper*, who enters therapy at someone else's direction and may not be motivated to change. The MRI therapist wants to meet with the family members who are *motivated* to change. Contrary to most family therapy approaches, this may mean that the IP who does not want to be in treatment will not be seen in the initial interview. Moreover, the IP may never enter treatment. However, the MRI model of brief

therapy is able to produces changes in the presenting problems even if
seemingly important family members do not attend therapy. Change will
occur in nonattending members when the family members who are motivated for change and who are attending therapy identify their ineffective solutions to the family problem and develop and implement new
and more effective solutions.

Several specific techniques have been developed to bring about change
using MRI brief therapy. The most important technique is to understand
that the problem is maintained by ineffective attempts to resolve it. The
therapist's key function is to help the family implement *new solutions.*

A second technique is to develop an achievable goal for therapy.
This goal may not be total change in the problem but a small step in the
right direction. Segal (1991) manages this therapeutic task by structuring
the goal setting in this way: "Since we only have 10 sessions, we need
to define a goal of treatment that would tell us you are beginning to solve
the problem. You're not completely out of the woods, so to speak, but
you'll have found a trail and can find your way on your own. So, what
would be the smallest, concrete, significant indicator of this?" (p. 182).
Brief therapy is time limited, thus a concrete, achievable goal must be
set. Once the family has achieved the goal, therapy is terminated with
the expectation that they will continue to implement their new solutions
to the old problem and experience relief as a result.

A third technique is for the therapist to *avoid the minefield.* The
minefield is the family's ineffective thoughts, feelings, and ideas about
how the problem *should* be solved. Avoiding the minefield means that
the therapist understands and appreciates but does not accept the family
members' positions and is able to avoid ineffective, "more of the same"
solutions to the problems. If the therapist accepts family members' positions and gives directives that are similar (more of the same) to those
already in place, change will not occur, and the problem may get worse.
For example, if a family is seeking help in having their son be more involved in family activities, a therapist would be in the minefield with
any directive that attempted to help the parents encourage or direct the
son to be more involved in more effective ways. If this approach were
implemented, the son's lack of involvement is likely to become more
pronounced.

A fourth technique is to seek a 180° shift or U-turn away from the
attempted solution and implement a new and more creative solution
(Fisch et al., 1982). In the example above, a 180° shift would be to direct

the family to encourage the son to develop autonomy and independence. In so doing, the family could feel good about helping their son become independent, and the son may well respond by spending more time with a supportive—rather than a controlling—family. Implementing this 180° shift with the family is often difficult. Such a shift often creates a solution that is counterintuitive to the family and makes no logical sense. "How can we get closer to our son by encouraging him to be distant?" they might wonder.

At this point, clients will need support in performing therapist-initiated directives that appear counterintuitive (Segal, 1991). To accomplish this task, the therapist employs a key technique called *reframing*. Reframing is a technique defined by Watzlawick et al. (1974) that

> changes the conceptual and/or emotional setting or viewpoint in relation to which a situation is experienced and places it in another frame which *'fits the facts'* of the same concrete situation equally well or even better, and thereby changes its entire meaning. (p. 95)

For example, a client who insisted that she was powerless to improve her marriage complained that no matter what she did to improve her relationship, it did not work because she was convinced that no improvement could occur unless her husband acknowledged and explored his dysfunctional family of origin and his previous problematic marriage. The more she tried to get him to "do his therapy," the more he resisted. She became extremely angry and depressed, and, of course, their relationship deteriorated further. The client truly believed she was working to improve her marriage by insisting that her husband do family-of-origin work. The therapist *reframed* the situation by pointing out that the client was making it difficult for her husband to demonstrate his unique attempts to improve their relationship when she recognized only *one way* for him to demonstrate his desire to improve the relationship. The client was surprised and shocked by this reframe and claimed angrily that she had no desire to create difficulties for her husband. Yet, she was able to accept the directive that she not work so hard at making the marriage better for a few weeks "just to see what happens." After several weeks of implementing this new 180°, counterintuitive solution of "not trying," the client reported she was less angry and depressed and that her husband was indeed trying new ways to respond to her needs.

In this scenario, the reframe worked because it placed the information reported in a different context. Her efforts to improve the relationship through demanding her husband do family-of-origin work was reframed as her not recognizing and appreciating his other ways of showing love and affection. This technique is effective because it has the power to reset the relationship stage for clients in a way that permits new solutions to old and persistent problems.

Brief therapy employs a set of techniques that are considered paradoxical. The 180° solution may be considered an example of paradox. Change is created by directing the family to engage in solutions that seem the opposite of what should be helpful. Other examples of paradox include a directive that asks clients to engage in more of the symptomatic behavior or to perform a problematic behaviors only at specific times. This technique is called *symptom prescription* and is effective for two reasons. First, if clients follow the directive and increase symptomatic behavior intentionally, they are *controlling the symptom* through doing more of it. They are also demonstrating that they will follow the therapist's unusual directives. If clients can *increase* the frequency of their symptom, they can use this same ability to *decrease the frequency* of their symptom. Second, if clients resist the directive, as many clients do, and do not increase symptomatic behavior, the symptoms are decreased through the resistance.

Other paradoxical techniques include directing the client to go slowly in changing (Fisch et al., 1982). This is known as *restraining change*. This is simply another 180° shift for a client who has been desperately attempting to create change quickly. By going slowly, the client's anxiety may be reduced, and other directives for change may be employed with less urgency and with more likelihood of success. Conversely, if the client is not progressing rapidly and is experiencing discouragement, the therapist's directive to go slowly will support the gradual change that may be about to happen. Moreover, the therapist should be prepared to *predict relapse,* another paradoxical technique, so that clients are prepared to deal with setbacks and do not view these setbacks as failure, or the client may strive to prove the therapist wrong by not having a relapse. Either outcome is positive; thus, effectively implemented paradoxical directives create win–win results.

Segal (1991) warned that beginning therapists must not erroneously assume that paradox is the essence of brief therapy. It is more important to understand the usefulness and power of the 180° shift in the attempted solution to the problem and learn to develop and implement effective reframing techniques to support new solutions to persistent family problems.

Segal (1991) suggested that termination of therapy occurs when (p. 189)

- a small but significant change has been made in the problem,
- the change appears to be durable, and

CASE EXAMPLE

MRI Approach to Brief Family Therapy

The author of this text worked with a family who complained that their son was rebellious because he did not go to bed when instructed and, in fact, turned the light on in his room and read Hardy Boys mysteries into the night. All attempts to correct the behavior with verbal warnings and restrictions failed. The parents were becoming increasingly angry and coercive, to no avail. The parents framed the problem (and took the position) that they had a rebellious child who did not respect his parents. The couple was asked what small goal might indicate that things were getting back to normal. They reported that they would like to see their son getting more sleep. The presenting problem was reframed by the therapist. He described the "acting-out" son as a seemingly intelligent young man who loved to read (a positive) and was able to function well with very little sleep (another positive). The parents accepted this reframe because it was true: It described the original situation with the same facts in a way that portrayed the son's behaviors in positive and different ways. The parents accepted the reframe and the accompanying 180° reversal solution. They were to tell their son each night that they appreciated his intelligence and interest in reading and his ability to function on so little sleep. Further, they were to tell him they trusted him to turn his light off and go to sleep when he was tired.

When the couple returned for the second session, they reported that they had employed the new solution each night for a week. For the first two nights, the boy read into the wee hours, but beginning with the third night, he turned his light out earlier and earlier. In fact, after one week of implementing the new solution, the parents felt the problem was solved.

- the patient implies or states an ability to handle things without the therapist.

The therapist must be careful to ensure that clients assume responsibility for making changes rather than crediting the therapist for them. It is also important to remind clients that relapse may occur but that they have the tools to handle future problems. If clients resist termination, the therapist may frame the termination as a temporary break from therapy while the clients consolidate their learning (Segal, 1991).

Strengths and Limitations of Brief Therapy

The MRI approach to brief therapy has several strengths. The most notable is that problem resolution frequently occurs quite rapidly. Additionally, this approach specifically identifies and attempts to change the pattern of ineffective attempted solutions to the problem. As families learn to employ unique and sometime counterintuitive solutions to their problems, rapid change is possible. Finally, the MRI brief therapy model does not look at individuals as mentally ill. The model looks at problems as the result of ineffective attempts to manage them.

There are also limitations to the approach. Brief therapy is criticized because it does not look at historical aspects of the problem and therefore focuses only on symptoms, not their cause. Others criticize the approach as too directive and not respectful of client families. They also claim that paradoxical techniques are not genuine and are often manipulative.

Multisystemic Therapy with Families

Multisystemic therapy (MST) is a pragmatic and goal-oriented treatment that specifically attempts to change specific factors exhibited by acting-out adolescents. This approach identifies and intervenes in all significant subsystems within the social network that are affecting and maintaining the antisocial behavior. Moreover, MST is an empirically validated treatment approach, based on a large body of outcome research that supports its effectiveness. MST was developed to treat adolescents who may present an array of serious behavioral problems (Curtis, Ronan, & Borduin, 2004; Saldana & Sheidow, 2005). MST has been demonstrated to be particularly effective with adolescents who are at risk for out-of-home placement. IPs may exhibit a range of behaviors, including substance abuse; severe impulsivity; antisocial acting out, including violating the law; severe emotional disturbances; or a combination of these behaviors (Henggeler, Schoenwald, Borduin, Rowland, & Cunningham, 1998; Henggeler, Schoenwald, Rowland, & Cunningham, 2002).

The ultimate goals of MST are to provide parents with the skills and resources that they need to address, without continued therapeutic support, the difficulties that arise when rearing teenagers and to give the acting-out adolescents the skills to cope with family, peer, school, and neighborhood influences (Saldana & Sheidow, 2005). This approach is systemic in nature. The treatment system is community based. Therapy usually includes the IP, the IP's family, people in the neighborhood, friends, schoolteachers, school counselors, classmates, and other individuals and organizations that have impact on the IP's behavior.

Basic MST concepts were developed and investigated in the 1970s by Scott Henggeler and his doctoral students. The theory became more widely recognized and accepted after Henggeler established the Family Services Research Center at the Medical University of South Carolina in 1992, with the mission of developing, improving, and validating cost effective services for youths presenting serious mental health problems and for their families (Saldana & Sheidow, 2005, p. 28). Community agencies from across the country became interested in MST based on a series of successful outcome research studies validating the efficacy of MST with difficult adolescents' problems. In response to the demonstrated success of MST, demand for information and training in the approach exploded. In response, MST Services, a commercial enterprise, was formed to deliver the MST treatment model to agencies that wished to implement it in their work with adolescents with serious antisocial behavior problems. MST Services owns the license to the MST treatment model, technology, and training modules and provides ongoing quality control to the agencies that have contracted with MST Services to employ the approach.

MST research has demonstrated that strict adherence to the MST therapy protocol is essential for successful outcomes. Thus, MST Services markets the model, provides training, and grants licenses to agencies that complete the intensive training and apply the treatment consistently and with fidelity in accordance with the MST treatment protocol (Saldana & Sheidow, 2005; Family Services Research Center, n.d.).

In order to become an MST service provider, interested agencies must complete a comprehensive application process and undergo a through review to ensure the organization can apply MST concepts and procedures with fidelity. The outcome research evaluating the effectiveness of MST interventions suggests that the approach must be applied rigorously and with consistency. Thus, agencies are screened and guided through a rigorous and systematic training curriculum prior to final acceptance as an MST provider. The following steps are used in the application, program development, and program maintenance process:

- Initial information collection
- MST needs assessment
- MST critical issues session
- Site readiness review meeting
- Staff recruitment & orientation training
- Ongoing implementation support

Moreover, MST Services will continue to play an ongoing role in the training and delivery of services and in providing continuing support after the program is implemented (MST Services, 2010).

Philosophical Tenets and Key Theoretical Constructs

MST is an approach to treating serious behavior problems in adolescents at risk for out-of-home placement employing systems theory concepts. It is based on Bronfenbrenner's social ecological theory, which recognizes the interplay between the individual and other larger organizations to which the individual belongs. MST utilizes the concepts of pragmatic family systems theories including structural family therapy, FFT, and brief solution focused theory, such as the MRI model. All three of these approaches were presented in the previous sections of this chapter. MST also applies concepts from cognitive and behavioral theories as required by the needs of the various subsystems and their responses to MST interventions. In accordance with systems theory, the client in the MST approach is the *community system,* or this ecology of interconnected subsystems, within which the individual is embedded, rather than the acting-out adolescent IP. The MST approach, based on pragmatic systems theory, assumes that all individuals in treatment are linked through a network of interconnected relationships and subsystems that encompass individual, family, and other significant parties including friend, school, and neighborhood subsystems. MST therapists provide interventions in any one or a combination of these systems. (Saldana & Sheidow, 2005; (MST Services, 2010).

MST is a home-based, team approach to treatment. Members of the therapeutic team travel to the family and to visit other members of involved subsystems to provide interventions. The home-based approach virtually eliminates the barrier to treatment created by requiring that families travel to therapists to receive therapeutic assistance. In-home treatment eliminates this problem for the family by taking the services to the family at a time and place that is convenient for them. This contributes to the continuity of the treatment, eliminates most missed appointments, and increases the likelihood of successful outcome. The therapeutic team of 3 or 4 therapists trained by MST Services in the strict application of MST interventions makes multiple visits to the family and community subsystems each week. Regular involvement of the community subsystems is essential to the treatment process and significantly increases the probability of producing and maintaining change in the behaviors of at-risk adolescents (Saldana & Sheidow, 2005; MST Services, 2010).

Why Families Request Treatment

Families with a full range of adolescent acting-out problems request treatment with the hope of helping their son or daughter function more effectively at home, in school, with friends, and in the workplace (Henggeler, Schoenwald, Borduin, et al., 1998; Henggeler, Schoenwald, Rowland, et al., 2002). Families request treatment from MST providers for several reasons:

- MST has a track record of effectiveness with acting-out teenagers.
- MST includes all relevant subsystems, not just the family, in treatment.
- MST services are intensive, with several meetings with relevant parties each week, rather than a traditional weekly hour-long meeting with the family.
- MST providers implement targeted interventions and evaluate change and improvement on a regular basis from several perspectives and provide feedback to the participants on these evaluations. Corrections to the treatment may be made based on these evaluations.

- MST providers work on a team with several therapists familiar with the problems who are committed to helping the family construct solutions.
- MST removes barriers to receiving treatment by meeting the family in its home and other involved subsystems at their location.

Main Therapeutic Interventions

Although MST is a family-based treatment model that has similarities to other family therapy approaches, several substantive differences are evident (Saldana & Sheidow, 2005).

- MST places considerable attention on factors in the adolescent's and family's social networks that are linked with antisocial behavior. For example, MST priorities include removing offenders from deviant peer groups, enhancing school or vocational performance, and developing an indigenous support network for the family to maintain therapeutic gains.
- Most important, MST has well-documented long-term outcomes with adolescents presenting serious antisocial behavior and their families. The strongest and most consistent support for the effectiveness of MST comes from controlled studies that focused on violent and chronic juvenile offenders.

MST Treatment Principles

MST treatment can take numerous potential directions based on the dynamics of the community system of which the IP is part. However, MST has several key treatment principles (Henggeler, Schoenwald, Rowland, et al., 2002):

- MST is a highly controlled approach to treatment and uses specific interventions to affect the IP's social context. The goal is to modify all aspects of the system in ways that promote and reinforce responsible behavior by the adolescent.
- The treatment plan is based on the needs of the family and developed in collaboration with the family. The plan specifically identifies and modifies factors in the adolescent's social network that contribute to and maintain the negative behaviors.

- Interventions might include focusing on developing and reinforcing family rules and discipline, helping family members identify and express their feelings to one another, decreasing or eliminating the IP's association with influential acting-out peers, and developing positive recreational and vocational activities.
- When these and other interventions are complete, it is essential that a support network of extended family, neighbors, and friends is prepared to help caregivers achieve and maintain behavioral changes.
- Treatment usually last about 4 months. Major improvements are possible in this short period of time because of the interventions by multiple therapists several times per week with a variety of important community subsystems, including the family.

Strengths of the Approach

MST has several strengths and advantages already described. Five specific advantages are that the approach is empirically validated, takes the therapy to the family and other important subsystems at their locations, is time limited, is delivered by a team of three or four professionals, and cannot be implemented with clients until the professionals selected to provide treatment are fully trained in the use of the MST treatment approach.

Weaknesses of the Approach

Some therapists might consider the following to be potential weaknesses of MST. First, the costs associated with contracting with the MST organization and becoming certified to deliver the approach prevents some agencies from implementing it. Second, while studies have shown the cost effectiveness of MST, some agencies may not have sufficient personnel to implement the team approach. Third, the requirement that providers adhere to a strict treatment protocol might limit innovation and creativity in the treatment.

Despite these potential limitations, MST is a treatment approach that has demonstrated much promise in the treatment of adolescents with severed behavioral problems.

CASE EXAMPLE

Multisystemic Therapy with Families

The Williams family contacted the Family Services Agency based on the recommendation of the local Teen Court. Their oldest daughter, Monica, had been detained and required to go to court twice in the past month for shoplifting and fighting with a knife with other girls after school. These violations appeared to be gang related. The judge told Monica and her parents that if there were another offense, Monica would go to regular court and might be placed in a juvenile detention facility for up to 3 years.

The Agency made an appointment with the family and met at their residence. Working with the family, the team determined what the goals of the family were and identified the subsystems that had the most influence on Monica.

Some members of the team worked with the family in establishing more effective rules and ways of implementing consequences for Monica. Other team members established relationships between the Williams family and the school, Monica's place of work, and her closest friends. These relationships evolved into a network of concerned individuals who were coordinated to help Monica avoid illegal and irresponsible behaviors. By coordinating the efforts of the family, school, courts, police department, and Monica's non–gang member friends, procedures and communication networks were put in place that helped her increase positive behaviors and decrease her negative actions. Monica's contact with the gang was eliminated. The therapy team and all involved subsystems worked collaboratively several times per week for 6 weeks evaluating behavioral changes by frequently using MST assessment instruments. Six weeks after treatment began, significant changes had occurred in Monica, in her family, and in the ways that important subsystems in the community were engaged in her positive behavior changes.

The likelihood that the change will be maintained is enhanced because all elements of Monica's environment were changed. Monica was different, her family was different, her friends were different, her teachers and counselors were different, and others with influence were enlisted to support the changes in Monica's ecology. MST therapist followed up regularly with the Williams family and provided "booster" interventions as needed.

Summary

In this chapter, I have described four family systems approaches with their roots in cognitive–behavioral theory. Structural family therapy, functional family therapy, MRI brief therapy, and multisystemic therapy seek to help families understand their behavior and employ powerful change techniques to help them function more effectively. All four approaches are readily understood by beginning family therapists because the principles of each theory are clearly explained and the change techniques closely follow the major constructs of the theory. In the next two chapters, we examine individual- and systems-based theories with humanistic and existential assumptions.

Suggested Readings

Alexander, J., & Parsons, B. V. (1982). *Functional family therapy*. Pacific Grove, CA: Brooks/Cole.

Fisch, R., Weakland, J. H., & Segal, L. (1982). *The tactics of change: Doing therapy briefly*. San Francisco: Jossey-Bass.

Henggeler, S. W., Schoenwald, S. K. C., Bourdin, C. M., Roland, M. D., & Cunningham, P. B. (1998). *Multisystemic treatment of antisocial behavior in children and adolescents*. New York: Guilford Press.

Henggeler, S. W., Schoenwald, S. K. C., Roland, M. D., & Cunningham, P. B. (2002). *Serious emotional disturbance in children and adolescents: Multisystemic therapy*. New York: Guillford Press.

Minuchin, S., & Fishman, C. (1981). *Family therapy techniques*. Cambridge, MA: Harvard University Press.

Helping Families
Using Humanistic
Individual Theories

In this chapter, three humanistic approaches to family
therapy are introduced. These include the person-
centered approach of Carl Rogers; the Gestalt approach
to family counseling developed by Walter Kempler, built
upon the work of Fritz Perls; and the psychodrama approach of J. L. Moreno. These approaches have similar
philosophical roots and a common focus on subjective
states of being.

Key Concepts

- Human capacities
- Self-awareness
- Self-determination
- Subjective experience
- Existential death
- Search for meaning
- Autonomy
- Self-actualization
- Existential aloneness
- Phenomenological view
- Reflection of content/feelings
- Self-disclosure
- Unfinished business
- Role playing
- Family sculpture

Questions for Discussion

1. How would a person-centered family therapist communicate unconditional positive regard to a family?
2. What ethical issues might be raised by using a person-centered approach in family therapy?
3. How might a therapist work with a family member who does not want (or is afraid) to take part in an empty-chair Gestalt experiment?
4. How might a Gestalt-oriented family therapist work with a family member who is avoiding personal responsibility?
5. What are some of the possible psychological risks associated with using psychodrama techniques with a family?

Humanistic theories focus on the subjective perceptions of clients and on the importance of the relationship between client and therapist. This chapter introduces three humanistic individually-oriented theories that may also be used in family treatment. Philosophical leaders of the humanistic existential movement include Rollo May, Carl Rogers, Fritz Perls, Walter Kempler, Abraham Maslow, James Bugenthal, Viktor Frankl, and philosophers Martin Buber and Jean-Paul Sartre.

Because they base their interventions on a core philosophical position, humanistic therapists can utilize diverse methods to work with families including cognitive, behavioral, and feeling-oriented methods. Generally regarded as the *third force* in psychology, the humanistic approaches to therapy tend to be largely experiential and relationship centered (Weinhold & Hendricks, 1993).

Humanistic theorists argue that human behavior cannot be fully understood by objective and cognitive methods. For example, a therapist using a humanistic approach with a family that seems to be struggling with conflicts in destructive and self-defeating ways might structure the first session by saying:

> "I understand that you have come to therapy because you are not able to resolve the conflicts in your family. Further, it seems to me that you care about your family and hope to find some solutions to your dilemma. A good place to begin the search for solutions is for each of you to describe what you think and feel about the problems you are facing. As each of you describes your view of the problem, I want the rest of the family members to listen carefully to what is being said rather than thinking of how you will defend or justify your own position. Also, each of you might add something about how you would like your family to be different as a result of counseling. Who would like to begin?"

This initial session is designed to have each family member share her subjective or phenomenological world. Sharing these unique perceptions with other family members and the therapist has a therapeutic effect on all present, particularly if family members are listening carefully to each other.

Goals of Humanistic Family Therapy Approaches

The goals of humanistic family approaches are to increase each client's self-awareness and each client's awareness of the perspectives of other family members concerning the family's style of interacting and the nature of the problems presented. Family counseling is designed to help family members become aware of their patterns of behavior, choices, and decisions as well as their options and potentials for change (Watson, 1977). Another goal is to increase autonomy and self-actualization, or the ability to be more fully oneself in the present moment. Rather than merely adjust to societal or family norms, family members are encouraged to discover how they want to live their lives. Important therapeutic goals include helping clients accept their own freedom to change and grow along with accepting responsibility for their existence and the quality of the relationships within their family. Because existential qualities including anxiety and uncertainty are an important aspect of humanistic approaches, these feelings often accompany the acceptance of freedom and responsibility. A fundamental goal of the humanistic approach is to support clients and respond effectively to the uncertainty and anxiety that will inevitably arise as a result of their challenges to old thoughts, feelings, and behaviors and as they contemplate change and choose how to be in the future.

The Process Used in Humanistic Approaches

The helping process in family counseling focuses both on what happens *within* individual members and also on what happens *between* family members. Thayer (1991) introduced a series of progressive developmental stages that are typical of the process of family therapy, using a humanistic framework:

1. *Client uncertainty and need for structure.* At first, clients are confused and uncertain about the purpose of the therapy. They ask, "Why are we here? What is going to happen? What should we do?"

2. *Resisting therapy.* Family members are resistant to sharing their thoughts and feelings. They wonder if it is safe to do so.

3. *Talking about the past.* Members describe past happenings and their feelings about these events. They are focused on the "then and there."

4. *Negative feelings.* Members begin to share their negative feelings toward each other or the therapist. They may be testing the safety of the therapy situation. They ask themselves, "Is it safe to be me, even the negative me?"

5. *Expressing and exploring personally relevant issues.* At this stage, there may be enough trust to permit open expression and exploration of personally relevant information. Family members begin to feel as if they can help change themselves and the family. They begin to work toward what they want it to be.

6. *Fully expressing feelings in the here and now.* Members express moment-to-moment feelings toward one another. Changes in the family structure begin to take place.

7. *Healing capacity of family members.* Family members begin to turn their attention to helping each other heal the pain and suffering of others in the family. A climate of trust and freedom allows for acceptance and understanding to emerge.

8. *Self-acceptance and change.* Family members begin to accept themselves as they are in the family and accept the inevitable changes that take place in the family. Members take responsibility for their actions and are in control of changing their own behavior rather than trying to change the behavior of other family members. All feel safe enough to ask others for what they want in each relationship and to suggest how others might eliminate behaviors or add new behaviors to enhance relationships.

9. *Fading facades.* A sense of realness develops among family members, and this becomes a norm. Those who are less real or defensive are challenged to reveal their deeper feelings and thoughts.

10. *Feedback.* Family members get and give feedback to each other. They seek feedback about themselves so they can grow even more.

11. *Confrontation.* Any remaining defensiveness is confronted as members drop their politeness and protectiveness. They recognize the interpersonal strengths in each other and recognize that all are able to hear and respond effectively to confrontation.

12. *Understanding the family unit.* Each family member begins to experience the family as an interconnected unit, with each member

affecting the others. They recognize that changes in one family member affect all other members. A family bond develops and is felt by all members. Simultaneously, family members recognize each other's autonomy and embrace the knowledge that members are differentiated; that is, they know that the family is composed of individuals with lives and activities apart from the family.

13. *Fuller expression of closeness.* Family members have warm and genuine feelings toward each other. They have learned to listen to and accept each other's feelings, both positive and negative. Disputes are now resolved with less conflict and anxiety.

14. *A changed family.* The members now experience both oneness and separateness in their interactions with each other. They have learned a process by which they can continue to explore and clarify values, examine and make decisions, and challenge issues that come up in the family. They are able to be as open with each other in their day-to-day interactions as they were in their family therapy sessions.

While these stages are progressive and developmental, therapists should not be surprised when families regress to an earlier stage or perhaps temporarily skip a stage or two in their therapy process.

Advantages and Limitations of the Humanistic Approaches

A substantial body of literature supports these approaches (Anderson, 1989; Clarke, 1978; Corey, 2009; Kempler, 1991; Rogers, 1961, 1980). Among the advantages of the humanistic philosophy are the following:

- It empowers people to take responsibility for their actions and provides a framework for understanding universal human concerns.
- It presents the positive, hopeful view that humans can continually actualize themselves and reach their potential and that families have the potential to resolve many of their own problems.
- It has contributed much to understanding the essential ingredients of the therapeutic relationship.
- Because the theory emphasizes that techniques should follow understanding, the danger of abusing the techniques is lessened.

The humanistic approach has limitations as well (Fenell & Weinhold, 2003):

- It may use abstract concepts and language that some clients find difficult to understand.
- Therapy is not usually brief. Several sessions may be required to complete the growth process.
- The theory may not work as well with families who are in severe crisis and require immediate and directive interventions.
- It may focus too much attention on individual growth and development instead of targeting problematic family interaction patterns.
- There are no set standards for training family therapists to use this approach, leading to wide variance in expertise and training.

Person-Centered Family Therapy

Carl Rogers (1902–1987) considered that his theory of person-centered therapy could be used effectively with couples and families as well as individual clients. Rogers (1961) translated the principles of his individual person-centered model to an approach that was useful in helping couples and families. The person-centered model fits rather naturally with family therapy because of its emphasis on developing close interpersonal relationships (Rogers, 1961). Yet, to most effectively employ the person-centered approach with families requires an expansion of traditional person-centered theory (Anderson, 1989; Thayer, 1991). Rogers theorized that family members will become more trusting of each other if the therapist is able to create the right climate in the therapy sessions. The basic conditions required for this climate to develop are genuineness, openness, caring, acceptance, positive regard, and reflective listening.

Some of Roger's followers (Levant, 1978; Thayer, 1991; Van der Veen, 1977) have made advances in the practice of person-centered family therapy. While the individual's self-concept is at the heart of person-centered individual therapy, the family concept is at the heart of person-centered family therapy (Raskin & Van der Veen, 1970). The term *family concept* describes the feelings, attitudes, and expectations a person has toward his family of origin and present family. This relatively stable concept organizes and influences much of a person's behavior.

According to this theory, for a family to change, the members have to acknowledge their problems and change their family concept. As the family comes to think about itself in new and more productive ways, each member makes changes that acknowledge and strengthen the new family concept. As the family members experience their family differently and more positively, a recursive process is initiated, as the new attitudes members hold about the family and each other serve to strengthen each person's self-concept, which in turn further strengthens their positive feelings about the family.

Philosophical Tenets

Epistemology is the branch of philosophy that studies the nature of knowledge, in particular its foundations, scope, and validity. Rogers and other person-centered family therapists adopted an *epistemology,* or way of knowing, based on humanistic and phenomenological beliefs about human nature. According to this view, the most important source of knowledge is the experience and perceptions of each individual. When applying the humanistic approach in counseling, the therapist pays close attention to and acknowledges the subjective and personal view of the world and of other people held by the client. The primary target of the interventions is usually the client's feelings and perceptions of self and the relationship between the self and others. Simply stated, the humanistic approach examines and privileges the client's subjective experience in therapy sessions. The therapist's best source of knowledge about a client and her problems is based on an accurate understanding of and empathy with the client's views of her experiences (Rogers, 1961).

According to this approach, *ontology,* which is concerned with the nature of being, is based on the individual's subjective perspective of his own existence and personal reality. But there are differences between a purely existential view of being and a purely humanistic one. The existential position, as stated by Sartre, says that although we learn of our essence through our existence, that essence is largely unknowable. The humanistic view, which is more phenomenological, says that the perception of our essential nature is what we use to guide our behavior. The humanistic theorists are more concerned with discovering this perception than with finding the ultimate truth.

The source of people's values, according to this approach, is a set of universal principles that cannot be totally known but is reflected in the consciousness of each individual. People are essentially good at their core, and as they become more aware or conscious, they are better able to live a life based on this inherent goodness and their values. Counseling is seen as a way to help the client increase self-awareness and encourage the natural process of personal growth and essential goodness to occur.

Theoretical Constructs

Two relevant theoretical constructs are the theory of problem formation and the theory of change.

Theory of Problem Formation

Rogers asserted that people developed problems because their lives are incongruent. While he fully believed that each human has the capacity for self-actualization and a satisfying life, problems develop for some people because they live in ways that are not authentic and genuine. They look toward others to see how they should think, feel, and act rather than behaving in ways that are true to themselves. This incongruence results in anxiety or other symptoms and leads the person to seek counseling. In the same manner, families can live in incongruent ways, and when they do, it is likely that one or more members of the family may develop symptoms that reflect the family's incongruence and inability to find within itself the resources for authentic living.

According to the person-centered approach, people develop emotional problems because they are unable to effectively communicate what they think and feel to others. They tend to withdraw from other people. Thayer (1991) identified the family problems that person-centered family therapy is best able to deal with. These include the following (Thayer, 1991):

- Lack of realness in relating to other family members
- Denial or lack of expression of important feelings in the family
- Failing to see the individuality of each family member
- Failing to listen with accurate empathy to others
- Ineffective communication in the family
- Family members' inability to resolve conflicts as they arise

Theory of Change

The person-centered family therapist believes that the individual family members and the family unit itself, not the therapist, are responsible for making desired changes. The role of the therapist is to create the proper conditions to allow the untapped inherent potential of the individual and family to be explored and integrated (Thayer, 1991). Rogers (1980) believed that individuals have within themselves vast resources for self-understanding and for altering their self-concept, basic attitudes, and self-directed behavior. Moreover, these resources can be tapped if the therapist is able to provide a predictable climate of facilitative psychological conditions to each of the family members and to the family as an entity itself. The most important facilitative conditions, according to Rogers (1961), are genuineness, empathy, and unconditional positive regard. The therapist teaches these qualities through modeling and by demonstrating how these qualities help the family members release these untapped qualities.

Genuineness is the quality of being real and authentic with self and others. The counselor must be able to demonstrate this characteristic if an effective relationship is to be established with family members. If the family does not feel a sense of trust in a genuine counselor, they are not likely to allow the therapist access to the important details of their inner family system. When the therapist responds authentically with genuine caring to the pain or grief of family members, it has a powerful effect on the family system and enhances trust and the therapeutic relationship.

Empathy, the ability to enter the phenomenological world of another, is an important counselor characteristic in providing effective family therapy. Empathy is the therapist's ability to understand the family members as they understand themselves and to communicate this understanding to them. Unconditional positive regard is another key ingredient in successful therapy and blends smoothly with genuineness and empathy. *Unconditional positive regard* is the ability of the counselor to communicate to clients in a way that demonstrates valuing, care, and concern for each family member without conditions. When present, this quality helps clients to feel safe enough to release long-held feelings.

Main Therapeutic Interventions

The person-centered family therapist believes that the core therapeutic conditions developed by Carl Rogers described above, plus the communication skills identified below, are both *necessary* and *sufficient* to facilitate therapeutic change. The role of the therapist is to establish therapeutic relationships with each family member that model empathy, respect, genuineness, unconditional positive regard, and congruence. By demonstrating these therapeutic conditions and the following communication skills, the therapist teaches family members how to employ these qualities in their relationships with one another (Fenell, 1998; Rogers, 1961):

- *Being attentive* is a way of deepening the therapist's contact with the client (Thayer, 1991). Attending verbal and nonverbal skills are necessary if the therapist wishes to follow the process of the family's interaction patterns.
- *Reflection of content* communicates respect and assures family members that the therapist truly understands their perceptions of the family situation.
- *Reflection of feelings* is crucial in humanistic approaches. The therapist's ability to be comfortable with client's emotions and to be able to reflect empathy is essential. The therapist must pay close attention to verbal and nonverbal behavior and attach accurate affective meaning to these interactions. Therapists also need to confront discrepancies between verbal and nonverbal messages when they occur in therapy.
- *Immediacy* is utilized to model effective communication and is usually a response to something that happens in the session *at that very moment.* For example, the therapist might say: "When you tell that to John and then look away, I feel sad and wonder why you don't look at him when you say things that are important to you." The immediate reaction of the therapist is the feeling of sadness, which is disclosed to the family, modeling honesty, trust, and risk taking to improve relationships.
- *Showing respect* is a skill that person-centered therapists use to demonstrate caring and concern for family members. The therapist shows respect by communicating his belief that the family members have all the relationship resources necessary to make desired personal and family changes.
- Utilizing *intuitive hunches* is another important therapeutic skill (Thayer, 1991). The therapist has to draw upon all of her senses to develop gut reactions or hunches about what is occurring in the family. The therapist appropriately shares these intuitive feelings, and this often helps family members reach deeper levels of awareness and growth. Moreover, this modeling by the therapist helps family members learn to share their own hunches and gut reactions with one another.

O'Leary (1989) identified the complex role of the person-centered family therapist as twofold. First, the therapist has to be able to respond to the individual meanings of each family member. Second, the therapist must be able to assess and respond to the objective reality of the family's interactional patterns. Skills that the person-centered therapist generally does not employ include *questioning,* which often implies leading and directing, and *interpretation.* The main goals are to reflect and model, leaving the interpretation to each family member.

Strengths of Person-Centered Family Therapy

Person-centered family therapy has several strengths. The main strength is that this approach, more than any other, emphasizes the importance of the relationship between the therapist and all members of the family. Moreover, many of the fundamental skills employed by the person-centered family therapist are those that have been identified by researchers as the common factors that appear to be necessary and present in all therapy models (Duncan, 2010). Finally, this approach has a positive view of the human conditions and conveys to family members the empathy, unconditional positive regard, and respect needed to activate their internal resources and bring about family change.

Limitations of Person-Centered Family Therapy

This approach can work effectively in the early stages of therapy with families that have serious and long-standing problems, because the family members feel understood, validated, and hopeful. However, the approach often must be coupled with other, more directive, action-oriented interventions for significant changes in the family structure to take place. The caring attitudes and skills demonstrated by skillful person-centered therapists are necessary but may not be sufficient to generate lasting change in some severely dysfunctional family systems.

A second limitation of the approach is that it requires the therapist to be able to tolerate loose structure and ambiguity. This absence of direction and focus on the client rather than therapist as the change producer may raise the anxiety of family members more than they can tolerate and lead to premature termination. Third, if therapists rely solely on empathic and reflecting techniques without significant personal disclosure, they may remain hidden as persons. Thus, therapists may become outer-directed and remain cut off from their own feelings and reactions.

Fourth, nondirective therapists do not use formal screening and assessment tools. Therefore, the therapist may spend considerable time obtaining information that could have been obtained more expeditiously. Finally, some practitioners object to the lack of formal certification or academic training of many person-centered family therapists. The use of minimally trained therapists is supported by research (Carkhuff, 1969b), but this lack of extensive training has led to some other highly trained professionals' reluctance to accept this approach.

Gestalt Family Therapy

The call for self-awareness in Gestalt-oriented family therapy cannot be considered an original idea developed by Fritz Perls (1883–1970). The self-awareness fostered through Gestalt family therapy has been understood as important in relationships throughout human history. It is

---

CASE EXAMPLE

Person-Centered Therapy

Bob and Joan have been married 6 years. They came to therapy because they were "not getting along with each other." Neither seemed to know why, and neither seemed to know what to do about it. Using a person-centered approach, the therapist decided to build a relationship with each of them and, in the process, hoped to teach them how to get along with each other. The therapist started with Bob and began by talking to Bob about his job and his interests outside of the relationship with Joan. This formed a good foundation for the breakthrough, which began when the therapist was talking to Joan.

Therapist: Tell me more about your fear of Bob leaving you.

Joan: I'm having another feeling right now, and I think I'm going to cry.

(continued)

Person-Centered Therapy *(continued)*

Therapist: You're feeling touched because of what I asked you.

Joan: Yes, it suddenly dawned on me that you really care what happens to me. I don't know if it was what you said so much as it was the way you said it. There was real caring in your voice.

Therapist: Sounds as though you experienced a deep sense of being cared for, something you need very much, and perhaps you are realizing for the first time how much you miss that.

Joan: I think I've wanted Bob to care about me more than he seems to. I didn't know that was behind my loneliness.

Bob: I can see what you mean. I, too, felt the caring in his voice. I do care for you, Joan, but I don't know how to tell you. Please help me.

Joan: You just did. I felt it in my body just now. Usually I'm not open to you this way. I'm guarded when you talk to me, always afraid you're going to tell me I've done something wrong. (long pause)

Therapist: Joan, you opened yourself to me and stayed open to what Bob said to you, and our words touched a place deep within you where you have hidden this tender, somewhat fragile need of yours. I'm glad you trusted us enough to let us in. I have warm feelings toward you right now. Bob, how are you feeling toward Joan right now?

Bob: I'm feeling lots of love and compassion. I didn't know you felt that way, Joan. I think I sensed your fear, and not knowing what it was, I held back saying things to you.

The relationship the therapist built with each of the clients helped both to lower their barriers to intimacy with each other. By helping family members experience a positive relationship with the therapist, they learn skills to build better relationships with each other.

described in Socrates' admonition "Know thyself." Today, the philosophy of Gestalt-oriented family therapy is that direct and accurate knowledge of the self is the key to good mental health and happy, productive relationships (Kempler, 1991).

Leaders of the Gestalt approach are Fritz Perls, Walter Kempler, Irving and Miriam Polster, and Joseph Zinker. Kempler broke away from Perls because he objected to Perls confrontational *one-up, hot seat* approach, in which Perls would frustrate, confront, and confuse clients deliberately to produce an emotional reaction, leading to client self-awareness, followed by behavior change. Kempler believed that Perls kept himself, *one-up,* or in a more superior role, and personally detached from the therapy situation. Kempler thought that therapists were more effective when personally involved in the therapy as an interactive participant and that they should share personal thoughts and feelings with clients, as is often done in person-centered family therapy.

Gestalt therapy was initially practiced as an individual or group therapy approach to treatment. However in 1961, because he saw the promise of gestalt therapy applications with couples and families, Walter Kempler founded the Kempler Institute for the Development of the Family, focusing primarily on couple and family therapy. Besides Kempler's (1965, 1968, 1981, 1991) pioneering works, only a handful of books in the literature deal with Gestalt-oriented family therapy. These include Bauer (1979), Goulding and Goulding (1979), Hatcher (1978, 1981), Kaplan and Kaplan (1978), and Rabin (1980).

The goals of Gestalt-oriented family therapy are:

- to help individuals within a family structure develop better boundaries between themselves and other family members, and
- to help individuals become more self-aware and present focused so they can complete unfinished business and change persistent family patterns.

Because the therapist attempts to balance the treatment of individual intrapsychic problems with the treatment of interpersonal problems that are present in family interactions, the therapy can rapidly shift between an in-depth focus on the individual and a broader focus on family interactional patterns. The gestalt family therapist must be skilled at making a smooth transition from the individual to the family system in a way that supports and includes all family members and does not neglect individual growth.

Philosophical Tenets

Although Gestalt psychology is also a phenomenological approach, it has epistemological differences with the person-centered approach. Perls, who was influenced by psychoanalytic theory, placed much greater emphasis on the inner or intrapersonal sources of knowledge than the outer or interpersonal sources of knowledge emphasized by the person-centered approach. Both theories, however, share an emphasis on the importance of the phenomenological field of the individuals' perceptions as reality.

Perls borrowed heavily from the existential framework. The name of his theory, Gestalt therapy, is based on the German word *gestalt*, or whole. Perls believed life was a process of trying to bring together the various aspects of our lives into a coherent whole, or gestalt. The more whole (and less fragmented) a person's life is, the more psychologically healthy she will be.

His most significant contribution is a focus on the present moment, or the *here and now,* as he called it. A focus on the immediate present in therapy is an existential concept. Perls's theory has a good news–bad news message. He asserted that people are solely responsible for their own conflicts and their life problems (the bad news); however, Perls also held forth that people have the capacity to resolve their conflicts and problems (the good news). He argued that all unresolved conflicts from our past are with us in the here and now and therefore are resolvable through experiential psychotherapy with a focus on bringing the past into the present. Talking about something that happened in the past puts the person in an observer's role, removed from the emotions inherent in the conflict situation. Perls encouraged clients to act out their conflicts in the present moment, bringing the elements of the original conflict to life and providing opportunities for resolution in the here and now.

This approach hypothesizes that people move through life unaware and oblivious to much of what is occurring around them and within their own minds and bodies. Perls thought that healthy people embraced the *awareness* of moment-to-moment encounters, feelings, and thoughts. Therapy is designed to be experiential and facilitate this awareness, which is a requirement for psychological health and personal growth. Gestalt therapists believe that *awareness alone* can produce change in clients. As clients become self-aware, they make different and more effective choices. Perls claimed that all people have *unfinished business* in their lives. Unfinished business is some interaction or goal or desire that has not been fulfilled or a past relationship that was problematic and remains so. The more aware people are of their unfinished business, the more likely they are to resolve it and to *complete their gestalt* and become people who are more whole and complete. Gestalt therapy does not try to help people adjust to a set of social values, which are viewed as transitory ways to remain unaware. The Gestalt therapist sees awareness as the path to this wholeness and designs therapy to create awareness through interactional experiences with the therapist. With awareness, people can recognize, face, and reintegrate parts of themselves they have disowned and thus become more unified and whole (Corey, 2007).

Theoretical Constructs

Theoretical constructs include the theory of problem formation and the theory of change.

Theory of Problem Formation

Gestalt-oriented family therapy is based on the premise that people have the ability and desire to understand and resolve their own problems when they are aware of, and take full responsibility for, all aspects of their personality and behavior. When a person's quest for awareness is blocked, disturbing behavior may result. Anger, fear, and sadness are natural reactions to the blockage and are ways of expressing a need to move to a state of enhanced awareness. The causes of this blocked awareness are often forgotten in the past but remain acted out in the here-and-now behavior of each person.

Blocked experiences (incomplete gestalts) occur in a person's interactions with the family of origin during childhood. The therapist attempts to help the client bring these experiences back to life *in the present moment* so the client can begin to gain awareness, discover what was causing the problem, and complete its resolution in the present.

Theory of Change

A model called the Gestalt experience cycle (Rabin, 1980) identifies the main elements of an experience and the way to complete an incomplete experience. The cycle begins with sensations and perceptions that are learned in childhood. These include messages about what we should or should not do and what we can or cannot do. Because of these experiences, we are sensitive to certain stimuli in present interactions, and when we experience these stimuli, we recall some of the original events from the past.

Awareness results from the ability to remain focused on a sensation. When clients are confused about what really happened in their childhood, they may have trouble bringing this sensation into awareness. Enhancing awareness and helping people understand their perceptions of what happened during their childhood is central to Gestalt therapy. As clients become more aware of these events, their bodies are stimulated to action. Clients who are blocked in their awareness may experience tension or pain; others may take ineffective action. The therapist must help the client develop appropriate ways to experience and act out the conflict in the here and now.

Contact is the next and probably the most crucial stage of the cycle. People who are disturbed resist making genuine contact. Their resistance takes these forms:

- *Projection*—making contact with disowned parts of the self rather than with other people; seeing one's own weaknesses in others, when in fact those weaknesses are not present
- *Introjection*—incorporating aspects of the other into the self; being the way others expect rather than true to oneself
- *Retroflection*—turning against oneself
- *Confluence*—confusion in the boundaries between self and others
- *Deflection*—erecting a wall to avoid contact

In family therapy, the therapist confronts these attempts to avoid contact and helps the family members learn new ways to make contact with each other, gain awareness, and complete unfinished business.

The final stage of the cycle is *withdrawal,* which occurs after experiences have been completed. An inability to withdraw and let go of an experience usually means that the unfinished business in relationships is still present. The therapist helps the family members work through the unfinished business until they are able to let go of it and are able to resolve the inner conflicts.

Main Therapeutic Interventions

The goals of Gestalt-oriented family therapy are to help family members develop clear boundaries between the self and others and to increase self-awareness so they can break free from persistent ineffective patterns and experience themselves and their lives more fully.

Views about the most effective ways to use Gestalt therapy with families differ. Hatcher (1978) recommended a blend of individual and family therapy. He suggested that a focus on the individual is appropriate when dealing with intrapersonal and boundary issues and that family therapy is appropriate when dealing with interpersonal and transactional issues. He suggested building a contract with a family that permits the shift back and forth within the context of the family therapy session rather than scheduling separate sessions.

Bauer (1979) suggested a similar arrangement using the empty-chair technique as a tool for resolving an individual's contact–boundary problems. The empty chair technique facilitates awareness by permitting a family member to confront unresolved issues with a person from the past in the here and now. The therapist instructs the client to sit in one chair and imagine the other party is in the empty chair. The client is encouraged to interact with the person in the empty chair in a way that helps resolve past unfinished business in the present therapeutic moment. Although he focused on the family as a whole, Bauer recommended using the empty chair technique and other Gestalt experiments to increase family members' awareness in therapy.

Kaplan and Kaplan (1978) focused on the process of family therapy to determine whether to intervene with the individual, with a particular subsystem, or with the family as a whole. They described three functions or skills that therapists must have to promote change: observing, focusing, and facilitating.

1. By *observing* the process carefully, the therapist can help the family become more aware of its dynamics.
2. *Focusing* means helping the family better understand specific aspects of its process, which may include the use of exaggeration techniques to highlight specific behaviors and enhance family members' awareness.
3. *Facilitating* is defined as helping the family move toward constructive reintegration. Experiential activities are used in this part to help produce self-awareness and a new integration and completion of a gestalt.

The concept of *polarities* is extremely important in Gestalt therapy. Every choice a person makes has a polar opposite that may be a disowned aspect of the client's personality. For example, a client could choose to go along with a family member's description of a situation in therapy; however, an equally valid choice and perhaps a better one could be for the client to say that he disagrees and present his own perceptions of the situation. Helping clients identify, own, and take responsibility for the polarities in their personality is a significant part of Gestalt therapy and is a powerful tool in increasing awareness (Perls, 1969).

Strengths of Gestalt-Oriented Family Therapy

Gestalt family therapy is a powerful model for creating change in family members. It often employs an individual focus, even when working with entire family systems. It uses a variety of effective experiential activities that serve to enhance family members' awareness in the here and now and, through increased awareness, change perceptions, behaviors, and family relationships. The approach is particularly helpful in dealing with unresolved issues from the past. Rather than taking the family member back in time, the therapist deals with the thoughts, feelings, and resulting behaviors precipitated by the past even in the here and now. Thus, the client is able to complete unfinished business in the present with family members in the room. The family members will gain in their own awareness as they watch the client grow through completing the unfinished business. Finally, the concept of *polarities* is powerful in helping clients come to recognize that choices *not made* are choices just the same as choices *made* and that all have people have positive as well as negative attributes. Awareness of both the good and bad qualities allows family members to choose and be responsible for their choices ... whether they are socially approved choices or not.

Limitations of Gestalt-Oriented Family Therapy

A limitation of Gestalt-oriented therapy is that it involves a philosophy that discounts the importance of cognitive understanding. Gestalt practitioners emphasize experience and feelings rather than build cognitive structures with clients. In addition, some Gestalt techniques can be offensive because of a danger of therapist taking a one-up role with clients. Gestalt therapists may be so directive that they create dependency relationships with clients, who come to rely on their direction. Therapists may utilize experiential activities that create dramatic catharsis and then insist that their clients create personal meaning from the catharsis without helping them work through and integrate the experience. Gestalt therapists can easily hide behind their techniques and may emphasize a "quick fix" instead of encouraging clients to grow and change over time.

Another weakness of Gestalt therapy is that the jargon that the therapist and client use can result in avoiding deeper issues. Phrases such as, "Stay in the here-and-now" or "take responsibility" can become rigid rules and lose their important meaning for the change process. Finally, little research has been done on Gestalt therapy, and virtually none has been done on Gestalt-oriented family therapy.

CASE EXAMPLE

Gestalt Therapy

Husband: What can I do? She stops me at every turn.

Therapist: (sarcastically, to provoke him) You poor thing, overpowered by that terrible lady over there.

Husband: (ducking) She means well.

Therapist: You're whimpering at me, and I can't stand to see a grown man whimpering.

Husband: (firmer) I tell you, I don't know what to do.

Therapist: Like hell you don't (offering and at the same time pushing). You know as well as I that if you want her off your back, you just have to tell her to get the hell off your back and mean it. That's one thing you could do instead of that mealy-mouthed apology, "She means well."

Husband: (looks quizzical; obviously is not sure if he wants to chance it with either of us but is reluctant to retreat to the whimpering child posture again) I'm not used to talking that way to people.

Therapist: Then you'd better get used to it. You're going to have to shape up this family into a group that's worth living with instead of a menagerie where your job is to come in periodically and crack the whip on the little wild animals.

Husband: You sure paint a bad picture.

Therapist: If I'm wrong, be man enough to disagree with me and don't wait to get outside of here to whimper to your wife about how you didn't know what to say here.

(continued)

Gestalt Therapy *(continued)*

Husband: (visibly bristling and speaking more forcefully) I don't know that you're wrong about what you're saying.

Therapist: But how do you like what I'm saying?

Husband: I don't. Nor do I like the way you're going about it.

Therapist: I don't like the way you're going about things either.

Husband: There must be a more friendly way than this.

Therapist: Sure, you know, whimper.

Husband: (with deliberate softness) You're really a pusher, aren't you?

Therapist: How do you like me?

Husband: I don't.

Therapist: You keep forgetting to say that part of your message. I can see it all over you, but you never say it.

Husband: (finally, in anger) I'll say what I damn please. You're not going to tell me how to talk . . . and how do you like that? (socks his hand)

Therapist: I like it a helluva lot better than your whimpering. What is your hand saying?

Husband: I'd like to punch you in the nose, I suppose.

Therapist: You suppose?

Husband: (firmly) Enough. Get off my back and stay off.

Therapist: (delighted to see his assertion) Great. Now, about the rest of them (waving to the family). I'd like to see if there's anything you'd like to say to them.

Husband: (looks at each one of them and then settles on his wife) He's right. I take an awful lot of nonsense from you, and I hate it (still socking his hand). I don't intend to take any more. I'll settle with the kids my way. If you don't like it, that's too bad.

Source: From *Experiential Therapy with Families* (pp. 178–179), by W. Kempler, 1981, New York: Brunner/Mazel.

This excerpt from a case study shows how Gestalt-oriented family therapy might be used to help a client re-own something that has been disowned or projected. Unlike the typical empty-chair technique, the therapist acted out the polarity of the client's aggressive side until the client took over the part.

Psychodrama with Families

J. L. Moreno (1889–1974) created psychodrama in Vienna in 1921. In that year, he opened the Theatre of Spontaneity. Those who participated as actors in the theater were laypersons and did not use scripts. Instead, the performers acted out in a spontaneous manner the events reported in the daily newspaper or topics suggested by members of the audience. After an event or topic was acted out, the actors and audience were invited to comment on their experiences during the performance. Moreno found that both the actors and those in the audience experienced a catharsis or release of pent-up feelings as a result of being in the play or observing the play. As a result of this experiment, Moreno began to develop specialized therapeutic techniques that became the foundation for psychodrama.

Psychodrama is designed to help people express their feelings in a spontaneous and dramatic way through role play. Because the work involves many different players, it is effective in a group setting and lends itself to family therapy as well. Although it is interpersonally oriented, psychodrama is intended to help people explore intrapersonal facets of their lives. Psychodrama recognizes the importance of the social environment and of acting out conflicts in front of an observing audience to resolve family problems (Moreno, 1983).

Psychodrama was the precursor of many other action-oriented approaches, including Gestalt, encounter groups, behavioral approaches, guided fantasy, play therapy, and improvisational dramatics. Other family systems approaches, such as family sculpting and family role playing, use psychodrama techniques originally developed by Moreno.

Philosophical Tenets

Like Perls, Moreno based his ideas on the notion that people are the product of their experiences and are responsible for their actions. This existential position is similar to the philosophies of Camus and Sartre, both of whom emphasized that people are alone in the universe of their experience. This aloneness, however, provides a common experience for all people, a concept that forms the epistemological basis of existentialism. People share the common experience of *being* as well as the common fear of *nonbeing*. The belief that death is absolute also frees people to choose to either accept their fate and to enjoy life in the present moment or to try to deny or run away from the inevitable and therefore be ruled by fear and guilt.

Like Sartre, Moreno believed that experiences determine a person's essence. People *are* what they *do* or *experience*. Those holding this view do not deny the possibility of preexisting human nature but do not believe it is possible to discover it and therefore ignore its role in human development. The only reality worth considering is a person's experience. According to this view, the source of value is *self-awareness* and the commitment to *take responsibility* for oneself as well as exercising one's ability to respond. Evil involves the failure to act according to one's ability.

Theoretical Constructs

Two theoretical constructs are the theory of problem formation and the theory of change.

Theory of Problem Formation

Moreno clearly delineated the role of social forces in causing disturbances. Forces of the family, society, occupational groups, and religious groups all shape the personality. Moreno theorized that one of the main results of this socialization process is that most people lack spontaneity and live a sort of "as if" existence, never fully entering into their experiences. Moreno observed that young children are able to enter into spontaneous role playing and fantasy situations and freely express their feelings, but adults have great difficulty in doing so. He saw that people develop limiting scripts for their lives and rigid, stereotyped responses to most situations.

Instead of meeting eye-to-eye and face-to-face, Moreno suggested that parents see in their children only what they want to see and are unable to truly mirror for the child. At the same time, children look at their parents and see omnipotent, perfect gods instead of scared, limited human beings. This condition may cause identity confusion for the child.

With this confusion as a base, most children grow up with distorted views of how the social order works. These distortions are best diagnosed through role playing or action drama. If these distortions are not uncovered and removed before children leave their families, the children's perceptions of the larger cultural milieu also are distorted, which leads to distortion at the universal level.

As a result of all these distortions, people live in a world they hardly even recognize. Most people adapt to their own distortions; they are cut off from their own life force and spontaneity, living life in a bubble, unable to break out, and unable to grow and develop very much without feeling crowded and restricted (Moreno, 1951).

Theory of Change

The cure, so to speak, lies in the client's willingness to risk breaking the bubble through action. In this approach, insight and awareness come as the result of some action. Moreno saw the psychodrama method as the way to break through the bubble and learn how to be spontaneous. The method uses five instruments: the stage, the client, the director, the auxiliary egos, and the audience.

1. The *stage* provides the client with a living space that is multidimensional and highly flexible. The client's reality is usually much too limited, and the stage allows for a new freedom to emerge. The clients are asked to be themselves on the stage and to portray their own private world. Once they are warmed up to the task, clients are asked to give a spontaneous account of some problem in their daily lives.

2. The *client* is encouraged to become involved with all the people and things present in this problem, which can mean encountering internal parts of the self as well as other people—past, present, and future—who are involved in some way with the problem.

3. The *director* is the therapist and serves as the producer, counselor, and analyst. As the producer, she develops the production in line with the client's life script, never letting the production bog down or move too fast. As the therapist, she confronts, reflects feelings and content, summarizes, and gives information. The analyst interprets and helps the client integrate the material into his life space.

4. *Auxiliary egos* are extensions of the client and are used to portray the actual or imagined personas of his real life drama. They help model and teach the client new ways to act in this and other similar situations.

5. The *audience* is used as a sounding board of public opinion, helping the client see overlooked aspects of the drama. The client also helps the audience, as people from the audience see aspects of their own life drama being played out on the stage.

Psychodrama has three phases: the warm-up phase, the action phase, and the discussion or sharing phase. The therapeutic element in psychodrama is *catharsis,* or release. This catharsis is produced only if a climate fostering spontaneity can be created in the *warm-up* stage. To create an open and effective therapeutic climate, the client and all other members of the psychodrama must feel safe and trust the direction. If this occurs, the expression of emotions, an attitude of playfulness, and a willingness to explore novel behavior emerges.

During the *action* phase, the spontaneity of the drama produces a catharsis that enables the client to experience repressed feelings and distorted thoughts. A skillful director can then utilize this expression of feelings and thoughts to enable a new drama to emerge. With the help of the auxiliary egos, the director produces the new drama with the client and allows for new roles and actions to occur within the safety of the therapeutic setting. These new dramas can be properly rehearsed and reinforced by the director, the auxiliary egos, and the audience before the client tries them out in his life space.

During the *discussion* stage, the director protects the client from interpretive or negative feedback because the client is in a vulnerable position. This protection is necessary to help the client integrate what he just experienced. The director requests personal sharing by audience members, asking them how the psychodrama helped them. The catharsis that occurs in members of the audience connects the audience to the client (Moreno, 1983).

Main Therapeutic Interventions

A number of psychodrama techniques lend themselves to family therapy:

- *Self-presentation.* The therapist lets all family members present how they see themselves in relationship to every other family member. This technique enables the therapist to discover who is enmeshed in the family system and who is an outsider.
- *Presentation of the other.* The therapist who wishes to know how family members see each other may ask them to present other family members as they see them. The therapist may wish to interview the person who is presenting another family member to get a more complete picture of how she sees the other family member.
- *Role playing.* This is an extension of the presentation of the other, with a possible role reversal. Two or more family members reverse

roles and act out some scene. The therapist encourages maximum expression of feelings in conflict situations. The technique helps to quickly reveal the distortions in the relationships and to correct them, and it can produce new options and much insight into conflict situations.

- *Double technique.* Sometimes the therapist or another family member has to act as a double, standing behind the client and speaking for the client when necessary or requested. This technique helps the family member recognize and express feelings and content that has been blocked or repressed. This technique is often used as a catalyst to get a family member to express feelings or thoughts that have been inhibited. Multiple doubles can be used to help portray mixed or conflicting feelings as well. For example one double could express love and closeness for the client and the other anger and resentment.

- *Family sculpture.* In this technique, the therapist asks all the family members to sculpt the family the way they see it in relationship to themselves and to each other. This means physically placing people in postures and having them hold the position as a freeze frame for examination and reactions by all family members and the therapist (Duhl, Kantor, & Duhl, 1973). This technique can also be used to choreograph new patterns by experimenting with different sculpture formations and allowing the family to change in ways that members would like and direct in the sculpting exercise. This powerful intervention can help realign family relationships (Papp, 1980).

Strengths of Psychodrama-Oriented Family Therapy

Psychodrama is a powerful approach to dealing with family issues. It is effective when employed with an unrelated group experiencing family problems or with a family unit. The process is clear, roles are delineated, and the outcome of the dramas leads to new self-awareness and psychological clarity. The important family therapy technique of family sculpting is a direct descendant of Moreno's psychodrama approach to treatment.

Limitations of Psychodrama-Oriented Family Therapy

Although feelings and repressed material can be uncovered quickly using this technique, it requires an experienced and sensitive therapist to use the material effectively. Another problem with the technique is

CASE EXAMPLE

Psychodrama

Mr. and Mrs. Thomas, their 17-year-old son John, and their 15-year-old daughter Ann came to family therapy because of unresolved conflicts that had beset the family. In the initial interview, the major problem discussed was Mrs. Thomas's criticism of her daughter, comparing her unfavorably with her older brother. Ann was asked to present or role-play the way she experienced her mother, and she was happy to show her unexpressed feelings in the safety of the family therapy session as she portrayed her mother's attacks. She said, as her mother, "Ann, you're so lazy. Look at you—you don't do anything but sit around watching TV. John is always busy with his job, school activities, and his friends, and all you do is sit there."

Mrs. Thomas had initiated the family therapy, and it turned out that she was also critical of Mr. Thomas, who she said was always too busy at work. Mr. Thomas defended himself, saying that he stayed away because she was always nagging him.

The therapist attempted to uncover their patterns and help them discover new ways of behaving with each other through role playing. Ann became John, Mrs. Thomas became Ann, and John and Mr. Thomas reversed roles. The therapist helped them all express their feelings toward the rest of the family members. Ann, as John, said, "I feel isolated and alone inside this family. Everyone just expects me to do well, but I don't feel they like me, and I'm always afraid I'll screw up." Mr. Thomas, as John, said, "I'm a lot like Dad. I run away from conflict and just keep busy." Later Mrs. Thomas reversed roles with Mr. Thomas. As Mr. Thomas, she said, "I wish I could bring some order to this family."

The therapist worked with Mr. Thomas to show him what he could say and do to help bring order to the family. Using the double technique, with the coaching of the therapist, he tried out several possibilities. To his surprise, the family members responded positively. The therapist suggested scheduling a regular meeting time during which they could clear their feelings and plan family activities. Mr. Thomas was assigned the role of leading these meetings. The family role-played an actual meeting during one session to learn how it might use this type of meeting to resolve conflicts.

that, like other experiential models, this approach does not have a strong research base (Rudestam, 1982). It requires specialized training and supervised experience, yet many practitioners utilize psychodrama techniques without additional training or supervision.

Summary

This chapter has introduced the reader to individual counseling theories that are especially effective in work that requires a sustained and intense therapeutic relationship with the client or family. These theories focus on and privilege the client's phenomenological perceptions and strive to validate the client's perceptions of self, others, and the world and work within the framework of those perceptions. The first theory presented described how the counselor can use the principles of Carl Roger's person-centered therapy to help couples and families. In this approach, the therapist communicates unconditional positive regard to the clients and demonstrates empathy, respect, and genuineness in relationships with them. This theory posits that families can make substantial change in the safety of this type of caring therapeutic relationship.

The next theory presented was Walter Kempler's gestalt family therapy. Kempler used the principals of Fritz Perls's work with individuals and groups, applying them to family therapy. This approach challenges clients to experience their phenomenological realty in new ways within the context of a safe relationship, creating new and more complete awareness. This awareness is by itself change producing and can lead to changed family relationships. Families working within this framework are challenged to experience themselves, other family members, and their relationships in new ways, creating new awareness and changes in the family's interactional patterns.

The last theory presented was Moreno's psychodrama-based family therapy. This approach is used to help individuals work through family issues with a cast of role players who take on the functions of the family members and enact behaviors that create new insights and awareness for the client as the psychodrama unfolds. Clients learn about their own behaviors in the family based on feedback from the role players and also gain appreciation for new ways to behave with their real family. This approach was modified by contemporary family therapists for use with intact families. The revised approach is called family sculpting.

The following chapter will introduce the reader to the humanistic systems theories that have become increasing popular with family therapist over the past decade.

Suggested Readings

Fenell, D. L. (1998). The use of Rogerian techniques in marital therapy. In T. Nelson & T. Trepper (Eds.), *101 more interventions in marriage and family therapy.* Binghamton, NY: The Haworth Press.

Kempler, W. (1982). *Experiential therapy with families.* New York: Brunner/Mazel.

Moreno, J. L. (1946). *Psychodrama.* Boston: Beacon House.

Rogers, C. R. (1951). *Client centered therapy.* Boston: Houghton Mifflin.

Rogers, C. R. (1972). *Becoming partners: Marriage and its alternatives.* New York: Dell.

Thayer, L. (1991). "Toward a person-centered approach to family therapy." In A. Horne & J. L. Passmore (Eds.), *Family counseling and therapy* (2nd ed.). Itasca, IL: Peacock.

Helping Families Using Humanistic Interpersonal Systems Theories

In this chapter four systemically-based theories of couple and family therapy based on interpersonal and humanistic concepts and assumptions are presented. The theories of Virginia Satir (1983, 1988) and Carl Whitaker (1976, 1981) emphasize systemic, interactional, and contextual dimensions of the family while recognizing individual differences and the humanistic belief in human potential. The narrative and conversational approach to therapy developed by Michael White and David Epston (1990) will also be presented. This approach includes elements of postmodern and constructivist theory (Gehart, 2010) and the human potential movement (Rogers, 1961). Each of these movements suggests the ability of individuals to recreate themselves and their families through the use of new and more effective language and metaphors. The last theory presented in this chapter is emotionally focused therapy developed by Sue Johnson (2004) and Les Greenburg. As indicated in its title, this theory incorporates an interpersonal and emotional focus in systemic family therapy that is designed to sooth and repair damaged relationships.

Key Concepts

- Self-concept
- Family communication
- Architects of the family
- Family rules
- Placater
- Blamer
- Computer
- Distracter
- Softening
- Attachment theory
- Battle for structure
- Battle for initiative
- Cotherapy
- Three-generation therapy
- Externalization
- Therapeutic letters
- Reauthored narrative
- Primary emotions
- Deepening affect
- Healthy dependence

Questions for Discussion

1. According to Satir's communications theory, what creates an individual's psychological problems?
2. Why did Satir believe the personal qualities of the counselor are so important in family therapy?
3. What major techniques did Satir use to help family members develop self-esteem?
4. What are the characteristics of a healthy family according to Whitaker?
5. What are the battles for structure and initiative? Why are these important in therapy?
6. Why is having a cotherapist important in Whitaker's family therapy?
7. According to Whitaker, what common errors do family counselors make? How can these errors be avoided?
8. What is the goal of linking elements of the historical approach to treatment with elements of brief therapy in the narrative approach?
9. How would you use therapeutic letters in your treatment of families? Do you think the time involved in preparing the letters would be justified? Why or why not?
10. What is externalization of problems and why is it important in narrative therapy?
11. What are exceptions and why are they important in narrative therapy?
12. What is softening emotions in emotionally focused therapy and why is this intervention important?
13. What are attachment needs in humans? Do you believe adults have attachment needs? Defend your answer.

The four systems theories presented in this chapter—those of Virginia Satir, Carl Whitaker, Michael White and David Epston, and Sue Johnson and Les Greenburg are based in a belief in individual differences and human potential. Humanistic/interpersonal systems therapists believe that individuals and families have a drive toward wholeness and health. Therapy should encourage the family members to identify and come into full contact with their experiences. This process of focused experiencing and awareness is the vehicle for enhanced self-worth and family improvement. Humanistic therapists are far more interested in what is currently occurring in the family than in past memories or events.

The overall goal of humanistic family systems therapies is to encourage family members to have a corrective experience based on an enhanced awareness of feelings, thoughts, and actions in the here and now. They participate directly in family issues though internal encounters with perceived elements of the self and external encounters with their family members. Through that corrective experience, clients learn how to deal creatively with individual and family issues that may emerge in the future.

The presentation of Satir's communications theory is followed by a description of the symbolic–experiential therapy formulated by Whitaker; the narrative approach used by White, Epston, and others; and emotionally focused therapy used by Johnson and Greenburg.

Satir's Communications Theory

Virginia Satir (1916–1988) completed her graduate degree in psychiatric social work and began training as a family therapists at the Illinois State Psychiatric Institute in Chicago in 1955. In 1959, she became one of the founding members of the Mental Research Institute in Palo Alto, California, where she worked with Don Jackson, Jay Haley, and others who were completing research on communication in schizophrenic families. In *Conjoint Family Therapy*, first published in 1964, she put forth her family therapy model. In a revised edition (Satir, 1983), she began to define the humanistic, existential foundation of her communications theory. Satir's humanistic theory was strongly influenced by her work as director of the residential training program at Esalen Institute, Big Sur, California, the historic home of the encounter group movement. Her legacy continues today because the theoretical approach she developed is one of the most widely respected and emulated family therapy models. Virginia Satir's genuine warmth and caring for families, which seemed to be always present, was the hallmark of her successful career. Satir died in 1988 at 76 years of age. Her ashes were scatted in the Rocky Mountains, near Crested Butte, Colorado.

Philosophical Tenets and Key Theoretical Constructs

Satir viewed her theory as dynamic and evolving rather than as a set of rigid principles. As such, she considered her model of therapy with families to be constantly in process. She was continually seeking to improve the model by refining her techniques. In her work with families, Satir attempted to identify the ubiquitous processes that occur in all relationships involving human beings. She wanted to help heal human relationships, which then would promote the growth and development of the self-concepts of family members. According to Satir, every relationship is an encounter between two people at a given moment in time. Satir's theory was developed to create genuine encounters between family members, allowing them to experience, identify, and work with their concealed feelings and thoughts in order to help heal the pain in the family.

Satir (1988) believed that an effective family therapy theory integrated the four basic parts of the self, which is composed of the mind, the body, the report of the senses, and social relationships. The order of this list, identifying individual aspects of the self before contextual ones, suggests that Satir placed more emphasis on the functioning of individuals within the family than many of the other systems theorists included in this book. Satir believed that relationships would be stronger and more functional if the individual members of the family possessed strong self-concepts. Thus, she placed much of the emphasis in therapy on developing strong self-concepts in the individual family members. She accomplished this through implementing interventions that created powerful emotional encounters between family members that would lead to enhanced self-awareness followed by new and more positive ways of interacting. These positive interactions in turn contributed to the development of stronger self-concepts in family members.

In keeping with her fluid and open process approach to therapy, Satir employed principles and ideas obtained from the disciplines of dance, drama, religion, medicine, communications, education, and the behavioral sciences. She believed that effective family counselors do not omit any useful tool to help the family, whether it comes from a discipline typically associated with psychotherapy or not (Satir, 1988). Satir made three key points concerning therapy and change:

1. The individual needs to develop self-awareness by observing the self in interaction with significant others within the family system.
2. The individual needs to come to recognize how behavior and self-concept are products of the relationships within the family system itself.
3. In healthy, evolving families *all* members need to understand the points above. This awareness may occur in treatment where therapeutic encounters between and among members allows them to experience each other genuinely and practice new interactional behaviors.

Further, Satir believed that effective therapy, to be most helpful, must be flexible and variable. She may have counseled families for an hour, or she may have worked with them in a marathon session lasting over a weekend. Thus, for Satir, the *time* of therapy is flexible and variable. Satir may have treated families in her office, their home, at a park, or in their workplace. Thus, the *place* of therapy is flexible. After meeting with the family as a unit and gaining a solid understanding of the situation, Satir would meet with individuals, couples, siblings, spouses, or any other important family subsystem. Thus, for Satir, *who* will be seen in therapy is flexible and variable. She worked alone, with a cotherapist, or with more than one cotherapist. The cotherapist could have been of either gender. Thus the nature of the *therapy team* that works with the family is flexible and variable. Satir used techniques from virtually any discipline that she believed would be helpful for the family. Thus, *techniques and procedures* for therapy are flexible and variable. This ability to use a wide variety of approaches and therapeutic plans is characteristic of therapists who work from a humanistic theoretical orientation. However, because of the flexibility and the variability employed in these approaches, the treatment methods of humanistic therapists like Satir are extremely difficult to duplicate. Family therapists seeking to emulate Satir's unique therapy style and interventions often have difficulty doing so. Moreover, researchers who have tried to identify the effective elements within her treatment approach have difficulty designing the research protocol because of the flexibility and variability of treatment delivery (Gurman & Kniskern, 1981b).

Like most therapists, Satir (1983) was interested in effective outcomes for family treatment. She believed that the therapist's answers to the following questions strongly influence the type of therapy provided:

- What causes family problems?
- What helps to resolve those problems?
- What helps people grow?

Satir sought answers to these questions and developed a model of treatment based upon those answers. She argued that family problems result when individuals are unable to establish the types of relationships they desire with the people who are most important to them. Specifically, Satir theorized that family relationships became dysfunctional because of an inability of the family members to communicate effectively with each other. Family problems are resolved when family members are able to honestly and openly relate to those who are important to them without fear of rejection and threat to their self-concepts. When family members communicate honestly and openly, self-awareness and individual growth is likely to occur. Satir believed these goals could be accomplished through therapy that emphasizes emotional encounters between the individuals in the family accompanied by the open discussion and resolution of important personal and family-related concerns that emerged through these encounters.

As a growth-oriented therapist, Satir did not believe that resolution of a presenting problem is sufficient. She believed that her therapy would be effective only if she were able to create an environment for the family that supported the continued positive growth of both the individuals and the relationships in the family.

Finally, in growth-oriented family therapy, the warmth and genuine caring of the therapist is particularly important. Satir was willing to risk herself in therapy, to be spontaneous, and to establish intimate contact with family members to support their growth and self-esteem. The use of self in this manner is unique to the humanistic approaches to family therapy. The techniques are not designed to achieve specific behavioral outcomes. Rather, therapy and the encounters that occur within the therapy are designed to help individuals become more self-aware, congruent, genuine, caring, and more capable of taking risks in their relationships with other family members.

Main Therapeutic Interventions

Because Virginia Satir held the optimistic worldview that individuals have within them the potential for growth and wholeness, her techniques and therapeutic interventions were designed to allow people to fully express their potential in relationships with other family members. This approach stresses individual growth and development within the context of the family. It encourages individuals to take risks, to openly express their feelings to those they care about, and to take responsibility for their own behavior. Specifically, Satir believed that growth can take place only when the family communicates effectively and is able to validate and enhance the self-worth of its members.

In her book, *The New Peoplemaking,* Satir (1988) described the family as a factory that is in the business of producing people. More specifically, she focused on the adults in the family as the *peoplemakers.* Thus, as the architects of the family, Satir placed special responsibility on the parents for nurturing their children and maintaining of an effective and loving family environment.

Families that selected Satir as their therapist tended to be experiencing problems in one or more of the following ways:

- Family members had low self-concepts.
- Family members were unable to honestly share thoughts and ideas.
- Communication was vague, indirect, and was not candid.
- Family rules were autocratically developed, rigidly enforced, and everlasting.
- The family's link to the societal system was based on fear, acquiescence, and blaming.

Using her creative, flexible, and humanistic growth-oriented approach to family therapy, Satir helped the family members develop increased self-worth; clear, direct, and honest communication; flexible and appropriate rules; and open and hopeful links to society (Satir, 1983).

Virginia Satir exemplified and modeled for her clients the characteristics she hoped to help them develop in therapy. Because she was warm and caring, her ability to develop meaningful relationships with family members was exceptional. Thus, she was able to ask important and possibly threatening questions of family members very early in the therapy process without jeopardizing the relationships she had developed and nurtured.

For instance, Satir might ask each family member how it felt to be a member of the family right now. With this type of question, Satir accomplished at least two goals: (1) She introduced affect, or feeling, to the therapy ("How does it feel?") and (2) she introduced the importance of immediate interaction in the *here and now*. Such questions elicit varied responses from family members that provide the therapist with data about the self-worth of members, communication within the family, family rules, and the family's link with society.

In *Conjoint Family Therapy,* Satir (1983) described in detail the role and functions of the therapist. To connect effectively with the family, the therapist must recognize that the family members will be fearful and unsure whether therapy will help or hurt their situation. They are afraid to ask questions of other family members and the therapist because they fear that they may learn things in therapy that they really do not want to know. This means that the therapist must be confident because *when the family is afraid, the therapist must be unafraid.*

The effective therapist must also have the ability to create an environment that permits family members to take the risk of looking clearly at themselves, their feelings, thoughts, behaviors, and interactions with other members. With this self-awareness, the family members are encouraged by the therapist and one another to use their feelings and thoughts to open productive dialogue with other members and to guide them in making changes to problematic behaviors. The confident therapist asks the questions necessary to allow the family members to experience and express this openness. The therapist is always supportive and sensitive to the risk the family members are taking as they disclose their feelings.

The effective therapist must be skilled at creating a therapeutic environment that supports and facilitates risk taking. Because all families are idiosyncratic, the therapist checks out all assumptions, including those made by family members and those of the therapist. The therapist gains the family's trust by being skilled in helping the family explore the thoughts, feelings, and behaviors of its members, as well as clarifying the family conflicts that exist but have not been clearly expressed.

Family functioning is guided by unspoken assumptions and implicit rules. The therapist plays the key role in creating a trusting environment to support the therapeutic process. Moreover, the therapist allows the family to develop confidence in the treatment by demonstrating to them that therapy has direction and purpose and by asking questions that elicit the information the therapist and family members need to bring about family growth and change. After ensuring that an effective therapeutic relationship has been established, the therapist continues to help family members examine themselves more objectively and talk to one another about what they are learning about themselves and about other members. Thus, the therapist encourages feedback among the family members about how each member may be experienced by others in the family. This feedback must be given in a helpful and nonjudgmental way, so family members are taught basic communication skills prior to this phase of therapy (Rogers, 1980). Most people do not receive direct, honest, and caring feedback in day-to-day living. Clients recognize this fact and usually appreciate the opportunity to receive honest and caring feedback from the therapist and other family members. When appropriate, the therapist provides the family with specific information about their interactional style and models effective communication by providing nonjudgmental feedback with clarification when needed.

Honest, caring, and nonjudgmental feedback from family members and therapist helps the family members heal and grow. A foundational principle of Satir's family therapy approach is that effective treatment must provide the opportunity for family members to grow and develop positive self-esteem. If family members are going to relate effectively to others and honestly present their own points of view, they must feel good about themselves and be confident in expressing their thoughts and feelings to other family members. In other words, they must have a strong sense of self-esteem. The self-esteem movement has received harsh criticism in recent years, as children now compete in sporting events where score is not kept in order to preserve self-esteem. Satir would have criticized this as well. Her notion of self-esteem centered on the ability of individuals to openly and honestly express themselves to family members and others persons of importance to them. She would not support the idea of artificially protecting individuals from life's inevitable struggles like experiencing failure. Learning to respond to life's disappointments is necessary in developing a strong self-concept.

The core of Satir's theory is based on the premise that effective therapy must help family members develop self-worth. To a accomplish this, family therapists employ these techniques (Satir, 1983):

- Making *I value you* comments to the client that have a basis in fact rather than kind but meaningless platitudes
- Identifying client strengths and reporting these to the client
- Asking the client questions that are in his area of expertise, thereby helping the client to demonstrate and feel competence
- Encouraging family members to ask for clarification if the therapist's communication or the communication of other family members is not clear
- Asking each family member to describe what she might do to bring happiness to other members

Building self-esteem is critical to the therapy. Satir's communications theory emphasizes the idea of the therapist and the family working together as a team to solve family problems. The therapist must be perceived as a knowledgeable expert who works at the same level as members of the family, cares for them, and helps them along rather than tells them how they should proceed.

The therapist also needs the ability to structure the therapy sessions. The therapist sets rules for therapy that encourage clients to listen to each other and respect the opinions of other members. For instance, an important therapy rule is that each person must speak for himself. Another important rule is that family members make *I want* statements so that they take full responsibility for what they communicate. Another important rule is that the family members refrain from activities that disrupt the therapy process. By providing this structure, family members will feel secure, realizing that the therapist has effective boundaries. This will hasten their trust and willingness to explore their issues in therapy and suggests a model the family may adopt in creating a structure for itself at the termination of therapy. In summary, the therapist structures the therapy sessions and sets rules and boundaries while at the same time remaining nonjudgmental and demonstrating care and warmth to the family members.

Satir's theory increases the self-esteem of family members through their development of effective communication skills. Once these skills are developed, they may be used to maintain and enhance self-esteem, negotiate family rules, and connect the family with the external social system. Satir (1988) developed a creative description of the types of dysfunctional communication patterns or styles that family members may adopt.

- *Placater*—People in this role strive to keep others from becoming upset. Placaters say, "Whatever." They tend to go along with others' desires and wants and appear to be fine on the surface. However, placaters actually feel that they are of no value and that they are unable to change.
- *Blamer*—People in this role communicate in a way that makes other people believe they are at fault or wrong and that the communicator is without fault and always correct. Blamers always seem to say, "You can't do anything right" and "I am perfect." In reality, they feel unsuccessful and lonely.
- *Computer*—People in this role communicate in a highly logical and overly reasonable way that takes the emotion out of any situation. They establish their self-worth by winning and out-thinking others. These "super-reasonable computers" appear calm and in control but use their style to cover the vulnerability and insecurity they feel in life.
- *Distracter*—People in this role attempt to move the focus of attention away from a potentially threatening issue to some irrelevant or tangential situation. Distracters use themselves to deflect attention from family problems. Distracters often seem flighty and scatterbrained, but inside they are sad and feel they are not valued or cared about.

The therapist teaches family members about these roles and the communication styles associated with the roles. The therapist encourages family members to identify which communication patterns they and others in their family use. The therapist then works with the family in developing ways to eliminate these ineffective styles and replace them with open, congruent, and direct communication.

Satir (1983) believed treatment should terminate when family members:

- can complete transactions and seek clarification without threat;
- can recognize hostility from others and reflect this interpretation to the sender;

- become able to understand how others view them;
- can provide nonblaming feedback to others about their behavior;
- can openly share hopes, fears, and expectations;
- can disagree;
- can make choices;
- can learn through practice;
- are no longer bound by past models and inappropriate rules; and
- can be congruent in communication with a minimum of hidden messages.

Satir used her unique communications model and personal style to help families develop these characteristics. She attempted to help families establish an environment that is a haven for nurturing children to develop into responsible persons with high self-esteem. She believed that effective communication is the most critical element in this process. Satir believed that the parents, as architects of the family, need to take responsibility for ensuring that healthy communication exists in the family. Many family therapists have lauded Virginia Satir as a therapist with a warm, humanistic approach to treatment who brought a breath of fresh air to a profession dominated by technique-oriented theories.

Strengths of Satir's Communications Theory

Satir's approach to family therapy is one of the most widely accepted by therapists who are trained in individual psychotherapy because it has the stated goal of increasing the self-worth of the individual family members. Increased self-worth is often one of the chief goals of individually-oriented counseling theories. Thus, a major strength of this approach is that it is readily accepted by therapists working with individuals and is an excellent first theory for counselors to employ in family therapy. Other strengths of the approach are the following:

- It emphasizes the therapist's personhood. Family therapists are more than well-trained technicians. They are warm, caring, and empathic to the needs of the family.
- It recognizes and responds to the feelings of individual members of the family in treatment. Identification and exploration of feelings is an important component of the therapy.
- It recognizes the importance of excellent communication skills in acknowledging family members' feelings. By openly recognizing and

CASE EXAMPLE

Satir's Communication Theory

Mr. and Mrs. Smith sought family therapy because their daughter was experiencing feelings of hopelessness about her future. The therapist requested that the entire family come for the initial sessions. At the first session, all members were present. Mr. Smith was a successful systems analyst for a data-processing firm. Mrs. Smith was a homemaker with numerous interests and talents in the arts. Debby, the IP, was 15 years old and had average grades as well as a tremendous drive to play basketball, which her parents did not support. John was 7 years old. The family members viewed him as being very cute and not part of the problem.

The therapist began by gathering information about the family and how it resolved issues. During the information-gathering period, the therapist worked to develop the self-concept of each family member by identifying their strengths. The therapist introduced the concept of communication styles and asked the family members to evaluate their styles. Dad was found to be a super-reasonable computer, Mom was a placater trying to make everyone else happy at her own expense, Debby was a blamer who was angry at Dad for not encouraging her in her sports activity, and John was a distracter who could be counted on to be cute whenever family tensions increased.

Once the therapist helped the members recognize their communication styles, work began on developing effective communication patterns. As communication improved, Mom, Dad, Debby, and John expressed their hidden feelings, and Debby's symptoms of depression lifted. Mom became less concerned with making the family run smoothly and began to develop her artistic interests. Dad became more playful and had less need to analyze the feelings of family members. Finally, John remained cute, but his cuteness was no longer needed to distract family members from emerging issues in the family.

responding to feelings using healthy communication patterns, family members gain more respect from others and a heightened sense of self-worth. This increased self-worth through effective communication leads to a healthier family.

Limitations of Satir's Communications Theory

The major limitation of Satir's approach to family therapy is that, although her charismatic style of treatment has attracted thousands of students, the approach remains uniquely Satir's. Her personal ability to connect with each family member in her own warm, loving, and nurturing way had a major influence on the family's ability to change in treatment. Because the success of treatment relies heavily on the therapist's personality, training therapists in this approach may be difficult. Thus, the major limitation of Satir's growth-oriented approach to family therapy is that it is not a systematic method for family treatment that other therapists can easily replicate (Gurman & Kniskern, 1981b).

Whitaker's Symbolic–Experiential Family Therapy

Carl Whitaker (1918–1995), a psychiatrist, had been active in family therapy before its formal recognition in the early 1950s. He developed and refined his model of family therapy, called symbolic–experiential family therapy (Whitaker & Keith, 1981), through collaboration with several colleagues, including David Keith and Augustus Napier. Previously trained as an obstetrician/gynecologist, Whitaker was board certified in psychiatry during World War II. His early experience was as a psychiatric administrator at a small hospital, and he later received training in child guidance and play therapy. He treated family members separately, as was the practice in those days.

Whitaker said he began to formulate ideas about mental illness and its treatment because of what he learned from his early experiences as a psychiatrist. In his work with patients, Whitaker noticed that his interventions were most effective when he acted *spontaneously* and *genuinely* in a situation presented by a patient rather than when he attempted to intervene based on some theoretical construct. Thus, Whitaker began to hypothesize that change is the result of *client and family experiences* that take place both within and outside the therapy sessions rather than therapeutic education and clinical wisdom dispensed by the therapist.

A classic example of the development of Whitaker's experience-based model occurred when he used a baby bottle left by a previous client's child as a prop that he presented to nurture subsequent adult patients who were expressing child-like responses to the dilemmas they were facing. This "technique" provided a unique, and perhaps startling, experience for Whitaker's clients. This experiential intervention was effective for patients with all sorts of problems as long as Whitaker was invested in the notion of nurturing the clients. As he began to move on to other ideas about treatment, the baby-bottle experience became ineffective.

In a second classic example, Whitaker became bored and dozed off during an interview with a client. When he awoke he apologized but reported that the clients must not be talking about their most relevant issues or he would not have become bored and dozed off. He used his experience to provide feedback to the client and shared his dream as a part of the therapeutic process. This intervention proved valuable when it was a spontaneous and experiential part of treatment. But when it became a therapeutic technique to be taught to others, it lost its effectiveness.

As with many of the family therapy pioneers, Whitaker began to formulate ideas about family interaction in psychopathology based on work with schizophrenic patients and their families. His most widely recognized work began at Emory University in Atlanta, Georgia, and was continued when he accepted a position at the School of Medicine at the University of Wisconsin in 1965. As one of the senior members of the family therapy profession, Whitaker was a sought-after speaker and conducted numerous workshops throughout the country and the world.

Philosophical Tenets and Key Theoretical Constructs

Some professionals question classifying symbolic–experiential family therapy as a humanistic theory. Whitaker believed that theory itself can be harmful to clients because it allows the therapist to remain removed from the intimate contact he believed necessary for therapeutic change (Whitaker, 1976). Thus, Whitaker's approach to family therapy may be viewed as a moment-to-moment encounter with the family based on the *therapist's own experience* as well as caring for the family members. This moment-to-moment nature of symbolic–experiential therapy, coupled with the importance Whitaker placed on the therapist's ability to become genuinely involved with the family, leads to the classification of this "non-theory" in the humanistic grouping.

Key tenets of symbolic–experiential family therapy are developed with caution because therapists using this approach do not want to establish a set of rules for therapy. Rather, this theory is constantly open to change and depends ultimately on the therapist's intuition and understanding of family problems and systemic interactions between and among the family members. Whitaker and Keith (1981) identified key tenets of this treatment model in their description of the healthy family. Family health is a process of perpetual becoming, and healthy families are constantly evolving. Therapy is designed to help families develop the following qualities of family health:

- The healthy family is able to use constructive negative input to improve functioning.
- A healthy family is composed of three generations that maintain healthy separation and autonomy.
- Family roles are flexible, and members are encouraged to exchange roles and explore various family roles.
- The distribution of power in a family is flexible.
- Healthy families develop an "as if" structure that allows tremendous latitude in behaviors tolerated in the family.
- Family members are free to behave temporarily in irrational ways without being viewed as permanently deviant by the family.
- The healthy family continues to grow despite adversities.
- The healthy family develops a functional reality about itself that is evolutionary and changes as necessary.
- Healthy families are not symptom free; rather, they are able to deal with inevitable problems and challenges as part of family growth and development.
- Problems with children are opportunities for parents to look at themselves and determine how they will grow from the challenge. Whitaker believed that parents get the children they need to help then develop as parents and as individuals.
- Healthy families are aware of the stresses each member experiences.

- Healthy families do not permanently focus on the anxiety and problems of one member. The IP in a healthy family moves from person to person rather than remaining fixed on one member.
- Healthy families change through crisis.
- Healthy families encourage expression of both positive and negative feelings. Children and parents should know they are loved and hated.
- In a healthy family, intimacy and separateness go hand in hand. Members are free to be both intimate and distant as required to meet individual needs.
- The healthy family encourages and supports outside relationships for its members.

In summary, Whitaker's followers support maximum autonomy for their clients in therapy so each can experience a full range of human behaviors in family life. They encourage individuals to be serious as well as foolish to know that they can *choose* to be either, and to know that this *ability to choose* is healthy. They encourage families to experience both pain and joy in family living and to grow from those experiences. Families that are unable grow and change in response to their experiences are most likely to need and to seek therapy at some point in their development.

Main Therapeutic Interventions

The major goals of symbolic–experiential family therapy are to increase members' sense of belonging to the family and at the same time to create the opportunity for the members to individuate from the family. This objective can be accomplished by developing and exercising the creativity of the family in dealing with problems. To achieve these goals with a family in distress, certain therapeutic techniques may be employed. Mediating goals and ultimate goals are part of this theory. *Mediating goals* create a therapeutic environment, and the therapist and the family select *ultimate goals* to be attained through treatment (Roberto, 1991).

The Battle for Structure and Initiative

Two "battles" are typically waged as family treatment begins. The first, the *battle for structure,* must be won by the therapist. The battle for structure begins when the client family attempts to tell the therapist what is wrong in the family, what should be done about it, and who should be treated. The battle for structure begins with the first telephone contact between the therapist and a family spokesperson. To be effective, the therapist needs to be respectful of the predictable attempts by the family to organize and control the course of therapy. However, the therapist also knows that effective family therapy will only occur if the therapist is in charge of and manages the structure of therapy and the treatment plan. If the therapist gives up this role and loses this battle, the family will bring the same ineffective patterns and attempted solutions to the therapy that are fundamental in sustaining the problems in the family.

The symbolic–experiential therapist must be able to determine the unit of treatment, which for Whitaker was usually the entire family. If the client family resists this requirement for therapy, the therapist must be prepared to stand firm and be willing to refer the client to another therapist if the client rejects the proposed structure. Until the battle for structure is resolved, further therapeutic work cannot be accomplished, as the therapist and family will be engaged in a struggle for control rather than working together in a collaborative fashion to resolve the family's problems. Therapy cannot be effective until the family has decided to trust the therapist and give the therapist responsibility for structuring the therapy. Winning the battle for structure and control is paradoxical, however, because when the therapist has won the battle, she will frequently defer to the family members' wishes about what they want to do to help improve the family (Napier & Whitaker, 1978).

The second battle to be contested is the *battle for initiative*. This battle must be won by the family. Any initiative for change must come from, as well as be supported and maintained by, the family. The therapist cannot ultimately be responsible for the choices the family members make. Initially, members depend on the therapist and become reliant on the therapist's leadership. The therapist must reject this leadership role and instead support family members in making their own decisions about how to change the way problems are handled in their family.

These two critical battles uniformly occur in the initial stage of family therapy, and successful resolution is essential to an effective therapeutic outcome. The therapist must be in charge of therapy, and the clients must be in charge of the changes they will or will not make (Napier & Whitaker, 1978).

Cotherapy

Because symbolic–experiential family therapists become so intensely involved in their relationships with family members, a cotherapist is important for effective treatment to occur. Whitaker would often pay attention to his own experiencing of the family members in the immediacy of the moment and react to the family from his gut level. More often than not, Whitaker's experiential here-and-now reactions and interventions were therapeutic. On occasion, however, the therapist may become inappropriately involved with the family members and unable to withdraw from the intensity of the interaction.

At times like this, the cotherapist, who is also trained in this model of family treatment, intervenes and directs therapy while the other therapist regains perspective on what has occurred. The cotherapist in this situation might ask the other therapist and the family member involved in the exchange to describe what happened and use that interaction for growth for the family and the therapist alike. Using the experience and awareness gained from interactions in the immediate moment in the therapy is a necessary element of the change process according to Whitaker. Families (and therapists) have to be in the perpetual process of learning and growing (Rogers, 1980). They must be self-aware and able to make changes based on their life and therapeutic experiences (Napier & Whitaker, 1978).

Another reason to use cotherapy, according to Whitaker, is that healthy interactions between the cotherapists provide a model for family members to emulate. Cotherapists can support each other, disagree, be confused, teach each other, and engage in many functional behaviors. Observing this behavior is almost always helpful for the family (Whitaker & Keith, 1981).

Techniques

Whitaker and Keith (1981) described several specific techniques employed in symbolic–experiential family therapy. It is essential for the reader to remember that these therapeutic techniques will be useful only insofar as they function to create significant learning moments that promote deeper experiencing and lead to growth, self-awareness, and change.

- *Redefine symptoms as efforts for growth.* Family members enter therapy with complaints about the other members. The therapists redefine these painful or disruptive behaviors as signs that the family has reached a point in its development that requires growth and change in all members. For instance, the father may report that his son is neglecting his chores and behaving rudely at home. The therapist might suggest that the son is merely trying to get the parents to grow in their relationship and work together in their efforts to discipline him.

- *Teach family members to use fantasy alternatives rather than real-life behaviors.* For example, if a rebellious adolescent reports wanting to kill his "perfect" older sister, the therapist might ask the youth how he would do the deed and how it would help his situation. Thus, the youth's thoughts would not be considered precursors to an actual murder, because this matter of fact approach generally reveals that the threat is not real but the young man's expression of his own pain and dissatisfaction. Thus, rather than the family overreacting and perhaps hospitalizing the youth, the family learns that crazy thoughts do not necessarily mean that irrational behavior will follow. Whitaker believed that by accepting the violent or bizarre thoughts and encouraging the verbal expression of the fantasy, the need to turn the thought into action is dissipated. Confronting violent thoughts in family members is a difficult yet essential task and requires a confident and skillful therapist to perform the intervention effectively.

- *Assign homework that directs family members to change roles.* As family members change roles, they experience increased autonomy and flexibility in the family. Role changes, like father and son changing roles at dinner, with the son asking everyone about the day and the father focused on eating quickly in order to call a friend, break up rigid patterns in the family, allow the family to experience itself differently, and may support changes based on that experience.

- *Do not talk about the family therapy interviews between sessions.* Talking about the session between meetings depletes the emotional intensity of the family members. For symbolic–experiential family therapy to be most effective, this emotional intensity has to be present during the therapy session. This rule is important for cotherapists as well. Therapists are advised not to talk about the family during the week or in meetings before the session begins, as doing so will drain the therapists' energy from the previous encounter with the family and render them less effective.

- *Augment the despair of family members.* Family members are often at a loss about what to do when family members are feeling pain, fear, or sadness. Most therapists simply want the family members to feel better, and they do what they can to make it so. The symbolic–experiential therapist takes a counterintuitive position and employs interventions that intensifying the despair the family members feel. This demonstrates to family members that the therapist will not deflect the family member's pain and has the ability to go with the client through her despair. When a family member genuinely reveals intense pain, sadness, or fear to the family, this new experience prompts family members respond in new and more effective ways in supporting its members.

It is common for family members to rally together to provide support that was not present before. Whitaker emphasized that despair is a part of family life, and it must be acknowledged and respected. This concept is very difficult for most families and many therapists to grasp. Whitaker reminded us, family members and therapists alike, that denial of negative feelings leads to intensified family problems. Troubled families simply want everyone to feel better and frequently try to bury pain rather than encourage its expression and resolution. Symbolic–experiential family therapy is designed to help families uncover the pain, express it openly, and, through this experience, develop new and more effective ways of responding to the pain and supporting its members.

- *Engage in affective confrontation.* At times, the therapist will feel genuine affect, positive or negative feelings, toward family members based on their behaviors. The symbolic–experiential therapist confronts the family with this affective reaction. For example, a child may begin dismantling the therapist's office, and the parents may be ineffective in stopping the child's behavior. The therapist may say angrily, "Stop destroying my property and sit in your chair, now!" The child—and, perhaps more important, the parents—would experience and assimilate this affective confrontation, which could lead to the parents and child choosing to change their behavior patterns. The therapist's genuine reaction is grist for the mill in therapy and almost always leads to a discussion of what precipitated the therapist's reaction and how family members and the cotherapist felt about it. Most important, this discussion would help determine what, if anything, might be learned and what changes might be made by therapists and family members alike from the affective confrontation.

- *Treat children as children and not as peers.* This important principle states that family generational differences and boundaries must be acknowledged and respected at certain times. When children are treated as peers, an increasingly common situation in today's modern families, problems of discipline and family organization can emerge, because no clear leadership exists within the family to support family rules and expected behavior. By recognizing generational differences, the parents may win a "battle for structure" in their own family and develop a sense of order based on appropriate and flexible parental authority.

Symbolic–experiential family therapy is designed to support change in families through experiential interactions between family members and therapists. The therapy is designed to create new experiences for the family that offer the members the opportunity to respond in new and more effective ways to these experiences. It is essential to remember that symbolic–experiential family therapy is not about adhering to specific theoretical tenets or interventions. The cotherapy team along with the family members will create new situations that require spontaneous reactions with the expectation that new learning will take place.

Symbolic–experiential family therapy relies heavily on the therapists' judgments about and reactions to what is taking place within the family at any given moment. Because of the experiential nature of the therapy and the possibility of error even with a cotherapist present, Whitaker and Keith (1981) listed principles designed to help the cotherapists avoid errors:

- Do not become so connected with the family that it affects your ability to help.
- Do not become so aloof from the family that you operate as a technician rather than a compassionate human being.
- Do not pretend that you are immune to feelings of stress and inadequacy. Be genuine.
- Do not employ a technique for change if it will only create another serious problem in another family member.
- Move at the appropriate pace for the family.
- Do not expect insight to produce change. Insights must be acknowledged by the therapist and family members with the question, "How will this new awareness make a difference for your family?"
- Do not expect the family to operate from your value system.
- Do not revere your intuitive leaps. Intuition is only intuition, and it may not be appropriate for the family. If the family resists, back off

quickly. Use your cotherapist to help in the retreat and to move to a more productive area for discussion.

- Recognize when you have the family's trust. If you do not, you may waste time in the relationship-building phase when the family is ready to work.
- Do not create a new scapegoat in the family. Help the family understand that each person has a part in maintaining the problems.
- Realize the benefits of *not treating* someone. Not all families need therapy, and not all families will benefit from therapy.

Three-Generation Therapy

When therapy reaches an impasse, the symbolic–experiential therapist may attempt to break the impasse by inviting the older generation to participate in therapy to help unlock the process (Napier & Whitaker, 1978). The grandparents are not invited to therapy as clients but, rather, as consultants to help the cotherapists and family members break the impasse that has developed. The insights the grandparents bring to therapy frequently uncover a whole new arena of experience for the parents and the children to consider and promote additional family growth and development.

Strengths of the Symbolic–Experiential Approach

Symbolic–experiential family therapy as practiced by Whitaker and his colleagues has several important strengths. First, it fully recognizes the power of a family in maintaining its dysfunctional behavior patterns and the necessity for using a cotherapy team for work with families. Furthermore, Whitaker recognized the importance of the therapist's winning the battle for structure so the therapist, not the family, is in charge of how treatment shall proceed. Finally, this approach, more than any other, encourages the therapist to be spontaneous and creative in introducing new experiences to bring about family change.

Weaknesses of the Symbolic–Experiential Approach

The major limitation of this approach is that it lacks a systematic theoretical base for replication of the interventions in treatment. Because treatment in symbolic–experiential therapy is based primarily on the experiences and immediate reactions of the cotherapy team to the family members, no specific treatment interventions are suggested to intervene

CASE EXAMPLE

Whitaker's Symbolic–Experiential Family Therapy

Mrs. Green called to set up an appointment for her 12-year-old son, who was regularly truant from school. She wanted the therapist to work with her son for a while, and then she wanted to join the process. The therapist stated that he would need to see the entire family for his initial evaluation. Mrs. Green protested, and the therapist offered to give her the names of some therapists who would see the boy alone. Mrs. Green said she wanted to work with this therapist because he had been highly recommended by a trusted friend, so she would comply with his desire to see the whole family.

The first few sessions were devoted to learning about the family and the problems with the son, James, and winning the battle for structure. When the family began to trust the cotherapy team to direct therapy, the next phase of treatment began.

In the second phase of treatment, the therapists began to challenge the family's reality of James being the problem and suggested that the entire family seemed to be experiencing a problem. The therapist's challenge caused the family members to become defensive and angry. They were not the problem—it was James! The therapist used this in-session emotional experience to ask each family member what they should do to calm their emotions and improve family functioning. This gave each family member the opportunity to acknowledge immediate in-session feelings and to offer suggestions about how they could be more effective as a unit. The experience created by the therapist's challenge to the family produced the energy to make this growth step possible.

James's behavior was defined as his attempt to point out to the entire family that growth and changes were needed by all members. The rest of this phase of therapy was devoted to helping the family members discover what they needed to change about themselves to increase family intimacy while allowing and encouraging autonomy. As therapy progressed, James's truancy stopped and the family began redefining what members of the family should reasonably be expected to do. This process was handled with little assistance from the therapists, who suggested that the family was doing well on its own and that termination was in order.

in specific situations. Thus, the ability of other therapists to replicate this treatment approach is questionable. At best, therapists may attempt to develop their own version of this approach. Because of the difficulty in standardizing treatment from this approach, it is highly unlikely that symbolic–experiential family therapy could be rigorously investigated through controlled studies. Thus, this approach in not an evidence-supported treatment.

Another weakness of this approach is based on Whitaker's belief that the family system is more powerful than the cotherapy team and therefore ineffective treatment is unlikely to harm the family. Whitaker believed that the family unit is a powerful entity and is capable of growth but is unlikely to regress. The findings of research reviewed by Gurman and Kniskern (1978a & b) reported that ineffective treatment can make families worse. A final weakness of this family therapy model is that, although much has been written about symbolic–experiential family therapy, the claims of this approach have little empirical support in the literature.

White and Epston's Narrative Therapy

Many family therapists have heralded narrative therapy as the answer to the question, "How can we do in-depth family therapy with clients under the constraints of short-term managed care regulations?" Managed care insurance companies restrict the number of therapy sessions that will be funded. In-depth therapy typically exceeded the session limits imposed by the insurance companies until the narrative approach was introduced.

Narrative therapy developed primarily by Australian Michael White (1948–2008) and New Zealander David Epston. It is a postmodern constructivist approach to therapy that helps clients examine their family histories and the significant past experiences that impact how they function in the present. It helps clients consider how they came to possess the knowledge they have about themselves, their families, and their environment. The model holds great promise in helping family members do in-depth family therapy in relatively few sessions, thus meeting the session limitations set by managed care health insurance companies.

Philosophical Tenets and Key Theoretical Constructs

Narrative therapy is a postmodern, constructivist approach to helping people change. As a postmodern approach, narrative therapy is based on the tenet that our realities are *constructed* through the language we use in day-to-day discourse. Language is central in our lives because it shapes our identities as individuals and the way we know ourselves and our strengths and vulnerabilities. Moreover, our language defines what we and our clients identify as problems for therapy and what are not problems (Anderson, 1997). Narrative therapy is a constructivist approach because it is based on the premise that all truths and realities are *constructed* by individuals based on considerations that include (Gehart, 2010):

- their use of language,
- how personal meaning is created by an individual,
- how meaning is created through relationships, and
- how society and larger social systems contribute to creation of truth and meaning.

Narrative therapy is included in this chapter describing humanistic interpersonal family systems therapies because of the importance of the relationship between the therapist and the client. It is particularly relevant because of the importance of meaning creation as clients recreate their life narrative in a way that emphasizes strengths and positive personal qualities and that identifies how the client has been successful in dealing with presenting problems in the past. Rewriting the client's life narrative in a way that emphasizes success and strength is central to this theory.

Narrative therapy has been embraced by therapists who are guided by social justice maxims and recognize the inequalities among diverse groups within society. Narrative therapy recognizes that there are dominant discourses and local discourses in problem formation and problem resolution. *Dominant discourses* are rules of the road or the common knowledge that is adopted and accepted by the larger society and serves to set guidelines for social behavior. For example, the dominant discourse establishes what constitutes a healthy marriage, how children should behave, and how people are able to achieve success. Dominant discourses serve as a foundation for how people should behave in society and are often taken for granted (Gehart, 2010). *Local discourses* are knowledge that is private and conceptualized within the minds of individuals and diverse groups about themselves and their relationships to each other and society. Local discourses are behaviors that may not be consistent with those of the dominant culture but are accepted and valued in a minority cultural group. For example, ceremonies and rituals that are employed by Native Americans are accepted within their culture but may be foreign or unacceptable to the dominant culture.

Narrative therapists recognize the validity of both the dominant and local discourses within their respective contexts and further recognize that the dominant discourses are more widely recognized and accepted than local discourses. Narrative therapists and social justice advocates have identified the dominant discourse as being *privileged* over local discourses. By that they mean that the realties of local discourse concerning what is good and bad and what should and should not be done may conflict with the principles embedded in the dominant discourse. In such cases, the knowledge of the dominant discourse is given higher stature or is privileged compared to the local discourse. When an individual or family from a minority background is operating in a larger social context by adopting behaviors based on local knowledge, they may be perceived as rejecting the dominant, privileged discourse and may suffer consequences for their behaviors. For example, prior to the women's movement, the dominant and privileged discourse was that a woman should remain at home and care for the children. Within certain groups, a local discourse emerged avowing that women could and should contribute in more ways than as a homemaker. The first women to challenge the dominant discourse were criticized and mocked. However, through their persistence, the discourse is evolving and women are accepted both in the workplace and as homemakers.

Narrative therapists are experts at helping their clients develop an understanding of the impact of dominant social discourses on members of communities that operate from local discourses. This unique feature of narrative therapy makes it especially relevant for providing help to minority group families (White & Epston 1990).

The principles of narrative therapy are straightforward, yet, like most therapies, they are difficult to implement without competent training and clinical practice. Narrative therapy is an approach that focuses on individual client narratives or life stories. The approach often includes other family members in the treatment, because an individual's narrative is embedded in the narratives of other family members. As clients write a new narrative, the support of all family members is necessary to ensure the new narrative is reinforced and privileged. Some sessions may be conducted with only the identified client present while other sessions include family members.

The narrative therapist establishes a warm, caring relationship with the client and family members and facilitates the client's descriptions of her concerns, how the concerns developed over the client's life, and how the problems have affected the client and client's family. Through this process, the client is creating a *narrative* that uses language to construct and describe a personal life story for the therapist. The telling of the client's narrative life story will include the precipitating elements of the problem situation. Also embedded in the client's telling of the narrative will be explanations rooted in the past that bring into focus how the past has influenced and maintained the client's present symptoms and current difficulties with life.

Through a series of steps that will be described in detail later, the narrative therapist assists the client in developing new language that *externalizes* the problem so the problem, not the client, is understood as the reason for treatment. Many clients, along with other family members, enter therapy using language describing the client as the problem. The skillful therapist must alter this view if the narrative approach is to be successful. The problem must not be the client. Instead, the problem is the impact of forces that are external to the client on the client's life.

After the client accepts the postmodern creation of the externalized problem, the narrative therapist helps the client reconstruct her life story by emphasizing and punctuating the narrative in new ways, using different language that identifies the client's positive characteristics and strengths rather than problems. Other family members may be included in this process to affirm the client's strengths. Narrative therapists call the reconstruction and retelling of the client's narrative *reauthoring*. As the client and family members come to accept the reauthored narrative, significant life changes become possible and often occur (White & Epston 1990).

Narrative therapists have great respect for the client's past. By revealing his history, the client begins to realize he has strengths and abilities that were previously unrecognized. Moreover, the client finds that he has the personal power to reshape his life and to begin to live in new, more productive ways. Unlike psychodynamic theories, which assume that problems are the result of internal personality difficulties, narrative therapy helps the client look at the larger ecological system consisting of dominant and local discourses as well as all other forces, past and present, that have shaped the individual and family's attitudes and behaviors.

Narrative theory assumes that clients adopt identities and behaviors based on numerous life influences. These influences define a *problem-focused identity* because clients assume that societal norms, family members' rules and opinions, and influences from other important relationships have the power and authority to define what is good or bad and what is a psychological problem. Narrative therapy helps clients understand the forces that have affected them over the years and make conscious choices to reshape and redefine their responses to these influences (White, 1986).

Externalization of problems is one of the keys to successful narrative therapy. *Externalization* is the fundamental understanding that the "person is never the problem; the problem is the problem" (O'Hanlon, 1994, p. 23). Through the therapy process, usually based on a series of specific questions, clients come to recognize that they are not the problem but that some external forces are influencing them to behave, think, and feel in ways that are unproductive. Externalization (White, 1986) of the problem gives clients a sense of their own personal worth as well as creating an active adversary to fight against—the externalized problem. The therapist enlists other family members in recognizing the externalized problem and in helping the client combat it (White & Epston 1990). For example, a client may enter therapy believing she is a depressed person. The narrative therapist works with the client to help her understand that she has been influenced by societal messages to believe she is a depressed person and that she is the problem. In reality, however, the "forces of depression" are working on the client, and these forces of depression are the problem, not the client herself. Family members are also enlisted to help support the externalized problem and to help the client fight against it.

When clients realize that they are not the problem, they come to understand that they need to develop new responses to combat the problem. Once they gain this important insight, powerful and creative responses are possible. Externalization puts clients in the position of being responsible and accountable for the choices they make in responding to the problem. In the example above, the client might be asked how depression has been controlling her life. Then the therapist might ask what the client could do to fight depression and keep it from ruling her. This type of *narrative questioning* empowers the client and shows respect for the client's ability to respond in effective ways to the problem (O'Hanlon, 1994). In summary, the key element of this theory is the ability to separate, through the use of language, the problem from the client's personal identity. When family members are effective contributors to the therapy, they reinforce the separation of the problem from the client.

Continuing to use the "forces of depression" as the problem, Freedman and Combs (1996) developed the following externalizing narrative questions to help clients separate themselves as individuals from the problems that have troubled them.

- What made you vulnerable to the forces of depression so that they were able to dominate your life?
- In what situations are the forces of depression most likely to take over?
- What types of things usually happen that allow the forces of depression to take over?
- What have the forces of depression influenced you to do against your better judgment?
- What effects do the forces of depression have on your present life and relationships?
- How have the forces of depression led you to the difficulties you are now experiencing?
- How are you able to see your strengths and resources when the forces of depression are attacking you?
- Tell me about the times when you have been able to get the better of the forces of depression, times when forces of depression could have taken over but you kept them out of the picture.

Each of these questions serves to externalize the problem of depression and attempt to help the client recognize times that she was able to overcome the externalized problem. Of course, the narrative therapist will continue to emphasize the times that the client is successful in overcoming the problem while minimizing those times when the client was not successful. Once again, family participation in validating the new narrative and responding to the client in ways identified by the new narrative help to enhance growth and change.

O'Hanlon (1994) listed the following fundamental steps in the narrative approach:

1. Establish collaborative relationships with the client and family.
2. Have all members mutually agree upon a name for the problem. For example, a depressed mother might name the depression "Agony."
3. Personify and externalize the problem—give it its own identity—and attribute oppressive characteristics to it. For example, Agony is

identified as a powerful entity that steals the client's pleasant memories and time with family members.

4. Investigate how the problem has been disruptive, dominating, and discouraging for the client and the family. For example, ask family members to describe how Agony has disrupted their lives and been a demoralizing factor for the family. This description encourages the family to mobilize resources to combat Agony. Do not use the *linear causality* model by suggesting that the problem "causes" client behaviors. The force of the problem only influences, tricks, confuses, or tries to recruit the client into certain unproductive actions, thoughts, or feelings. The language used in narrative questioning must employ the *circular causality* model by emphasizing the client's choices in response to the problem.

5. Discover, through narrative questioning, moments when the problem has not dominated or discouraged the family members. For example, ask the client in this situation to describe the longest period she has not been influenced by depression. By identifying times when she is symptom free—which are exceptions to the rule of being depressed—the client begins to understand that she has power over the problem in some situations. Next, seek ways to help the client develop power over the problem in most situations.

6. Discover historical evidence to support and reinforce the view that the client is competent enough to have stood up to, defeated, or escaped from the dominance of the problem. In this stage of the therapy, the client begins to rewrite her life story through narrative. The therapist and the client *deconstruct*, by taking apart the previous narrative and reconstructing a reality very different from the one that brought the client to therapy. In this newly discovered reality, the client is competent and powerful and able to respond effectively to the problem. The therapist might ask, "As you continue to overcome the forces of depression, tell me how your life will be different from the one that Agony had planned for you?"

7. The narrative therapist is a coauthor to both the IP and the family members. The therapist asks the family members to speculate on their future in a family with a strong, competent person who is able to overcome the forces of the problem. This speculating becomes the family's reauthoring of the *family's narrative reality* and reinforces the reauthoring accomplished by the IP through the process of therapy.

8. Narrative therapists recognize that the new narrative must be supported and reinforced in order to endure. Therefore, narrative therapists help families establish *communities of concern* to help the IP continue to be successful in overcoming the forces of the externalized problems. Communities of concern provide an audience for the client that will support and reinforce the new life story and the new identity created by this story. Because problems develop in social contexts, it is important for the client to be in a context that supports the reauthored life script. Involving family members and others close to the client is one way of developing the new audience and the community of concern.

9. The therapist must involve the family members in a thorough discussion about how they will continue to live according to their new life story in support of the IP's new narrative. This discussion is a critical part of the termination phase of the narrative approach.

The Use of Therapeutic Letters

Epston (1994) found that narrative conversations with clients may be extended by the use of therapeutic letters to the clients that may be reread days, weeks, months, or years after the therapy has terminated to reinforce the new narrative. Epston (1994) suggested that therapists use a letter to the family after most sessions. In addition to reinforcing the new narrative explored in therapy, the letter provides clients and the therapist with a record of what has occurred in treatment in previous sessions and provides a baseline of information to work from in future sessions. Although letters are initially time consuming, with practice and effective in-session note taking, most therapists can write a meaningful letter in about 30 minutes (Epston, 1994).

Nylund and Thomas (1994) conducted research concerning the efficacy of therapeutic letters. In a survey of 40 clients, 37 respondents found them to be "very useful" and three found them to be "useful." The "average worth" of one letter was 3.2 sessions. The clients believed that more than 50% of the gains in therapy were a result of the letters alone. The average length of therapy was 4.5 sessions. These results strongly suggest that therapeutic letters are powerful tools and clients as a whole support the use of letters in narrative and other therapies.

Nylund and Thomas (1994) proposed a format for therapeutic letters to help the novice begin using this powerful tool. They suggested the following four areas to be covered in the letter:

1. In an introductory paragraph, join with the clients and reconnect them to the therapy process.
2. Record statements that define how the problem is influencing the client and reinforce the concept of externalization of the problem.
3. Ask questions that could have been asked during the session but were not. For example: "I wish I had asked which of your family and friends will be most likely to support the changes you have made in resisting the influence of depression."
4. Document and reinforce elements of the session that show the client as competent and able to resist the influences of the problem. The focus on client strengths in the letter helps the client maintain changes by the rereading the letter between sessions.

Obviously, letters to clients are not a panacea. But they offer the therapist an additional avenue of intervention and support for client change.

Strengths of Narrative Therapy

Narrative therapy offers an answer to the therapist's dilemma of how to attend to the client's past and yet focus on present change. Through the use of narrative, language, and the reauthoring of client life stories, significant changes may be made in relatively brief therapeutic encounters. The therapist is able to work with the client as a colleague, supported by family members and other communities of concern in this process and does not have to take a more powerful and directive position in the therapy. The skillful use of powerful questions helps the IP and the family members deconstruct their previous unhappy narrative and reauthor a new and more effective one. The use of postsession letters to reinforce the gains made in therapy is an important intervention and one that might be employed in other approaches. Narrative therapy is particularly appropriate for use with minority cultures, as it clearly recognizes the impact of privilege associated with dominant discourses on cultures that operate from local discourses.

Limitations of Narrative Therapy

Criticisms of the narrative approach suggest that the postmodern constructivist approach denies the existence of absolute truth and emphasizes

CASE EXAMPLE

Narrative Therapy

The Albertson family entered therapy because their son was anxious and fearful in most situations and was unwilling to go to school or to other places where he would be with strangers. The therapist used standard techniques in joining with family members. In the joining process, he had the family members come up with a name for the anxiety. The family called the anxiety "Mr. Fear." This personalization of the anxiety began the process of externalizing the problem.

In the next phase of treatment, the therapist asked family members questions demonstrating that the problem, Mr. Fear, was oppressive and was creating havoc for the IP and family members. Next, the therapist investigated with the family the many ways in which the problem was disruptive to the family. All members were able to list several ways the externalized problem had adversely affected the family, and all agreed that the forces of Mr. Fear were great and very disruptive.

In the next phase of the narrative, family members were asked to identify times when Mr. Fear had not been influencing the family and the client had been able to withstand the power of the problem. This created a situation in which the IP and family members began to focus on times when the client and the family had been able to function in the face of the problem. If the problem had been successfully defeated in the past, perhaps this could be done again in the future. The family was asked to record specific instances in their history when Mr. Fear was not in control and to discuss how the family worked to make such times happen.

Continuing the narrative approach, the therapist asked family members to speculate on how the family's life would be different without the power and influence of Mr. Fear. The family responded quickly to ways they would be more productive and able to focus their energies on projects that up to now were impossible to contemplate.

Finally, the therapist and the family searched for ways to create a context that would support the newly developed narrative suggesting that the client and the family could make choices that

(continued)

Narrative Therapy *(continued)*

would defeat the influence and tricks of Mr. Fear. This context or audience is crucial to reinforcing and maintaining the new narrative.

A few weeks after termination of therapy, the therapist sent the family a letter outlining the process of the therapy and specifically reminding the IP and family members what they did to overcome the powers of the externalized problem, Mr. Fear.

---

a process of reality creation that may not take into consideration the power and influence of the dominant culture. At the same time, the narrative approach creates its own truth about how problems may be resolved with the collaborative efforts of client, communities of influence, and the therapist. These interventions may set the client up for significant discomfort if the larger culture does not recognize and validate the changes that were made in therapy. Fish (1993) criticized White and Epston, stating the they engage in therapy that "denies the existence or relevance of differences in power at an interpersonal level" (p. 228) and does not deal with the realities of interpersonal power and power politics. Moreover, he posits that the reauthoring of life stories cannot exist outside the sphere of political, social, and economic truths and realities. Another criticism is that by externalizing problems, therapists may ignore or minimize the internalized feelings that clients have about their problem situations and about themselves.

Johnson and Greenburg's Emotionally Focused Therapy

Sue Johnson and Les Greenburg developed emotionally focused therapy (EFT), an approach for helping couples and families repair distressed and damaged relationships. Minor modifications to the model have been made to provide treatment to families in addition to couples. EFT is an empirically validated and evidence-based treatment approach that blends elements of person-centered therapy with elements of humanistic, experiential, and structural family therapy (Johnson & Greenburg, 1995).

This approach is relatively brief and implemented with most couples in 15–20 sessions. EFT has been included in this chapter covering humanistic interpersonal systems theories, as the interventions are heavily focused on interactions that occur in the present moment. According to EFT, the feelings experienced by couples are expressions of their innate need for a secure and trusting *attachment* to each other. EFT helps couples develop that secure attachment by focusing upon and emphasizing the importance of here-and-now experiencing and expression of deeply held feelings. In addition, successful implementation of EFT is dependent upon a genuine empathic relationship between the clients and therapist. The techniques of empathy, warmth, and unconditional positive regard identified by Carl Rogers (1961, 1980) create this relationship.

Johnson and Greenburg (1995) asserted that their theory best fits in the category of psychodynamic system theories, because its foundational principle is based on the psychodynamic concept of attachment theory. While this is certainly true, the importance of the relationship between therapist and the couple and the couple themselves builds heavily on interpersonal and humanistic concepts. Thus, emotionally focused therapy is included in this chapter.

In addition to the importance of the therapist–clients relationship, EFT employs concepts from attachment theory, as well as humanistic and experiential therapy models that are combined effectively with systems-based interventions. As the title of the theory implies, the emotions of the family members are tapped and utilized systemically to repair damaged and distressed relationships. EFT is based on John Bowlby's (1988) attachment theory. Johnson and Greenburg contended that attachment theory is the most informed model for understanding loving, adult relationships and for describing the importance of developing and maintaining secure attachment in loving relationships. Moreover, these authors argued that secure attachment is necessary to develop healthy relationships and to maintain psychological health.

In much of Western culture, and according to other family therapy theories, dependency is considered to be a personal weakness. Johnson and Greenburg disagreed, countering that dependency is necessary and present in all intimate relationships. Further, they asserted that all human beings have an *innate need for secure attachment* and the ability to depend on one another in healthy and functional ways. The clinical question is whether the innate dependency needs present in all people are met through healthy and secure attachments or whether attempts to meet these needs emerge as relationship dysfunction and create insecure attachments.

Philosophical Tenets and Key Theoretical Constructs

Johnson and Greenburg (1995) succinctly summarized their view concerning the formation of interpersonal relationship problems in their comprehensive description of EFT, based on the tenets of attachment theory. They stated:

> EFT views marital distress from an integrative interpersonal–intrapsychic perspective, synthesizing experiential and systemic concepts into a theory of marital dysfunction. Interactional positions in distressed couples tend to be rigidly defined and interact to create powerful, repetitive, negative interactional cycles. From an EFT perspective, these positions are maintained by both the compelling emotional experiences of the partners and the prototypical interactional patterns that take on a life of their own and become self-reinforcing. These patterns then restrict accessibility and responsiveness, which are the basis of a secure sense of attachment and emotional connectedness. (p. 121)

In order to respond to attachment problems, EFT takes steps to identify the patterns couples use as they ineffectively communicate their affective experiences related to their interpersonal distress to each other. In distressed relationships, the pattern used by the partners to express emotions is generally to repress true feelings or, if the feelings expressed are true, to communicate them in ways that are anger-based, hurtful, and not congruent. This style of relating tends to keep the couple locked in conflict. The conflict may express itself in an attacking pattern between the partners or an attack by one and withdrawal by the other. These patterns ensure that the couple will not develop a secure attachment. A key principle of EFT is that *contact between partners is needed to develop secure relationships*. Therefore, EFT identifies and focuses on the deeper primary feelings of the partners to help create emotional connectedness. The therapy is designed to help the partners identify these primary feelings and learn to express them to each other in ways that lead to trust and the development of a secure attachment. As this occurs, the partners develop new, self-reinforcing patterns of relating and creating healthy dependency and connection.

Several key assumptions undergird EFT. The most significant of these assumptions include the following (Johnson, 2004):

- Attachment is a motivating force for individual behavior. People, for better or worse, behave in ways designed to create an attachment bond.
- Developing *secure dependence* in relationships is the goal of therapy. Independence is not possible because of the innate biological need in humans for secure attachment.
- Attachment offers safety from stress and provides the ability to risk, explore, and disclose.
- Secure attachment allows for emotional accessibility and responsiveness.
- Fear and uncertainty activate attachment needs that may create stress and discord in significant relationships.
- The results of loss of attachment are predictable. Common responses are anger, clinging, depression, and despair.
- There are three insecure attachment styles: anxious and hyperactivated, avoidant, and a combination of anxious and avoidant.
- Secure, high-quality attachments in key relationships promote healthy self-concepts, or the perception of the self as lovable, worthy, and competent.
- Isolation and loss are inherently traumatizing experiences.

EFT therapists use these key assumptions to identify and understand the causes of relationship problems and develop interventions to remedy these problems to help partners establish healthy attachments and secure relationships.

Key Tasks of EFT

Emotions are the critical element in couple and family treatment. This is so because emotions are the vital link between the internal processes occurring within each individual and the social and interactive process that occurs between each person. Thus, clients must tap, express, and understand emotions so they are able to gain insight and recognize the link between their internal experiencing and their overt behaviors toward one another. Because of the critical importance of feelings in EFT, providing the link between internal experiences and external behaviors, Johnson and Greenburg (1995) identified two major tasks of therapy:

1. Therapists must help clients identify, explore, clarify, and deepen the significant emotions that are at play in the relationship.
2. Clients must disclose and share emotions with one another. The therapist helps clients use this information to *change their interaction patterns.* As functional patterns replace dysfunctional patterns, trust, openness, vulnerability, and empathy will lead to a more secure attachment and an improved relationship.

Johnson and Greenburg (1995, p. 126) cautioned therapists using their approach to be aware of three types of emotions that may emerge in therapy. Each of the three types of emotions should be treated in different ways.

1. *Primary emotions* are viewed as genuine and adaptive feelings that emerge to help individuals respond to external forces and to meet their own goals and needs. For example, anger expressed because of being discounted or violated in some way is a primary emotion, as is sadness at the loss of the partner's affection or fear in the face of a partner's rejection. Clients may not be aware of their primary emotions; therefore, the therapist must be skilled in identifying these feelings by helping clients access them and attach meaning to them. This will aid in facilitating changes to the couples' interactional patterns.

   It is important for the therapist to recognize that primary emotions are generally adaptive. However, maladaptive primary emotions such as rage in response to compassion or fear in response to kindness are usually reactions to trauma or particularly negative childhood experiences. These negative primary emotions are detrimental to the relationship and must be recognized and dealt with in therapy with the goal of modifying them. When this occurs, therapy is more intensive and of longer duration.
2. *Secondary emotional responses.* These feelings are reactive and are not directed toward resolving immediate issues and attaining desired goals. Secondary emotions are reactions to primary emotions being thwarted. For example, the secondary emotion of shame might occur when one feels sad or scared. The internal message is, "I should not feel this way." Secondary emotions are usually very much in the

client's awareness and may be an impotent feature of their problems. Johnson (2004) advised therapists to not to focus on or deepen secondary emotions. Rather, they should recognize them as indicators that will lead the clients and therapist to the more important underlying experiences related to the client's primary emotions.

3. *Instrumental emotional responses*. These emotional behavior patterns are learned rather than organic to the person. They are used to *influence people* and are expressed to achieve some intended effect on others. For example a person might cry to evoke sympathy or become angry in order to get his way. Instrumental emotional responses provide the therapist with information about how clients consciously use their emotions to attempt to get their way and to project a desired image to others, including the therapist. Johnson and Greenburg suggested that instrumental emotional responses may be confronted, identified, and interpreted to clients to enhance their self-awareness, or they may be bypassed in order to focus on primary emotions. They caution against excessive focusing and deepening of these feelings.

As therapists become adept at identifying the types of emotions their clients express, they will use this information as a guide to help determine the therapeutic goals and the interventions that will be most useful in establishing healthy attachments.

The Process of Therapy

EFT is a relatively brief treatment approach, with therapy generally terminating within 20 or fewer sessions (Johnson & Greenburg, 1995). The approach follows a series of systematic steps designed to help couples and families resolve their presenting complaints. The first step in the therapeutic process is to establish a secure and trusting working relationship with the clients. The therapist must achieve a *positive alliance* with the clients. This means that the clients must believe that the approach and tasks the therapist employs are relevant and that the goals of the therapeutic process are likely to help resolve the presenting problems. The therapist must be perceived as trustworthy, accepting, and supportive, with the ability to create a bond with the clients and an environment of safety that facilitates the clients' willingness to be vulnerable and reveal their deepest thoughts and feelings. Once the therapist establishes a positive working alliance, she implements the following steps:

- The therapist identifies the core issues in the relationships.
- By encouraging the couple to interact with each other in the session around various concerns, the therapist identifies the negative patterns of interaction.
- The therapist helps the clients begin to access and identify their unacknowledged feelings associated with the negative interaction patterns.
- The therapist uses the information obtained in the steps above to reframe the problem. Reframing means that the therapist presents the problem to the couple in a novel and innovative way, emphasizing the dysfunctional interactional cycles, the lack of connection between the couple or family members as a result of their inability to recognize and share their feelings, and the lack of secure attachment in the relationship.
- As the clients acknowledge and accept the new explanation provided by the therapist, they become better able to identify their disowned needs and feelings and to communicate them to each other.
- The vulnerability and openness demonstrated by the couple or family members to each other leads to a *softening* of the attitudes of each and to a new closeness and openness to accepting the partner in a nondefensive way. This change in behavior leads to a change in the interactional pattern between the clients and a new closeness. One of the indicators of positive movement in therapy is the softening that occurs in each of the partners.
- The clients are more willing and able to be vulnerable and begin to behave in ways the increase emotional engagement.
- The new patterns, enhanced trust, and closeness, lead to discovering new solutions to old problems.
- The couple or family tries and implements new solutions, consolidating into new relationship patterns.

Strengths of the Theory

EFT has several strengths. It is an empirically validated approach, which means therapists who use the model are likely to be reimbursed by managed care insurance companies. Moreover, EFT is based on attachment theory, a well-respected model describing human interaction. EFT emphasizes the importance of feelings and incorporates feelings into a systemically-based treatment model. This conceptualization was a major leap forward for systems thinkers who had difficulty

CASE EXAMPLE

Emotionally Focused Therapy

Luke and Christina Brown came to therapy because the tension in their marriage had become unbearable to each of them. They reported that they seemed to have lost all love for each other and that they were more like business partners who did not get along and did not like each other than a loving husband and wife. They reported that they were very much in love when they married and everything was fine until Christina became pregnant and lost the couple's baby to a miscarriage. At this point, Luke complained that Christina was unable to let go of her grief and that her grief left no room for him. Christina complained that Luke was unsupportive and spent all his time at work or involved with sports, both as a participant and spectator.

The therapist used the Rogerian relationship-building skills of empathy, respect, warmth, and unconditional positive regard to establish a strong alliance with both Luke and Christina. With a trusting working alliance established, the therapist asked Christina and Luke to talk to each other about their disagreements. By observing the interaction patterns, she noted that Christina was ineffectively trying to establish secure attachment by pursuing Luke in an attacking and critical manner. Luke, in response, withdrew and gave up, saying that Christina never let go of her anger at losing the child and everything he did to try to help her failed. The therapist carefully identified this pattern to the couple, ensuring that they understood it and agreed that this pattern was indeed occurring in their relationship.

The therapist then began the important step of reframing this dysfunction and painful interaction pattern as a pattern that provided some hope of change. So the therapist said to Christina and Luke, "I can tell that each of you has a great deal of emotion caught up in your troubled marriage. The feelings that you seem to be expressing are anger from Christina and withdrawal and indifference from Luke. This pattern seems to be getting stronger and stronger. Now, what I see in this marriage is an ineffective attempt by each of you to establish that loving connection and trust

(continued)

Emotionally Focused Therapy *(continued)*

that you had before the miscarriage." Then the therapist checked with the couple to see whether they indeed do want a close attachment and trust in the relationship. Both Christian and Luke agreed that that is what they wanted.

Next the therapist began exploring the primary emotions under the anger and indifference expressed by the couple. Christina revealed that under her anger was a deep sadness. She told Luke that she needed him to want and accept her and for him to realize the depth of her pain at the loss of their child. She wanted to know that he cared and was hurt by the miscarriage as well. When Luke heard this, his attitude softened considerably. He told Christina that, by his withdrawal into work and sports, he was hiding the fear that he would lose Christina. He interpreted her anger as a signal that she did not love him. He withdrew to conceal his hurt and fear.

With this trust and willingness to be vulnerable, the couple came to understand the dysfunctional interaction patters in a new way and were able to begin the process of revealing other deeper feelings they had for each other. This major shift in the couple's willingness to be vulnerable and their ability to accept and empathize with one another created a new and more productive pattern of vulnerability and an openness to share their feelings in a context of love and safety. Through this process, the couple began to feel closeness and developed a secure attachment and healthy dependency.

incorporating affect in to treatment. Another strong point of this approach is its use of humanistic and experiential interventions in the here and now with couples and families. Therapists use emotionally charged in-session experiences to help couples recognize their need for attachments and a secure dependency in their relationships. EFT therapists are especially well qualified to establish effective working relationships with couples and families and are careful to ensure that a trusting therapeutic relationship is established before delving into deeply held emotions.

Weaknesses of the Theory

EFT is not well suited for all relationship problems. It is not as useful with couples who are highly defensive and unwilling to assume their own responsibility for their problems. EFT is not effective in relationships in which a basic sense of trust and good will is absent and cannot be developed. This is especially true for clients who have already determined to leave a relationship or who have been so severely traumatized that allowing themselves to become vulnerable is impossible. This approach is also not generally effective in relationships where expressions of violence preclude expressions of vulnerability (Johnson & Greenburg, 1995). Another weakness of this approach is its dependence on emotions to move to improved relationship functioning. This may not be effective with clients who are cognitively oriented and have difficulty connecting with the premises of the approach.

Summary

This chapter explored four systems-based theories of family therapy that are of particular interest to therapists who believe family treatment must consider and emphasize the uniqueness of the individual within the family context. The theories of Virginia Satir, Carl Whitaker, Michael White and David Epston, and Sue Johnson and Les Greenburg all place a premium on the genuine encounter between the therapist and the family members. Moreover, they insist that this relationship is central to the family change process. These four theories all consider that the ability and necessity of the client to create meaning and develop life truths through experiences and relationships are fundamental to resolving individual and family problems.

Suggested Readings

Johnson, S. M. (2004). *The practice of emotionally focused couples therapy: Creating connections* (2nd ed.). New York: Brunner/Routledge.

Johnson, S. M., & Greenburg, L. S. (1995). The emotionally focused approach to problems in adult attachment. In N. Jacobsen & A. Gurman (Eds.), *Clinical Handbook of Couple Therapy* (pp 121–141). New York, Guilford Press.

The legacy of Virginia Satir. (1989). *Family Therapy Networker, 13*(1), 26–56.

Napier, A. Y., & Whitaker, C. A. (1978). *The family crucible*. New York: Harper & Row.

The promise of narrative. (1994). *The Family Therapy Networker, 18*(6), 18–49.

Satir, V. M. (1982). "The therapist and family therapy: Process model." In A. M. Horne & M. M. Ohlsen (Eds.), *Family counseling and therapy*. Itasca, IL: Peacock.

Satir, V. M. (1983). *Conjoint family therapy* (3rd ed.). Palo Alto, CA: Science and Behavior Books.

Satir, V. M. (1988). *The new peoplemaking*. Palo Alto, CA: Science and Behavior Books.

Whitaker, C. A., & Keith, D. V. (1981). Symbolic–experiential family therapy. In A. S. Gurman & D. P. Kniskern (Eds.), *Handbook of family therapy*. New York: Brunner/Mazel.

White, M., & Epston, D. (1990). *Narrative means to therapeutic ends*. New York: Norton.

Part Three

Special Issues in Marriage and Family Therapy

Chapters

Counseling Military Families

The United States and her allies have been involved in the Global War on Terrorism for almost 10 years. Nearly three million military personnel have been deployed to Afghanistan and Iraq during this period. Many of these combat veterans have been deployed two, three, four, or more times. Multiple deployments have had a profound effect on warriors and their families. Many have experienced combat stress reactions while deployed, returning home as changed people and in need of counseling support. Moreover, military families have had to develop strategies to continue to function effectively when one parent or, in the case of dual-career military couples, both parents are deployed. This chapter is based on the premise that counseling provided to combat veterans is more effective when all family members, key military colleagues, available military support systems, and leaders from the military unit are included in treatment. In this chapter, I often use the inclusive term *warriors* to describe military personnel serving in the Army, Navy, Marine Corps, Air Force, and Coast Guard.

Key Concepts

- Impact of deployment on the extended family system
- Deployment cycle stages
- Stigma and reasons for not seeking counseling services
- Use of psychotropic medications by military personnel and their families
- Combat stress reactions
- Posttraumatic stress disorder
- Traumatic brain injury
- Military suicides
- The veteran in the larger systems
- The military as a distinct culture

Questions for Discussion

1. Describe what you consider the greatest stressor faced by military families?
2. Which values that you hold would be most important if you were counseling a combat veteran?
3. How would you work with a military couple who came to you concerned that the returning warrior had PTSD?
4. What are the pros and cons of using psychotropic medications for veterans deployed in combat?
5. How would you use your knowledge of the deployment cycle in counseling a military couple preparing for their first deployment?
6. What are the causes of military suicides?
7. What do you think might reduce the number of suicides in the military?

The Global War on Terrorism has placed incredible stress on the nation's military personnel and their families. The frequency and severity of the psychological problems experienced by veterans returning from combat and their spouses and children who remain at home continue to increase as the War on Terrorism moves into its 10th year. More than three million combat deployments have been ordered since September 11, 2001. Approximately 800,000 warriors have deployed two, three, four, or more times since the beginning of the conflict (Tan, 2009). While the impact of these separations is greatest for the couple and their children, others are also affected. Parents, grandparents, siblings, other relatives, and friends may feel emotions associated with these separations. For example, if the wife of a deployed warrior is having difficulties with children and in other areas of life, it is not unusual for the grandparents, members of the older generation, to assist with frequent visits whenever possible or to invite their offspring and children to move back "home" during the deployment. Thus, combat deployments can have widespread impact on the larger family system.

The Need for Mental Health Services

The frequency and duration of combat deployments to Afghanistan and Iraq have resulted in an increase in psychological problems for the combat veteran, spouse, and children. In January 2011, approximately 92,000 troops were deployed in Afghanistan and 85,000 in Iraq and Kuwait. Many of these combat veterans are on their second, third, or fourth deployments. Moreover, there are approximately 150,000 veterans who are not deployed at the present time but have been previously deployed and are likely to be deployed again. These warriors and their families have experienced stressors resulting from the deployments, and many would benefit from counseling support. A survey conducted by the Rand Corporation in 2008 concluded that nearly 300,000 veterans returning from combat showed symptoms of posttraumatic stress disorder (PTSD).

This was 20% of the total number of veterans surveyed. The study further reported that only slightly more than 50% of these warriors received treatment (Gould, 2010). The reasons given for not seeking treatment included the following:

1. The stigma associated with being treated for a psychological disorder could damage a military career.
2. Fellow warriors would lose confidence in the help seeker.
3. Medications might be prescribed and could cause unwanted side effects.
4. Because exhibiting some *symptoms* of PTSD is not the same has having the disorder, many of the 300,000 warriors in the study may have been misdiagnosed and would have improved without seeking behavioral health treatment.

Concerning the possible unwanted side effects of psychotropic medications cited in the third point above, it is significant that according to the March 8, 2010, issue of *Army Times*, approximately one out of every six service members is on some type of psychotropic medication, and military personnel are being deployed to combat while taking psychotropic medications. Regulations preclude deploying military personnel if they are taking antipsychotic medications. However, if the drugs are being used to treat moderate depression, reduce nightmares, or mange symptoms of PTSD, exceptions can be made. Since the beginning of the War on Terrorism, prescriptions for antipsychotic medications for military personnel have increased 234%, prescriptions for anticonvulsant drugs have increased 68%, and prescriptions for antidepressant drugs have increased 39%. When surveyed by *Army Times*, 10% of military respondents acknowledged taking psychotropic medications, with 73% using antidepressants, 56% using sleep medications, 12% using pain medication, and 10% using tranquilizers. Fifty-seven percent reported using the medications after a deployment, and 19% used the medications during a deployment. The widespread prescription of psychotropic medications has raised the issue of the role these medications may play, if any, in the growing suicide rate within the military (Tilghman & McGary, 2010) and in their relationship to the increase in PTSD symptoms noted in returning warriors.

The stressors experienced by the children of combat veterans have resulted in a dramatic increase in the prescription of psychotropic medications, despite some reports that certain drugs may increase the likelihood of suicide (Jowers & Tilghman, 2010). In 2009, psychiatric drugs were prescribed to more than 300,000 children under 17 years of age served by the military's health insurance program. This is an 18% increase since 2005. The most commonly prescribed medications are for attention deficit hyperactivity disorder (ADHD), anxiety, and depression. The authors reported that when a parent is deployed, outpatient visits for behavioral and stress disorders increased by almost 20% compared to children whose parents were not deployed. The prescription of psychotropic medications is designed to help alleviate painful psychological symptoms of which the deployment may be a contributing factor. However, the frequent use of medications may also be a result of insufficient numbers of trained mental health professionals with the knowledge and skills to provide counseling services to military families.

Frequently Occurring Psychological Problems

The most common psychological problems reported by returning military personnel include combat stress reaction, PTSD, and traumatic brain injury (TBI). Depression, suicidal ideation, anxiety, and substance abuse disorders are also prevalent. Sexual assault can be a concern for deployed female and some male warriors. Finally, the transition from the military to civilian life has been problematic for many veterans.

Combat Stress Reaction

Combat stress reaction is not an official diagnosis that appears in the *Diagnostic and Statistical Manual for Mental Disorders* (DSM-IV-TR; APA, 2000). Rather it is a preliminary and temporary assessment used to identify a myriad of psychological symptoms that may occur as a result of being under fire in combat, including fear and anxiety, sleep disturbance, and feelings of hopelessness. The assumption is that the combat stress reaction symptoms are temporary and will decrease and ultimately disappear when the veteran is removed from combat. Improvement often occurs when the warrior is directed to step away from the combat situation and get some recuperation time, allowing the stress of the mind and body to return to normal. The Chairman of the Joint Chiefs of Staff, Admiral Mike Mullen, encouraged the use of the term combat stress rather than PTSD, because the stigma associated with a diagnosis of PTSD might prevent a warrior from seeking treatment.

Posttraumatic Stress Disorder

PTSD is a formal DSM-IV-TR diagnostic category that has gained widespread notoriety in the mental health professions as well as in the media. PTSD includes a constellation of symptoms that create significant impairment in the veteran's ability to carry out normal military duties and especially to engage the enemy effectively in combat. The cause of PTSD is thought to be experiencing or witnessing an event that was life threatening and that involved feelings of intense fear, helplessness, or horror. The primary symptom is a reexperiencing of the event through flashbacks or nightmares. Other symptoms include feeling numb, withdrawal from social contact, hyperarousal, insomnia, irritability, aggression, and poor concentration.

David Dobbs (2009), in his *Scientific American* article, suggested that PTSD is overdiagnosed. In his critique, Dobbs proposed that the symptoms are often normal responses to traumatic events in combat and that, for many, the symptoms will eventually subside with a return to normal functioning. He contended the symptoms of PTSD are too broad and overlap with other diagnoses such as anxiety reactions, depression, and, the other signature diagnosis of the War on Terrorism, TBI. He further asserted that by assigning the PTSD diagnosis to returning warriors, the natural healing process may be delayed. Finally, Dobbs was concerned that the PTSD diagnosis will lock warriors into a Veterans Administration (VA) system that allocates its services and compensation based on disability, dysfunction, and the maintenance of symptoms rather than on the return to psychological health. For example, a veteran preparing to leave military service who is experiencing psychological symptoms that do not reach the threshold level for financial compensation and medical treatment from the VA may be so concerned about the possibility of needing treatment in the future that the associated stress may intensify the duration and number of symptoms. This increase in symptoms may ultimately qualify the veteran for VA assistance while at the same time making the veteran less functional and less able to obtain gainful employment after leaving military service. The veteran's increased disability was needed to qualify for lifetime VA care and compensation while at the same time potentially diminishing the ability to return smoothly to civilian life.

Traumatic Brain Injury

TBI is a concussion-like injury that has been diagnosed in more than 161,000 combat veterans. TBI is usually the result of the detonation of an improvised explosive device, commonly known as an IED or roadside bomb. These devices have become highly sophisticated since the beginning of the war. The most effectively engineered devices are very powerful and are capable of penetrating armored vehicles and inflicting tremendous damage and loss of life and limb. TBI occurs when a warrior experiences a blast or other physical head trauma. The damage to the brain can vary from slight to severe. Most athletes in contact sports such as football have experienced mild head trauma, and most recover, as do most soldiers who encounter mild head trauma. However, powerful and destructive explosions capable of overturning heavy military vehicles present the possibility of more severe brain injury. A recent report in *Army Times* (Kennedy 2008) found that warriors hospitalized as a result of traumatic brain injury were prone to major depression that is frequently accompanied by anxiety, poor cognitive functioning, aggression, and higher rates of suicide. The study recommended that depression screening and systematic mental health services be integrated in to the treatment of TBI.

PTSD can be confused with or accompany TBI. Table 14.1 demonstrates the possible overlap of symptoms of these two disorders. Counselors must be certain to carefully evaluate the information provided by military clients to determine what types of traumatic events were experienced and in determining appropriate mental health treatment.

Depression

Depression is another frequently diagnosed disorder in returning combat veterans. The symptoms of hopelessness, feelings of worthlessness, and an inability to function effectively may be a reaction to the death of friends in combat or a sense of purposelessness that occurs for some when removed from combat or when unable to readjust to home and family life. Some warriors become so dependent on experiencing the stress of combat and the adrenaline rush that is involved that the return to normalcy can trigger feelings of loss and symptoms of depression. The death of, or severe injury to, fellow veterans may lead to feelings of depression. Multiple deployments have taken a toll on many marriages. Being unable to readjust to family life or learning that a spouse wants a

Table 14.1 Overlap of Symptoms of PTSD and TBI

Post Traumatic Stress Disorder	Traumatic Brain Injury
Insomnia	Insomnia
Impaired memory	Impaired memory
Poor concentration	Poor concentration
Depression	Depression
Anxiety	Anxiety
Irritability	Irritability
Ringing in ears	Emotional numbness
Fatigue	Hyper-vigilance
Headaches	Flashbacks and nightmares
Dizziness/impaired vision	Avoidance of people/situations
Noise and light intolerance	Anger outbursts

divorce can cause feelings of loss and depression, especially if the veteran does not want to end the marriage. Finally, depression can be a symptom of PTSD, TBI, or both.

Anxiety Reactions

Fear and anxiety are normal reactions to combat. However, when these normal feelings are heightened and not well controlled in vulnerable individuals, preventive steps should be taken. Anxiety reactions may occur as a result of functioning in high-stress combat environments for a prolonged period of time. A sense of fear and dread begins to emerge in the warrior's mind, especially as the pace of constant combat operations continues. Rest and talking about the feelings with a chaplain, mental health professional, or caring fellow service member often diminishes these feelings. When anxiety does not diminish with primary care and support, the individual may need to be removed from the combat environment and transported to the rear in order to recuperate and receive more extensive behavioral health care.

Alcohol and Substance Abuse

Alcohol and substance abuse is a frequent problem for returning combat veterans. Alcohol and drugs are not readily available in Afghanistan and

Iraq, as US commanders strive to respect Muslim prohibitions on alcohol and drug use by issuing orders that US troops abstain. This prohibition sets the stage for binge drinking and drug abuse upon redeployment, the return home from the combat environment. Another key reason for drinking and drug use is to numb the painful feelings of loss and dread that some returning warriors experience related to their experiences in combat. In 2003, about 6,000 soldiers sought alcohol treatment. In 2009, this number increased to almost 10,000 soldiers diagnosed and treated for alcohol abuse. According to Army Vice Chief of Staff, General Peter Chiarelli, there is little doubt that fighting a war on two fronts with multiple deployments and issues associated with family separations have had an effect on the numbers of alcohol diagnoses. Alcohol is a much larger problem than drug abuse, accounting for 85% of the substance-abuse treatment caseload. The Army is trying to reduce stigma and increase voluntary treatment by allowing soldiers to seek counseling without notifying their commanders and perhaps damaging their military careers (Smith, 2010).

Sexual Assault

Sexual assault is more common in the military than in civilian life. Reports of sexual assault have increased more than 11% in combat areas compared to 8% overall. Women are increasingly important to the effective functioning of the armed forces. Women and men are assigned to combat zones together with only a few combat specialty areas restricted to men.

When sexual contact is forced, it damages the human spirit and can result in depression or other behavioral health problems. Sexual assaults in combat zones may be military on civilian or civilian on military, but the most common reported assaults, 53%, are by military personnel on military personnel. Of these assaults, 87% were male on female and 7% were male on male. One of the reasons that statistics have increased is that reporting sexual assault has been encouraged and prosecution has been timely. The victim reporting the assault can choose *restricted reporting,* meaning that the military commander will not be informed of the assault, and there will be no further investigation; however, behavioral health and medical care will be provided (Youssef, 2010). Counselors helping returning combat veterans, especially women, will want to determine whether sexual assault is an area that needs to be explored.

Suicide

Suicide completions by active duty and reserve military personnel have skyrocketed since the beginning of the Global War on Terrorism. 2009 was the worst year on record for military suicides. The Army reported as many as 160 confirmed suicides among active duty soldiers. Seventy-eight suicides were reported among members of the reserve components who were not on active duty when the suicide occurred. The majority of military suicides were by gunshot wound or hanging.

The Marine Corps, a much smaller force than the Army, reported 52 completed suicides. Suicide rates have also increased in the Navy and Air Force. The upward trend in military suicides is clear. In 2005 the Army reported 87 completed suicides, and the Marine Corps reported 25. In 2007 the Army reported 115 suicides, and the Marine Corps reported 42.

In the past, the military has boasted of a lower suicide rate than the general population. This is no longer true. The Marine Corps had the highest suicide rate of the military services in 2009, with 24 suicides per 100,000 Marines. The Army's rate was 21.7 suicides per 100,000 soldiers, and the Air Force rate was 13 suicides per 100,000 airmen. The suicide rate for the nation, last tabulated in 2006, was 20 suicides per 100,000 people. The most common explanations for the increased suicide rates are the impact of War on Terrorism, which is in its 9th year, and the effects of multiple combat deployments associated with this prolonged conflict. While frequent combat deployments may be the most significant factor associated with suicide, other data revealed that approximately 30% of the 2009 suicides in the Marine Corps were by those who had never deployed. The Marine Corps reported 52 suicides in 2009. Of these, 16 Marines had no deployment history, 11 completed suicide while deployed, and 25 had previous combat deployments but were not deployed at the time of the suicide (Kovach, 2010).

While multiple combat deployments appear to be a key factor associated with completed military suicides, other circumstances need to be examined in an effort to reduce the problem. The following factors have been identified as potential contributors to the increase in military suicides:

- The Global War on Terror has created a personnel shortage for the Army and, to a lesser extent, the Marine Corps. A personnel shortage means that the military has a fewer recruits to carry out its mission than are needed. In order to resolve this problem, the military services have relaxed some of the qualifications to be accepted into the military. For example, enlistment waivers for service in the Army have been granted to individuals without a high school diploma, with past criminal and substance abuse behavior, and for previously disqualifying physical and psychological problems. The implication of granting these waivers is that the recruits who graduate from basic training enter the military with previously existing psychological and personal vulnerabilities that may make them more susceptible to combat stress, depression, family problems, alcohol and drug abuse, and suicidal ideation.

- Military training is difficult. It is purposefully designed to challenge and enhance the ability of individuals to withstand stress in combat and other situations. It is also designed to identify and to eliminate those who cannot perform effectively. In times of personnel shortages, individuals with personal and psychological problems, who would have been eliminated in other times, are allowed to enter the services. These vulnerable individuals typically have fewer resources to deal with the challenges of military life, are more likely to feel personally ineffective, and are more prone to considering suicide as an alternative to dealing with the challenges they face.

- Marital problems are another factor that contributes to the military suicide epidemic. Multiple deployments take a toll on relationships. When a warrior discovers that a spouse has been unfaithful or wants a divorce, this knowledge can create a sense of failure and despair. These feelings can be exacerbated and lead to severe depression, especially if the veteran desires to work on the marriage in counseling and the spouse does not. If other stressors such as alcohol abuse accompany the ended relationship, suicide might be considered as an option.

- Combat stress reactions leading to PTSD and depression can have devastating effects on the combat veteran. If the warrior does not receive help, this sense of futility can increase, leading to contemplation of suicide. Of course, untreated combat stress reactions will also adversely impact the warrior's job performance and relationships and is often accompanied by alcohol abuse. All of these factors compound the sense of futility felt by the veteran and may lead to suicidal thinking.

- Severe combat wounds are often the result of violent roadside bomb explosions. Many wounded veterans have overcome their disabilities with personal determination and the love and support of family, friends, and military colleagues. Some wounded warriors have returned to active duty in the military, and others have successfully transitioned to civilian life. However, some warriors are unable to accept the reality of the disability, and for many a context of family support is absent. These individuals understandably have a pessimistic view of the future and may experience depression with suicidal ideation.

- The "dirt bag" syndrome is a group phenomenon in the military where members of a military unit label a warrior who can do nothing right the "dirt bag." This individual has the role that parallels that of the identified patient in a family described in previous chapters of this book. The other members of the unit ostracize this individual and make his or her life miserable. Before long, the ostracized individual gives up trying to be part of the group, and depression sets in. Alcohol abuse may be present to decrease the pain, however, this behavior further highlights the ineptness of this person. The haplessness and helplessness the individual feels within the unit may lead to depression and possible suicidal ideation (Fenell, 2009; Kovach, 2010; Tan, 2010).

- Another significant factor in this serious epidemic of military suicides is that reserve component members not on active duty can be affected as well. These reserve personnel often live a great distance from military mental health support facilities and may not receive the counseling services they need (Kovach, 2010; Tan, 2010). Civilian mental health professionals need to be available to support returning Reserve and National Guard military personnel who deploy from their region. Moreover, counselors need to be available to help the families of these veterans during their deployment (Fenell & Fenell, 2003).

A warrior is more likely to consider the option of suicide as the number of negative life factors described above increases and as the ability to deal with these stressors decreases. The senior leadership in the military is very concerned about the growing number of suicides and has commissioned a major study to determine the factors that contribute to and predict the potential for suicide (Tan, 2010).

Military mental health professionals have not yet determined how to stem the tide of increasing suicides. However, several strategies have been implemented to respond to the problem. The first line of defense is for members of the military unit to use the buddy system. The buddy system directs all personnel to keep a watch on other members of the unit for displays of unusual or erratic behavior such as talking about death, describing feelings of haplessness, misuse of weapons, alcohol or drug abuse, mood swings with intense anger, impulsivity and an attitude of not caring, withdrawing from family and friends, and giving away possessions. Noticing is not enough. Talking with the distressed individual and identifying professional help is required. Moreover, military leaders must become more vigilant and make contact with all warriors in their units on a regular basis to communicate caring and concern and willingness to provide help if emotional problems are evident. These actions by the military leadership will do a great deal to reduce the stigma associated with acknowledging psychological vulnerabilities and seeking treatment (Fenell, 2008). Members of the unit and family members must not be afraid to ask the tough question, "Are you thinking about hurting yourself?" If the answer is yes, stay with the individual and get help immediately (Kennedy, 2010).

Elmore and Van Dyke (2010) identified several common elements of successful behavioral health treatment for combat veterans who have become suicidal:

- Use a simple and understandable approach.
- Identify and clarify for the client the factors that have contributed to the feelings of hopelessness.
- Explain the benefits of treatment and engender hope.
- Identify and strengthen the client's skill deficits.
- Emphasize self-awareness and personal responsibility.
- Teach crisis management skills.
- Remove weapons or other means of committing suicide.
- Use effective methods to keep the client engaged in therapy.

Transition to Civilian Life

Transition to civilian life can be difficult for some combat veterans, especially if the warrior's difficulties in adjusting are caused by combat stress reactions. The military services have career counseling programs designed to help veterans find civilian employment. Many employers want to hire experienced veterans because they realize that military service instills a sense of personal pride in its members and creates individuals with integrity and the desire to complete the mission assigned without complaint. However, veterans who are struggling with emotional issues as a result of their experiences in the military may embody these values but be unable to exhibit them in the workplace. These individuals may be underemployed or unemployed. Personal counseling is provided by the VA that is focused on dealing with the veteran's emotional concerns. The employment counseling service provided by the VA is charged with helping the veteran find gainful civilian employment.

The information provided above highlights the most common psychological and emotional issues that have emerged for many combat veterans of the Global War on Terrorism. There can be little doubt that highly qualified professional counselors, both military and civilian, are needed to meet the ever increasing psychological needs of our military combat veterans (Fenell, 2010). Each of the potential problem areas that I have described may have immediate and profound consequences for the warrior's relationships with a spouse or partner, children, other relatives, and military comrades. In the following sections, the systemic implications of combat stressors on all relationships will be described.

The Veteran: A Member of a Larger System

The counseling profession must not forget that each warrior is a member of a family, a social network, and a military unit. The warrior influences the actions of these larger systems, just as the actions of the larger systems influence the veteran. The previous chapters in this book have emphasized the importance of assessing and understanding the reciprocal influence of the individual on the system and the system on the individual. Effective treatment of returning combat veterans will incorporate the members of the larger system in the therapy process to support healthy changes in the warrior and family.

The Military as a Distinct Culture

The need for behavioral health services for returning warriors and their families is great. This chapter has described problems that are specific to the combat veterans, but, make no mistake, family, coworkers, and friends are affected by these problems as well. The warrior's spouse, partner, children, friends, and military colleagues can have a significant impact on the veteran's problems, for better or for worse. Therapists are encouraged to include members of the warriors' network of support—family, friends, and coworkers—in the counseling process. The use of systems-based interventions will facilitate the effective participation of the members of the network in ways that help resolve, rather than exacerbate, presenting problems.

To successfully engage the warrior, family, and military network in treatment, the counselor has to be perceived as credible and professional. The first step in achieving professional credibility is by establishing effective counseling relationships (joining) with all participants in treatment. To accomplish this, the therapist demonstrates an understanding of, and respect for, the military culture and those who serve in that culture (Fenell, 2008).

Most civilian counselors have limited exposure to military life and military culture. Without an informed frame of reference, it is possible for counselors to adopt stereotypical and biased views about combat veterans and military organizations. The counselor's thoughts and feelings about violence as well as combat, killing enemies, and global political and military strategy might predispose either a negative or positive perception of the military client (Fenell & Fenell, 2008).

Military personnel and their families are likely to be patriotic, organized and systematic in behavior, rule conscious, and are often religious. Warriors, freely and without mental reservation, take a sacred oath to protect and defend the Constitution of the United States and to obey, without question, the lawful orders of those appointed over them. In combat, those lawful orders require the warrior to inflict deadly force on the enemy and to willingly engage the enemy in extremely dangerous, life-threatening situations that are incomprehensible to most civilian therapists. The ethos and duties of the warrior may conflict with the values and beliefs held by the counselor (Fenell & Wehrman, 2010). Counselors who hold negative perceptions about military personnel and the duties they perform may not be best suited to help these clients. Military clients can detect a counselor who has difficulty demonstrating respect and empathy for those who serve the profession of arms and will not usually remain in treatment with such a counselor. When an incompatablity of values is severe and likely to negatively affect the counseling process, the ethical therapist will refer to a qualified colleague.

The demand for counselors qualified to provide support to military personnel is growing rapidly. Most well-trained counselors have studied multicultural counseling and understand the skills needed to be a successful multicultural counselor. To be a successful counselor to military families, the therapist recognizes and accepts that the military is a unique culture. Counselors who are trained to use multicultural counseling skills in the treatment of combat veterans and their families are likely to be successful even if unenthusiastic about military values and the War on Terrorism. The counselor's key to successful treatment of military clients is the ability to manage personal views about the military and to ensure that personal values are not inappropriately interjected in to the counseling process. This is true for the counselor, especially when the client himself is criticizing the military. Those within the profession of arms are entitled and even expected to "gripe" about the military, but those who have not served must use caution. To be a successful therapist, the following cultural competencies, presented by Sue and Sue (1992) and modified by Fenell for the military culture (2008, 2010), are important when working with military clients:

- The effective counselor is aware of personal values and biases about war and military service that may prejudice the counselor's perception of the client.
- The counselor performs a thoughtful self-assessment to determine whether he or she is able to value and work comfortably with military clients and their families.
- The counselor has an understanding of the barriers, including stigma, that prevent military personnel from seeking counseling services.
- The counselor has a basic understanding and appreciation of military history, values, and culture.
- The counselor is comfortable with a variety of theoretical approaches and has the ability to shift the approach as needed to respond the unique needs presented by the military client.

Effective counselors for military clients are generally mature individuals who have successfully incorporated the following three multicultural counseling competencies in their repertoire.

Self-Awareness and Adaptability

Self-awareness and adaptability are essential qualities for the military counselor. Counselors, based on their own life experiences, family roles, culture, and ethnicity, bring assumptions, values, and biases about the military to the counseling session. Counselors who have not had frequent contact with the military may hold perceptions and biases about the military culture and its members that hinder development of an effective counseling relationship. Counselor should be actively involved in the process of becoming aware of their assumptions about human behavior, values, biases, and preconceived notions as they relate to military service and military clients. The military, like other cultures, has been stereotyped. Effective, self-aware counselors examine their stereotypes about the military and have the adaptability needed to develop the knowledge and skills required to ensure any personal biases do not adversely impact the counseling process. If the military client detects counselor incongruence about the military, the client is unlikely to return. Counselors should be genuine about their beliefs and values without letting those beliefs and values negatively impact their ability to demonstrate respect and understanding of the military client's worldview (Fenell, 2008).

Ability to Understand and Accept the Client's Worldview

Effective counselors must be able to empathize with the military client and understand and accept the client's worldview. The military client's worldview is shaped by the events of childhood as well as later life experiences in ways that are similar for all people. However, the military client's worldview is further shaped by an intensive basic military training program that molds the individual into a warrior. The training experience in the Marine Corps is called the *crucible*, because during this process individuals are tested through arduous training and forged in to a unified, team-oriented, and hardened military force. After basic training, a warrior may receive more specialized training, followed by combat deployments and other military experiences. These experiences further shape the warrior's worldview and many develop a "military mindset." Effective counselors must be able to link with the military client's worldview in a way that communicates respect. As described previously, if the military client detects counselor incongruence about the military, the client is not likely to return to counseling.

To join with the worldview of military clients, counselors need to recognize several common values shared by military personnel, including the following:

- Always maintain physical fitness.
- Train hard before deployment to reduce casualties.

- Never abandon your fellow warriors in combat.
- The mission and the unit always come before the individual.
- Never show weakness to fellow warriors or to the enemy.

The effective therapist also recognizes that the stigma associated with seeking counseling is real for the warrior. These combat veterans do not want to appear weak to their comrades. They are also concerned that seeking treatment from military therapists will not be confidential. Moreover, the awareness that seeking psychotherapy can negatively impact the veteran's military career is still widespread despite efforts to change this perception. Because of this concern, many warriors and their families will seek counseling from civilian providers rather than military therapists. This fact makes it even more important that civilian therapists have the cultural and clinical skills required to understand and demonstrate respect for the warrior's worldview (Fenell, 2008).

Skills to Meet the Needs of Military Clients

The effective multicultural counselor needs specific skills to work within the military culture. While members of the military culture share common values and beliefs, it is a mistake to view military clients in a monolithic fashion. As is the case in any cultural group, there are as many differences among individuals within the group as there are differences between different cultural groups.

The effective counselor will be equipped to apply the following counseling skills:

- Demonstrate empathy
- Listen accurately
- Reflect content and feelings
- Deliver precise summarizations of client disclosures
- Encourage the client to *teach the therapist* about military life, values, traditions, and expectations

Moreover, the counselor must be able to employ an array of counseling interventions based on a variety of theoretical orientations to best meet the needs and personality style of the client. The therapist will eventually want to focus on the client's main problems in the here and now. However, it may be necessary to spend time establishing the relationship by exploring past issues and difficulties with the client, including experiences from combat as well as from the family of origin, prior to focusing on the present difficulties. When military clients feel understood, heard, and respected by the counselor, they are more likely to deepen the counseling process by taking interpersonal risks and delving into the significant issues that have brought them to counseling.

Finally, counselors should be adept at employing consultation when needed. It is possible that the client will present issues with which the therapist is not familiar or comfortable. In these situations, seeking consultation and making a referral, if necessary, is an important counselor skill in working with military clients.

The demand for well-qualified, culturally competent counselors to provide services to military personnel is significant. The demand will only grow as the War on Terrorism continues. Professional counselors will be successful in working with military clients if they have an understanding of the military culture and utilize the multicultural competencies presented in this section to their work with military clients (Fenell, 2008, 2010).

The Systems Theory Approach to Helping Military Clients

The military is a culture based on a disciplined, organized, and uniform approach to completing assigned missions. While teamwork is critical to success in the military, accountability focuses on the individual within the unit. For example, when a unit performs a mission and that mission is determined to be effective or ineffective, the commander is ultimately held accountable for the outcome. When awards are presented, they most often go to individuals; likewise, punishment in the military is delivered to individuals who do not perform to expectations. While military units perform as teams, individuals within the team are held accountable for how that team functions. Similarly, when psychological problems occur within the military unit or family system, the military approach is to identify these problems as *individual concerns* and to respond to them with individual or group counseling interventions or both. Of course there are times when this approach is effective. At other times, however, a systemic and contextual approach to treatment is more beneficial. Whenever possible, the therapist should attempt to engage as many members of the family and military system in the resolution of any problems for the warrior or family members that result from combat deployments.

The remainder of this chapter will describe the deployment cycle model (Fenell & Fenell, 2003; Fenell & Wehrman, 2010)). The deployment cycle model identifies the predictable phases that military families transition through in their preparation for deployment, their separation, and their reunion. Each phase of the deployment cycle has expected and recognizable challenges. These challenges are more effectively met when military families have knowledge about the deployment cycle and are able to anticipate potential difficulties during this difficult transition. Counselors are more effective in supporting military families when they clearly understand the phases of the deployment cycle and the potential problems associated with each phase of the cycle. In this following description of the deployment cycle, systems theory approaches to treatment are recommended for helping military families with the predictable problems they encounter as they deal with their deployments.

The Deployment Cycle

Fenell and Fenell (2003) described a three-phase model that identifies the key events in the mobilization, deployment, and reunion of military personnel. This model is developmental and based on a review of research on the effects of combat deployments on military families (Fenell & Wehrman, 2010).

Preparation for Separation

The first phase of the deployment cycle begins when the warrior first learns that a combat deployment will occur in the near future. This information is relayed to the spouse and children. All the children should be informed of the impending separation by the both parents presenting the information together. However, the couple must be certain that the news is delivered to children in developmentally appropriate ways. Older children comprehend differently than young ones. Young children may need to be informed separately after older children are told. Older children are then able to help the parents support younger offspring who may not fully understand the concept of deployment but who are fully able to detect the new anxiety introduced in to the family system (Fenell & Fenell, 2008).

Once the family is informed, each person, in his own way, experiences the emotions of anticipating the separation. After the reality of the news sets in, the parents and children begin making plans for the effective functioning of the family during the combat deployment. During the preparation phase, all legal processes must be completed, giving the spouse remaining at home the authority to manage all the duties of caring for family and home. Childcare arrangements may be required. Updating wills and powers of attorneys heightens the anxiety of the pending separation and introduces the awareness of the dangers inherent in combat. Often these fears remain undisclosed but emerge in unproductive ways, such as angry outbursts or withdrawal from contact. If this occurs, couples and families may talk with a family counselor to facilitate the open discussion of these normal fears and anxieties.

During the preparation for separation phase of the deployment cycle, the family wants to spend as much time together as possible. However, the warrior will likely be spending 10- to 12-hour days training for the deployment; many weekends may also be reserved for training. The inability to be together often creates frustrations and marital tensions for the couple and resentment for the children. Couple counseling can be very helpful for those who experience this conflict. An effective therapist will normalize the anxiety by helping the couple and children recognize the frustration is normal, yet unavoidable, and is the result of the caring the family members have for one another rather than relationship problems.

Couples who have responded to several deployments are often prepared for the disappointments that are inherent in the preparation for separation phase of the deployment cycle. Veteran couples who have been through the process before can be helpful to first-time couples who may not know what to expect or how to deal with the inevitable emotions that arise. Military families strive to ensure that the family is prepared for the separation and that all important tasks are completed so there will not be any unexpected challenges. When warriors who deploy to Iraq or Afghanistan are preoccupied with worries about their spouse or partner and children at home, they have difficulty focusing on their dangerous combat missions, and they will not be combat effective and may be vulnerable to enemy attack. Therefore, if relationship, parenting, or other family issues remain unresolved, couple or family therapy should be considered prior to the deployment to address these concerns. Therapy will help the stay-at-home parent and children, as well as the warrior, feel more comfortable with their difficult situation (Fenell & Fenell, 2003).

The Separation

The second phase of the deployment cycle is the separation. This phase is generally the easiest for the warrior and the most difficult for the family members who remain at home. This phase is easiest for the warrior, because a daily routine begins that involves doing the mission, eating, and sleeping. Then the next day, the same sequence starts all over again. The warrior has no domestic responsibilities. The warrior's domestic responsibilities, as well as the normal responsibilities of the spouse or partner and children, are being managed by the nondeployed adult and children. So the work of the nondeployed spouse or partner doubles while the warrior's work load is lessened. Of course, the warrior may be involved in life-threatening duties, and these terror-filled moments can make the warrior's work challenging as well.

Some outposts in Iraq and Afghanistan have many of the amenities of a military base in the United States. It is common for many, but not all, warriors to have daily access to email, Skype, and phone connections with their family at home. The ability to have frequent contact has many benefits, as the warrior is able to maintain contact with the family. However, when problems occur in the relationship because of frustrations with children or the overwhelming responsibilities of managing the home and family alone, resolution via cyberspace can be difficult. It is frustrating for the partner at home to have regular contact but no actual support in dealing with the myriad problems that occur. It is frustrating for the deployed warrior because he or she wants to "do something." Unfortunately, little can be done from half a world away other than demonstrate caring and concern. Mental health professionals deployed with the combat unit can help resolve some of these issues by communication with the couple via email or other means, suggesting interventions to stabilize problematic situations, thus permitting those concerns to be addressed, perhaps in family therapy, after the deployment is completed (Fenell & Fenell, 2003).

The separation phase of the deployment cycle may begin with the nondeployed partner feeling abandoned and insecure. However, over time, these change to feelings of confidence as new and successful routines are initiated, leading to a greater sense of self-reliance, independence, and differentiation (Bowen, 1978). This new confidence and self-reliance in the nondeployed spouse or partner is often an unexpected change for the warrior and can create problems during the reunion phase. Veterans returning from combat are provided reintegration training prior to the reunion. They are told to be prepared for a more independent partner and children as well as a new set of rules and expectations guiding the family. The warrior is encouraged to be patient and to let the process of including the returning veteran into the new family structure to unfold. When the returning partner is not finding a place in the family structure, couple and family counseling can help the couple and children work through these positive but potentially difficult changes.

Children also change during the deployment. In effective deployments, the children contribute to the functioning of the family and gain considerable self-confidence and independence. In problematic situations, children can feel scared, angry, and abandoned. They may begin acting out at home or develop academic and/or behavior problems at school (Fenell, Fenell, & Williams, 2010). Problems with children can be especially difficult when the deployed parent has traditionally been the disciplinarian. Problems with children also tend to exacerbate if the parent remaining at home is not handling the deployment well. As a rule, the children do well if the nondeployed parent is functioning well during the separation. Children are more likely to experience problems during the deployment when the parent is struggling with the separation. Family therapy with a military-sensitive therapist can be particularly helpful for the nondeployed parent and children in working through many of the personal and family issues resulting during the deployment (Fenell & Fenell, 2003, 2008).

Another serious problem that may occur during the separation phase is infidelity. Some deployments have been as long as 18 months in duration. If the marriage or committed relationship was vulnerable prior to the deployment, partners might seek emotional support outside the marriage. Most believe that the nondeployed partner is more likely to engage in an extramarital affair. However, the deployed member may also engage in an extramarital affair while deployed. The major military installations in Afghanistan and Iraq have significant male and female populations. While fraternization is discouraged, men and women find ways to spend time together during deployments, often with negative effects on their marriages (Fenell & Wehrman, 2010). Infidelity by the deployed warrior is almost as likely as infidelity by the nondeployed member. If the infidelity is discovered, it may have devastating effects on the combat effectiveness of the deployed warrior and on the effective functioning of the nondeployed spouse or partner.

Relationship problems that existed before the deployment do not improve. They remain and may become worse during the separation (Fenell & Fenell, 2003). Some relationships strained by deployment can be salvaged afterward if the couple recognizes the problems and commits to intensive couple therapy. For other couples, the deployment intensifies and clarifies the incompatibilities in the relationship, leading to separation and divorce. If divorce is the decision, it is important for the family to seek counseling to ensure the divorce is as amicable as possible and that the children are supported through the process.

The Reunion

As the deployment draws to a close, the family begins to anticipate the homecoming and reunion. As the family members prepare for the reunion, expectations may exceed the reality of the event. The first kiss may not have the magic that was anticipated. The kids may not be as glad to see the returning warrior as hoped. The first few days of the reunion are the honeymoon. During this period the couple and kids are on best behavior and all enjoy being together again. After the honeymoon, family reconstitution begins. This process is often a challenge because *all* family members have changed; some have changed a lot, others not as much, but everyone is different after the deployment. The warrior has changed as a result of the war and the experiences of the deployment. The nondeployed spouse or partner has changed as well. She has become more self-reliant and independent, or, if the deployment was particularly difficult, frustrated, angry, and less confident. The children have changed because they are older and more mature. Problems may occur when one partner criticizes the other, saying, "You are not the way you were before the deployment. You have changed in ways that I don't like," while not recognizing the changes that have occurred in his or her own personality. This potential problem, if viewed as an opportunity for growth, can bring excitement into the relationship. Growth will occur in all members if the family is able to accept the reconstitution as a time to get reacquainted and to evolve into a more effective and loving family unit. The challenge for the family is to get to know each other again as they are now—rather than how they were before. The family members have changed gradually but significantly during the deployment. They do not recognize their changes, but the returning warrior does. The returning warrior does not recognize the changes that he has made, but the family does. The deployed warrior often has a "freeze frame" vision of the family and is surprised and perhaps disappointed that life has gone on during the deployment. Moreover, the nondeployed partner has taken charge of areas of family life that had previously belonged to the warrior. New ways of doing things have been instituted and there may not seem to be a "place" in the family for the returning warrior.

If the family has made progress toward healthy reintegration within 4 weeks, family therapy should be considered to help work through the inevitable rough spots. The old saying that "absence makes the heart grow fonder" may have some truth to it; however, marriages that have significant problems before the deployment are not likely to improve during a deployment. The problems remain and may even be worse when the honeymoon is over (Fenell & Fenell, 2003).

A component of the reunion phase of the deployment cycle is supposed to be stabilization. *Stabilization* is the last element of the reunion phase and is that period in which the family can "get back to normal." Unfortunately, stabilization is not happening for most military families. As soon as Army and Marine Corps units return from combat, they are back in the cycle for their next deployment. The preparation for separation begins almost immediately without a significant stabilization period and time for the family to get back to normal. Because the Global War on Terrorism continues with no end in sight, those families who are making a career of the military can expect these deployments to continue. Recently, the Chief of Staff of the Army proposed a new deployment model. Within the next year the goal is that a 6- to 9-month deployment will be followed by an 18-month reunion and stabilization period. Implementation of this new model will have a positive impact on the mental health of all military family members (Jowers, 2010).

Conclusion

The Global War on Terrorism will likely continue for years to come. Millions of warriors have been deployed to combat operations. Family members have been crucial in supporting these deployments, and they have experienced significant stressors in their roles. Countless numbers of combat veterans and their family members will require counseling services, now and for many years into the future. Well-trained family therapists with the ability to treat families using a strength-based, systems theory approach will be among the best equipped professionals to provide this need support. While this chapter has highlighted many of the challenges facing military families, it would be a mistake to assume that all, or even most, returning warriors have combat related difficulties. Most warriors return to stable though changed families and reconstitute without experiencing serious problems.

Counseling Families
with Special Needs

Family therapy was developed as a method for helping families with serious psychological problems.
Later, this method of intervening was employed with
families exhibiting a variety of problems. More recently,
family systems theories have been applied to specific
family constellations, including blended families, ethnically diverse families, same-sex relationships, families
with children with disabilities, alcoholic and substance
abusing families, physically abusive families, families
experiencing divorce, families with a member who is
HIV-positive, families with a depressed or suicidal member, and rural families. Each of these family situations is
discussed briefly in this chapter.

Key Concepts

- Blended families
- Families with a depressed member
- Alcoholic and substance abusing families
- Families with a child with special needs
- Abusive families
- Culturally diverse families
- Divorcing families
- Same-sex relationships
- Gender issues in family therapy
- Rural families
- Families with an HIV-positive member

Questions for Discussion

1. What important issues should a remarrying couple resolve prior to the wedding?
2. What is the best preparation for family therapists helping culturally and ethnically diverse families?
3. In what ways are the dynamics of families with children with special needs similar to those of families that do not have children with disabilities? In what ways do the dynamics of these family types differ?
4. What special problems should the family therapist be aware of when helping a family with a substance abusing member?
5. What are the critical issues to consider when helping a family with a physically abusive member?
6. What are the significant steps in the divorce process?
7. Should the family therapist hold values that suggest trying to save a marriage or committed relationship? Defend your answer.
8. How can depression in one family member be maintained by the behaviors of other family members?
9. How would you help a family with a member who has suicidal thoughts?
10. How might gender stereotyping affect the process of family therapy?
11. What are your values concerning same-sex marriage? How would you help a couple seeking premarital counseling?
12. What are your thoughts concerning power differentials between males and females in a marriage or committed relationship? If a differential is present, what do you recommend as an alternative?
13. What would be your concerns when helping a family with an HIV-positive member? What skills would be most important?
14. What family therapy skills are important to help rural families?

As family therapy has matured and earned respect from the mental health community, new responsibilities have emerged for the profession. Family therapy clinical research has increased, and information has emerged that suggests the importance of employing specific approaches for assisting families with special needs. This chapter provides the reader with strategies for helping these families.

Blended Families

Blended families are created when one or both partners bring children from a previous relationship into a new one. Divorce and remarriage is a frequently occurring phenomenon in the United States. Glick (1989) reported that an estimated 69% of children in the United States lived with both parents, and, for children born in the 1980s, 59% could expect to live with only one parent for a period of time, and 35% could expect to live with a stepparent before the age of 18.

The most pervasive problem for the remarried or blended family is that family members attempt to reconstitute as a traditional nuclear family (Visher & Visher, 1979). After the new relationship is established, the stepparent will attempt to assume the role of the "real," biological, mother or father. If the stepchild does not accept this attempt, an escalating battle to determine who will define the adult–child relationship may rapidly emerge. As this situation intensifies, the biological parent frequently enters the fray on the side of his own child, compounding the problem by creating a conflict between the adults in the relationship.

When a blended family enters therapy, the therapist should effectively join with each member by understanding the challenges inherent in the roles of parent, stepparent, child, and stepchild. After establishing credibility as a caring and knowledgeable expert about stepfamily problems, the therapist describes the "myth of the nuclear family." This myth, which is embraced by many remarrying couples (or unmarried but committed couples entering a new relationship), requires that stepfamilies constitute themselves and act in ways that are similar in most respects to traditional families (Visher & Visher, 1979). Once the family recognizes that they are different in many ways from a first marriage or first unmarried committed relationship, this myth will no longer determine the family's behavior. The family will stop attempting to replicate the traditional family, permitting the family members to discuss and negotiate how they would like their blended family to function. This intervention gives stepparents the opportunity to hear directly from the stepchildren how they would like the relationships to develop rather than assume the stepparent will be immediately embraced. Therapy should also provide an opportunity for the couple to discuss with each other how they wish their children to be treated by the stepparent and how they will support each other when dealing with their stepchildren (Carter & McGoldrick, 2005).

Therapy with a blended family can be an extremely positive experience after the family releases some of its idealistic notions concerning how blended families function. Structured premarital or relationship preparation counseling (Brunn & Ziff, 2010; Fenell, Nelson, & Shertzer, 1981; Fenell & Wallace, 1985) can help couples prepare for certain problems associated with blended families and is advised whenever possible.

Culturally Diverse Families

Most family therapists will have the opportunity to work with client families of diverse cultural and ethnic backgrounds. This can be challenging, as different cultural groups value and respond to therapy in their own unique ways (McGoldrick, Pearce, & Giordano, 1982). When therapists meet a client family from a different cultural background, how should they respond? Each person and, indeed, each family is unique, and therapists must value that uniqueness. If therapists are open to the process of learning about, understanding, and respecting the values and behaviors of all families, they are likely to take the time to understand the uniqueness of any family that they encounter in the therapy room. This ability to relate to the uniqueness of all families is the key characteristic of therapists who are effective with a wide range of culturally and ethnically diverse families.

An alternative point of view contends that effective family counselors must be familiar with the fundamental characteristics of a variety of ethnic groups to be able to respond effectively to them in therapy.

This point of view maintains that understanding the most typical values and behaviors of a variety of ethnic groups and the characteristics of these groups better prepares therapists to work effectively with each specific group. A criticism of this approach is that the therapist may form stereotypical ideas about members of certain cultural groups that, while valid for the majority of members of the group, may not apply to the specific individuals who are in family therapy. Thus, therapists might believe that they understand the context of the family before actually learning from the family what that context is. This is a recipe for ineffective therapy, regardless of the family's ethnic background.

All counselors must remember that a specific ethnic group may have as much diversity within the group as it does when compared to another distinct ethnic group. To assume knowledge that has not been validated through conversation with the family members is bad therapy indeed. For example, the within-ethnic group differences between an African American who is a US citizen born in Nigeria and educated in England and an African American born in poverty in New Orleans is likely to be as significant as the between-group differences of an Asian American and a Hispanic American.

The key is to let the family educate you, the therapist. As you come to know the family, you will be better able to develop interventions that are consistent with the family's cultural values. Discovering and respecting the values and beliefs of culturally diverse families is really no different from what any effective family counselor does with any family encountered in treatment.

McGoldrick, Preto, Hines, and Lee (1991) contended that the best preparation for family therapists who will work with ethnically diverse clients is for them to thoroughly study their own ethnic identity. By so doing, therapists will come to understand the unique characteristics of their own cultural group and recognize that the values of the group, while understandable and useful for its members, might not be useful for other groups. Therapists come to understand that the values of each ethnic group are born out of the context and experiences of each group's members and are clearly understandable when they realize the forces that have shaped the group. Further, it is critical that effective multicultural therapists recognize when they are operating out of a personal, culturally-based value in therapy. If therapists are able to transcend their own ethnic identity, they can develop a multiethnic perspective, and they no longer feel the need to convince clients to adopt their own values.

It is more important for effective therapists to know how to think about ethnic and cultural differences and to be able to recognize how these differences could have an impact on therapy than to possess a wealth of specific academic knowledge about a variety of ethnic groups. For example, various ethnic groups may have differing responses toward suffering, different attitudes about helping professionals, a more formal or informal interactional preference with strangers, and differing attitudes about the appropriateness of children's expressiveness. Therapists, to be effective, will have to be sensitive to each of these and numerous other possible conditions in therapy.

While well aware of the problems associated with stereotyping members of ethnic groups and with no intention of doing so, McGoldrick and Rohrbaugh (1987) conducted a study that characterized differences among groups to help clinicians become aware of the range of values brought to therapy experience. Some of the most striking modal characteristics of several groups identified in the study are the following:

- Jewish families
  - marry within group,
  - value success and education,
  - encourage children,
  - talk out problems,
  - have shared suffering, and
  - use guilt to shape children's behavior.

- White Anglo-Saxon families
  - are expected to be strong and make it alone,
  - are independent,
  - have self-control,
  - suffer in silence, and
  - hide conflicts.

- Italian American families
  - hold nothing more important than family,
  - are expressive and enjoy a good time,
  - follow traditional sex roles,
  - relate through eating,
  - accomplish tasks through personal connections, and
  - tend to have male-dominant roles.

- African American families
  - ○ exhibit strength to survive,
  - ○ are religious,
  - ○ are able to make it alone,
  - ○ see women as strong, and
  - ○ want children to succeed.

- Asian American families
  - ○ always have time for family members,
  - ○ respect elders for their wisdom,
  - ○ believe that bad behavior reflects on the whole group,
  - ○ worry about children doing well in school, and
  - ○ want children to succeed.

- Hispanic American families
  - ○ take responsibility for care of elderly,
  - ○ always have time for family members,
  - ○ have defined roles: men protect and women nurture,
  - ○ respect elders for their wisdom, and
  - ○ consider "losing face" as catastrophic.

The authors emphasized that these characteristics come from a preliminary study; they are based on average behaviors and should not be used to stereotype any group. Understanding the uniqueness of each family remains one of the most important tasks of the family therapist in dealing with ethnic minority families, or any family, for that matter.

Families with a Child with Special Needs

Fenell, Martin, and Mithaug (1986) described therapy with a family with a child with special needs. They suggested that once the initial distress associated with the reality of having a child with a disability subsides and the family is able to accept the reality of the situation, the parents begin working together to provide the best possible environment for their child. At this point, two problems may arise:

1. The parents may focus so much of their energy on the child that they neglect their own relationship and perhaps the needs of their other children.

2. The family may do so much for the child with a disability that the child does not learn what she is able to accomplish without assistance.

The first problem often precipitates the need for therapy, as the parents begin to experience problems their own relationship because of the tremendous amount of time, money, and effort spent on supporting the child with special needs. The relationship tension is frequently accompanied by one of the other children in the family beginning to demonstrate behavioral problems.

The therapist's first task is to communicate that he understands and appreciates the sacrifices each member has made for the child with special needs. Then the therapist points out that the family has not been able to make time for other members because they have organized their lives around the child with a disability (Berger, 1982). Helping the family find time to reestablish other relationships requires patience and understanding on the therapist's part.

When the child with the disability is the identified patient (IP), the situation differs from typical family therapy situations because the child often has physical or mental impairments that are unlikely to change in any significant ways. An IP without special needs is likely to make dramatic changes as the family system improves. Thus, parents and children must be aware that only small improvements by the child with a disability are likely, but that family functioning will still improve markedly through the therapy process.

Even though family members may be overinvolved in supporting the child with special needs to the detriment of other relationship and family responsibilities, the child's behaviors are primarily the result of the disability rather than the stressed family environment. Therapy should devote considerable effort toward helping the other family members create an environment for the child with the disability that will allow the child to fully develop her potential, regardless of how limited that might be, and permit other members to lead their lives as normally as possible (Grossman & Okun, 2009).

This objective may be accomplished by strengthening the key subsystems in the family, especially the executive subsystem and the subsystems between parents and children without special needs. Parents may not know what resources are available in the community to help them with their child. Furthermore, they may feel guilty about placing the child in short-term care, even though that service allows the family to enjoy some time away from the challenges the child's disability presents. The therapist must support the family in using childcare, acknowledge the guilt feelings, and emphasize and support the need for time away from the child with special needs. The therapist should be ready to help the family by providing necessary information about available support systems and, more important, by normalizing the parents' concern about leaving the child in short-term care. The parents and the child both need to spend time away from each other.

When the parents begin taking some of their focus off the child with special needs, they may recognize deficits in their own relationship. The couple may need support and training in communication to begin to relate to each other in meaningful ways as individuals. As the family begins to balance its time and energy better, the child with a disability may be able to accomplish some of the tasks that the parents and siblings had previously done for him. This change has a systemic effect on the parents and siblings, who then begin to encourage further appropriate autonomy for the child with a disability and commit more time and energy to their own and other important family relationships.

Families with a Member Who Abuses Alcohol or Other Substances

Families with a member who abuses alcohol or other substances often are treated with family therapy (Edwards & Steinglass, 1995). Many professionals consider alcohol and substance abuse a disease, and others believe it is a behavioral problem. Regardless of the therapist's definition, the abusing member clearly affects the individuals in the family, and the family members affect the abuser's behaviors (Kaufman & Kaufman, 1979; Pattison, 1982).

Family therapists have criticized treatment approaches for substance abuse that do not incorporate the family constellation, and many drug and alcohol therapists have criticized family therapists for assuming that substance abuse can be cured simply by eliminating dysfunctional family patterns. Almost all problems of substance abuse may be treated most effectively by interrupting the cycle of abuse through a combination of individual therapy for the abuser and family therapy incorporating all involved members. The purpose of family therapy is to modify the family environment so the family does not inadvertently encourage and reinforce patterns of alcohol and drug abuse.

Pattison (1982) identified four themes in the interaction of the alcoholic member and the family. These themes are also present in families with a drug abusing member.

1. The substance abusing member places significant stress on the family system. Family members may have to adopt roles to cope with the abusing member that are not in their own best interests. For instance, a young daughter may have to assume a parental role and prepare meals because her parent is frequently drunk.
2. Therapists must understand the effects that the family has on the substance abusing member. Conflict in the marriage or committed adult relationships or with children may precipitate excessive drinking or drug abuse and maintain the dysfunctional pattern. Thus, substance abuse may serve as (a) a symptom of family dysfunction; (b) a method for coping with family stress; (c) a consequence of dysfunctional family rules, roles, and structure; or (d) a combination of these functions.
3. Alcoholism and drug abuse is a family disease. It may be transmitted from one generation to the next. If one generation has a substance abusing family member, the chances increase that the next generation also will have an abusing member. Sons and daughters of substance abusers who do not, themselves, abuse frequently marry an alcoholic or dug abuser, thus maintaining the intergenerational pattern. Researchers are attempting to determine whether the transmission of this behavior has a genetic basis, is learned from parents and other family members, or results from a combination of factors (Schuckit, 1987).
4. Family participation in the treatment of an alcoholic or drug abuser improves the prognosis. Pattison (1982) reported that family participation in aftercare greatly enhances the positive outcome of treatment. He argued that it is critical to include family members in the treatment of substance abuse.

However helpful it may be, family therapy alone is rarely sufficient in treatment. Alcoholic and drug abusing persons suffer from major physical, emotional, social, and vocational impairments. These problems often must be treated with specific rehabilitation methods, which may include inpatient therapy to break the substance abuse cycle (Pattison, 1982).

When couples and families with a substance abusing member seek family therapy, they rarely present their problem as being based in substance abuse. Rather, some other symptom almost always precipitates the decision to enter therapy. As a result, family therapists too often do not explore the possibility of an alcohol or drug problem in the family, and this oversight ensures that many alcoholic families remain untreated. Usher and Steinglass (1981) encouraged family therapists to routinely explore the possibility of a substance abuse problem in the family. If a substance abuse problem is detected, the authors maintained that the drug or alcohol problem must be dealt with before any other symptoms can be effectively treated. However, this approach may mitigate the commitment of family members to exploring their role in the maintenance of the behaviors of the substance abuser.

For family therapists, effective treatment of the family requires diagnosing the alcoholism or the drug dependence as a family problem. All family members must understand that each of them has a role to play in resolving this family problem. The therapist's substance abuse diagnosis will not be helpful unless the family members accept the diagnosis and recognize the role of the family in both the maintenance and resolution of the problem. Thus, the therapist must carefully gather and present data to support the diagnosis sensitively and firmly.

The first requirement of effective treatment is to interrupt the pattern of substance abuse. The therapist will prepare the family members for "slips" so that expectations are not too high. Participation in groups such as Alcoholics Anonymous (AA), Alanon, and Alateen are often useful adjuncts for the family while the cycle is being interrupted. However, the therapist must remember that not all substance abusers or family members subscribe to or accept the 12-step process advocated by AA. In these instances, other types of support systems should be identified if possible.

After the drinking or drug abuse has stopped, the therapy focuses on reestablishing intimacy in the family that is built upon the genuine caring and respect of family members for one another rather than the episodes of alcohol and drug abuse. Removing drugs and from the family system may create an intense void in family functions, because family members no longer know how to act or what to do when not responding to the chaos created by the substance abuse in the family. Family therapy can help the members move through this confusing and frightening phase to more productive family functioning. Although family therapy is no panacea in the treatment of alcoholism and the abuse of other substances, it often is useful (Edwards & Steinglass, 1995).

Gender Issues in Marriage, Couple, and Family Therapy

The feminist critique of family therapy was one of the most powerful trends in the field during the 1980s and 1990s and continues as a powerful force in the profession today. Feminist family therapists questioned the notion of circularity in assessing families and the resulting conclusion that all family members are equally involved in maintaining a pattern of behavior (Goodrich, Rampage, Ellman, & Halstead, 1988). Feminists insisted that many family systems are unequal, with men having significantly more power than women. Moreover, those writers condemned critics who conceptualized systematically at the expense of an individual within the family, often a woman (Sprenkle, 1990).

Family therapists in the past conceptualized systemically and advocated that all members played an equal and important role in changing and maintain family behaviors. However, their interventions frequently were not congruent with their theory. In response to this criticism, family therapists have looked closely at the role of gender in family treatment. In the past, many therapists assumed that families in treatment held traditional gender roles. This is no longer the case. Therapists now need to consciously involve previously marginalized family members and all others, attempting to understand how each individual views healthy family functioning and how each person would like to be treated by the therapist and other family members.

Therapists also need to examine client family patterns to determine whether those patterns are maintained by family hierarchical structures supported by implicit or explicit threat to other members. When a therapist identifies such structures, it is essential to clarify the effects of this subtle force with all family members. Helping families develop alternative and more equal structures would be a goal of treatment.

In a special section of the *Journal of Marital and Family Therapy*, several authors commented on the role of men in marriage. Doherty (1991) warned that moving men from the pedestal to the mud and women from the mud to the pedestal will not solve the gender problems. Doherty's concern was that we have moved from a model that recognized women as men with deficits to an equally problematic deficit model of recognizing men as women with deficits.

Berg (1991) criticized the movement to make men more like women and women more like men. She challenged the assumption that obliterating the differences between men and women will solve gender problems. Rather, Berg (1991) suggested an intervention that asks the question: How can this particular woman learn to obtain what she wants in life using her strengths and talents? How can this particular man learn to obtain what he wants from life using his unique assets? How are men and women the same and how are they different? Let us make these commonalties and differences work for us separately and together (pp. 311–312).

How do mental health professionals develop a more gender-sensitive approach to our work? Storm (1991) suggested that therapist training is crucial to this shift. She developed a training module placing gender at the heart of the training program. Although this approach to family therapy training emphasizes the importance of systems theory in treatment, it challenges the axioms and assumptions of systems theory throughout the training program. In order to determine whether modified training programs have an effect on family therapists' behaviors and attitudes, Black and Piercy (1991) developed a research scale for assessing students' attitudes toward a feminist-informed perspective on therapy. As new family therapists enter the profession trained by educators who are sensitive to gender issues, discrimination in families will continue to abate.

Same-Sex Relationships

Unions between members of the same sex are becoming more accepted and visible in the United States. Most states recognize the legitimacy of same-sex committed relationships. However, strong disagreement persists about whether these legal committed relationships are the same as a marriage between a man and a woman. As this book goes to press, legal challenges in several states seek to sanction or prevent recognition of same-sex committed relationships as marriages. Irrespective of how theses challenges are resolved, the family therapist will likely be called upon to help same-sex couples resolve their relationship difficulties (Olson & DeFrain, 2006).

Relationship problems between gay or lesbian couples are in most respects no different from the issues the therapist encounters in therapy with a man and woman. Problems appear in communication, childrearing, in-laws, finances, and infidelity. The skills the therapist needs are the same as those required in couple therapy with a man and woman. One notable therapist characteristic, however, can impede successful treatment of same-sex couples. Successful treatment is unlikely when the therapist holds strong values that view homosexuality as a wrong or a deviant behavior and that marriage is only between a man and a woman. If the therapist holds these values, he must be able to effectively keep them from impeding therapy, or, if this is not possible, refer the same-sex couple to a therapist who does not hold these values.

Families with an HIV-Positive Member

In the zenith of the AIDS epidemic, the Centers for Disease Control and Prevention (CDC) reported 665,000 cases of AIDS and 99,000 cases of HIV infection in the United States (Serovich & Mosack, 2000). Since then, tremendous strides in treatment and prevention have been developed, and rates of infection are much lower. Nonetheless, providing therapy to families with an HIV-positive member has created certain challenges for counselors.

When a family member has AIDS, the information may or may not be disclosed to other family members. Because of widespread ignorance about the disease as well as reactions to an HIV-positive diagnosis, the impact on family members is likely to be difficult and disrupt typical family functioning (Serovich & Mosack, 2000). The presence of a skilled family therapist to help family members openly discuss and begin to deal with the issues involved can be critical in maintaining family stability and support for the infected member.

To deal effectively with this issue, the therapist must be educated about the disease and be aware of the most recent information available. Information on HIV changes rapidly, and the counselor must remain current to provide the help these families need. Moreover, the therapist must be skilled in working with emotionally laden topics such as death, discrimination, drug abuse, and sexuality. Involvement of all immediate and extended family members may be useful in understanding the disease and its implications and in developing effective support for the patient and those who love her.

Ethical issues involving the disclosure of potentially life threatening communicable diseases such as HIV/AIDS to client families and other significant persons their lives arises when an infected client discloses that he is engaging in unprotected sexual relationships. Pais, Piercy, and Miller (1998) and Serovich and Mosack (2000) offered guidelines for therapists when this situation arises. The American Counseling Association (ACA) addressed infectious diseases in its ethical standards. The ACA *Code of Ethics* of 2005 "is one of the few codes that addressed the issue of contagious or communicable diseases, such as HIV/AIDS. Unlike almost all other codes it gives therapists some guidelines in regard to confidentiality and disclosures" (Zur & Smith, 2011). The standards state that the counselor is justified in breaking confidence and warning prospective partners. Other professional associations are wrestling with the issue. Members of the American Medical Association (AMA) encourage the patient to disclose to sex partners. If they will not, the physician is to report to the local health department and finally to those at risk if the health department does not act (Serovich & Mosack, 2000).

Domestic Violence

The effective treatment of domestic violence has long presented difficult problems for mental health professionals. It is especially difficult because physical abuse is a violation of the law as well as a threat to the family structure of those involved (Margolin, 1987). When abuse or neglect involves a child, therapists should be aware that they have a legal obligation to report the abuse in most states (Huber, 1994). Because abusive adults often were abused as children, their self-concepts are often low. Their ability to control their impulses and consider alternatives in highly stressful situations is limited.

From a family systems perspective, physical abuse of a spouse, partner, or a child is considered to be part of a pattern of behavior that involves several family members. Unlike most other types of presenting problems, however, the family therapist should not attempt to take the focus off the abuser, as this approach leads family members and community service agencies to believe that the therapist is excusing the violent acts. Families often enter treatment shortly after an abusing incident has taken place. At this time, the perpetrator usually feels bad about the violent actions and is ready to work at improving the family relationships and eliminating the abuse. Other family members are also hopeful that therapy will eliminate the abuse.

When the family enters treatment, the therapist has three basic goals. First, the therapist helps the perpetrator and victim identify the typical pattern that ultimately leads to the violence, with each sharing thoughts and feelings that occur as the pattern evolves. Second the abusive member is taught to delay acting on impulses. Third, the therapist helps the abused client and the abuser to develop the ability to recognize and consider several alternatives to potentially violent situations. Through this process, it is hoped that the abuser will learn to recognize and select alternatives to violence in the situations that had triggered abuse in the past (Hatcher, 1981).

The first session often requires crisis intervention. The therapist might be the first person outside the law enforcement system with whom the family has been able to discuss the problem. Therefore, the therapist must talk with each family member and allow all unexpressed feelings to be presented without allowing those feelings to escalate. At this point in treatment, escalation of feelings could engender anger and regression to old behavior patterns, creating a tense and potentially abusive situation that the family is not yet ready or able to handle.

As the therapist discusses the family members' feelings with them, he must be certain not allow the feelings to escalate. He asks each member to speak to him, not to other family members, and asks how that person has been able to manage the feelings effectively in the past by ensuring they do not escalate in the present moment of the session. This helps the family members begin to develop confidence that they have control over stressful situations. Perhaps for the first time, they are able to discuss what has happened without escalation. Managing feelings in the therapy session is the first step toward impulse control. As family members begin to share their feelings, the therapist reinforces the aspects of the discussion that demonstrate control of their behavior. This initial process sets the stage for the family to begin to deal with anger within controlled limits— a characteristic that families suffering domestic abuse must develop.

It is important that therapists understand the cycle of violence that occurs in families. Davidson (1978) proposed a modified version of the cycle:

- Tension builds in the family.
- The abuser becomes violent.
- The violent member is remorseful and seeks sympathy and understanding. Apologies are made and forgiveness given.
- The family returns to a stable state (homeostasis) with no violence while anticipating and dreading the next occurrence of the cycle. (see Figure 15.1)

From a systems point of view, the violent incident can be understood through the provocation–response cycle. When victims sense the tension building and realize that a violent incident is going to occur, they may precipitate the incident to speed movement through the violence stage to the remorseful stage and ultimately to stability. If the therapist discovers that this behavior is occurring, it should be identified in a way

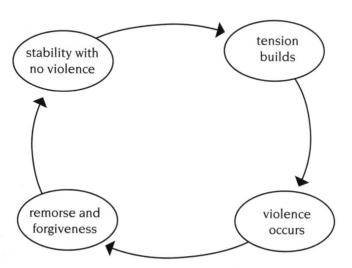

Figure 15.1 Cycle of Domestic Violence

that reveals the pattern to the couple or family but that does not remove the responsibility of committing violence from the abuser. Again, the therapist must ensure that all family members understand that the abusive behavior is not acceptable while helping each member recognize (and eventually modify) the roles played by all in maintaining the behavior. Furthermore, the therapist must ensure that the family knows that if the abuser does not learn to manage the violent behavior, the police and courts will intervene, and the issue will be settled by others. Ultimately, the therapist and family members all must agree that the behavior is unacceptable, and all must constantly reaffirm this value in therapy (Hatcher, 1981).

The therapist should develop a contract with the family. In this contract, family members agree that when tension is building and violence is likely, the victims will leave the home to a safe location. The contract should specify that the family will be in a "safe house" for an agreed-upon length of time and that a call will be made to the abuser and to the therapist to ensure a safe environment before the family considers returning home. The place where the family will go should be arranged in advance but should not be known to the violent member. If this is not possible, the person agreeing to help the victims must be prepared to contact the police if the violent member precipitates a potentially dangerous situation at the safe house (Hatcher, 1981).

After the situation deescalates, each family member involved is instructed to call the therapist to describe how he or she managed the situation. These calls to the therapist are important because they reinforce that the leaving behavior on the victims' part is appropriate and that the victims have helped the violent member by leaving. It also provides the therapist with more information about the cycle of violence and may offer new ways to intervene. When the victims leave the home prior to the violence, actual physical harm does not occur. This is a positive step and a major shift in the pattern and may offer opportunities for the family to make further changes. The therapist must be aware that the perpetrator may initially view the leaving behavior by the victim(s) as a challenge and affront. The therapist needs to prepare the abuser for this possible reaction before initiating this intervention. The abuser must understand that when the family leaves the home, this is good behavior, designed to strengthen the family relationships, and not abandonment. The therapist plays an important role in helping the abuser recognize and accept these facts.

In the initial sessions, the therapist should attempt to develop a basic contract with the family. Refinements take place in later sessions. If the family cannot agree on the contract or if a contract is not finalized, the therapist may suggest that a temporary separation is needed if the welfare of the family members is of concern. If the therapist believes there is reasonable probability that harm will befall one of the family members, the therapist is ethically bound to report this to the police or human services department.

After the family has been in therapy for several sessions, the members should be establishing a pattern for impulse control and considering options other than violence. At this point, the family members might benefit from attending support groups. These support groups for victims and perpetrators help the family members know that they are not alone in their struggle and that they have the understanding and support of those who have been in similar circumstances. Furthermore, these groups provide support to the family as they make difficult systemic changes.

It is well known that most perpetrators suffer from low self-esteem. One of the major contributors to long-term success with violent families is to help the violent member gain self-esteem. Accomplishing this objective may require working individually with key family members in counseling sessions designed to enhance their self-esteem, too.

A final caveat for the therapist working with an abusive family is the potential threat to the therapist. If a threat is made or implied, the therapist should take the threat seriously and deal with it in a matter-of-fact manner. If the threatening client is not appropriately responsive, the therapist should not be reluctant to discontinue treatment, contact authorities, and take other appropriate protective measures (Benedek, 1982).

The need to provide treatment to families with an abusive member is unquestionably crucial. But outcome studies on the effects of treatment have been discouraging. Hamberger and Hastings (1993) found no conclusive studies to suggest effective intervention for domestic violence other than the permanent separation of the conflictual parties. Even given these grim statistics, many families do not want to end their relationship and are unwilling to implement permanent physical separation. These couples return to their old patterns, waiting for the abuse to cycle once again or may elect to seek help in eliminating abuse. Even though treatment may not be effective for many families, it can be helpful for some.

Families with a Depressed or Suicidal Member

All therapists encounter depressed clients numerous times during their careers. Olin and Fenell (1989) completed a study suggesting that when one spouse in a marriage is depressed, the other may be depressed as well. They suggested marital therapy as an effective treatment for such depressed marriages. Often, the depression becomes severe and life threatening, and the depressed family member contemplates suicide. These findings are likely to hold true for couples who are not married but in committed relationships.

Depression in Families

As in other life-threatening situations, the systems therapist should focus treatment initially on the presenting problem, the depression and potential suicide. Although a systemic conceptualization of the patterns of interaction in the family is helpful in understanding the family dynamics that support the suicidal ideation, it is a mistake to take the focus away from the presenting problem and onto the behaviors of other family members until the suicidal ideation has been explored thoroughly and steps have been taken to remove the immediacy of the suicide threat.

Thus, in the first phase of therapy, the therapist should attempt to learn from the family members what has occurred in the past to lead to the depressed and suicidal feelings in the family member. It is not uncommon for the therapist to discover that the intense worry about the suicidal member experienced by other family members causes them to overload the identified patient (IP) with love and concern, which paradoxically can contribute to the person to feeling less competent, more depressed, and more hopeless. The therapist can help family members learn to express just the *right level of concern* to the depressed member, that is, not showing too much concern and possibly overloading the individual or too little concern, perhaps seeming not to care. This change in the family's behavior will usually take some of the pressure off the IP and begin to mitigate the depression and hopeless feelings.

Because depression and suicidal thoughts frequently occur together, the therapist should assess the client's life situation and explore the history that has resulted in depression. Individuals who identify their family-of-origin experiences as positive are less likely to experience depression or other health problems than those who recall their family-of-origin experiences as being problematic (Canfield, Hovestadt, & Fenell, 1992).

When a longstanding history of depression is identified, the client may be referred for an examination by a psychiatrist to determine whether antidepressant medication may be helpful in stabilizing the hopeless and helpless feelings that accompany depression. When medication is indicated, it often helps to stabilize the client's mood and enable more effective work to take place in family therapy (Conye, 1987). The therapist should caution the family that antidepressant medication is dangerous if taken in excessive amounts. Some studies have suggested that antidepressants are associated with childhood suicide (Gibbons, Kwan, Bhaumik, & Mass, 2006). The family should be instructed to monitor the patient's use of the medication, especially during the early weeks of treatment when effects of the medication may not be evident and when the depression is severe (Conye, 1987).

Suicidal Family Member

Nothing brings family therapy to a screeching halt faster than the statement by one of the members that she is contemplating suicide. All the systemic goals and creative conceptualizations are "out the window," and the focus shifts from system reconstruction or individual growth to keeping the person alive (Jurich, 2001). Suicidal behavior exists on a continuum from a thought about self-destruction to a carefully conceptualized plan. The therapist must determine as accurately as possible the client's point on the continuum.

Most people have suicidal thoughts from time to time when life is not going well and they are in emotional pain. But the vast majority of these individuals recognize that the alternative is not a good one, and they do not become overtly suicidal. A few clients, however, do reach a point at which they prefer death to their currently painful life.

The therapist should assess five major dimensions to determine the significance of the situation:

1. Are any physical factors affecting the client? Does she have health issues such as cancer that seem to be out of control and have left the client feeling helpless and hopeless?
2. Is the client experiencing any personal crises that she cannot meet successfully? Are factors such as legal proceedings or the inability

to provide food and shelter for herself and her family stressing the individual?

3. If the client is a child, is he having relationship problems with parents, teachers, or peers? Is the child a victim of bullying?

4. Have family issues such as divorce or an affair by the spouse left the client feeling hopeless and rejected?

5. Does the client have problems with peer relationships? Does the client have any friends and support systems?

The therapist must assess the problems in each of these areas and determine the magnitude of the stress created by the demand and the client's resources to respond to that stress. When stressors on the client are greater than the resources available to meet them, the therapist must consider how to best support and keep the client alive until the suicidal impulse passes.

Jurich (2001) uses the information gained in interviewing the client to answer four questions:

1. Is the client's level of pain and isolation high enough to move suicidal ideation into action?

2. Does the client have the resources and family support to overcome the suicidal impulses?

3. What are the client's perceptions that support death over life and what might the family and therapist do to modify these perceptions?

4. If the client has a plan for suicide, how lethal is that plan, and how can the therapist ensure that the plan is not implemented?

In addition to the interview with the client and family, the therapist can employ one of the many commercially available brief assessment instruments to lend support to or perhaps disconfirm the initial diagnosis of lethality.

The behavior of family members toward the suicidal member is important. The therapist and family members must provide the client a forum to openly discuss the pain and isolation that he feels. When the client feels that those family member and close friends are aware of the pain, the intensity of the impulse often subsides. The therapist must be able to facilitate this process and prevent family members from attempting to "correct" the client's perceptions. Acceptance of and concern for the suicidal person's feelings and thoughts by the other family members, without appearing devastated, is critical at this stage of treatment.

All those involved in the treatment must be concerned and attentive, but in a way that communicates to the suicidal person that the helpless feelings are understandable and that, with the help of therapy as well as changes in the family system and environment, these feelings can be managed. Their attitude should communicate respect for the client's ability to work through the situation. In situations in which the family cannot develop the appropriate level of concern (either overinvolved or not sufficiently responsive), the therapist may begin sessions with only the depressed individual present and gradually integrate the family into the sessions as the suicide thoughts become less intense and the family is better able to support the IP. The therapist must engage the entire family in treatment as soon as possible because, if the therapist treats the IP alone, the family members may come to believe that no change is required of them; only the suicidal member must change.

One helpful way to begin treatment of a family with a depressed or suicidal member is to develop a *no suicide contract* with client and the family. In this contract, the suicidal member agrees not to attempt suicide while involved in treatment. Whenever possible, other family members should identify in the contract specifically what they will and will not do to assist the suicidal member in getting back to normal. By including all family members in developing the contract, a systemic base is established that begins to broaden the family's understanding of the problem as a family problem that the behaviors of all its members may be maintaining.

The contract is helpful for the suicidal member because it formally offers a way for the person not to take her own life. Agreeing with the therapist and other family members to a contract not to commit suicide often removes a tremendous burden from the suicidal member. A caution is in order, however: A contract will not stop a person who is determined to take her own life. If the therapist suspects that the client will attempt suicide despite a contract, hospitalization or some other type of inpatient treatment should be arranged in coordination with the family.

Once the immediate threat of suicide has subsided, more traditional family therapy should begin. Rather than focusing on helping the suicidal member stay alive, the treatment now focuses on other members and their impact on each other and on the family's overall health.

Therapy with Divorcing Families

Divorce is a widespread phenomenon in American society. Most therapists will deal with divorce-related problems in their practices, and the effects of divorce will touch the majority of adults and children in the United States in some way (Everett & Volgy, 1991). Kitson and Morgan (1990) reported that as many as one half to two thirds of marriages contracted in 1990 may end in divorce. Fenell (1993b) reviewed the literature suggesting the potential harmful impact of divorce on children, extended family members, and the divorcing couple themselves. Despite the potential pain associated with divorce, it remains common.

The process leading to divorce is developmental and sequential. The therapist may be contacted at various points in the process and with various clients. For example, a therapist may work with:

- a couple in marriage counseling who discover that they do not want to stay together,
- a spouse whose partner has informed him that the marriage is to end and is devastated by the news,
- an acting-out child who is responding to the recent divorce of her parents, or
- a couple who intends to divorce and wants the process to be as positive as possible for all concerned.

Everett and Volgy (1991) developed a framework for the divorce process to help therapists understand and treat the various aspects of divorce with specific interventions. They postulated a series of steps and suggested that therapists be prepared to intervene at any of the steps. The most important steps in the divorce process as identified by these authors are the following:

1. *Heightened ambivalence.* The couple begins to have serious doubts about the marriage. It is during this stage that children usually become aware that a problem exists. The therapist may be involved here, or the couple may let the relationship deteriorate without seeking help.

2. *Distancing.* The marriage relationship begins to be characterized by both physical and emotional distance. This distancing also may occur with extended family and some friends. During this phase, the

couple may become aware that outside help is essential if the relationship is to improve.

3. *Preparation fantasies and actions.* Here the partners begin to imagine that they will have their needs met by a return to the family of origin or by living a less restricted life, perhaps with another partner, after the divorce.

4. *Physical separation.* The couple moves apart and the reality of the divorce begins to have an impact on the children. This is often when the children enter therapy if they are not already involved.

5. *Pseudo-reconciliation.* Events such as problems with the children or financial difficulties sometimes bring the couple back together. Although this coming together has signified reconciliation, this is usually not the case. Moreover, this phase fuels children's fantasies that the parents will get back together, which can be devastating when the reconciliation is short lived. After the temporary reconciliation, old problems resurface and reconfirm for the spouses why they are seeking a divorce. At this stage, they may become more open about their plans. As children recognize the reality of the divorce, they can develop physical symptoms or behavioral problems that unite the parents temporarily and slow the divorce process. At this point, therapy focuses on helping the children adjust while working to smooth the divorce process.

6. *Decision to divorce.* During this stage, the legal system becomes actively involved, and the therapist may need to consult with a network of family law specialists to best provide help to the divorcing family.

7. *Recurring ambivalence.* This stage resembles the earlier attempt at reconciliation. This time the overwhelming forces of the legal process lead one or both spouses to reconsider the decision to divorce. During this stage, children's hopes for reconciliation are renewed, and sometimes these hopes are rewarded as the divorce process is discontinued.

8. *Dealing with potential disputes.* The divorcing couple may choose to deal with disputes through the use of mediation or through adversarial methods. If they choose the adversarial method, the therapist must be aware of the possibility of being called into court to testify concerning the case and to help the children sort out the malice expressed by their parents.

9. *Postdivorce coparenting.* Once the divorce is finalized, the couple and children begin to establish clearly defined rules and responsibilities

for the parenting of the children. This clear set of rules and expectations is essential to eliminate disagreements and confusion about custody and shared parenting. If coparenting problems arise, therapy can be of great value. The sooner the couple gets unbiased help in resolving these issues, the better off the children will be. When the divorced parents are at odds, they may suffer; however, the children are the ones who are hurt the most.

10. *Remarriage.* Most couples who divorce will eventually remarry. More than 65% of women and 70% of men remarry after divorce (Norton & Mooreman, 1987). Many of these remarriages will require intervention by the family counselor to help the new family link with the ex-spouse to define roles, rules, and responsibilities.

11. *Dual family functioning.* In this stage, both partners from the former marriage are remarried and share children with their new spouse and their former spouse. This combination of relationships creates a myriad of potential problems. When the problems are not resolved, a family therapist can be helpful in responding to this complex undertaking that requires skill and perseverance from the adults and children to be successful.

Glang and Betis (1993) developed the following list of suggestions to help children through the divorce process.

● The parents together convene the family and tell the children, with care and concern, about the plan to divorce.
● The parents give children ample advance warning before one parent moves out.
● Both parents ensure that the children do not feel they are being divorced from either parent.
● Each parent spends individual time with each child.
● The parent with whom the child spends the most time is the "anchor" parent and will be the one to experience most of the child's anger and sadness.
● The parents should explain the divorce to kids in words they will understand, reassuring them that the divorce is the result of the adults' shortcomings, not the children's.
● Children should see the parents' emotions and know that the parents are human. However, too much emotionalism may lead children to believe they have no strong adult to rely on, and consequently they may feel overwhelmed and frightened.

- Neither parent should criticize the former spouse in front of the children. The children will find fault with both parents. The kids, not the parents, should be able to bring up these faults.
- The kids should see a parent's new home as soon as possible and be assured some space of their own. They may have a room, a closet, or perhaps only a chest of drawers, but it must be their own private space.
- Children often wish their parents would reconcile, even years later. Parents should be aware of this and accept their children's feelings even though reconciliation is out of the question.
- The parents should help kids look forward to the stay with the other parent. These transitions can be difficult and stressful for the children, and parents must work together to help smooth the process. While the discussion in this section has focused on divorce after marriage, the dynamics, problems and solutions apply equally to committed relationships with children that are ending through permanent separation.

No couple marries with the intention of divorcing. Couples are aware of the potential negative impact of divorce on thier children. Nonetheless, marriages do fail and counselors are called upon to help. Counselors' awareness of the stages of divorce and of the ways to most effectively help families through this painful process can help families successfully negotiate these most difficult times.

Rural Family Therapy

Rural families have unique needs that are consistent with their lifestyle. Problems in rural communities are often caused by the relative lack of privacy in that setting. The closeness characteristic of rural communities is one of their strengths, but at the same time it can magnify problems. Closeness can be a blessing when rural families support each other through times of crisis. Closeness can be a curse when the entire community knows too much detail about a family's private issues.

As social and economic pressures mount throughout the United States, rural communities, accustomed to a conservative and low-stress lifestyle, feel them uniquely. With urban demands impinging on their lifestyle and economic uncertainties emerging, rural communities are experiencing significant mental health problems in both number and intensity that may be treated best in a family therapy context (Fenell, Hovestadt, & Cochran, 1985).

Providing mental health services to families in rural communities offers unique challenges to the family counselor. Hovestadt, Fenell, and Canfield (2002) identified several important skills of effective family therapists working in rural communities.

The first, and perhaps most important, is appreciation and understanding of the rural community. This characteristic simply states that the successful therapist will enjoy rural life, appreciate the people, and understand the workings of the community. Rural values are often more conservative that those of the typical family therapist. If the therapist has strong value differences with the dominant rural community values, the therapist will be isolated and marginalized. But if the therapist truly appreciates the community, people, and values, joining the community will be relatively easy, and the therapist can anticipate acceptance and the possibility of doing much good.

A second key ability is the therapist's knowledge of systems theory and the skill to apply this knowledge to the rural community. The rural community is a large system with key subsystems that the therapist must acknowledge and join if the community is to accept her. If the Lions Club is the place where key community members meet, the therapist will want to join the club, actively participate, and thus come to be accepted and valued by members of the community.

Successful counselors in rural communities do much more than work with families. They must be generalists, a third key ability. Although some work in rural communities is family related, the ability to do individual and group therapy is essential, as is the ability to consult with community organizations. Mental health services are few and far between in rural communities, and the therapist must be skilled in a variety of interventions to provide the most assistance.

A fourth characteristic of effective therapists in rural settings is the ability to be comfortable meeting clients in social and other community settings. In a small community, the ability to see clients only during sessions is not possible. The therapist will encounter clients in the hardware store, at church, and in restaurants. If the therapist is not comfortable meeting clients socially, the rural setting probably is not a good fit.

Rural therapists with a background in systems therapy are well prepared to work in the rural environment. Rural communities are simply larger systems with interactions, strengths, and dysfunction similar to a family. If the family therapist is able to establish effective relationships in the rural community and develop each of the key skills described in this section, he can be effective in helping rural families and individuals resolve many of the issues that are emerging as urban values begin to subsume the rural way of life.

Summary

For marriage and family counselors to be best able to serve clients' divergent needs, they must have specific knowledge about numerous family-related problems. In this chapter, I have introduced and briefly discussed several specific family problems that family counselor will encounter in clinical practice. I suggest that the reader use this chapter as an introduction and springboard to a more comprehensive study of each of these important issues, as well as other specific family relationship problems not covered here.

Suggested Readings

Brunn, E. L., & Ziff, A. (2010). *Marrying well: The clinicians' guide to premarital counseling*. New York: Norton.

Carter, B., & McGoldrick, M. (2005). Remarried families. In B. Carter & M. McGoldrick (Eds.). *The expanded family life cycle* (3rd ed.). Boston: Allyn & Bacon.

Goodrich, T. J., Rampage, C., Ellman, B., & Halstead, K. (1988). *Feminist family therapy: A casebook*. New York: Norton.

Grossman, N. S., & Okun, B. F. (2009). Challenges in family forensic psychology: Families with special needs children. *The Family Psychologist, 25*(1), 15–16.

Wallerstein, J. (1989). *Second chances: Men, women and children after divorce*. New York: Ticknor & Fields.

Research in Marriage, Couple, and Family Therapy

Because of the complexity involved in identifying changes that occur within family systems, much of the research in family therapy has focused on individual change within the system—change by the identified patient (IP) and other individual family members. The preponderance of research has demonstrated that family therapy is effective in working with a variety of presenting issues that are addressed within this chapter. Even though the majority of the research conducted has shown that family therapy is effective in producing changes at the individual subsystem level, research methodology has not been successful in evaluating systemic changes involving subsystems of two or more family members. The research cited in this chapter presents some of the classic, yet still relevant, findings concerning marital, couple, and family therapy. More recent research describing evidence-based therapies, common factors, and model dependent research is presented in Chapter 4. Future researchers are challenged to develop methodologies appropriate for evaluating systems therapy and multiperson changes within families, rather than trying to "shoehorn" systems therapies into a linear, cause-and-effect research model.

This chapter presents an overview of some of the classic research on psychotherapy in general, followed by more specific information about the research in MCFT.

Key Concepts

○ Meta-analysis
○ Marital satisfaction research
○ Effects of divorce on children
○ Family therapy effectiveness
○ Gottman's research
○ Randomized studies

Questions for Discussion

1. Why is research important in marriage, couple, and family therapy?
2. Why is family therapy research so difficult?
3. How does divorce affect the children involved? Do you agree with Wallerstein's findings? Why or why not?
4. What MCFT research question do you believe needs to be investigated? Why is this important?
5. What professional journals are most useful to you? Why do you enjoy them?

Family therapy research is difficult for several reasons. First, if the treatment is designed to change the family system, what assessment instrument can be used to demonstrate change in each of the members of the family and, more important, the larger family system itself? It is relatively easy to identify changes over time in an individual's behavior. However, what is the best way for a researcher identify and measure changes to a family system? Family research outcomes are complex and difficult to operationally define. For instance, two families may come to therapy, each with a rebellious child. One family might adjust its rules and roles, normalize the rebelliousness, and leave therapy feeling successful. This family has improved, therapy has been successful, yet the behaviors of the IP have not changed in measurable ways while the attitudes about the child's behavior held by the other members of the family system (which were not a focus of assessment) have changed. In the second family, the parents learn to become more united and assertive, confronting the rebellious child directly. The change in the parents' behavior can be measured, as can the changes made by the IP based on the family interventions. Both families have improved, but in a very different ways. How does the researcher make sense of this? And how can a therapist decide which approach is most effective for a particular type of family problem? This example highlights the importance of understanding how system changes in families can look quite different and occur with very different intervention approaches yet still contribute to successful therapy.

Early Studies

In 1952, Hans Eysenck threatened the world of psychotherapy with the results of his research on the effectiveness of psychotherapy. Eysenck reported that, according to his analysis, about 67% of neurotic patients improved within 2 years whether they received therapy or not. Eysenck challenged psychotherapists to demonstrate that the effectiveness of their approaches was superior to the improvement that occurred in symptomatic individuals who received no therapy. If unable to do this, therapists should concede that their approaches were not useful (Eysenck, 1952).

Bergin (1967, 1971) was one of the first researchers to respond to the Eysenck criticism. His reevaluation of Eysenck's data revealed that psychotherapy was at least moderately effective with neurotic patients, as 65% improved within 2 years *with* psychotherapy, while only 43% of untreated neurotic patients improved within 2 years.

Despite Bergin's findings, the challenge to demonstrate the effectiveness of psychotherapy remains. Ethical mental health practitioners are persistently searching for information about the most beneficial treatment for their clients. How can therapists know what kinds of treatments are most beneficial unless effective research is conducted to demonstrate the results of various approaches? Ethical therapists commit a portion of their daily activities to reading professional publications that describe family therapy approaches and the research. Therapists need to know, within the limits available, whether the treatment they plan to implement works (Levant, 1984).

Paul (1967) phrased a question that described what psychotherapy research attempts to discover. His question clearly identified the complexities involved in conducting psychotherapy research. He asked, "What treatment, by whom, is most effective for this individual with that specific problem, and under what set of circumstances?" Attempting to respond to Paul's question has been, and will continue to be, a major challenge for psychotherapy researchers.

Following the publication of Bergin's (1967, 1971) findings, investigators began to identify deterioration in clients as a result of psychotherapy (Lambert, Bergin, & Collins, 1977). *Deterioration* means that the client becomes worse as a result of therapy. It was discovered that deterioration occurred in less than 10% of the clients treated, and the rate was higher for more disturbed clients. While this rate is fairly low, therapists are cautioned to evaluate for client deterioration and, if identified, discuss the problem with the client, change approaches, or refer to another therapist.

Several research projects investigated the effects of the level of therapist empathy, warmth, and genuineness on the outcome of therapy (Duncan, 2010; Mitchell, Bozarth, & Kraft, 1977; Rogers, 1957; Truax

& Carkhuff, 1967; Truax & Mitchell, 1971). Although the results of these studies consistently suggested that these therapist qualities are important to client change, the mechanism for these results, as well as how widely the findings can be generalized, have been questioned (Mitchell et al., 1977; Sexton, Ridley, & Kleiner, 2004). Nonetheless, when various theories of counseling are compared, the results indicate that one approach is generally just as effective as another (Blow, Sprenkle, & Davis, 2007; Luborsky, Singer, & Luborsky, 1973; Smith & Glass, 1977; Sprenkle & Blow, 2004; Strupp & Hadley, 1979). Thus, researchers have not been able to conclude precisely what it is about psychotherapy that brings about improvement.

However, these studies do lend indirect support to the findings of researchers who have concluded that the *therapist qualities* of empathy, warmth, and genuineness are factors that facilitate change. Refer to Chapter 4 for a more detailed explanation of common factors research in psychotherapy.

Subsequent studies by Bergin and Lambert (1978) suggested that *short-term therapy* lasting 6 months or less was effective in providing symptom relief for the client. Smith and Glass (1977) completed a meta-analysis of 375 controlled-outcome studies, which suggested that the typical client in therapy is better off than 75% of individuals with similar problems who are not treated. Thus, a fairly solid body of research has been compiled suggesting that psychotherapy is effective.

This summary of several important psychotherapy outcome studies sets the stage for a review of the specific research in marriage, couple, and family therapy. The same problems that exist in research with individual clients persist in family therapy research, but with additional complications. In MCFT research, change is more difficult to assess. Are we looking for change in the IP, change in other family members, change in the family subsystems, or change in the family system itself? Without knowing what to look for, specifying what change is expected, and knowing where within the family system that change will occur, it is difficult to reliably assess outcome (Gurman & Kniskern, 1981b). Olson, Russell, and Sprenkle (1980) stated that, to evaluate family therapy, researchers need ways to identify and measure family system changes. A significant amount of work remains to be completed before researchers are able to reliably identify and accurately measure system change.

Major Research Reviews

Several comprehensive reviews of the research literature concerning the outcome of MCFT have been conducted (DeWitt, 1978; Gurman & Kniskern 1978a; Liddle & Rowe, 2004; Olson et al.,1980; Pinsof & Wynne, 1995a, b; Wells & Dezen 1978). Specific findings based on these comprehensive reviews indicate the following conclusions:

- Improvement rates in MCFT are similar to improvement rates in individual therapy.
- Deterioration rates in MCFT are similar to deterioration rates in individual therapy.
- Deterioration may occur because:
  - the therapist has poor interpersonal skills,
  - the therapist moves too quickly into sensitive topic areas and does not handle the situation well,
  - the therapist allows family conflict to become exacerbated without moderating therapeutic intervention,
  - the therapist does not provide adequate structure in the early stages of therapy, or
  - the therapist does not support family members.
- Conjoint couple therapy (with both partners present) is the treatment of choice over individual therapy for couples experiencing marital or other serious relationship problems. Lower improvement rates and higher deterioration rates are found when couples are treated separately for marital or relationship problems (Gurman & Kniskern, 1978b).
- Family therapy is just as effective as individual therapy for problems involving marital, relationship, and family conflict and even for treating an individual's problems.
- Brief therapy, limited to 12 sessions or fewer, seems to be as effective as open-ended therapy.
- Participation of the father in family therapy increases the probability of a successful outcome.
- Cotherapy, even though more expensive to provide, has not been demonstrated to be more effective than single-therapist family therapy.
- Therapist relationship skills have an influence on the outcome of therapy. Good relationship skills produce positive outcomes, and poor relationship skills may produce deterioration.

- When the identified patient has severe diagnosable psychological problems, a successful outcome is less probable.
- Modified structural family therapy has been used to successfully treat psychosomatic problems, eating disorders, (Minuchin, Rosman, & Baker, 1978) and drug and alcohol problems (Stanton, 1978; Stanton & Todd, 1979, 1981).
- Multisystemic therapy and functional family therapy have been demonstrated to be effective in treating problems of acting-out adolescents (Sexton & Alexander, 2004).
- Family type, family interaction style, and family demographic factors have not been demonstrated to be related to the outcome of family therapy (Gurman & Kniskern, 1981b; Sprenkle & Blow, 2003).

Shadish et al. (1995) conducted a meta-analysis of 163 randomized studies. A meta-analysis takes a number of related studies and quantifies the results to determine any significant overall effects. The results of this study demonstrated that MCFT works with a variety of presenting problems. But no orientation was shown to be more effective than another, and individual therapy was as effective as MCFT. Moreover, the authors concluded that MCFTs are conducted in different ways and are difficult to compare in meta-analyses. More specific findings concerning the efficacy of family therapy are presented next.

Family Therapy with Schizophrenic Disorders

Goldstein and Miklowitz (1995) and Aderhold and Gottwalz (2004) reviewed the research evaluating the use of family therapy with families who have a member with schizophrenia. The authors challenged early theories (Bateson, Jackson, Haley, & Weakland, 1956; Bowen, 1960) suggesting that the family climate and relationships precipitate the onset and maintenance of the illness. More recent research presents an almost exclusive biological basis for the disorder. Nonetheless, the authors found that family therapy interventions, especially psychoeducational approaches, coupled with appropriate medications, are helpful in treating schizophrenic disorders. Specifically, family psychoeducation was found to be far more effective than routine care in preventing relapse.

The unit of treatment for the psychoeducational family therapy included (a) the family and the patient, which encompassed skill-building, problem-solving, case-management, and crisis-intervention strategies; (b) the family without the patient in sessions, focusing on providing support and developing approaches to cope with the disorder; and (c) multifamily support groups that also did not include the patients.

Goldstein and Miklowitz (1995) suggested common ingredients in an effective psychoeducational family therapy intervention program. They reported that it is important that the family be engaged early in treatment and that the family treatment does not imply that the family is responsible for the patient's illness. The counselor should also present factual information on schizophrenia—including causal factors, prognosis, and the reasons for various treatments. Moreover, the program must include recommendations for coping with the disorder and problem-solving techniques. Finally, the sessions should help the family members communicate effectively and deal successfully with crises if they occur. Alderhold and Gottwalz (2004) asserted that psychoeducational family therapy can be used effectively with disorders other than schizophrenia.

Liddle and Rowe (2004) reviewed the literature on the treatment of families with a schizophrenic member. They identified several key findings:

- Family-based interventions are effective.
- Interventions are more effective when employed in conjunction with medication.
- Interventions that help family members deal with the stress of caring for a schizophrenic member are important.
- Family support networks are helpful.
- Teaching family members patient-management and crisis-intervention strategies is helpful.
- Communication training for family members is helpful.

The research shows that family-based psychoeducational interventions coupled with medication and family support can ease the family's burden of managing and supporting a family member with schizophrenia.

Family Therapy Treastment of Depression and Anxiety

Liddle and Rowe (2004), in their review of the literature, found evidence suggesting that depression and anxiety in children and adolescents may develop and be maintained by certain family patterns such as the following:

- Insecure or problematic attachment relationships

- Dysfunctional and incongruent communication patterns
- Negative messages from parents to children
- Consistent and severe parent–child conflict
- Rejection of child by parents
- Severe parental depression

On the positive side, the authors reported that supportive and cohesive families that are able to adapt to changing circumstances can make depression in children less likely.

The Liddle and Rowe review (2004) found that problems in marriage were prevalent in depression in adults. Depression has been linked to the following relationship problems:

- Infidelity
- Marital separation
- Lack of fulfilling relationship
- Lack of intimacy with poor communication
- Ineffective problem-solving abilities

Marital, couple, and family dysfunction, especially high levels of criticism, has been linked to poor prognosis in the alleviation or depression and contributes to relapse (Liddle & Rowe, 2004). While there is less research investigating anxiety in family members, many of the family concerns reported above are likely to contribute.

The largest and most comprehensive study to date of the effects of individual therapy on depression is the NIMH Collaborative Depression Study (Shea et al., 1992). This study compared cognitive therapy, interpersonal therapy, and therapy using psychotropic medications. Even though initial results for all forms of treatment were promising, some 40% of the clients relapsed. This result led Prince and Jacobson (1995) to conclude, "Individual treatment may be overlooking some critical factors in the etiology, maintenance and resolution of affective disorders" (p. 378). This hypothesis suggested that marital and family therapies might provide the contextual focus that is missing from individual treatments.

Prince and Jacobson (1995) reviewed three well-designed studies comparing individual therapy and conjoint marital therapy for depressed couples in which the woman was diagnosed with unipolar depression. Results of the studies suggested that conjoint marital therapy is as effective as individual therapies for treating depressed women in distressed marriages and that conjoint treatment is more effective than individual treatment in alleviating marital distress. Even with these results, the authors noted that success requires improvement in both reduced depression and enhanced marital quality. Unfortunately, the authors discovered that, even with notable success for many couples, some of the couples did not improve significantly on these dimensions.

The Liddle and Rowe (2004) review of the research literature favored cognitive and behavioral family treatments as holding most promise for helping families with depressed or anxious members. Systemic behavior family therapy (SBFT) and cognitive behavioral family therapy (CBFT), while still being studied, show promise. For depression in marriage, behavioral couples therapy has shown the most promise.

Marital Therapy for Conflict and Divorce

After reviewing the literature on the effects of marital therapy on marital conflict and divorce, Bray and Jouriles (1995) concluded that marital therapy is effective in the short run for resolving marital conflict. Long-term follow-up studies, however, suggest that marital therapy is less effective for the long run (Gottman, 1999). One of the reasons for this may be that couples do not return for periodic "booster shots" of therapy that might help them maintain the early gains of treatment.

Moreover, no type of marital therapy treatment has been shown to be more effective than another. Most of the research has been conducted on behavioral couple therapy (BCT), and this therapy is not used much outside the academic environment. On a more positive note, Bray and Jouriles (1995) found that marital therapy is successful in preventing divorce. They reported that even though in the short run treatments are successful in stabilizing the marriage, about 50% of those treated in marital therapy are not helped in the long run. A way to reach those not helped through traditional therapies is desperately needed.

Family Therapy in Treating Alcoholism and Drug Abuse

Edwards and Steinglass (1995) did a modified meta-analysis of 21 studies examining the effects of family interventions on alcoholism. They found that the spouse's commitment to therapy led to alcoholics (especially men) entering treatment significantly more often than alcoholics whose spouse did not participate. Studies evaluating outcome at 6-month follow-up found that alcoholics treated with family therapy did better than those treated individually or not at all. This gain, however, did not hold up over longer periods. Finally, Edwards and Steinglass found that family involvement in aftercare was related to continuing abstinence for up to 2 years after treatment began.

Liddle and Dakof (1995) reviewed 18 studies dealing with adult and adolescent drug abuse and found overwhelming support for family treatment in engaging adolescent drug abusers and their families in therapy and the concomitant reduction in drug use. The findings considering family therapy for adult drug abusers are not as compelling. Results of the studies are mixed. Though some show family therapy to be as effective in engaging families in treatment, others suggest that family therapy is no better than other treatments—which often are not very effective. Liddle and Dakoff (1995) reminded the reader that many of the family interventions used in the studies they reviewed are embedded in a broader treatment approach, so it is impossible to determine whether the family component is uniquely responsible for the change.

Liddle and Rowe (2004) found in their review of the family therapy literature strong support indicating that dysfunctional interactions among members contributes to substance abuse among individuals in the family. Strong and consistent evidence also shows that family-based treatments, especially more contemporary evidence-based treatments involving the family and larger systems that follow strict protocols described in published manuals, can be helpful in resolving substance abuse problems in adolescents and, to a lesser extent, among adult substance abusers.

Family Therapy with Childhood and Adolescent Behavior Disorders

Estrada and Pinsof (1995) reviewed the research on the use of family therapy in treating selected behavioral disorders of childhood, using the age of 14 as the cutoff between childhood and adolescence. They concluded that most so-called family therapy studies for the treatment of behavioral disorders were some form of parent management training (PMT). This training was typically behavioral, and the family component was part of a larger treatment protocol. Thus, isolating the change-producing factors is impossible. Nonetheless, Estrada and Pinsoff did find evidence to support the efficacy of family therapy as described in the treatment of childhood conduct disorders, phobias, anxiety, and autism. Their review of the data did not support the superiority of brief PMT for ADHD children when compared to treatment with Ritalin.

Chamberlain and Rosicky (1995) extended the research on the treatment of adolescent conduct disorders by reviewing seven studies published since 1988 that used specific, manual-based independent treatment variables, a control or comparison group, and some form of family treatment that targeted adolescent conduct disorders. Independent variables that have been described in detail in treatment manuals are applied consistently according to a documented procedure. Changes resulting from manualized treatments are more reliable than changes that have not used standardized treatments.

Treatments in the studies reviewed were based on social learning theory with families, structural family therapy, and a multimodal family therapy. Results of several studies suggested that family therapy interventions seem to decrease conduct problems when compared to standard individual therapy and no treatment. The researchers cautioned that even though these results are promising, several families participating in the studies were not satisfied with the outcome of the family treatment.

Liddle and Rowe (2004) reviewed the research literature concerning childhood and adolescent behavior disorders and concluded that negative family interaction patterns contribute to the development and maintenance of oppositional defiant behavior disorder (ODD); attention deficit hyperactivity disorder (ADHD); and conduct disorder (CD). Much of the research strongly implies that antisocial behavior is learned and that it emerges at an early age when certain negative qualities exist in the family. Family behaviors that foster acting out in children and adolescents include the following:

- Constant conflict and aggression within the family
- Family aggression patterns generalized to school and other environments
- Acting-out behaviors interrupting parental conflict
- Overly coercive parenting practices
- Poor parental oversight of children's activities and behaviors
- Parental substance abuse and antisocial behavior

Positive family patterns can minimize these problems of childhood and adolescence. Positive qualities identified in the literature include parents who are attuned to their children and react in a caring way to their needs and requests, parental acceptance, parental oversight that is caring and not punitive, and caring connections among family members.

Liddle and Rowe (2004) identified three family therapy approaches that have been shown to be effective in treating behavior problems of children and adolescents. These include parent management training, functional family therapy, and multisystemic therapy. These approaches were discussed more fully in Chapter 4 under evidence-based treatments.

Marriage Research

This section examines some fundamental issues concerning marriage. According to the US Census Bureau, the overall percentage of adults who were married declined to 54.1% in 2010 from 57.3% in 2000 (US Bureau of the Census, 2010). Is marriage a necessary institution and a positive experience? Or is it an archaic relic, no longer needed, one that inhibits the growth of its participants? Is divorce preventable, or is it sometimes the right answer for a couple? How does it impact children? If marriage is still important to our society, what are the characteristics of successful long-term marriages? In preparing the following discussion, empirical, descriptive studies, and case-study research was reviewed.

Advantages of Marriage

In their comprehensive review on marriage, Waite and Gallagher (2000) reported that, on the average, married men and women live longer, are healthier, happier, more solvent financially, and more satisfied sexually than their unmarried counterparts. While the research often shows men benefiting more than women from marriage, husbands and wives alike are better off than their unmarried peers. Coombs (1991) reported that married persons generally have lower incidences of alcoholism, lower rates of suicide, longer lifespan, lower incidences of mental illness, and greater happiness than unmarried persons. Coombs cautioned that the benefits of marriage are likely predicated on the positive qualities of the marriage. It is hard to imagine a person in an extremely unhappy marriage leading a pleasant and satisfying life. More recent research has suggested that unmarried women, especially well-educated women, are leading very satisfying lives as well.

Divorce and Its Consequences

Divorce can have devastating consequences to the partners and children involved. Morgan (1990) and Wallerstein, Lewis, and Blakeslee (2000) described the multiple consequences of divorce. Divorce contributes to poor physical and mental health, economic problems, and problems in social adjustment as a single person. Coombs (1991) reported higher suicide rates among divorced individuals than married individuals. Wallerstein and her colleagues' landmark longitudinal study of children of divorce reported that, contrary to much of today's conventional wisdom that suggests leaving a bad marriage has few negative consequences, divorce often does have devastating effects on children. Children of divorce on the average are less physically and mentally healthy, less well-educated, and less successful in their careers and their own relationships than children from intact marriages (Waite & Gallagher, 2000; Wallerstein et al., 2000). Although divorce is necessary in certain situations, many researchers believe that couples willing to work together with integrity can resolve many of the issues that otherwise would result in divorce (Fenell, 1991, 1993a; Gottman, 1999; Wachtel, 1999). Michelle Weiner-Davis (1992), in her books and presentations, developed a program called "divorce busting." This program is designed to help improve and sustain marriages that are experiencing problems that are leading towards divorce.

Fenell Study: Successful Marriages

Fenell (1993a) conducted a survey of 147 couples in satisfactory first marriages of longer than 20 years in duration. These couples were middle class, were from an urban or suburban environment, and ranged in age from 39 to 65 years of age. One of the criticisms of previous research on characteristics of long-term marriages is that the studies often examined marital duration without considering marital quality (Glenn, 1990; Lewis & Spanier, 1979). The Fenell (1993a) study responded to this criticism by administering the Dyadic Adjustment Scale (Spanier, 1976) to all participants to ensure the presence of marital quality. People who were not in satisfactory marriages as identified by the scale were eliminated from the study.

A survey was developed through a modified Delphi process that resulted in a questionnaire listing 59 potential marital strengths. Each of the 59 items was a potential strength that could contribute to a successful long-term relationship. The survey was administered to each of the 294 participants to determine the major characteristics of long-term marriages. A key finding of this study was that men and women in successful marriages demonstrated considerable congruence in what they believed contributed to their successful long-term relationships. The top 10 characteristics contributing to the long-term and high quality marriages, as identified by the participants, are the following:

1. *Lifetime commitment to marriage.* This was the most frequently endorsed characteristic contributing to the successful and long-term marriages considered in this study. The participants believed that commitment was the glue that held the marriage together during the inevitable bad times. When couples do not feel committed to each other, their commitment to the institution of marriage can sustain the relationship until better times come. Couples with less commitment to the institution of marriage might be more prone to leave the marriage during troubled times.

2. *Loyalty to spouse.* This was the second most frequently endorsed characteristic. This quality suggests the importance of standing with and supporting the other, especially during rough times in the marriage.

3. *Strong moral values.* Although the values held by each couple in the study varied, the importance of value congruence in successful marriages is noted throughout the literature (Murstein, 1976, 1987). The moral values referred to here were not made explicit by the study participants. Nevertheless, based on list of characterizes of successful marriages reported here, some of the important values may be inferred.

4. *Respect for spouse as a best friend.* This characteristic is important as the marriage endures and the initial passions fade (Flowers, 2000; Rowe & Meridith, 1982; Swensen, Eskew, & Kohlhepp, 1984). Couples with solid friendships enjoy each other and sustain their relationships at a high level. Good friends are self-disclosing—revealing their feelings to each other—and are empathic and understanding. Both self-disclosure (Hansen & Schuldt, 1984; Hendrick, 1981; Knapp & Vangelisti, 1991) and empathic understanding (Mackey & O'Brien, 1995) have been identified as important characteristics in successful relationships. Moreover, a good friendship can serve as a buffer for the marriage when the stress levels are high (Shapiro, Gottman, & Carrere, 2000).

5. *Commitment to sexual fidelity.* Without trust and sexual exclusivity in the relationship (Mackey & O'Brien, 1995), it rarely is possible to attain marital quality and, thus, divorce becomes more likely. Although an affair does not automatically lead to divorce, the pain the affair causes may make repair of the relationship quite difficult (Bader, Pearson, & Schwartz, 2000).

6. *Desire to be a good parent.* Although a body of research suggests that the transition to parenthood can cause the relationship to decline in quality (Glenn, 1990; Shapiro et al., 2000), participants in this study believed that their shared desire to be good parents was an important contributor to the success of their marriages.

7. *Faith in God and spiritual commitment.* This finding is identified in numerous other studies (Abbot, Berry, & Meridith; 1990; Olson, Sprenkle, & Russell, 1983; Schumm, 1985; Stinett & Saur, 1977; Thomas & Rogharr, 1990) and is not surprising, given the religious nature of many of the populations selected for study. Nonetheless, the religious and spiritual faith of couples in the long-term marriages served as a guide, especially during difficult times in the marriage. This religious dimension of long-term marriages strongly emphasizes preservation of marriage over divorce when possible. Married couples who have differing views on the role of religion and spirituality in marriage may have difficulties when their deeply held but differing values clash. In contrast, couples with religious or spiritual convictions that encourage marital preservation may "weather the storm" of marital difficulty and later move to a period of marital happiness and marital stability (Robinson & Blanton, 1993; Schumm, 1985; Weiner-Davis, 1992).

8. *Desire to please and support the spouse.* This characteristic encourages successful marriage by recognizing the importance of appreciating the partner, identifying the partner's needs, and having the desire and ability to respond to those needs. Winch (1958) developed the theory of complimentary needs in marriage and postulated that when those needs were met for both partners, the relationship was strengthened. A spouse who engages in behaviors that please and support the other spouse must also be the recipient of pleasing and supporting behaviors from the partner. Reciprocity of positive behaviors is important in successful marriages. If one spouse does all the giving and the other all the taking, marital problems are likely (Jacobson, 1978).

9. *A good companion to the spouse.* This characteristic is similar to the fourth characteristic, respect for spouse as a best friend. It differs, though, in its emphasis on companionship—being with the spouse physically, emotionally, and with deep commitment to the partner and the marriage. As partners spend more enjoyable time together as companions, their appreciation of each other increases and strengthens the marriage.

10. *Willingness to forgive and be forgiven.* The couples in this study were in successful, long-term marriages. These happy couples, however, did encounter significant problems in their marriages that could have, but did not, result in divorce (Fenell, 1991). The couples in this study emphasized the importance of being able to forgive the partner for real and perceived transgressions during the long-term marriages. Equally important was that the spouse who had offended the partner recognized how it hurt the other person and the relationship, was apologetic, and was both willing and able to receive the partner's forgiveness. Forgiving oneself can be difficult for some. Without forgiveness and the ability to receive forgiveness, marriages labor with unspoken resentments and guilt—qualities that do not support successful marriage.

Fenell (1993a) used the results of this study to develop a *Marriage Characteristic Worksheet* (see Figure 16.1) and has used the worksheet in his treatment of couples experiencing marital difficulties.

Other Studies of Successful Marriages

Other marital researchers have identified characteristics of successful marriages. Berger and Kellner (1977) suggested that creating an existential shared meaning is the hallmark of successful marriages. They believe that couples construct a shared reality as they redefine the individual realities that each brings to the marriage. The shared reality provides meaning to the relationship.

To the extent that the shared meaning encompasses the most salient personality traits of each partner, the relationship is strengthened. If the shared meaning excludes individual traits that the other member of the relationship considers essential, consensus and cooperation become difficult. Thus, a successful marriage must develop a mutually reinforcing shared reality in which the couple values the characteristics that each

Your Name: _____

Date: _____

DIRECTIONS

Ten important characteristics of long-term marriages are listed below. Under each characteristic, list two or three specific ways your partner could demonstrate this characteristic in your relationship. When you and your partner have finished this worksheet, we will discuss your responses. If the characteristic is not important to you, please indicate this below the characteristic.

CHARACTERISTICS

Lifetime commitment to marriage
  1.
  2.
  3.

Loyalty to partner
  1.
  2.
  3.

Strong moral values
  1.
  2.
  3.

Respect for spouse as a best friend
  1.
  2.
  3.

Commitment to sexual fidelity
  1.
  2.
  3.

Desire to be a good parent
  1.
  2.
  3.

Faith in God or spiritual
  commitment
  1.
  2.
  3.

Desire to please and support
  partner
  1.
  2.
  3.

Good companion to partner
  1.
  2.
  3.

Willingness to forgive and be
  forgiven
  1.
  2.
  3.

Figure 16.1   Marriage Characteristic Worksheet

partner possesses. Wallerstein and Blakeslee (1995) conducted a longitudinal study of 50 couples married from 9 to 40 years. They found no single model of marital success and discovered that no marriages were free from conflict, tragedy, and other hardships. Results of the study showed that successful marriage partners were good friends, respected each other, and enjoyed each other's company. The couples believed that their marriages were works in progress, not finished products. Many of these findings are similar to those of Fenell (1993a), Flowers (2000), and Robinson and Blanton (1993).

Robinson and Blanton Study

Robinson and Blanton (1993) conducted a study of 15 couples in long-term marriages, using an unstructured interview format. They interviewed each spouse separately and asked each to report the strengths of the partner, strengths of the relationship, and strengths of within themselves. In addition, the participants were asked to discuss times when they felt close to their spouse, difficulties in the relationship, and the most important things one should know about marriage.

Results of the Robinson and Blanton (1993) study revealed several key characteristics of these successful marriages.

- *Intimacy.* Defined as closeness to one's spouse, intimacy was the central concept identified by the participants in this study. The elements of intimacy they reported include: shared interests, activities, thoughts, feelings, values, pains, and joys; involvement through good times and bad; and interdependence. Although the couples reported high levels of connectedness, the authors concluded that this was a healthy and mutual intimacy rather than fusion (Bowen, 1978), which is a way of completing an incomplete sense of self and may be dysfunctional and stressful in a marriage. In addition, the participants reported that strong friendships (Fenell, 1993a; Flowers, 2000) were a component of intimacy and that time spent together was mutually enjoyable.
- *Commitment.* Defined as an expectation by the partners that the marriage would endure, commitment was a second key characteristic of these long-term marriages. The participants reported that the influence of an external commitment—an expectation by society to remain in the relationship (Lewis & Spanier, 1979)—and internal commitment—a deeply held personal value—were equally important to the

success of their relationships. In addition, the couples reported feeling a deep level of commitment to their spouse and to the marriage (Fenell, 1993a; Lauer & Lauer, 1986; Weishaus & Field, 1988).

- *Communication.* In this study, communication was defined as emotional transparency, including a sharing of thoughts and feelings, discussing problems, and listening to the other's point of view. Couples used their communication skills to resolve many of the problems experienced in their marriages. Communication was important in facilitating shared decision making and conflict resolution. Effective communication also enabled participants to interact effectively and minimize negative feelings. Couples who reported higher intimacy levels also had stronger communication abilities. Noler and Fitzpatrick (1990) reviewed the literature on communication in marriage, and this review further supported the relationship between good communication and marital quality.

- *Congruence.* The married couples in the study identified similar strengths in their relationship. The spouses had strong congruence in their perceptions of communication, commitment, intimacy, family orientation, and religious orientation. The couples also expressed congruence in certain areas of relationship weaknesses. Partners who share congruent and positive perceptions of their relationship are more likely to be in well-adjusted and satisfactory marriages (Fields, 1983; Robinson & Blanton, 1993; Sporakowski & Hughston, 1978). In his study of long-term, successful marriages, Fenell (1993a) found that the marital strengths identified by the husbands and wives were highly correlated and congruent. Future research might investigate whether congruence in happy marriages was present in the beginning of the relationship, whether it evolved over time, or whether it was some combination of these.

- *Religious orientation.* Research by Schumm (1985) suggested that religious orientation is the key characteristic of the successful relationships he studied. Furthermore, he found that this characteristic influenced all other relationships. Robinson and Blanton (1993) and Fenell (1993a) concurred that religion, spirituality, or belief in a greater power is an important variable in enduring relationships, but their research did not identify religion as the main factor influencing all others. All 15 couples in the Robinson and Blanton research were affiliated to some extent with a specific religious denomination, so this finding is not surprising. A majority of participants indicated that they received social, emotional, and religious support from their faith. Commitment to the marriage and an expectation for family togetherness were reinforced through the values of religion. Moreover, religious faith helped the couples deal with adversity in their marriages and provided a common value base for marital and family decision making.

Robinson and Blanton (1993) did not find a strong relationship between religiosity and marital quality in their subjects. Although religious orientation was an important characteristic, some of the less religiously involved couples seemed to have stronger marriages than some couples who were more involved in their religion. The importance of religious orientation, though controversial, appears in much of the research on long-term marriages (Abbott et al., 1990; Fenell, 1993a; Schumm, 1985; Stinett & Saur, 1977; Thomas & Rogharr, 1990) and merits consideration along with other qualities in contributing to successful marriages.

Critics have suggested that the relationship between religious orientation and successful marriages is spurious. A number of the long-term studies on marriage obtained their samples from predominantly religious populations and, thus, the participants' reports of the importance of religion to their successful marriages make sense.

Lewis and Spanier Model

Finally, Lewis and Spanier (1979) developed one of the most comprehensive models for successful marriage. They examined premarital variables, marital variables, and external contingencies that lead to successful marriages. Their model considered the couple's similarity, premarital resources, exposure to adequate role models, and support from significant others as key premarital predictors. The following were found to be the most important relationship variables:

- Satisfaction with lifestyle, including employment roles, economic adequacy, community support, and optimal family size
- Rewards from spousal interaction, including positive regard, emotional gratification, communication, role fit, and amount of interaction

The two external contingencies that impact marriage are (a) alternative attractions, such as an emerging affair or significant workplace involvement and (b) pressures to remain married. This pressure includes factors such as family approval and sanctions from church and society. When marital dissatisfaction is present, the power of alternative attractions from the marriage become more powerful. Satisfaction with the marriage strengthens the external pressures that couples feel to remain married.

Research by Gottman and Colleagues

Gottman (1999), one of the most prolific and respected researchers in the field of MCFT, conducted an extensive series of longitudinal studies on marriage quality involving nearly 700 couples. These studies were based on the careful observation, coding, and analysis of actual couple behaviors recorded in his Couples Laboratory at the University of Washington. Based on an exhaustive review of the outcome research on marital therapy, Gottman contended that most marriage counseling interventions are not effective in the long run in enhancing marital quality. Even with marriage counseling, only between 11% and 18% of the couples in therapy maintain the initial gains achieved in treatment. After reviewing the research on relapse rates in marital therapy, Gottman estimated that 35% of the couples treated experienced positive changes in the relationships and an improved marriage. But his review of available studies suggested that 30% to 50% of the couples who initially improve relapse after a year.

Based on Gottman's review of the marital therapy research and his analysis of marital treatments, he concluded that many widely used approaches to the treatment of marital problems have not been successful. Moreover, Gottman insisted that to be deemed successful in the future, effective marital interventions must be based on demonstrated empirical studies that clearly define what is functional and what is dysfunctional in marriages. To accomplish this task, he designed an elaborate research laboratory to observe, record, and evaluate the actions, communication, and physiological responses of hundreds of married couples and identified research-based conclusions on what contributes to satisfactory and enduring marriages.

Some of Gottman's findings are controversial, as they contradict much of the "shared wisdom" of the profession of marital therapy. The findings, however, are based on highly controlled observations of marital couples and extensive follow-up with those couples. Gottman (1999) asserted that his research has provided a picture of what leads to divorce and the characteristics that make couples resistant to divorce. He developed a model that identifies the four major causes of divorce and reported several ways to improve marriages (Gottman, Gottman, & DeClaire, 2007).

Gottman (1993, 1999) found that conflict was present in happy and distressed marriages alike and that the process of resolving conflict was a key predictor in whether the marriage was successful or ended in divorce. Couples in happy marriages had the ability to repair the relationship, whereas couples in unhappy marriages did not. Gottman pointed out that repairing the relationship does not imply resolving all the conflict. His studies found that most couples had ongoing conflicts that were never fully resolved. The happy couples possessed the mechanisms in their relationships to repair the conflicts but not necessarily resolve all of them.

Specifically, Gottman's research found that couples in happy, stable marriages had an overall level of positive affect. Based on observations of couples in happy marriages, he found that the first key is a ratio of positive to negative exchanges in their marriages of at least 5 to 1. This means that happily married couples performed at least five affirming affective behaviors for every negative behavior. Examples of positive affect are showing interest, showing caring, being affectionate, being empathic, being appreciative, showing concern, accepting the partner, using appropriate humor, and sharing joy.

A second key ability found in couples in happy marriages was the ability to reduce the negative affect during conflicts. Couples in distressed marriages established patterns of escalating negative affect in their conflicts. Moreover, couples in unhappy marriages held perceptions of the partner's hurtful behavior as permanent, unchangeable, and an internal part of the partner's personality. In contrast, couples in happy marriages viewed the partner's hurtful behavior as temporary and a result of external causes such as a bad day at work rather than some everlasting character defect.

Gottman (1994, 1999) was able to predict with a high degree of accuracy the marriages that will endure and those that will end in divorce. Based on behavioral, self-report, expert observation, and physiological data recorded from participating couples, he predicted with 95% accuracy which couples' marriages would strengthen and which would deteriorate (Gottman, 1991, 1999). He identified three styles of conflict and conflict resolution. Many therapists think that two of the three styles often contribute to the deterioration of marriage. The Gottman research, however, showed that all three styles can result in satisfactory marriages:

1. *Validating style*. This is the style that most marriage therapists encourage couples to develop during therapy. The communication is clear and direct, spouses express a moderate amount of affect, and they provide support for each other.
2. *Volatile style*. This style has high levels of expressed feelings, frequent arguments, and lots of bickering. Most marital therapists consider this to be a dysfunctional marital style. Gottman agreed that it presents more potential for problems than the validating style but can produce happy marriages.
3. *Conflict-avoiding style*. This style is characterized by repressed feelings and by minimizing marital problems. The partners are eager to compromise, see the other's point of view readily, and are willing to suppress their own thoughts and feelings to preserve the marriage. Minimizing the conflict is their strategy for dealing with controversial issues that emerge in the relationship. Many therapists consider this style as dysfunctional because it lacks the openness and disclosure believed necessary for happy marriages. Yet this style also produces happy marriages.

Gottman (1999) discovered that all three styles may produce happy marriages. What is most important in each style is the partners' ability to interact in ways that present positive affect in a ratio of at least five positive messages for each negative message. Moreover, the happy couples are able to *initiate repair mechanisms* in their arguments and to reduce the negative feelings the arguments generate. Gottman discovered that not all problems will be resolved and that some become perpetual issues that recur. The ability to repair the relationship by *soothing the negative affect* expressed by the partners when perpetual issues are negotiated is one of the key characteristics that differentiate happy and unhappy marriages.

To understand how to make marriage successful, it is important to understand what occurs when the marriage is in difficulty (Gottman, 1999; Gottman et al., 2007). His observational research identified four specific characteristics of marriages in trouble:

1, Criticism
2. Defensiveness

3. Contempt
4. Stonewalling

These characteristics occur in sequence. First one partner criticizes the other. Then the criticized partner becomes defensive and escalates the conflict. This portion of the sequence exists in happy and distressed marriages alike. In distressed marriages, however, the conflict escalates and contempt for the partner emerges. Finally, the couple stonewalls, closeting off interaction and causing escalating negativity.

In Gottman's research, criticism, defensiveness, and stonewalling were found in both happy and distressed marriages. But contempt was identified only in distressed marriages. In happy marriages, couples were able to activate the repair mechanism discussed previously and did not move into the contempt phase. Unhappy couples were not able to trigger repair mechanisms, and their fighting escalated to the contempt phase. Contempt is such a strong predictor of marital unhappiness that Gottman (1999) encouraged marital therapists to "label contempt as psychological abuse and as unacceptable" (p. 47) in the treatment of couples trying to improve their marriages.

A significant and instructive finding about successful marriages emerging from Gottman's research is that, in the first months of thriving marriages, wives are better able to identify negativity in the relationship. Moreover, in these marriages, wives were more likely to raise negative issues for consideration. In troubled marriages, wives were more likely to adjust their "negativity threshold," by accommodating the increasing negativity displayed by the husbands. This adaptation by wives was frequently a precursor to more severe marital distress and divorce. Wives who identified and challenged the negativity rather than accommodating it were more likely to be in happy marriages (Gottman, 1999).

Another of Gottman's important findings was that couples with higher expectations for their marriages tended to have better marriages than couples with lower expectations. Thus, couples who expected much from marriage were more likely to get it and to be in happy marriages. Still another important finding was that husbands who are able to *self-soothe,* as Gottman calls it, by lowering their levels of anger during conflict, were more likely to be in happy marriages.

Even though the Gottman research provided a new view of the causes of marital happiness and distress and new ideas about what are successful and unsuccessful marriages, many of his specific techniques for maintaining happy marriages are similar to those identified by other researchers. Developing skills to repair disagreement and conflict in marriage is seen as essential to happy relationships. For example, Gottman contended, like Berger and Kellner (1977), that happy couples create a shared meaning and that, to maintain a happy relationship, the partners need to communicate more positives than negatives (Jacobson, 1978) to each other. Moreover, Gottman, like Robinson and Blanton (1993), agreed that couples who learn to communicate complaints clearly rather than criticize, express genuine caring and validation to the partner, use nondefensive listening and speaking skills, and identify and alter thoughts that perpetuate relationship problems are more likely to be in successful marriages.

Gottman (1999) and Gottman et al. (2007) identified four strategies for maintaining and improving a marriage:

1. Identify emotional reactions to a situation and make an effort to calm down.
2. Speak nondefensively using good communication skills.
3. Use validation to let your partner know you understand and are empathic. Gottman considered this is especially important for men, who tend to become hyperrational.
4. Overlearn the previous skills by practicing them again and again so they are used automatically when conflicts inevitably arise.

Summary of the Research

The research reviewed in this chapter suggests that MCFT may be useful in a variety of problem situations including the following:

- Family psychoeducation with schizophrenic disorders (Aderhold & Gottwalz, 2004; Goldstein & Miklowitz, 1995)
- Affective disorders (Prince & Jacobson, 1995)
- Selected behavioral disorders of childhood (Estrada & Pinsof, 1995)
- Adolescents with conduct disorders (Chamberlain & Rosicky, 1995)
- Treatment of alcoholism (Edwards & Steinglass, 1995)
- Drug abuse (Liddle & Dakof, 1995)
- Physical illness (Campbell & Patterson, 1995)
- Marital dysfunction (Fenell, 1993a; Gottman, 1999)

Pinsof and Wynne (1995a & b) summarized contemporary family therapy research. They reported that family therapy treatment in its many forms is more effective than no treatment at all and does not seem to have negative effects on clients. They reported that family therapy is more effective than standard individual treatment for depressed outpatient women in distressed marriages, adult schizophrenia, marital distress, alcoholism and drug abuse, anorexia in young women, and in the treatment of several medical problems. Although not all studies confirm these findings, many do. Moreover, family involvement is an important ingredient but is not sufficient by itself to bring about change in some of the studies reviewed. Finally, no one type of family therapy has been found to be superior to any other.

Future research efforts should address a series of issues:

- The disorder and the symptoms of the problem being treated should be clearly operationalized and the severity of the symptoms controlled.
- The independent or treatment variables have to be clearly defined. Research using manualized treatments is attempting to address this issue.
- Research should be methodologically sound with control groups; larger sample sizes; assessments with standardized, reliable, and valid instruments appropriate for the treatment being employed; and assessment made for both short-term and longer-term outcomes.

Psychotherapy research is still in a relatively primitive state, and the findings reported here should be considered with this limitation in mind.

The most important professional journals that report the results of marital and family therapy research are:

- *American Journal of Family Therapy*
- *Family Journal: Counseling and Therapy for Couples and Families*
- *Family Process*
- *Family Systems Medicine*
- *Family Therapy*
- *Psychotherapy Networker*
- *Journal of Family Psychology*
- *Journal of Marital and Family Therapy*
- *Journal of Marriage and the Family*
- *Journal of Sex and Marital Therapy*
- *Journal of Strategic and Systemic Therapies*

Future research should focus on evaluating specific aspects of treatment on specific behaviors in the family system. Common factors that produce change should be identified as well as model-specific change elements. Further, future research designs should use a control group whenever feasible so findings can be generalized to broader populations. In addition, findings should be useful in practical ways to clinicians as well as statistically significant to researchers. Finally, researchers need to conduct follow-up evaluations of their subjects to determine the long-term effects of treatment (Gurman & Kniskern, 1981b; Pinsoff & Wynne, 1995a & b). In addition to providing practicing clinicians with information about the efficacy of certain treatment approaches, research in psychotherapy provides a continuous flow of information to the increasingly critical public concerning the effects of treatment for psychological difficulties.

Summary

This chapter has introduced the reader to the complexities involved in conducting research on therapy outcomes. The problems are especially difficult when attempting to isolate which variables in family systems theories are change producing. While the available research suggests that, for most problems, treatment is preferable to no treatment, researchers are still in the primitive stages of determining what therapeutic interventions are best for treating a variety of family problems. If the family therapy profession is to advance in the future, more high-quality controlled studies will be required to determine efficacy of the treatments provided.

Suggested Readings

Duncan, B. L. (2010). *On becoming a better therapist.* Washington, DC: American Psychological Association.

Gottman, J. M. (1999). *The marriage clinic: A scientifically-based marital therapy.* New York: Norton.

Gottman, J. M., Gottman, J. S., & DeClaire, J. (2007). *10 lessons to transform your marriage.* New York: Three Rivers Press.

AAMFT Code of Ethical Principles for Marriage and Family Therapists

eprinted by permission of the American Association for Marriage and Family Therapy. This revised
code was approved effective July 1, 2001. The AAMFT
can make further revisions of the code at any time the
association deems necessary.

Preamble

The Board of Directors of the American Association for Marriage and Family Therapy
(AAMFT) hereby promulgates, pursuant to Article 2, Section 2.013 of the Association's
Bylaws, the Revised AAMFT Code of Ethics, effective July 1, 2001.

The AAMFT strives to honor the public trust in marriage and family therapists by
setting standards for ethical practice as described in this Code. The ethical standards define professional expectations and are enforced by the AAMFT Ethics Committee. The
absence of an explicit reference to a specific behavior or situation in the Code does not
mean that the behavior is ethical or unethical. The standards are not exhaustive. Marriage
and family therapists who are uncertain about the ethics of a particular course of action
are encouraged to seek counsel from consultants, attorneys, supervisors, colleagues, or
other appropriate authorities.

Both law and ethics govern the practice of marriage and family therapy. When making decisions regarding professional behavior, marriage and family therapists must consider the AAMFT Code of Ethics and applicable laws and regulations. If the AAMFT Code of Ethics prescribes a standard higher than that required by law, marriage and family therapists must meet the higher standard of the AAMFT Code of Ethics. Marriage and family therapists comply with the mandates of law, but make known their commitment to the AAMFT Code of Ethics and take steps to resolve the conflict in a responsible manner. The AAMFT supports legal mandates for reporting of alleged unethical conduct.

The AAMFT Code of Ethics is binding on Members of AAMFT in all membership categories, AAMFT-Approved Supervisors, and applicants for membership and the Approved Supervisor designation (hereafter, AAMFT Member). AAMFT members have an obligation to be familiar with the AAMFT Code of Ethics and its application to their professional services. Lack of awareness or misunderstanding of an ethical standard is not a defense to a charge of unethical conduct.

The process for filing, investigating, and resolving complaints of unethical conduct is described in the current Procedures for Handling Ethical Matters of the AAMFT Ethics Committee. Persons accused are considered innocent by the Ethics Committee until proven guilty, except as otherwise provided, and are entitled to due process. If an AAMFT Member resigns in anticipation of, or during the course of, an ethics investigation, the Ethics Committee will complete its investigation. Any publication of action taken by the Association will include the fact that the Member attempted to resign during the investigation.

1. Responsibility to Clients

Marriage and family therapists advance the welfare of families and individuals. They respect the rights of those persons seeking their assistance, and make reasonable efforts to ensure that their services are used appropriately.

1.1 Marriage and family therapists provide professional assistance to persons without discrimination on the basis of race, age, ethnicity, socioeconomic status, disability, gender, health status, religion, national origin, or sexual orientation.

1.2 Marriage and family therapists obtain appropriate informed consent to therapy or related procedures as early as feasible in the therapeutic relationship, and use language that is reasonably understandable to clients. The content of informed consent may vary depending upon the client and treatment plan; however, informed consent generally necessitates that the client: (a) has the capacity to consent; (b) has been adequately informed of significant information concerning treatment processes and procedures; (c) has been adequately informed of potential risks and benefits of treatments for which generally recognized standards do not yet exist; (d) has freely and without undue influence expressed consent; and (e) has provided consent that is appropriately documented. When persons, due to age or mental status, are legally incapable of giving informed consent, marriage and family therapists obtain informed permission from a legally authorized person, if such substitute consent is legally permissible.

1.3 Marriage and family therapists are aware of their influential positions with respect to clients, and they avoid exploiting the trust and dependency of such persons. Therapists, therefore, make every effort to avoid conditions and multiple relationships with clients that could impair professional judgment or increase the risk of exploitation. Such relationships include, but are not limited to, business or close personal relationships with a client or the client's immediate family. When the risk of impairment or exploitation exists due to conditions or multiple roles, therapists take appropriate precautions.

1.4 Sexual intimacy with clients is prohibited.

1.5 Sexual intimacy with former clients is likely to be harmful and is therefore prohibited for two years following the termination of therapy or last professional contact. In an effort to avoid exploiting the trust and dependency of clients, marriage and family therapists should not engage in sexual intimacy with former clients after the two years following termination or last professional contact. Should therapists engage in sexual intimacy with former clients following two years after termination or last professional contact, the burden shifts to the therapist to demonstrate that there has been no exploitation or injury to the former client or to the client's immediate family.

1.6 Marriage and family therapists comply with applicable laws regarding the reporting of alleged unethical conduct.

1.7 Marriage and family therapists do not use their professional relationships with clients to further their own interests.

1.8 Marriage and family therapists respect the rights of clients to make decisions and help them to understand the consequences of these decisions. Therapists clearly advise the clients that they have the responsibility to make decisions regarding relationships such as cohabitation, marriage, divorce, separation, reconciliation, custody, and visitation.

1.9 Marriage and family therapists continue therapeutic relationships only so long as it is reasonably clear that clients are benefiting from the relationship.

1.10 Marriage and family therapists assist persons in obtaining other therapeutic services if the therapist is unable or unwilling, for appropriate reasons, to provide professional help.

1.11 Marriage and family therapists do not abandon or neglect clients in treatment without making reasonable arrangements for the continuation of such treatment.

1.12 Marriage and family therapists obtain written informed consent from clients before videotaping, audio recording, or permitting third-party observation.

1.13 Marriage and family therapists, upon agreeing to provide services to a person or entity at the request of a third party, clarify, to the extent feasible and at the outset of the service, the nature of the relationship with each party and the limits of confidentiality.

2. Confidentiality

Marriage and family therapists have unique confidentiality concerns because the client in a therapeutic relationship may be more than one person. Therapists respect and guard the confidences of each individual client.

2.1 Marriage and family therapists disclose to clients and other interested parties, as early as feasible in their professional contacts, the nature of confidentiality and possible limitations of the clients' right to confidentiality. Therapists review with clients the circumstances where confidential information may be requested and where disclosure of confidential information may be legally required. Circumstances may necessitate repeated disclosures.

2.2 Marriage and family therapists do not disclose client confidences except by written authorization or waiver, or where mandated or permitted by law. Verbal authorization will not be sufficient except in emergency situations, unless prohibited by law. When providing couple, family or group treatment, the therapist does not disclose information outside the treatment context without a written authorization from each individual competent to execute a waiver. In the context of couple, family or group treatment, the therapist may not reveal any individual's confidences to others in the client unit without the prior written permission of that individual.

2.3 Marriage and family therapists use client and/or clinical materials in teaching, writing, consulting, research, and public presentations only if a written waiver has been obtained in accordance with Subprinciple 2.2, or when appropriate steps have been taken to protect client identity and confidentiality.

2.4 Marriage and family therapists store, safeguard, and dispose of client records in ways that maintain confidentiality and in accord with applicable laws and professional standards.

2.5 Subsequent to the therapist moving from the area, closing the practice, or upon the death of the therapist, a marriage and family therapist arranges for the storage, transfer, or disposal of client records in ways that maintain confidentiality and safeguard the welfare of clients.

2.6 Marriage and family therapists, when consulting with colleagues or referral sources, do not share confidential information that could reasonably lead to the identification of a client, research participant, supervisee, or other person with whom they have a confidential relationship unless they have obtained the prior written consent of the client, research participant, supervisee, or other person with whom they have a confidential relationship. Information may be shared only to the extent necessary to achieve the purposes of the consultation.

3. Professional Competence and Integrity

Marriage and family therapists maintain high standards of professional competence and integrity.

3.1 Marriage and family therapists pursue knowledge of new developments and maintain competence in marriage and family therapy through education, training, or supervised experience.

3.2 Marriage and family therapists maintain adequate knowledge of and adhere to applicable laws, ethics, and professional standards.

3.3 Marriage and family therapists seek appropriate professional assistance for their personal problems or conflicts that may impair work performance or clinical judgment.

3.4 Marriage and family therapists do not provide services that create a conflict of interest that may impair work performance or clinical judgment.

3.5 Marriage and family therapists, as presenters, teachers, supervisors, consultants and researchers, are dedicated to high standards of scholarship, present accurate information, and disclose potential conflicts of interest.

3.6 Marriage and family therapists maintain accurate and adequate clinical and financial records.

3.7 While developing new skills in specialty areas, marriage and family therapists take steps to ensure the competence of their work and to protect clients from possible harm. Marriage and family therapists practice in specialty areas new to them only after appropriate education, training, or supervised experience.

3.8 Marriage and family therapists do not engage in sexual or other forms of harassment of clients, students, trainees, supervisees, employees, colleagues, or research subjects.

3.9 Marriage and family therapists do not engage in the exploitation of clients, students, trainees, supervisees, employees, colleagues, or research subjects.

3.10 Marriage and family therapists do not give to or receive from clients (a) gifts of substantial value or (b) gifts that impair the integrity or efficacy of the therapeutic relationship.

3.11 Marriage and family therapists do not diagnose, treat, or advise on problems outside the recognized boundaries of their competencies.

3.12 Marriage and family therapists make efforts to prevent the distortion or misuse of their clinical and research findings.

3.13 Marriage and family therapists, because of their ability to influence and alter the lives of others, exercise special care when making public their professional recommendations and opinions through testimony or other public statements.

3.14 To avoid a conflict of interests, marriage and family therapists who treat minors or adults involved in custody or visitation actions may not also perform forensic evaluations for custody, residence, or visitation of the minor. The marriage and family therapist who treats the minor may provide the court or mental health professional performing the evaluation with information about the minor from the marriage and family therapist's perspective as a treating marriage and family therapist, so long as the marriage and family therapist does not violate confidentiality.

3.15 Marriage and family therapists are in violation of this Code and subject to termination of membership or other appropriate action if they: (a) are convicted of any felony; (b) are convicted of a misdemeanor related to their qualifications or functions; (c) engage in conduct which could lead to conviction of a felony, or a misdemeanor related to their qualifications or functions; (d) are expelled from or disciplined by other professional organizations; (e) have their licenses or certificates suspended or revoked or are otherwise disciplined by regulatory bodies; (f) continue to practice marriage and family therapy while no longer competent to do so because they are impaired by physical or mental causes or the abuse of alcohol or other substances; or (g) fail to cooperate with the Association at any point from the inception of an ethical complaint through the completion of all proceedings regarding that complaint.

4. Responsibility to Students and Supervisees

Marriage and family therapists do not exploit the trust and dependency of students and supervisees.

4.1 Marriage and family therapists are aware of their influential positions with respect to students and supervisees, and they avoid exploiting the trust and dependency of such persons. Therapists, therefore, make every effort to avoid conditions and multiple relationships that could impair professional objectivity or increase the risk of exploitation. When the risk of impairment or exploitation exists due to conditions or multiple roles, therapists take appropriate precautions.

4.2 Marriage and family therapists do not provide therapy to current students or supervisees.

4.3 Marriage and family therapists do not engage in sexual intimacy with students or supervisees during the evaluative or training relationship between the therapist and student or supervisee. Should a supervisor engage in sexual activity with a former supervisee, the burden of proof shifts to the supervisor to demonstrate that there has been no exploitation or injury to the supervisee.

4.4 Marriage and family therapists do not permit students or supervisees to perform or to hold themselves out as competent to perform professional services beyond their training, level of experience, and competence.

4.5 Marriage and family therapists take reasonable measures to ensure that services provided by supervisees are professional.

4.6 Marriage and family therapists avoid accepting as supervisees or students those individuals with whom a prior or existing relationship could compromise the therapist's objectivity. When such situations cannot be avoided, therapists take appropriate precautions to maintain objectivity. Examples of such relationships include, but are not limited to, those individuals with whom the therapist has a current or prior sexual, close personal, immediate familial, or therapeutic relationship.

4.7 Marriage and family therapists do not disclose supervisee confidences except by written authorization or waiver, or when mandated or permitted by law. In educational or training settings where there are multiple supervisors, disclosures are permitted only to other professional colleagues, administrators, or employers who share responsibility for training of the supervisee. Verbal authorization will not be sufficient except in emergency situations, unless prohibited by law.

5. Responsibility to Research Participants

Investigators respect the dignity and protect the welfare of research participants, and are aware of applicable laws and regulations and professional standards governing the conduct of research.

5.1 Investigators are responsible for making careful examinations of ethical acceptability in planning studies. To the extent that services to research participants may be compromised by participation in research, investigators seek the ethical advice of qualified professionals not directly involved in the investigation and observe safeguards to protect the rights of research participants.

5.2 Investigators requesting participant involvement in research inform participants of the aspects of the research that might reasonably be expected to influence willingness to participate. Investigators are especially sensitive to the possibility of diminished consent when participants are also receiving clinical services, or have impairments which limit understanding and/or communication, or when participants are children.

5.3 Investigators respect each participant's freedom to decline participation in or to withdraw from a research study at any time. This obligation requires special thought and consideration when investigators or other members of the research team are in positions of authority or influence over participants. Marriage and family therapists, therefore, make every effort to avoid multiple relationships with research participants that could impair professional judgment or increase the risk of exploitation.

5.4 Information obtained about a research participant during the course of an investigation is confidential unless there is a waiver previously obtained in writing. When the possibility exists that others, including family members, may obtain access to such information, this possibility, together with the plan for protecting confidentiality, is explained as part of the procedure for obtaining informed consent.

6. Responsibility to the Profession

Marriage and family therapists respect the rights and responsibilities of professional colleagues and participate in activities that advance the goals of the profession.

6.1 Marriage and family therapists remain accountable to the standards of the profession when acting as members or employees of organizations. If the mandates of an organization with which a marriage and family therapist is affiliated, through employment, contract or otherwise, conflict with the AAMFT Code of Ethics, marriage and family therapists make known to the organization their commitment to the AAMFT Code of Ethics and attempt to resolve the conflict in a way that allows the fullest adherence to the Code of Ethics.

6.2 Marriage and family therapists assign publication credit to those who have contributed to a publication in proportion to their contributions and in accordance with customary professional publication practices.

6.3 Marriage and family therapists do not accept or require authorship credit for a publication based on research from a student's program, unless the therapist made a substantial contribution beyond being a faculty advisor or research committee member. Coauthorship on a student thesis, dissertation, or project should be determined in accordance with principles of fairness and justice.

6.4 Marriage and family therapists who are the authors of books or other materials that are published or distributed do not plagiarize or fail to cite persons to whom credit for original ideas or work is due.

6.5 Marriage and family therapists who are the authors of books or other materials published or distributed by an organization take reasonable precautions to ensure that the organization promotes and advertises the materials accurately and factually.

6.6 Marriage and family therapists participate in activities that contribute to a better community and society, including devoting a portion of their professional activity to services for which there is little or no financial return.

6.7 Marriage and family therapists are concerned with developing laws and regulations pertaining to marriage and family therapy that serve the public interest, and with altering such laws and regulations that are not in the public interest.

6.8 Marriage and family therapists encourage public participation in the design and delivery of professional services and in the regulation of practitioners.

7. Financial Arrangements

Marriage and family therapists make financial arrangements with clients, third-party payors, and supervisees that are reasonably understandable and conform to accepted professional practices.

7.1 Marriage and family therapists do not offer or accept kickbacks, rebates, bonuses, or other remuneration for referrals; fee-for-service arrangements are not prohibited.

7.2 Prior to entering into the therapeutic or supervisory relationship, marriage and family therapists clearly disclose and explain to clients and supervisees: (a) all financial arrangements and fees related to professional services, including charges for canceled or missed appointments; (b) the use of collection agencies or legal measures for nonpayment; and (c) the procedure for obtaining payment from the client, to the extent allowed by law, if payment is denied by the third-party payor. Once services have begun, therapists provide reasonable notice of any changes in fees or other charges.

7.3 Marriage and family therapists give reasonable notice to clients with unpaid balances of their intent to seek collection by agency or legal recourse. When such action is taken, therapists will not disclose clinical information.

7.4 Marriage and family therapists represent facts truthfully to clients, third-party payors, and supervisees regarding services rendered.

7.5 Marriage and family therapists ordinarily refrain from accepting goods and services from clients in return for services rendered. Bartering for professional services may be conducted only if: (a) the supervisee or client requests it, (b) the relationship is not exploitative, (c) the professional relationship is not distorted, and (d) a clear written contract is established.

7.6 Marriage and family therapists may not withhold records under their immediate control that are requested and needed for a client's treatment solely because payment has not been received for past services, except as otherwise provided by law.

8. Advertising

Marriage and family therapists engage in appropriate informational activities, including those that enable the public, referral sources, or others to choose professional services on an informed basis.

8.1 Marriage and family therapists accurately represent their competencies, education, training, and experience relevant to their practice of marriage and family therapy.

8.2 Marriage and family therapists ensure that advertisements and publications in any media (such as directories, announcements, business cards, newspapers, radio, television, Internet, and facsimiles) convey information that is necessary for the public to make an appropriate selection of professional services. Information could include: (a) office information, such as name, address, telephone number, credit card acceptability, fees, languages spoken, and office hours; (b) qualifying clinical degree (see subprinciple 8.5); (c) other earned degrees (see subprinciple 8.5) and state or provincial licensures and/or certifications; (d) AAMFT clinical member status; and (e) description of practice.

8.3 Marriage and family therapists do not use names that could mislead the public concerning the identity, responsibility, source, and status of those practicing under that name, and do not hold themselves out as being partners or associates of a firm if they are not.

8.4 Marriage and family therapists do not use any professional identification (such as a business card, office sign, letterhead, Internet, or telephone or association directory listing) if it includes a statement or claim that is false, fraudulent, misleading, or deceptive.

8.5 In representing their educational qualifications, marriage and family therapists list and claim as evidence only those earned degrees: (a) from institutions accredited by regional accreditation sources recognized by the United States Department of Education, (b) from institutions recognized by states or provinces that license or certify marriage and family therapists, or (c) from equivalent foreign institutions.

8.6 Marriage and family therapists correct, wherever possible, false, misleading, or inaccurate information and representations made by others concerning the therapist's qualifications, services, or products.

8.7 Marriage and family therapists make certain that the qualifications of their employees or supervisees are represented in a manner that is not false, misleading, or deceptive.

8.8 Marriage and family therapists do not represent themselves as providing specialized services unless they have the appropriate education, training, or supervised experience.

This Code is published by:
American Association for Marriage and Family Therapy
112 South Alfred Street, Alexandria, VA 22314
Phone: (703) 838-9808 — Fax: (703) 838-9805 — www.aamft.org

Ethical Code for the International Association of Marriage and Family Counselors

Reprinted with permission from the International Association for Marriage and Family Therapy. This draft of the code was approved by the board and published in 2002. IAMFC can make further revisions of the code at any time the association deems necessary.

Preamble

The International Association of Marriage and Family Counselors (IAMFC) is an organization dedicated to advancing practice, training, and research in couple and family counseling. Members may specialize in areas such as premarital counseling, couple counseling, family counseling, sex counseling, intergenerational counseling, separation and divorce counseling, relocation counseling, custody evaluation, and parenting training. Couple and family counselors may work with special populations, including stepfamilies, nontraditional couples and family systems, multicultural couples and families, disadvantaged families, and dual-career couples. In conducting their professional activities, members commit themselves to protect family relationships and advocate for the healthy growth and development of the family as a whole and each member's unique needs, while advocating for the counseling profession and the professionalism of counselors. IAMFC members recognize that the relationship between the provider and consumer of services is characterized as professional. However, IAMFC members should remain informed of social and cultural trends as well as scientific and technological changes affecting the foundation of the professional counseling relationship. This code of ethics provides a framework for ethical practices by IAMFC members and other professionals engaged in couple and family counseling. It is divided into the following nine sections: the counseling relationship and client well-being, confidentiality and privacy, competence and professional responsibilities, collaboration and professional relationships, assessment and evaluation, counselor education and supervision, research and publication, ethical decision making and resolution, and diversity. The observations and recommendations presented within these nine areas above are meant to supplement the current ethical standards of the American Counseling Association. Although an ethical code cannot anticipate every possible situation or dilemma, the IAMFC ethical guidelines can assist members in insuring the welfare and dignity of the couples and families who seek services. The ethical code of the IAMFC incorporates the ethics of principles and virtues. The IAMFC Ethical code articulates some specific principles and guidelines which protect consumers from potentially harmful practices, thereby empowering professionals to maintain high standards for effective practice. The IAMFC Ethical Code also addresses the character of the professional couple and family counselor. Ethics of character or virtue contribute to professional aspirations and values. Each of the nine sections includes aspirations and principles.

Section A: The Counseling Relationship and Client Well-Being

Couple and family counselors contribute to the healthy development and evolution of family systems. They are committed to understanding problems and learning needs from multiple contexts. Couple and family counselors, in particular, embrace models of practice based on family dynamics and systems. Professional counselors realize that their perspectives influence the conceptualization of problems, identification of clients, and implementation of possible solutions. Couple and family counselors examine personal biases and values. They actively attempt to understand and serve couples and families from diverse cultural backgrounds. Professional couple and family counselors are willing to remove barriers to the counseling relationship, act as responsible public servants, and become involved in advocacy in the best interests of couples and families.

1. Couple and family counselors demonstrate caring, empathy, and respect for client well-being. They promote safety, security, and sense of community for couples and families. Due to potential risks involved, couple and family counselors should not use intrusive interventions without sound theoretical rationale, research support, and clinical consultation or supervision.

2. Couple and family counselors recognize that each family is unique. Couple and family counselors do not promote bias and stereotyping regarding family roles and functions.

3. Couple and family counselors respect the autonomy of the families with whom they work. They do not make decisions that rightfully belong to family members. When indicated and possible, couple and family counselors share client's clinical impressions and recommendations, decision-making processes, problem-solving strategies, and intervention outcomes with clients.

4. Couple and family counselors respect cultural diversity. They do not discriminate or condone discrimination on the basis of race, gender, disability, religion, age, sexual orientation, cultural background, national origin, marital status, political affiliation, or socioeconomic status.

5. Couple and family counselors promote open, honest, and direct relationships with consumers of professional services. Couple and family counselors inform clients about the goals of counseling, qualifications of the counselor(s), limits of confidentiality, potential risks, and benefits associated with specific techniques, duration of treatment, costs of services, appropriate alternatives to couple and family counseling, and reasonable expectations for outcomes.

6. Couple and family counselors promote primary prevention. They advocate for the development of clients' cognitive, moral, social, emotional, spiritual, physical, educational, relational, and vocational skills. Couple and family counselors promote effective couple and family communication and facilitate problem-solving skills needed to prevent future problems.

7. Couple and family counselors have an obligation to determine and inform counseling participants who are identified as the primary client. The couple and family counselor should make clear to clients if they have any obligations to an individual, a couple, a family, a third party, or an institution.

8. Couple and family counselors who are IAMFC members have a professional duty to monitor their places of employment, making recommendations so that the environment is conducive to the positive growth and development of clients. When there is a conflict of interest between the needs of the client and counselor's employing institution, the IAMFC member works to clarify his or her commitment to all parties. IAMFC members recognize that the acceptance of employment implies agreement with the policies and practices of the agency or institution.

9. Couple and family counselors do not harass, exploit, coerce, or manipulate clients for personal gain. Couple and family counselors avoid, whenever possible, multiple relationships such as business, social, or sexual contacts with any current clients or their family members. Couple and family counselors should refrain generally from nonprofessional relationships with former clients and their family members because termination of counseling is a complex process.

10. Couple and family counselors are responsible for demonstrating there is no harm from any relationship with a client or family member. The key element in this ethical principle is the avoidance of exploitation of vulnerable clients.

11. Couple and family counselors have an obligation to withdraw from a counseling relationship if the continuation of services would not be in the best interest of the client or would result in a violation of ethical standards. If the counseling relationship is no longer helpful or productive, couple and family counselors have an obligation to assist in locating alternative services and making referrals as needed.

12. Couple and family counselors do not abandon clients. They arrange for appropriate termination of counseling relationships and transfer of services as indicated.

13. Couple and family counselors maintain accurate and up-to-date records. They make all file information available to clients unless there is compelling evidence that such access would be harmful to the client. In situations involving multiple clients, couple and family counselors provide individual clients with parts of records related directly to them, protecting confidential information related to other clients who have not authorized release. Couple and family counselors include sufficient and timely documentation in client records to facilitate delivery of services and referral to other professionals as needed.

14. Couple and family counselors establish fees that are reasonable and customary depending upon the scope and location of their practices. Couple and family counselors in community agencies, schools, and other public settings do not solicit gifts or charge fees for services that are available in the counselor's employing agency or institution.

15. Culturally sensitive couple and family counselors recognize that gifts are tokens of respect and gratitude in some cultures. Couple and family counselors may receive gifts or participate in family rituals that promote healthy interaction and do not exploit clients.

16. Couple and family counselors maintain ethical and effective practices as they address the benefits and limitations of technological innovations and cultural changes. Counseling may be conducted or assisted by telephones, computer hardware and software, and other communication technologies. Technology-assisted distance counseling services may expand the scope and influence of couple and family counseling. However, counselors are responsible for developing competencies in the use of new technologies and safeguarding private and confidential information.

17. When a conflict of values arises which inhibits the couples and family counselor's professionalism and/or objectivity in the counseling relationship, the couples and family counselor should refer the couple or family being served to another qualified counselor. Additionally, it is recommended that the counselor obtain supervision or counseling to address any issue that may inhibit the counselor's effective practice.

Section B: Confidentiality and Privacy

Couple and family counselors recognize that trust is the foundation of an effective counseling relationship. Professional counselors maintain appropriate boundaries so that clients reasonably expect that information shared will not be disclosed to others without prior written consent. Due to the nature of couple and family counseling, safeguards must be established in the counseling process to insure privacy of client disclosures without contributing to dysfunctional family secrets. Clients have the right to know the limits of confidentiality, privacy, and privileged communication, including the fact that family members may themselves disclose counseling-related information outside counseling. Thus, couples and family counselors should inform clients that while confidentiality may be maintained by the counselor, the counselor has no control over information that family members may share with one another. Therefore, in these instances, confidentiality, while desired, may not be guaranteed.

1. Couple and family counselors may disclose private information to others under specific circumstances known to the individual client or client family members. Ideally, the client consents to disclosure by signing an authorization to release information. Each person receiving counseling who is legally competent to sign a waiver of right to confidentiality should execute an authorization. The authorization should be time limited, consistent with legal statutes, and limited to the scope agreed to by the counselor and client. The client may rescind or withdraw the authorization.

2. Couple and family counselors inform parents and legal guardians about the confidential nature of the counseling relationship. When working with minor or juvenile clients, as well as adult clients who lack the capacity to authorize release of confidential information, couple and family counselors seek consent from the appropriate custodial parent or guardian to disclose information.

3. Couple and family counselors inform clients of exceptions to the general principle that information will be kept confidential or released only upon written client authorization. Disclosure of private information may be mandated by state law. For example, states require reporting of suspected abuse of children or other vulnerable populations. Couple and family counselors may have sound legal or ethical justification for disclosing information if someone is in imminent danger. A court may have jurisdiction to order release of confidential information without a client's permission. However, all releases of information not authorized by clients should be minimal or narrow as possible to limit potential harm to the counseling relationship.

4. Couple and family counselors inform clients who may have access to their counseling records, as well as any information that may be released for third-party payment or insurance reimbursement. State and federal laws may affect record keeping and release of information from client records.

5. Couple and family counselors store records in a way that protects confidentiality. Written records should be kept in a locked file drawer or cabinet and computerized record systems should have appropriate passwords and safeguards to prevent unauthorized entry.

6. Couple and family counselors inform clients if sessions are to be recorded on tape or digital media and obtain written consent authorizing recording for particular purposes. When more than one person is receiving counseling, all persons who are legally competent must give informed consent in writing for the recording. Couple

and family counselors inform clients that statements made by a family member to the counselor during an individual counseling, consultation, or collateral contact are to be treated as confidential. Such statements are not disclosed to other family members without the individual's permission. However, the couple and family counselor should clearly identify the client of counseling, which may be the couple or family system, and inform clients in writing who the identified client is. Couple and family counselors should inform clients that they do not maintain family secrets, collude with some family members against others, or otherwise contribute to dysfunctional family system dynamics. If a client's refusal to share information from individual contacts interferes with the agreed goals of counseling, the counselor may terminate treatment and refer the clients to another counselor. Some couple and family counselors choose to not meet with individuals, preferring to serve family systems.

1. Couple and family counselors provide reasonable access to counseling records when requested by competent clients. In situations involvingmultiple clients, counselors provide only the records directly related to a particular individual, protecting confidential information related to any other client.
2. Couple and family counselors provide reasonable access to counseling records of minor children when requested by parents or guardians having legal rights to custody and health decision making. However, counselors do not become embroiled in custody disputes or parent and child conflicts occasioned by records release. Professional counselors attempt to protect the counseling relationship with children by suggesting limits to disclosure appropriate to the particular situation.
3. Couples and family counselors keep counseling records following the termination of counseling services so that there is reasonable access to the records in the future, maintaining the records in accordance with state and federal statutes and applicable accreditation standards. Couples and family counselors should also follow the recommended procedures for records access and retention outlined by the American Counseling Association Code of Ethics.
4. Couples and family counselors take reasonable precautions to ensure clients' access to records and client confidentiality in the event of a counselor's death or incapacitation. Additionally, couples and family counselors are encouraged to have a written plan, such as a professional will, specifying individuals who take charge of client records if the couples and family counselor terminates his/her practice for any reason.
5. Couple and family counselors maintain privacy and confidentiality in research, publication, case consultation, teaching, supervision, and other professional activities. Ideally, counselors secure informed consent and authorization to release information in all professional activities.

Section C: Competence and Professional Responsibilities

Couple and family counselors aspire to maintain competency through initial training, ongoing supervision and consultation, and continuing education. They have responsibilities to abide by this ethical code as well as other professional codes related to professional identity and group membership. In particular, couple and family counselors should become active in professional associations such as the IAMFC and the American Counseling Association and encourage beneficial changes in professionals and the counseling profession.

1. Couple and family counselors have the responsibility to develop and maintain basic skills in couple and family counseling through graduate training, supervision, and consultation. An outline of these skills is provided by the current Council for Accreditation of Counseling and Related Educational Programs (CACREP) Standards for Marital, Couple, and Family Counseling.

2. Couple and family counselors recognize the need for familiarizing themselves with new developments in the field of couple and family counseling. They pursue continuing education afforded by books, journals, courses, workshops, conferences, and conventions.

3. Couple and family counselors accurately represent their education, expertise, training, and experience. Professional counselors objectively represent their professional qualifications, skills, and specialties to the public. Membership in a professional organization, including IAMFC, is not used to suggest competency.

4. Couple and family counselors insure that announcements or advertisements of professional services focus on objective information that enables the client to make informed decisions. Providing information, such as highest relevant academic degree, licenses or certifications, office hours, types of services offered, fee structure, and languages spoken, can help clients select couple and family counselors.

5. Couple and family counselors do not attempt to diagnose or treat problems beyond the scope of their training and abilities. They do not engage in specialized counseling interventions or techniques unless they have received appropriate training and preparation in the methods.

6. Couple and family counselors do not undertake any professional activity in which their personal problems might adversely affect their performance. Instead, they focus on obtaining appropriate professional assistance to help them resolve the problem.

7. Couple and family counselors do not engage in actions that violate the legal standards of their community. They do not encourage clients or others to engage in unlawful activities.

8. Couple and family counselors have the responsibility to provide public information that enhances couple and family life. Such statements should be based on sound, scientifically acceptable theories, techniques, and approaches. Due to the inability to complete a comprehensive assessment and provide follow-up, members should not give specific advice to an individual through the media.

9. Couple and family counselors produce advertisements about workshops or seminars that contain descriptions of the audiences for which the programs are intended. Due to their subjective nature, statements either from clients or from the counselor about the uniqueness, effectiveness, or efficiency of services should be avoided. Announcements and advertisements should never contain false, misleading, or fraudulent statements.
10. Couple and family counselors promoting tapes, books, or other products for commercial sale make every effort to insure that announcements and advertisements are presented in a professional and factual manner.

Section D: Collaboration and Professional Relationships

Couple and family counselors work to maintain good relationships with professional peers within and outside the field of counseling. Consultation and collaboration represent means by which couple and family counselors can remove barriers to underserved populations. Interdisciplinary teamwork may be required to best serve clients.

Couple and family counselors aspire to maintain competency through initial training, ongoing supervision and consultation, and continuing education. They have responsibilities to abide by this ethical code as well as other professional codes related to professional identity and group membership. In particular, couple and family counselors should become active in professional associations such as the IAMFC and the American Counseling Association.

1. Couple and family counselors are knowledgeable about the roles and functions of other disciplines, especially in the helping professions such as psychiatry, psychology, social work, and mental health counseling. Counselors work to strengthen interdisciplinary relations with colleagues.
2. Couple and family counselors enter into professional partnerships in which each partner adheres to the ethical standards of their professions. Couple and family counselors should not charge a fee for offering or accepting referrals.
3. Couple and family counselors do not engage in harmful relationshipswith individuals overwhomthey have supervisory, evaluative, or instructional control. They do not engage in harassment or other abuses of power or authority.
4. Couple and family counselors work to insure the ethical delivery of effective services in any agency or institution in which they are employed. Couple and family counselors engaging in consultation and collaboration take responsibility for the well-being and ethical treatment of clients. Counselors alert administrators about inappropriate policies and practices in institutions they serve.
5. Couple and family counselors working as subcontractors of counseling services for a third party have a duty to inform clients of limitations that the organization may place on the counseling or consulting relationship.

6. Couple and family counselors maintain good working relationships with team members and collaborators. They promote healthy boundaries and organizational climate. Couple and family counselors refrain from becoming involved in splitting, triangulation, and indirect forms of communication that could be harmful to colleagues or the organization they share.

7. Couple and family counselors do not offer services to clients served by other professionals without securing a referral or release. The counselor should be authorized by the client to contact the other professional to coordinate or transfer care. There may be special considerations regarding transfer of care in the termination of an abusive counseling relationship.

Section E: Assessment and Evaluation

Couple and family counselors are highly skilled in relational and interpersonal assessment. They recognize the potential values to clients from appropriate educational, psychological, and vocational evaluation. However, couple and family counselors are sensitive to misuse and abuse of assessment results. Counselors avoid, whenever possible, evaluation, assessment, or diagnosis that restricts the overall development and freedom of choice of individuals, couples, and families. Recognizing the origins of couple and family counseling in systems thinking, they avoid, whenever possible, assigning problems to individuals. Instead, professional counselors aspire to identify solutions that promote the well-being of family systems.

1. Couple and family counselors use assessment procedures to promote the best interests and well-being of the client in clarifying concerns, establishing treatment goals, evaluating therapeutic progress, and promoting objective decision making.

2. Couple and family counselors recognize that clients have the right to know the results, interpretations, and conclusions drawn from assessment interviews and instruments, as well as how this information will be used. Couple and family counselors safeguard assessment data and maintain the confidentiality of evaluation records and reports.

3. Couple and family counselors use assessment methods that are reliable, valid, and relevant to the goals of the client. Couple and family counselors using tests or inventories should have a thorough understanding of measurement concepts, including relevant psychometric and normative data. When using computer-assisted scoring, counselors obtain empirical evidence for the reliability and validity of the methods and procedures.

4. Couple and family counselors do not use inventories and tests that have outdated items or normative data. They refrain from using assessment instruments and techniques likely to be biased or prejudiced.

5. Couple and family counselors do not use assessment methods that are outside the scope of their qualifications, training, or statutory limitations. They consult with

psychologists, mental health counselors, or other professional colleagues in interpreting and understanding particular test results.

6. Couple and family counselors conducting custody evaluations recognize the potential impact that their reports can have on family members. They are committed to a thorough assessment of both parents.Therefore, custody recommendations should not be made on the basis of information from only one parent. Couple and family counselors only use instruments that have demonstrated reliability, validity, and utility in custody evaluations. They do not make recommendations based solely on test and inventory scores.

7. Couple and family counselors clarify the differences between forensic examination and counseling. When couples and family counselors are conducting forensic examination, they inform clients who may have access to the results of the examination and the circumstances under which information may be released.

8. Members strive to follow current guidelines and standards for testing published or disseminated by the American Counseling Association, American Educational Research Association, American Psychological Association, Association for Assessment in Counseling and Education, National Council on Measurement in Evaluation, and other groups dedicated to professional expertise in assessment.

Section F: Counselor Education and Supervision

Couple and family counselors are likely to engage in some training and supervision activities, including peer consultation and supervision. Couple and family counselors recognize potential power imbalances in teacher and student, supervisor and supervisee, and consultant and consultee relationships. They do not abuse power or influence and instead, work to protect students, supervisees, and consultees from exploitation. Couple and family counselors maintain appropriate boundaries that promote growth and development for all parties. They recognize and respect cultural differences, adjusting their professional efforts to fit the learning needs of trainees.

1. Couple and family counselors who provide supervision acquire and maintain skills pertaining to the supervision process. They are able to demonstrate for supervisees the application of counseling theory and process to client issues. Supervisors are knowledgeable about different methods and conceptual approaches to supervision.

2. Couple and family counselors who provide supervision respect the inherent imbalance of power in the supervisory relationship. They do not use their potentially influential positions to exploit students, supervisees, or employees. Supervisors do not ask supervisees to engage in behaviors not directly related to the supervision process, and they clearly separate supervision and evaluation. Supervisors also avoid multiple relationships that might impair their professional judgment or increase the possibility of exploitation.

3. Sexual intimacy with students or supervisees is prohibited.

4. Couple and family counselors who provide supervision are responsible for both the promotion of supervisee learning and development and the advancement of couple and family counseling. Supervisors recruit students into professional organizations, educate students about professional ethics and standards, provide service to professional organizations, strive to educate new professionals, and work to improve professional practices.

5. Couple and family counselors who provide supervision have the responsibility to inform students of the specific expectations regarding skill building, knowledge acquisition, and development of competencies. Supervisors also provide ongoing and timely feedback to their supervisees.

6. Couple and family counselors who provide supervision are responsible for protecting the rights and well-being of their supervisees' clients. They monitor their supervisees' counseling on an ongoing basis and maintain policies and procedures to protect the confidentiality of clients whose sessions have been electronically recorded.

7. Couple and family counselors who provide supervision maintain ethical standards for counselor supervision. Counselor educators and supervisors may consult publications of the Association for Counselor Education and Supervision to clarify ethical issues in supervisory relationships.

8. Couple and family counselors serving as supervisors utilize sound supervision and counseling theory in supervision practice. Additionally, couple and family counselors infuse their supervision with the Advocacy Competencies and the Multicultural Counseling Competencies endorsed by the American Counseling Association.

9. Couple and family counselors who are counselor educators encourage their programs to maintain the current guidelines provided in the CACREP Standards for Marital, Couple, and Family Counseling. They also encourage training programs to offer coursework and supervision indicated by particular accreditation boards.

10. Couple and family counselors involved in training and supervision, especially educators and students, should encourage, teach, and implement advocacy awareness for supervisees, as well as explore ethical principles and aspirational goals. Counselor educators must infuse ethical studies throughout the curriculum.

11. Couples and family counselors who serve as supervisors must promote ethical practice throughout their supervision.

12. Couple and family counselors refer to the current American Counseling Association Code of Ethics and ACES Code of Ethics as sources document or training and supervision in professional counseling.

Section G: Research and Publication

Couple and family counselors should engage in research and publication that advances the profession of couple and family counseling. They act to proactively prevent harm to research participants and produce results that are beneficial to couples and families. Couple and family counselors maintain high ethical standards of informed consent and protection of confidentiality when conducting research projects or producing publications. They solicit input from peers, institutional review boards, and other stakeholders to minimize risks and enhance outcomes.

1. Couple and family counselors shall be fully responsible for their choice of research topics and the methods used for investigation, analysis, and reporting. They must be particularly careful that findings do not appear misleading, that the research is planned to allow for the inclusion of alternative hypotheses, and that provision is made for discussion of the limitations of the study.
2. Couple and family counselors safeguard the privacy of their research participants. Data about individual participants are not released unless the individual is informed about the exact nature of the information to be released and gives written permission for disclosure.
3. Couple and family counselors protect the safety of their research participants. Researchers follow guidelines of a peer review committee or institutional research board. Prospective participants are informed in writing about any potential risk associated with a study and are notified before and during any study that they can withdraw at any time.
4. Couple and family counselors make their original data available to other researchers. They contribute to the advancement of the field by encouraging the research and publication efforts of colleagues.
5. Couple and family counselors only take credit for research in which they make a substantial contribution and give credit to all contributors. Authors are listed from greatest to least amount of contribution.
6. Couple and family counselors do not plagiarize. Ideas or data that did not originate with the author and are not common knowledge are clearly credited to the original source.
7. Couple and family counselors are aware of their obligation to be role models for graduate students and other future researchers. Thus, they act in accordance with the highest standards possible while engaged in research and publication.
8. Couple and family counselors review materials submitted for research, publication, and other scholarly purposes. They respect the confidentiality and proprietary rights of those who submit their products for review. Counselors engaged in reviews of manuscripts and presentation proposals use valid and defensible standards, act within the limits of their competencies, and refrain from personal biases. In this manner, authors and researchers are supported and the field of couple and family counseling is advanced.

Section H: Ethical Decision Making and Resolution

Couple and family counselors incorporate ethical practices in their daily work. They discuss ethical dilemmas with colleagues and engage in ethical decision making in all aspects of couple and family counseling. They hold other counselors to sound ethical principles and encourage professional virtues and aspirations in themselves and other counselors. Couple and family counselors work with other professionals to resolve ethical issues.

1. Couple and family counselors are responsible for understanding the American Counseling Association Code of Ethics, the Ethical Code of the International Association of Couple and Family Counselors, and other applicable ethics codes from professional associations, certification and licensure boards, and other credentialing organizations by which they are regulated.
2. Couple and family counselors have the responsibility to confront unethical behavior of other counselors or therapists. The first step must be discussing the violation directly with the caregiver, unless the confrontation would put a client at risk. If the problem continues, the couple and family counselor may contact the professional organization or licensure board of the counselor or therapist in question.
3. Couple and family counselors specify the nature of conflicts between work requirements and other demands of an employing organization and the relevant codes of ethics. Employment and consultation of couple and family counselors should not compromise ethical standards. They work toward beneficial changes in the organizations of which they are members.
4. Couple and family counselors do not engage in unwarranted or invalid complaints. Ethics violations are reported when informal attempts at resolution have failed or violations are likely to substantially harm an individual or organization. Couple and family counselors should follow the reporting requirements specified by laws and regulations in their jurisdictions.
5. Couple and family counselors cooperate with ethics committees and other duly constituted organizations having jurisdiction over the professional charged with an ethics violation. Counselors assist professional associations in promoting ethical behavior and professional conduct.

Section I: Diversity

Couples and family counselors respect the dignity, potential and uniqueness of couples and families within their cultural context. They infuse their counseling and supervision with advocacy strategies which facilitate client wellness. Furthermore, couples and family counselors advocate systems which facilitate wellness and positive human growth. They actively seek to eliminate oppression of human rights, understanding that advocacy enables client empowerment.

1. Couples and family counselors perform advocacy at multiple levels, including advocacy for clients, communities, and social systems. Further, couples and family counselors make efforts to remove barriers that oppress clients at all levels. Couples

and family counselors must be aware and understand how to implement the Advocacy Competencies endorsed by the American Counseling Association.
2. Couples and family counselors recognize diversity and its influence on themselves and their clients. Couples and family counselors are cognizant of the impact of world views, values, and cultural influences. Couples and family counselors must be aware of and understand how to implement the Multicultural Counseling Competencies endorsed by the American Counseling Association.

The members of the Ethics committee who completed the revision of the Ethical Code are the following: Bret Hendricks, Chair of the Ethics Committee, Department of Educational Psychology and Leadership, Texas Tech University. Loretta J. Bradley, Department of Educational Psychology and Leadership, Texas Tech University. Stephen Southern, Department of Counseling and Psychology, Mississippi College Marvarene Oliver, Department of Counseling and Educational Psychology, Texas A & M University–Corpus Christi. Bobbie Birdsall, Counselor Education Department, Boise State University.

Authors' Note

The 2010 Ethical Code of the International Association of Couple and Family Counselors (IAMFC) was written by members of the Ethics Committee and approved by the Board of IAMFC.

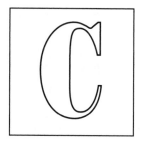

Glossary

AAMFT   American Association for Marriage and Family Therapy. Largest professional organization for couple and family therapists.

ABCDE theory   Albert Ellis's model for disputing irrational beliefs in rational–emotive behavior therapy.

ACA   American Counseling Association. Primary professional organization for professional counselors.

Accommodation   The counselor's adjusting to the family's style; useful in the joining process of family therapy.

Adaptability   The capability of families to respond effectively to unpredictable events. One dimension of the Circumplex model of family assessment.

Behavioral family therapy   Treatment mode that focuses on specific actions of family members and uses reinforcement to increase or decrease the frequency of those actions.

Blended family   A family formed by uniting members from two previously married families; stepfamilies.

Boundaries   Rules determining who is in and out of various family subsystems.

Brief therapy   A solution-focused, short-term approach to treating families.

CACREP   Council for Accreditation of Counseling and Related Educational Programs. Accrediting agency affiliated with the American Counseling Association; accredits marriage, couple, and family counseling, therapy, and other counseling emphases.

Certification   Designation of competence as psychotherapist awarded by a credentialing body; for example: Clinical Membership in AAMFT.

Circular causality   Actions in a feedback loop that view any cause as a reaction to a prior cause.

Circumplex model   A framework for assessing families based on the dimensions of adaptability, cohesion, and communication,

Codependency   Two or more people who depend on each other in a way that is not healthy; one member overfunctions while the other underfunctions.

Cohabitation   A couple living together with a level of commitment without the legal formality of marriage.

Cohesion   The family characteristic that governs its closeness or distance. A dimension of the Circumplex model.

Common factors theory   The premise that change that occurs in psychotherapy is the result of certain specific factors that occur in all therapies (e.g., a good relationship between family members and therapist).

Conceptual skills   The ability to think about and understand family functioning and family patterns.

Confrontation   Directly facing or being required to face personal shortcomings, attitudes, and how one is perceived by others.

Congruence   The interaction of honest and consistent actions, attitudes, and feelings.

Constructivism   Posits that reality is constructed by human interpretation and that objectivity is not possible.

Contracting   Making a formal agreement, usually in writing, that stipulates what changes the members involved in family therapy will make.

Couples' group therapy   A treatment group composed of couples in committed relationships to work on improving those relationships.

Cotherapy   Two therapists working together with a couple or family; brings varied therapeutic perspectives into the session.

Cybernetics   The concept of self-regulation of machines that has been extended to living systems; the mechanisms by which families and other living systems regulate their behaviors.

Differentiation   The application of learning to emotional experiences that leads to mature choices and actions; opposite of fusion.

Disengaged   Describes a family that has little real emotional contact with other members or those outside the family.

Disequillibrium   Absence of emotional and behavioral stability within the family system.

Division of Family Psychology   The group within the American Psychological Association for family psychologists.

Divorce therapy   Treatment to help a couple end their marriage without bitterness or other hard feelings.

Double-bind   A message with two incompatible parts; the responder is wrong no matter what the choice.

Escalation of stress   Counseling technique that puts pressure on the family system to cause disequillibrium, offering the opportunity for change.

Emotional cutoff   Withdrawing from one's family of origin, believing the cutoff will alleviate emotional pain.

Emotionally focused couple therapy   A treatment approach to couple therapy that strives to understand and incorporate emotions and attachment needs from a systemic perspective.

Empathy   Awareness of another's thoughts and feelings and their possible meanings.

Enactment   A counseling term referring to the family interacting with each other in usual ways, allowing the counselor to gain an understanding of the family's problems and dysfunctional interaction patterns.

Enmeshment   Blurring of boundaries between family members overinvolved in each other's activities, making autonomy impossible.

Evidence-based treatments   Models of psychotherapy that have been shown by a series of controlled studies to be effective in treating specific problems.

Executive subsystem   In structural family therapy, the husband–wife subsystem that ultimately is responsible for developing family structure.

Externalizing problems   A technique in narrative therapy that labels the problem as outside the individual, permitting the client to mobilize resources to overcome it.

Family life cycle   Stages families go through with unique tasks that must be accomplished at each stage.

Family of origin   A person's original family, parents, and siblings.

Family-of-origin therapy   An approach that examines relationships with the client's parents and siblings. The generations are often brought together in treatment to enhance communication and repair damaged relationships.

Family projection process   Playing out unresolved emotional issues of the parents with their families of origin through dysfunction in one or more of the children.

Feedback   Information provided to a family system that affects behavior; positive feedback indicates the need for the family to change; negative feedback signals all is well and maintains the homeostasis.

Fusion   An individual's emotions overpowering reason, leading to a loss of individuality and autonomy; opposite of differentiation.

Genogram   A diagram of one's family tree over three generations or more, allowing the client and counselor to identify recurring themes over the generations.

Homeostasis   A balanced state of equilibrium in the family; living systems adjust themselves to attempt to remain in this state at all times.

IAMFC International Association of Marriage and Family Therapist, a division of the ACA.

Identified patient The family member who bears the symptoms of a dysfunctional family system.

Internal family systems An intrapsychic model that hypothesizes the construction of a mental image of a family system within individuals. System concepts are applied to change dynamics of the internalized family system.

Interpersonal skills Critical relationship skills needed in functional family therapy and other treatment models.

Intrapsychic Competing forces within the mind, as opposed to competing forces in the family or broader environment.

Irrational beliefs Cognitions that are not valid and lead to self-defeating behaviors.

Joining Forming a working relationship with each family member.

Licensure Legal recognition by the State of professional competencies, rights, and obligations.

Linear causality The notion that one behavior directly causes another behavior. Contrasted with Circular Causality.

Live supervision A procedure in which the supervisor observes the counseling session and provides feedback during and immediately after the session.

Maneuverability A quality that family therapists try to maintain that permits the therapist to access the full range of intervention possibilities without threatening the family.

Manualized treatments See treatment manuals.

Marital dysfunction Problems in the relationship between husband and wife.

Meta-analysis Statistical technique that merges the quantitative results of several studies to produce an overall effect of the treatment; used in studies to determine whether therapy is effective.

Military family therapy Specific approaches to the treatment of military personnel and their families.

Multigenerational transmission process Murray Bowen's concept of emotional illness being transmitted from one generation to the next.

180° solution In brief therapy, a solution to a presenting problem that is the opposite of what the family currently is doing to resolve the problem.

Object relations theory A concept that emphasizes the resolution of attachment and differentiation issues as the key elements of psychological health.

Paradigm shift A change in basic assumptions about problem formation necessary to use systems theories effectively.

Paradoxical intervention   A command given to a client that creates a situation in which compliance or refusal leads to improved functioning; normally, the command is to continue the symptom, thereby demonstrating control of it or resisting and having the symptom become less frequent.

Postmodernism   The philosophical idea that reality and truth are constructed by humans based on experiences, that objective reality is impossible to determine because knowledge and truth are based on historical and cultural interpretations.

Posttraumatic stress disorder (PTSD)   A constellation of psychological symptoms that result after an individual has experienced or witnessed a horrifying life-threatening experience; one of the signature disorders of the global war on terrorism.

Pseudomutuality   A family condition that shows a façade of harmony while actually experiencing distress.

Quid pro quo   A behavioral exchange intervention of "something for something" used in many family therapy theories.

Reauthoring   A narrative therapy intervention in which the client composes a story about how he or she would like life to be; the therapist helps the new narrative become reality.

Reframing   Attributing positive motives to a situation that has been perceived to be negative.

Reinforcement   A behavioral event that increases the frequency of a specific response.

Restructuring   A technique that changes subsystem composition and power within the larger family system to create a more functional family.

Restraining change   A technique to overcome resistance by suggesting that family members not change; by resisting, they do change.

Rules   Overt or covert instructions that produce repetitive patterns of family behavior and regulate family functioning in a predictable way.

Same-sex unions   A marriage or legally binding contract between two members of the same sex.

Schizophrenic mother   Early family therapy concept, later shown to be incorrect, holding that schizophrenic offspring were the product of a family with an overinvolved, double binding mother and a disengaged, ineffectual father.

Sculpting   A nonverbal family therapy technique in which family members position themselves in a room to represent how each experiences significant aspects of the family.

Self-worth   Virginia Satir's term for the most important gift parents can give their children; parents without their own sense of self-worth cannot give it to their children.

Sex therapy   Using behavioral interventions to help couples improve the physical component of their relationship.

Single-parent families   Families with only one adult to provide and care for the children.

Subsystems   Smaller units of the family with their own organization and functions; may be determined by age, gender, interests, and other factors.

Therapeutic letters   A narrative therapy technique in which the counselor writes a letter to the client documenting how the client has overcome the forces of the externalized problem.

Transference   The client's projection of unconscious and unresolved issues onto the therapist; often the therapist is imagined as being like someone in the client's family of origin.

Traumatic brain injury (TBI)   A concussion resulting from a shock to the head; one of the signature disorders of military personnel participating in the global war on terrorism—usually caused by the detonation of roadside bombs.

Treatment manual   A detailed set of instructions that provide therapists with a step-by-step process for treating a specific psychological problem; often a component of evidenced-based treatments.

Triangulation   Stabilizing a conflictual relationship between two persons by bringing a third person into the relationship.

Unit of treatment   Describes who is seen in therapy. In family therapy, the unit is the whole family or various subsystems of the family.

Undifferentiated   An individual with a dependent need for emotional contact with his or her family of origin. Often lets feelings overrule reason.

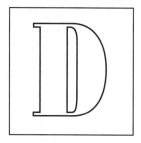

Marriage and Family Therapy Core Competencies

The marriage and family therapy (MFT) core competencies were developed through a collaborative effort of the American Association for Marriage and Family Therapy (AAMFT) and interested stakeholders. In addition to defining the domains of knowledge and requisite skills in each domain that comprise the practice of marriage and family therapy, the ultimate goal of the core competencies is to improve the quality of services delivered by marriage and family therapists (MFTs). Consequently, the competencies described herein represent the minimum that MFTs licensed to practice independently must possess.

Creating competencies for MFTs and improving the quality of mental health services was considered in the context of the broader behavioral health system. The AAMFT relied on three important reports to provide the framework within which the competencies would be developed: *Mental Health: A Report of the Surgeon General*; the President's New Freedom Commission on Mental Health's *Achieving the Promise: Transforming Mental Health Care in America*; and the Institute of Medicine's *Crossing the Quality Chasm*. The AAMFT mapped the competencies to critical elements of these reports, including IOM's 6 Core Values that are seen as the foundation for a better health care system: 1) Safe, 2) Person-Centered, 3) Efficient, 4) Effective, 5) Timely, and 6) Equitable. The committee also considered how social, political, historical, and economic forces affect individual and relational problems and decisions about seeking and obtaining treatment.

The core competencies were developed for educators, trainers, regulators, researchers, policymakers, and the public. The current version has 128 competencies; however, these are likely to be modified as the field of family therapy develops and as the needs of clients change. The competencies will be reviewed and modified at regular intervals to ensure the competencies are reflective of the current and best practice of MFT.

The core competencies are organized around 6 primary domains and 5 secondary domains. The primary domains are:

1. **Admission to Treatment**—All interactions between clients and therapist up to the point when a therapeutic contract is established.
2. **Clinical Assessment and Diagnosis**—Activities focused on the identification of the issues to be addressed in therapy.
3. **Treatment Planning and Case Management**—All activities focused on directing the course of therapy and extra-therapeutic activities.
4. **Therapeutic Interventions**—All activities designed to ameliorate the clinical issues identified.
5. **Legal Issues, Ethics, and Standards**—All aspects of therapy that involve statutes, regulations, principles, values, and mores of MFTs.
6. **Research and Program Evaluation**—All aspects of therapy that involve the systematic analysis of therapy and how it is conducted effectively.

The subsidiary domains are focused on the types of skills or knowledge that MFTs must develop. These are: a) Conceptual, b) Perceptual, c) Executive, d) Evaluative, and e) Professional.

Although not expressly written for each competency, the stem "Marriage and family therapists…" should begin each. Additionally, the term "client" is used broadly and refers to the therapeutic system of the client/s served, which includes, but is not limited to individuals, couples, families, and others with a vested interest in helping clients change. Similarly, the term "family" is used generically to refer to all people identified by clients as part of their "family system," this would include fictive kin and relationships of choice. Finally, the core competencies encompass behaviors, skills, attitudes, and policies that promote awareness, acceptance, and respect for differences, enhance services that meet the needs of diverse populations, and promote resiliency and recovery.

Domain 1: Admission to Treatment

Number	Subdomain	Competence
1.1.1	Conceptual	Understand systems concepts, theories, and techniques that are foundational to the practice of marriage and family therapy
1.1.2	Conceptual	Understand theories and techniques of individual, marital, couple, family, and group psychotherapy
1.1.3	Conceptual	Understand the behavioral health care delivery system, its impact on the services provided, and the barriers and disparities in the system.
1.1.4	Conceptual	Understand the risks and benefits of individual, marital, couple, family, and group psychotherapy.
1.2.1	Perceptual	Recognize contextual and systemic dynamics (e.g., gender, age, socioeconomic status, culture/race/ethnicity, sexual orientation, spirituality, religion, larger systems, social context).
1.2.2	Perceptual	Consider health status, mental status, other therapy, and other systems involved in the clients' lives (e.g., courts, social services).
1.2.3	Perceptual	Recognize issues that might suggest referral for specialized evaluation, assessment, or care.
1.3.1	Executive	Gather and review intake information, giving balanced attention to individual, family, community, cultural, and contextual factors.
1.3.2	Executive	Determine who should attend therapy and in what configuration (e.g., individual, couple, family, extrafamilial resources).
1.3.3	Executive	Facilitate therapeutic involvement of all necessary participants in treatment.
1.3.4	Executive	Explain practice setting rules, fees, rights, and responsibilities of each party, including privacy, confidentiality policies, and duty to care to client or legal guardian.
1.3.5	Executive	Obtain consent to treatment from all responsible persons.
1.3.6	Executive	Establish and maintain appropriate and productive therapeutic alliances with the clients.
1.3.7	Executive	Solicit and use client feedback throughout the therapeutic process.
1.3.8	Executive	Develop and maintain collaborative working relationships with referral resources, other practitioners involved in the clients' care, and payers.

1.3.9	Executive	Manage session interactions with individuals, couples, families, and groups.
1.4.1	Evaluative	Evaluate case for appropriateness for treatment within professional scope of practice and competence.
1.5.1	Professional	Understand the legal requirements and limitations for working with vulnerable populations (e.g., minors).
1.5.2	Professional	Complete case documentation in a timely manner and in accordance with relevant laws and policies.
1.5.3	Professional	Develop, establish, and maintain policies for fees, payment, record keeping, and confidentiality.

Domain 2: Clinical Assessment and Diagnosis

Number	Subdomain	Competence
2.1.1	Conceptual	Understand principles of human development; human sexuality; gender development; psychopathology; psychopharmacology; couple processes; and family development and processes (e.g., family, relational, and system dynamics).
2.1.2	Conceptual	Understand the major behavioral health disorders, including the epidemiology, etiology, phenomenology, effective treatments, course, and prognosis.
2.1.3	Conceptual	Understand the clinical needs and implications of persons with comorbid disorders (e.g., substance abuse and mental health; heart disease and depression).
2.1.4	Conceptual	Comprehend individual, marital, couple and family assessment instruments appropriate to presenting problem, practice setting, and cultural context.
2.1.5	Conceptual	Understand the current models for assessment and diagnosis of mental health disorders, substance use disorders, and relational functioning.
2.1.6	Conceptual	Understand the strengths and limitations of the models of assessment and diagnosis, especially as they relate to different cultural, economic, and ethnic groups.
2.1.7	Conceptual	Understand the concepts of reliability and validity, their relationship to assessment instruments, and how they influence therapeutic decision making.
2.2.1	Perceptual	Assess each clients' engagement in the change process.
2.2.2	Perceptual	Systematically integrate client reports, observations of client behaviors, client relationship patterns, reports from other professionals, results from testing procedures, and interactions with client to guide the assessment process.

2.2.3	Perceptual	Develop hypotheses regarding relationship patterns, their bearing on the presenting problem, and the influence of extra-therapeutic factors on client systems.
2.2.4	Perceptual	Consider the influence of treatment on extra-therapeutic relationships.
2.2.5	Perceptual	Consider physical/organic problems that can cause or exacerbate emotional/interpersonal symptoms.
2.3.1	Executive	Diagnose and assess client behavioral and relational health problems systemically and contextually.
2.3.2	Executive	Provide assessments and deliver developmentally appropriate services to clients, such as children, adolescents, elders, and persons with special needs.
2.3.3	Executive	Apply effective and systemic interviewing techniques and strategies.
2.3.4	Executive	Administer and interpret results of assessment instruments.
2.3.5	Executive	Screen and develop adequate safety plans for substance abuse, child and elder maltreatment, domestic violence, physical violence, suicide potential, and dangerousness to self and others.
2.3.6	Executive	Assess family history and dynamics using a genogram or other assessment instruments.
2.3.7	Executive	Elicit a relevant and accurate biopsychosocial history to understand the context of the clients' problems.
2.3.8	Executive	Identify clients' strengths, resilience, and resources.
2.3.9	Executive	Elucidate presenting problem from the perspective of each member of the therapeutic system.
2.4.1	Evaluative	Evaluate assessment methods for relevance to clients' needs.
2.4.2	Evaluative	Assess ability to view issues and therapeutic processes systemically.
2.4.3	Evaluative	Evaluate the accuracy and cultural relevance of behavioral health and relational diagnoses.
2.4.4	Evaluative	Assess the therapist-client agreement of therapeutic goals and diagnosis.
2.5.1	Professional	Utilize consultation and supervision effectively.

Domain 3: Treatment Planning and Case Management

Number	Subdomain	Competence
3.1.1	Conceptual	Know which models, modalities, and/or techniques are most effective for presenting problems.
3.1.2	Conceptual	Understand the liabilities incurred when billing third parties, the codes necessary for reimbursement, and how to use them correctly.
3.1.3	Conceptual	Understand the effects that psychotropic and other medications have on clients and the treatment process.
3.1.4	Conceptual	Understand recovery-oriented behavioral health services (e.g., self-help groups, 12-step programs, peer-to-peer services, supported employment).
3.2.1	Perceptual	Integrate client feedback, assessment, contextual information, and diagnosis with treatment goals and plan.
3.3.1	Executive	Develop, with client input, measurable outcomes, treatment goals, treatment plans, and after-care plans with clients utilizing a systemic perspective.
3.3.2	Executive	Prioritize treatment goals.
3.3.3	Executive	Develop a clear plan of how sessions will be conducted.
3.3.4	Executive	Structure treatment to meet clients' needs and to facilitate systemic change.
3.3.5	Executive	Manage progression of therapy toward treatment goals.
3.3.6	Executive	Manage risks, crises, and emergencies.
3.3.7	Executive	Work collaboratively with other stakeholders, including family members, other significant persons, and professionals not present.
3.3.8	Executive	Assist clients in obtaining needed care while navigating complex systems of care.
3.3.9	Executive	Develop termination and aftercare plans.
3.4.1	Evaluative	Evaluate progress of sessions toward treatment goals.
3.4.2	Evaluative	Recognize when treatment goals and plan require modification.
3.4.3	Evaluative	Evaluate level of risks, management of risks, crises, and emergencies.
3.4.4	Evaluative	Assess session process for compliance with policies and procedures of practice setting.
3.4.5	Professional	Monitor personal reactions to clients and treatment process, especially in terms of therapeutic behavior, relationship with clients, process for explaining procedures, and outcomes.

3.5.1	Professional	Advocate with clients in obtaining quality care, appropriate resources, and services in their community.
3.5.2	Professional	Participate in case-related forensic and legal processes.
3.5.3	Professional	Write plans and complete other case documentation in accordance with practice setting policies, professional standards, and state/provincial laws.
3.5.4	Professional	Utilize time management skills in therapy sessions and other professional meetings.

Domain 4: Therapeutic Interventions

Number	Subdomain	Competence
4.1.1	Conceptual	Comprehend a variety of individual and systemic therapeutic models and their application, including evidence-based therapies and culturally sensitive approaches.
4.1.2	Conceptual	Recognize strengths, limitations, and contraindications of specific therapy models, including the risk of harm associated with models that incorporate assumptions of family dysfunction, pathogenesis, or cultural deficit.
4.2.1	Perceptual	Recognize how different techniques may impact the treatment process.
4.2.2	Perceptual	Distinguish differences between content and process issues, their role in therapy, and their potential impact on therapeutic outcomes.
4.3.1	Executive	Match treatment modalities and techniques to clients' needs, goals, and values.
4.3.2	Executive	Deliver interventions in a way that is sensitive to special needs of clients (e.g., gender, age, socioeconomic status, culture/ race/ethnicity, sexual orientation, disability, personal history, larger systems issues of the client).
4.3.3	Executive	Reframe problems and recursive interaction patterns.
4.3.4	Executive	Generate relational questions and reflexive comments in the therapy room.
4.3.5	Executive	Engage each family member in the treatment process as appropriate.
4.3.6	Executive	Facilitate clients developing and integrating solutions to problems.
4.3.7	Executive	Defuse intense and chaotic situations to enhance the safety of all participants.
4.3.8	Executive	Empower clients and their relational systems to establish effective relationships with each other and larger systems.

4.3.9	Executive	Provide psychoeducation to families whose members have serious mental illness or other disorders.
4.3.10	Executive	Modify interventions that are not working to better fit treatment goals.
4.3.11	Executive	Move to constructive termination when treatment goals have been accomplished.
4.3.12	Executive	Integrate supervisor/team communications into treatment.
4.4.1	Evaluative	Evaluate interventions for consistency, congruency with model of therapy and theory of change, cultural and contextual relevance, and goals of the treatment plan.
4.4.2	Evaluative	Evaluate ability to deliver interventions effectively.
4.4.3	Evaluative	Evaluate treatment outcomes as treatment progresses.
4.4.4	Evaluative	Evaluate clients' reactions or responses to interventions.
4.4.5	Evaluative	Evaluate clients' outcomes for the need to continue, refer, or terminate therapy.
4.4.6	Evaluative	Evaluate reactions to the treatment process (e.g., transference, family of origin, current stress level, current life situation, cultural context) and their impact on effective intervention and clinical outcomes.
4.5.1	Professional	Respect multiple perspectives (e.g., clients, team, supervisor, practitioners from other disciplines who are involved in the case).
4.5.2	Professional	Set appropriate boundaries, manage issues of triangulation, and develop collaborative working relationships.
4.5.3	Professional	Articulate rationales for interventions related to treatment goals and plan, assessment information, and systemic understanding of clients' context and dynamics.

Domain 5: Legal Issues, Ethics, and Standards

Number	Subdomain	Competence
5.1.1	Conceptual	Know state, federal, and provincial laws and regulations that apply to the practice of marriage and family therapy.
5.1.2	Conceptual	Know professional ethics and standards of practice that apply to the practice of marriage and family therapy.
5.1.3	Conceptual	Know policies and procedures of the practice setting.
5.1.4	Conceptual	Understand the process of making an ethical decision.
5.2.1	Perceptual	Recognize situations in which ethics, laws, professional liability, and standards of practice apply.

5.2.2	Perceptual	Recognize ethical dilemmas in practice setting.
5.2.3	Perceptual	Recognize when a legal consultation is necessary.
5.2.4	Perceptual	Recognize when clinical supervision or consultation is necessary.
5.3.1	Executive	Monitor issues related to ethics, laws, regulations, and professional standards.
5.3.2	Executive	Develop and assess policies, procedures, and forms for consistency with standards of practice to protect client confidentiality and to comply with relevant laws and regulations.
5.3.3	Executive	Inform clients and legal guardian of limitations to confidentiality and parameters of mandatory reporting.
5.3.4	Executive	Develop safety plans for clients who present with potential self-harm, suicide, abuse, or violence.
5.3.5	Executive	Take appropriate action when ethical and legal dilemmas emerge.
5.3.6	Executive	Report information to appropriate authorities as required by law.
5.3.7	Executive	Practice within defined scope of practice and competence.
5.3.8	Executive	Obtain knowledge of advances and theory regarding effective clinical practice.
5.3.9	Executive	Obtain license(s) and specialty credentials.
5.3.10	Executive	Implement a personal program to maintain professional competence.
5.4.1	Evaluative	Evaluate activities related to ethics, legal issues, and practice standards.
5.4.2	Evaluative	Monitor attitudes, personal well-being, personal issues, and personal problems to insure they do not impact the therapy process adversely or create vulnerability for misconduct.
5.5.1	Professional	Maintain client records with timely and accurate notes.
5.5.2	Professional	Consult with peers and/or supervisors if personal issues, attitudes, or beliefs threaten to adversely impact clinical work.
5.5.3	Professional	Pursue professional development through self-supervision, collegial consultation, professional reading, and continuing educational activities.
5.5.4	Professional	Bill clients and third-party payers in accordance with professional ethics, relevant laws and polices, and seek reimbursement only for covered services.

Domain 6: Research and Program Evaluation

Number	Subdomain	Competence
6.1.1	Conceptual	Know the extant MFT literature, research, and evidence-based practice.
6.1.2	Conceptual	Understand research and program evaluation methodologies, both quantitative and qualitative, relevant to MFT and mental health services.
6.1.3	Conceptual	Understand the legal, ethical, and contextual issues involved in the conduct of clinical research and program evaluation.
6.2.1	Perceptual	Recognize opportunities for therapists and clients to participate in clinical research.
6.3.1	Executive	Read current MFT and other professional literature.
6.3.2	Executive	Use current MFT and other research to inform clinical practice.
6.3.3	Executive	Critique professional research and assess the quality of research studies and program evaluation in the literature.
6.3.4	Executive	Determine the effectiveness of clinical practice and techniques.
6.4.1	Evaluative	Evaluate knowledge of current clinical literature and its application.
6.5.1	Professional	Contribute to the development of new knowledge.

References

Abbott, D. A., Berry, M., & Meridith, W. H. (1990). Religious belief and practice: A potential asset in helping families. *Family Relations, 39,* 443–448.

Ackerman, N. W. (1958). *The psychodynamics of family life.* New York: Basic Books.

Aderhold, V., & Gottwalz, G. (2004). Family therapy and schizophrenia: Replacing ideology with openness. In J. Read, L. Mosher, & R. Bentall (Eds.). *Models of madness: psychological, social and biological approaches to schizophrenia.* New York: Brunner-Routledge.

Adler, A. (1927). *The practice and theory of individual psychology.* New York: Harcourt, Brace, Jovanovich.

Alexander, J. F. (1973). Defensive and supportive communications in normal and deviant families. *Journal of Consulting and Clinical Psychology, 40*(2), 223–231.

Alexander, J. F., & Barton, C. (1976). Behavioral systems therapy with families. In D. H. Olson (Ed.), *Treating relationships.* Lake Mills, IA: Graphic Press.

Alexander, J. F., & Parsons, B. V. (1973). Short term behavioral intervention with delinquent families: Impact on family process and recidivism. *Journal of Abnormal Psychology, 81*(3), 219–225.

Alexander, J. F., & Parsons, B. V. (1982). *Functional family therapy.* Pacific Grove, CA: Brooks/Cole.

Alexander, J. F., Barton, C., Schiavo, R. S., & Parsons, B. V. (1976). Behavior interventions with families of delinquents: Therapist characteristics and outcome. *Journal of Consulting and Clinical Psychology, 44,* 656–664.

Alexander, J., & Parsons, B. V. (1982). *Functional family therapy.* Pacific Grove, CA: Brooks/Cole.

American Association for Marriage and Family Therapy (AAMFT). (2001). *AAMFT Code of Ethics.* Washington, DC: Author.

American Association for Marriage and Family Therapy (AAMFT). (2004). *Marriage and family therapy core competencies.* Retrieved from http://www.aamft.org/imis15/Documents/MFT_Core_Competencie.pdf

American Association for Marriage and Family Therapy (AAMFT). (2007). The making of the MFT profession. *Family Therapy Magazine, 6* (4) 12–19.

American Association for Marriage and Family Therapy (AAMFT). (2011). *Clinical Membership Requirement.* Retrieved from www.aamft.org.

American Association of Family and Consumer Sciences. (2004). Retrieved from http://www.aafcs.org/

American Heritage Dictionary of the English Language (4th ed.). (2000). Boston: Houghton Mifflin.

American Psychiatric Association (APA). (2000). *Diagnostic and statistical manual of mental disorders* (4th ed., text rev.). Washington, DC: Author.

Anderson, H. (1997). *Conversation, language and possibilities: A postmodern approach to therapy.* New York: Basic Books.

Anderson, H., & Geheart, D. (2007). *Collaborative therapy: Relationships and conversations that make a difference.* New York: Brunner/Routledge.

Anderson, H., & Goolishian, H. (1992). The client is the expert: A not knowing approach to therapy. In S. McNamee & K. J. Gergen, (Eds.), *Therapy as a social construction.* Newberry Park, CA: Sage.

Anderson, W. J. (1989). Client/person-centered approaches to couple and family therapy: Expanding theory and practice. *Person-Centered Review, 4,* 245–247.

Anonymous. (1972). On the differentiation of self. In J. Framo (Ed.), *Family interaction: A dialogue between family researchers and family therapists.* New York: Springer.

Aponte, H. J., & Van Deusen, J. M. (1981). Structural family therapy. In A. S. Gurman & D. P. Kniskern (Eds.), *Handbook of family therapy.* New York: Brunner/Mazel.

Babcock, D., & Keepers, T. (1976). *Raising kids OK.* New York: Grove Press.

Bachelor, A., & Horvath, A. (1999). The therapeutic relationship. In S. D.Miller (Ed.), *The heart and soul of change: What works in therapy* (pp. 133–178). Washington, DC: American Psychological Association.

Bader, E., Pearson, P. T., & Schwartz, J. D. (2000). *Tell me no lies.* New York: St. Martin's Press.

Bandura, A. (1969). *Principles of behavior modification.* New York: Holt, Rinehart, & Winston.

Bandura, A. (1977). *Social learning theory.* Englewood Cliffs, NJ: Prentice Hall.

Barker, P. (1992). *Basic family therapy.* New York: Oxford University Press.

Barstow, S. (2010). What counselors need to know about health care reform. *Counseling and Human Development, 43*(1), 1–16.

Barton, C., & Alexander, J. F. (1977). Treatment of families with a delinquent member. In G. Harris (Ed.), *The group treatment of family problems: A source learning approach.* New York: Grune & Stratton.

Barton, C., & Alexander, J. F. (1981). Functional family therapy. In A. S. Gurman & D. P. Kniskern (Eds.), *Handbook of family therapy.* New York: Brunner/Mazel.

Barton, C., & Alexander, J. F. (1981). Functional family therapy. In A. S. Gurman & D. P. Kniskern (Eds.), *Handbook of family therapy.* New York: Brunner/Mazel.

Bateson, G., Jackson, D. D., Haley, J., & Weakland, J. (1956). Towards a theory of schizophrenia. *Behavioral Sciences, 1,* 251–264.

Bateson, G., Jackson, D., Haley, J., & Weakland, J. (1971). Toward a theory of schizophrenia. In G. Bateson, *Steps to an ecology of the mind.* New York: Ballentine.

Baucom, D. H., & Epstein, N. (1990). *Cognitive behavioral marital therapy.* New York, NY: Brunner/Mazel.

Bauer, R. (1979). Gestalt approaches to family therapy. *American Journal of Family Therapy, 7*(3), 41–45.

Beck, A. (1976). *Cognitive therapy and the emotional disorders.* New York: International University Press.

Beck, A. (1991). Cognitive therapy: A 30 year retrospective. *American Psychologist, 46,* 368–375.

Beck, A., Rush, A., Shaw, B., & Emery, G. (1979). *Cognitive therapy of depression.* New York: Guilford Press.

Bell, J. E. (1961). Family group therapy. *Public Health Monograph 64.* Washington, DC: US Government Printing Office.

Benedek, E. P. (1982). Conjoint marital therapy and spouse abuse. In A. S. Gurman (Ed.), *Questions and answers in family therapy* (vol. 2). New York: Brunner/Mazel.

Berg, I. K. (1991). Letter to the editor. *Journal of Marital and Family Therapy, 17,* 311–312.

Berger, M. (1982). Predictable tasks in therapy with families of handicapped persons. In A.

S. Gurman (Ed.), *Questions and answers in family therapy* (vol. 2). New York: Brunner/Mazel.

Berger, P. L., & Kellner, H. (1977). Marriage and the construction of reality. In P. L. Berger (Ed.), *Facing up to modernity: Excursion in society, politics and religion.* New York: Basic Books.

Bergin, A. (1967). Some implications of psychotherapy research for therapeutic practice. *International Journal of Psychiatry, 3,* 136–150.

Bergin, A. (1971). The evaluation of therapeutic outcomes. In A. Bergin & S. Garfield (Eds.), *Handbook of psychotherapy and behavior change.* New York: Wiley.

Bergin, A., & Lambert, M. (1978). The evaluation of therapeutic outcomes. In A. Bergin & S. Lambert (Eds.), *Handbook of psychotherapy and behavior change: An empirical analysis* (2nd ed.). New York: Wiley.

Berne, E. (1961). *Transactional analysis in psychotherapy.* New York: Grove Press.

Berne, E. (1972). *What do you say after you say hello?* New York: Grove Press.

Beutler, L. E., Bongar, B. M., & Shurkin, J. N. (1998). *Am I Crazy or Is it My Shrink?* New York: Oxford University Press.

Beutler, L. E., Harwood, T. M., Alimohamed, S., & Malik, M. M. (2002). Functional impairment and coping style. In J. C. Norcross (Ed.), *Psychotherapy relationships that work: Therapist contributions and responsiveness to patient needs* (pp. 145–170). New York: Oxford University Press.

Beutler, L. E., Malik, M. L., Alimohamed, S., Harwood, T. M., Talebi, H., Noble, S., et al. (2004). Therapist variables. In M. J. Lambert (Ed.), *Bergin and Garfield's handbook of psychotherapy and behavior change* (pp. 227–306). New York: Wiley.

Black, L., & Piercy, F. P. (1991). A feminist family therapy scale. *Journal of Marital and Family Therapy, 17,* 111–120.

Blow, A. J., Sprenkle, D. H., & Davis, S. D. (2007). Is who delivers the treatment more important than the treatment itself? *Journal of Marital and Family Therapy, 33,* 238-317.

Bodin, A. M. (1981). The interactional view: Family therapy approaches of the Mental Research Institute. In A. S. Gurman & D. P. Kniskern (Eds.), *Handbook of family therapy.* New York: Brunner/Mazel.

Bordin, E. S. (1979). The generalizability of the psychoanalytic concept of the working alliance. *Psychotherapy: Theory, Research, and Practice, 16,* 252–260.

Bowen, M. (1960). A family concept of schizophrenia. In D. Jackson (Ed.), *The etiology of schizophrenia.* New York: Basic Books.

Bowen, M. (1961). Family psychotherapy. *American Journal of Orthopsychiatry, 31,* 40–60.

Bowen, M. (1971). Family therapy and family group therapy. In H. Kaplan & B. Sadock (Eds.), *Comprehensive group psychotherapy.* Baltimore: Williams & Wilkins.

Bowen, M. (1976). Theory in the practice of psychotherapy. In P. J. Guerrin, Jr. (Ed.), *Family therapy: Theory and practice.* New York: Gardner Press.

Bowen, M. (1978). *Family therapy in clinical practice.* New York: Jason Aronson.

Bowers, M. (2007). The making of a profession: Standards, regulation and the AAMFT. *Family Therapy Magazine, 6*(4), 12–18.

Bray, J. H., & Jouriles, E. N. (1995). Treatment of marital conflict and prevention of divorce. *Journal of Marital and Family Therapy, 21*(4), 461–474.

Broderick, C. B. (1992). *Marriage and the family* (4th ed.). Englewood Cliffs, NJ: Prentice Hall.

Broderick, C. B., & Schraeder, S. S. (1991). The history of professional marriage and family therapy. In A. S. Gurman & D. P. Kniskern (Eds.), *Handbook of family therapy* (Vol. 2). New York: Brunner/ Mazel.

Brunn, E. L., & Ziff, A. (2010). *Marrying well: The clinicians' guide to premarital counseling.* New York: Norton.

Campbell, T. L., & Patterson, J. M. (1995). The effectiveness of family interventions in the treatment of physical illness. *Journal of Marital and Family Therapy, 21*(4), 545–584.

Canfield, B. S., Hovestadt, A. J., & Fenell, D. L. (1992). Family-of-origin influences upon perceptions of current family functioning. *Family Therapy, 19,* 55–60.

Carkhuff, R. (1969a). *Helping and human relations. Vol. 1: Selection and training.* New York: Holt, Rinehart, & Winston.

Carkhuff, R. (1969b). *Helping and human relations. Vol. 11: Practice and research.* New York: Holt, Rinehart, & Winston.

Carlson, J., Watts, R., & Maniacci, M. (2005). *Adlerian Therapy: Theory and Practice.* Washington, DC: American Psychological Association.

Carter, B., & McGoldrick, M. (2005). Remarried families. In B. Carter & M. McGoldrick (Eds.). *The Expanded Family Life Cycle* (3rd ed.). Boston: Allyn & Bacon.

Carter, B., & McGoldrick, M. (Eds.). (2005*). The expanded family life cycle: Individual, family and social perspectives.* Boston: Pearson.

Carter, E. A., & McGoldrick, M. (Eds.) (1980). *The family life cycle: A framework for family therapy.* New York: Gardner Press.

Chamberlain, P., & Rosicky, J. G. (1995). The effectiveness of family therapy in the treatment of adolescents with conduct disorders and delinquency. *Journal of Marital and Family Therapy, 21*(4), 441–460.

Chambless, D. L., & Hollon, S. D. (1998). Defining empirically supported therapies. *Journal of Consulting and Clinical Psychology, 66,* 7–18.

Clarke, J. (1978). *Self-esteem: A family affair.* Minneapolis: Winston Press.

Colapinto, J. (1991). Structural family therapy. In A. S. Gurman & D. P. Kniskern (Eds.) *Handbook of family therapy* (Vol. 2). New York: Brunner/Mazel.

Commission on Accreditation for Marriage and Family Therapy Education (COAMFTE). (2011). *Accreditation Standards.* Retrieved from http://www. aaamft.org/resources/On line_Directories/coamfte.htm

Conye, J. (1987). Depression, biology, marriage and marital therapy. *Journal of Marriage and Family Therapy, 13*(4), 393–407.

Coombs, R. H. (1991). Marital status and personal well-being: A literature review. *Family Relations, 40,* 97–102.

Corey, G. (2007). *Theory and practice of group counseling* (7th ed.). Belmont, CA: Thomson-Brooks/Cole.

Corey, G. (2009). *Theory and practice of counseling and psychotherapy* (8th ed.). Belmont, CA: Brooks/Cole.

Corey, G., Corey, M., & Callahan, P. (2006). *Issues and ethics in the helping professions* (7th ed.). Pacific Grove, CA: Brooks/Cole.

Council for Accreditation of Counseling and Related Educational Programs (CACREP). (2011). *Directory of accredited programs.* Retrieved from http://www.cacrep.org/di rectory/directory.cfm

Curtis, N. M., Ronan, K. R., & Borduin, C. M. (2004). Multisystemic treatment: A meta-analysis of outcome studies. *Journal of Family Psychology, 18,* 411–419.

Dattilio, F. M. (2006, September/October). Evidence based treatment may be too confining. *The National Psychologist, 23.*

Dattilio, F. M. (2010). *Cognitive behavioral therapy with couples and families: A comprehensive guide for clinicians.* New York: Guilford.

Davidson, T. (1978). *Conjugal crime.* New York: Hawthorne.

Davis, R. F., & Borns, R. F. (1999). *Solo dad survival guide: Raising your kids on your own.* New York: NTC Contemporary.

Davis, S. D., & Piercy, F. P. (2007). What clients of couple therapy model developers say about change: Parts I & II. *Journal of Marital and Family Therapy, 33*(3), 318–363.

DeWitt, K. (1978). The effectiveness of family therapy: A review of the outcome research. *Archives of General Psychiatry, 35,* 549–561.

Dilts, R., & Green, J. D. (1982). Neuro-linguistic programming in family therapy. In A. M. Horne & M. M. Ohlsen (Eds.), *Family counseling and therapy.* Itasca, IL: Peacock.

Dobbs, D. (2009). The post-traumatic stress trap. *Scientific American,* 64–69.

Doherty, W. J. (1991). Beyond reactivity and the deficit model of manhood: A comment on articles by Napier, Pittman, and Gottman. *Journal of Marital and Family Therapy, 17,* 29–32.

Duhl, F. J., Kantor, D., & Duhl, B. S. (1973). Learning, space and action in family therapy:

A primer of sculpture. In D. Bloch (Ed.), *Techniques of family psychotherapy.* New York: Grune & Stratton.

Duncan, B. L. (2010). *On becoming a better therapist.* Washington, D.C., American Psychological Association.

Edwards, M. E., & Steinglass, P. (1995). Family therapy treatment outcomes for alcoholism. *Journal of Marital and Family Therapy, 4,* 475–509.

Ellis, A. (1962). *Reason and emotion in psychotherapy.* Secaucus, NJ: Citadel Press.

Ellis, A. (1974). *Techniques of disrupting irrational beliefs.* New York: Institute for Rational Living.

Ellis, A. (1977). *Self-help report form.* New York: Institute for Rational Living.

Ellis, A. (1991). Rational–emotive family therapy. In A. Horne & A. Passmore (Eds.), *Family counseling and therapy* (2nd ed.). Itasca, IL: Peacock.

Ellis, A. (1993). The rational–emotive therapy approach to marriage and family therapy. *The Family Journal, 1,* 292–307.

Ellis, A. (1995). Rational emotive behavior therapy. In R. J. Corsini & D. Wedding (Eds.), *Current Psychotherapies* (5th ed.). Itasca, IL: Peacock.

Elmore, D. L., & Van Dyke, K. M. (2010, May). Warrior suicides. *Monitor on Psychology,* 20–21.

Epstein, N., & Dattilio, F. M. (2009, November/December). Responses to "legacies of the MFT pioneers"—Cognitive behavioral couple and family therapy: An integrative systemic approach. *8*(6), 64–68.

Epston, D. (1994). Extending the conversation. *The Family Therapy Networker, 18*(6), 30–37.

Erikson, E. H. (1946). *The psychoanalytic study of the child.* New York: International Universities Press.

Erikson, E. H. (1950). *Childhood and society.* New York: Norton.

Erikson, E. H. (1959). *Psychological issues.* New York: International Universities Press.

Estrada, A. U., & Pinsof, W. M. (1995). The effectiveness of family therapies for selected behavioral disorders of childhood. *Journal of Marital and Family Therapy, 21*(4), 403–440.

Everett, C., & Volgy, S. (1991). Treating divorce in family therapy practice. In A. Gurman & D. Kniskern (Eds.), *Handbook of family therapy* (Vol. 2). New York: Brunner/Mazel.

Eysenck, H. (1952). The effects of psychotherapy: An evaluation. *Journal of Consulting Psychology, 16,* 319–324.

Fairbairn, W. (1954). *Object-relations theory of the personality.* New York: Basic Books.

Falloon, I. (1991). Behavioral marital therapy. In A. S. Gurman & D. P. Kniskern (Eds.), *Handbook of family therapy* (Vol. 2). New York: Brunner/Mazel.

Family Services Research Center (2010). Retrieved from http://www.musc.edu/fsrc/

Feldman, J., & Kazdin, A. E. (1995). Parent management training for oppositional and conduct problem children. *The Clinical Psychologist, 48*(4), 3–5.

Fenell, D. L. (1982). Counseling dual career couples. *Arizona Personnel and Guidance Journal, 7,* 8–10.

Fenell, D. L. (1990, March). Unpublished paper presented at University of Colorado, Colorado Springs.

Fenell, D. L. (1991, Spring). Critical issues in long-term marriages. *International Association for Marriage and Family Counseling Newsletter,* 1–2.

Fenell, D. L. (1993a). Characteristics of long-term first marriages. *Journal of Mental Health Counseling, 15,* 446–460.

Fenell, D. L. (1993b). Using Bowen's differentiation of self scale to help couples understand and resolve marital conflict. In T. S. Nelson & T. S. Trepper (Eds.), *101 interventions in family therapy.* New York: Haworth Press.

Fenell, D. L. (1998). The use of Rogerian techniques in marital therapy. In T. Nelson & T. Trepper (Eds), *101 more interventions in marriage and family therapy.* Binghamton, NY: The Haworth Press.

Fenell, D. L. (2008, June). A distinct culture: Applying multicultural counseling competencies to work with military clients. *Counseling Today,* 8–9.

Fenell, D. L. (2009, October 4). *Treating trauma in military familes.* Presentaion to the Annual Conference of the American Association for Marriage and Family Therapy, Sacramento CA.

Fenell, D. L. (2010, September). *Marriage in the Military.* Paper presented at the American Association for Marriage and Family Therapy Conference, Atlanta, GA.

Fenell, D. L., & Fenell, R.A. (2003). Separated again: Personal and professional reflections of mobilization, deployment and well-being of military families. *Family Therapy Magazine, 2*(4), 18–23.

Fenell, D. L., & Fenell, R. A. (2008). The effects of frequent combat tours on military personnel and their families: How counselors can help. *Vista 2008 on-line.* Retrieved from http:// counselingoutfitters. com/vistas/vistas08/Fe nell.htm

Fenell, D. L., & Hovestadt, A. H. (1986). Family therapy as a profession or professional: Implications for training. *Journal of Psychotherapy and the Family, 1*(4), 25–40.

Fenell, D. L., Hovestadt, A. H., & Cochran, S. (1985). Characteristics of effective administrators of rural mental health centers. *Journal of Rural Community Psychology, 8*(1), 23–35.

Fenell, D. L., Hovestadt, A. J., & Harvey, S. J. (1986). A comparison of delayed feedback and live supervision models of marriage and family therapy. *Journal of Marital and Family Therapy, 12*(2), 181–186.

Fenell, D. L., Martin. J., & Mithaug, D. E. (1986). The mentally retarded child. In L. B. Golden & D. Capuzzi (Eds.), *Helping families help children: Family interventions with school-related problems.* Springfield, IL: Thomas.

Fenell, D. L., Nelson, R. C., & Shertzer, B. (1981). The effects of a marriage enrichment program on marital satisfaction and self-concept. *The Journal for Specialists in Group Work, 6*(2), 83–89.

Fenell, D. L., & Wallace, C. (1985). Remarriage: The triumph of hope over experience: A challenge for counseling professionals. *Arizona Counseling Journal, 10,* 12–18.

Fenell, D. L., & Wehrman, J. (2010). *Deployment counseling: Supporting military personnel and their families.*

Fenell, D. L., & Weinhold, B. K. (2003) *Counseling Families* (3rd ed.). Denver, CO: Love.

Fenell, R. A., Fenell, D. L., & Williams, R. (2010). The school counselor's role in supporting students with deployed parents. In J. Weber & J. Mascari (Eds.), *Terrorism, trauma and tragedies.* Alexandria, VA: ACA Foundation.

Fields, N. S. (1983). Satisfaction in long-term marriages. *Social Work, 28,* 37–41.

Fisch, R., Weakland, J. H., & Segal, L. (1982). *The tactics of change: Doing therapy briefly.* San Francisco: Jossey-Bass.

Fish, V. (1993). Poststructuralism in family therapy: Interrogating the narrative/conversational mode. *Journal of Marital and Family Therapy, 19,* 221–232.

Flowers, B. J. (2000). *Beyond the myth of marital happiness.* San Francisco: Jossey-Bass.

Flugel, J. D. (1921). *The psychoanalytic study of the family.* London: Hogarth Press.

Foley, V. D. (1974). *An introduction to family therapy.* New York: Grune & Stratton.

Framo, J. L. (1981). The integration of marital therapy with family of origin sessions. In A. S. Gurman & D. P. Kniskern (Eds.), *Handbook of family therapy.* New York: Brunner/Mazel.

Framo, J. L. (1982). *Explorations in marital and family therapy.* New York: Springer.

Freud, S. (1909). Analysis of a phobia in a five-year-old boy. *Standard Edition, 10,* 3–152. (original work published 1909)

Freud, S. (1949). *An outline of psychoanalysis.* New York: Norton.

Freud, S. (1963). *Collected papers* (Vol. 4). New York: Collier Books.

Fried, S., & Fried, P. (1996). *Bullies & victims: Helping your child survive the schoolyard battlefield.* New York: Evans.

Friedman, E. H. (1991). Bowen theory and therapy. In A. S. Gurman & D. P. Kniskern (Eds.), *Handbook of family therapy* (Vol. 2). New York: Brunner/Mazel.

Fromm, E. (1941). *Escape from freedom.* New York: Holt, Rinehart, & Winston.

Fromm, E. (1947). *Man for himself.* New York: Holt, Rinehart, & Winston.

Gaylin, N. L. (1989). The necessary and sufficient conditions for change: Individual versus family therapy. *Person-Centered Review, 4,* 263–279.

Gehart, D. (2010). *Mastering competencies in family therapy: A practical approach to theories and clinical case documentation.* Brooks/Cole: Cengage Learning.

George, R. L. (1990). *Counseling the chemically dependent: Role and function.* Englewood Cliffs, NJ: Prentice Hall.

Gibbons, R. D., Kwan, H., Bhaumik, D. K., & Mass, J. (2006). The relationship between antidepressant prescription rates and rate of early adolescent suicide. *American Journal of Psychiatry, 163,* 1898–1904.

Gill, S. J. (1982). Professional disclosure and consumer protection in counseling. *Personnel and Guidance Journal, 60,* 443–446.

Gladding, S. T. (2007). *Groups: A counseling specialty* (5th ed.). Upper Saddle River, NJ: Merrill.

Gladding, S. T. (2009). *Counseling: A comprehensive profession.* Upper Saddle River, NJ: Merrill.

Gladding, S. T. (2011). *Family therapy: History, theory and practice.* Upper Saddle River, NJ: Merrill.

Gladding, S. T., Burgraff, M. Z., & Fenell, D. L. (1987). A survey of marriage and family therapy training within departments of counselor education. *Journal of Counseling and Development, 66*(2), 90–92.

Glang, C., & Betis, A. (1993). Helping children through the divorce process. *PsychSpeak, 13*(4), 1–2.

Glenn, N. D. (1990). Quantitative research on marital quality in the 1980s: A critical review. *Journal of Marriage and the Family, 52,* 818–831.

Glick, P. (1989). Remarried families, stepfamilies and stepchildren: A brief demographic analysis. *Family Relations, 38,* 24–27.

Goldberg, P. D., Peterson, B. D., Rosen, K. H., & Sara, M. L. (2008, October). Cybersex: The impact of a contemporary problem on the practices of marriage and family therapists. *Journal of Marital and Family Therapy.*

Goldenberg, I., & Goldenberg, H. (2008). *Family therapy: An overview.* Belmont, CA: Brooks Cole.

Goldstein, M. J., & Miklowitz, D. J. (1995). The effectiveness of psychoeducational family therapy in the treatment of schizophrenic disorders. *Journal of Marital and Family Therapy, 21*(4), 361–376.

Goodrich, T. J., Rampage, C., & Ellman, B. (1989, Sept.–Oct.). The single mother. *The Family Therapy Networker,* 52–56.

Goodrich, T. J., Rampage, C., Ellman, B., & Halstead, K. (1988). *Feminist family therapy: A casebook.* New York: Norton.

Gottman, J. M. (1991). Predicting the longitudinal course of marriages. *Journal of Marriage and Family Therapy, 17,* 3–7.

Gottman, J. M. (1993). *Why marriages succeed or fail.* New York: Simon & Schuster.

Gottman, J. M. (1999). *The marriage clinic: A scientifically based marital therapy.* New York: Norton.

Gottman, J. M. (2002). *The seven principles for making marriage work.* New York: Three Rivers Press.

Gottman, J. M., Gottman, J. S., & DeClaire, J. (2007). *10 lessons to transform your marriage.* New York: Three Rivers Press.

Gottman, J., Notarius, C., Markman, H., Bank, S., Yoppi, B., & Rubin, M. (1976). Behavior exchange theory and marital decision making. *Journal of Personality and Social Psychology, 34,* 14–23.

Gould, J. (2010, June 14). Video conferences can shrink distance to mental health care. *Army Times,* p. 19.

Goulding, M., & Goulding, R. (1979). *Changing lives through redecision therapy.* New York: Brunner/Mazel.

Greenburg, L. S., & Johnson, S. M. (1988). *Emotionally focused therapy for couples.* New York: Guilford Press.

Grossman, N. S., & Okun, B. F. (2009). Challenges in family forensic psychology: Families with special needs children. *The Family Psychologist, 25*(1), 15–16.

Gumper, L. L., & Sprenkle, D. H. (1981). Privileged communication therapy: Special problems for the family and couples therapist. *Family Process, 20,* 11–23.

Gurman, A. S., & Kniskern, D. P. (1978a). Deterioration in marriage and family therapy: Empirical, clinical and conceptual issues. *Family Process, 17,* 3–20.

Gurman, A. S., & Kniskern, D. P. (1978b). Research on marital and family therapy: Progress, perspective and prospect. In S. L. Garfield & A. E. Lambert (Eds.), *Handbook of psychotherapy and behavior change: An empirical analysis* (2nd ed.). New York: Wiley.

Gurman, A. S., & Kniskern, D. P. (1981a). Family therapy outcome research: Knowns and unknowns. In A. S. Gurman & D. P. Kniskern (Eds.), *Handbook of family therapy.* New York: Brunner/Mazel.

Gurman, A. S., & Kniskern, D. P. (Eds.) (1981b). *Handbook of family therapy.* New York: Brunner/Mazel.

Gurman, A. S., & Kniskern, D. P. (Eds.) (1991). *Handbook of family therapy* (Vol. 2). New York: Brunner/Mazel.

Haley, J. (1971). Family therapy: A radical change. In J. Haley (Ed.), *Changing families: A family therapy reader.* New York: Grune & Stratton.

Haley, J. (1983). *Problem solving therapy.* San Francisco: Jossey-Bass.

Hamberger, L. K., & Hastings, J. E. (1993). Court mandated treatment of men who batter their partners: Issues, controversies and outcomes. In Z. Hilton (Ed.), *Legal responses to wife assault.* Newbury Park, CA: Sage.

Hansen, J., & Schuldt, J. (1984). Marital self-disclosure and marital satisfaction. *Journal of Marriage and the Family, 46,* 923–936.

Harris, T. (1967). *I'm O.K., you're O.K.* New York: Harper & Row.

Hatcher, C. (1978). Intrapersonal and interpersonal models: Blending Gestalt and family therapies. *Journal of Marriage and Family Counseling, 4*(1), 63–68.

Hatcher, C. (1981). Managing the violent family. In A. S. Gurman (Ed.), *Questions and answers in family therapy.* New York: Brunner/Mazel.

Hendrick, S. (1981). Self-disclosure and marital satisfaction. *Journal of Personality and Social Psychology, 40,* 1150–1159.

Henggler, S. W., Schoenwald, S. K., Bourdin, C. M., Rowland, M. D., & Cunningham, P. B. (1998). *Multisystemic treatment of antisocial behavior in children and adolescents.* New York: Guilford Press.

Henggler, S. W., Schoenwald, S. K., Rowland, M. D., & Cunningham, P. B. (2002). *Serious emotional disturbance in children and adolescents: Multisystemic therapy,* New York: Guillford Press.

Herrington, B. S. (1979). Privilege denied in joint therapy. *Psychiatric News, 14,* 1.

Hovestadt, A. H., Fenell, D. L., & Canfield, B. S. (2002). Characteristics of effective providers of marital and family therapy in rural mental health centers. *Journal of Marital and Family Therapy, 28*(2), 225–231.

Hovestadt, A. J., Fenell, D. L., & Piercy, F. P. (1983). Integrating marriage and family therapy within counselor education: A three-level model. In B. F. Okun & S. T. Gladding (Eds.), *Issues in training marriage and family therapists.* Ann Arbor, MI: ERIC/CAPS.

Howard, J. (2002). In A. Gore and T. Gore, *The spirit of family.* New York: Henry Holt.

Huber, C. H. (1994). *Ethical, legal and professional issues in the practice of marriage and family therapy* (2nd ed.). New York: Merrill.

International Association of Marriage and Family Counselors (IAMFC). (1993). *Ethical Code for IAMFC.* Denver, CO: Author.

International Association of Marriage and Family Counselors (IAMFC). (2001). *Ethical Code for IAMFT.* Denver, CO: Author.

Irving, P. (2003, Autumn). The family. *Country Web, 31,* 6–7.

Jacobsen, N. (1978). Stimulus control model for change in behavioral marital therapy: Implications for contingency contracting. *Journal of Marriage and Family Counseling, 4,* 29–35.

Jacobson, N. (1989). The maintenance of treatment gains following social learning based marital therapy. *Behavior Therapy, 20,* 325–336.

Jacobson, N. S., & Christensen, A. (1998). *Acceptance and change in couple therapy: A therapist's guide to transforming relationships.* New York: Norton.

James, M., & Jongeward, D. (1971). *Born to win.* Reading, MA: Addison-Wesley.

Johnson, H. C. (1987). Biologically based deficit in the identified patient: Indications for psychoeducational strategies. *Journal of Marital and Family Therapy, 13,* 337–348.

Johnson, S. (2004). *The practice of emotionally focused marital therapy: Creating connections* (2nd ed.). New York: Guilford

Johnson, S. M. (2003). Emotionally focused couples therapy: Empiricism and art. In T. L. Sexton, G. R. Weeks & M. S. Robbins (Eds.). *Handbook of family therapy: The science and practice of working with familes and couples* (pp. 263–280). New York: Brunner-Routledge.

Johnson, S. M., & Greenburg, L. S. (1995). The emotionally focused approach to problems in adult attachment. In N. Jacobsen & A. Gurman, (Eds.) *Clinical Handbook of Couple Therapy* (pp. 121–141). New York: Guilford Press.

Johnson, S. M., & Talitman, E. (1997). Predictors of success in emotionally focused marital therapy. *Journal of Marital and Family Therapy, 23,* 135–152.

Jowers, K., & Tilghman, A. (2010, December 27). Military kids taking more psychiatric drugs. *Army Times,* pp. 12–13.

Jowers, K. (2010, December 27). Military officials to focus on dwell time in '11. *Army Times,* p.15.

Jurich, A. P. (2001). Suicidal ideation and behavior. *AAMFT Clinical Update, 3*(6), 1–8.

Kaplan, M., & Kaplan, N. (1978). Individual and family growth: A Gestalt approach. *Family Process, 17,* 195–206.

Karasu, T. B. (1986). The specificity versus nonspecificity dilemma: Toward identifying therapeutic change agents. *American Journal of Psychiatry, 143,* 687–695.

Kaufman, E., & Kaufman, P. (1979). *The family therapy of alcohol and drug abusers.* New York: Gardner Press.

Kempler, W. (1965). Experiential family therapy. *The International Journal of Group Psychotherapy, 15,* 57–71.

Kempler, W. (1968). Experiential therapy with families. *Family Process, 7*(1), 88–99.

Kempler, W. (1981). *Experiential therapy with families.* New York: Brunner/Mazel.

Kempler, W. (1991). Gestalt family therapy. In A. Horne & J. L. Passmore (Eds.), *Family counseling and therapy* (2nd ed.). Itasca, IL: Peacock.

Kennedy, K. (2008). Report: Mild TBI linked to multiple ailments. *Army Times,* 18.

Kennedy, K. (2010, October 26). How did I miss the signs? *Army Times,* pp. 20–22.

Kerr, M. E. (1981). Family systems theory and therapy. In A. S. Gurman & D. P. Kniskern (Eds.), *Handbook of family therapy.* New York: Brunner/Mazel.

Kerr, M., & Bowen, M. (1988). *Family evaluation.* New York: Norton.

Kitson, G., & Morgan, L. (1990). Multiple consequences of divorce: A decade review. *Journal of Marriage and the Family, 52,* 913–924.

Klein, N. C., Alexander, J. F., & Parsons, B. V. (1977). Impact of family systems interventions on recidivism and sibling delinquency: A model for primary prevention and program development. *Journal of Consulting and Clinical Psychology, 45,* 469–474.

Knapp, M. L., & Vangelisti, A. L. (1991). *Interpersonal communication and human relationships* (2d ed.). Boston: Allyn & Bacon.

Kniskern, D. P., & Gurman, A. S. (1979). Research in training marriage and family therapists: Status, issues, and directions. *Journal of Marital and Family Therapy, 5,* 83–96.

Kovach, G. C. (2010, May 2). Suicide: The unseen enemy for Marines. *San Diego Union-Tribune.* Retrieved from http://www.signonsandiego.com/news/2010/may/02/suicide-unseen-enemy-marines/

Krumboltz, J., & Thoresen, C. (1969). *Behavioral counseling: Cases and techniques.* New York: Holt, Rinehart, & Winston.

Krumboltz, J., & Thoresen, C. (Eds.). (1976). *Counseling methods*. New York: Holt, Rinehart, & Winston.

Kuehl, B. (2008, September/October). Legacy of the family therapy pioneers. *Family Therapy Magazine, 7*(5), 12–49.

La Roche, M. J., & Christopher, M. S. (2009). Changing paradigms from empirically supported treatment to evidence based practice: A cultural perspective. *Professional Psychology: Research and Practice, 40,* 396–402.

Lambert, M. J. (1992). Psychotherapy outcome research: Implications for integrative and eclectic therapists. In J. C. Norcross & M. R. Goldfried (Eds.), *Handbook of psychotherapy integration*. New York: Basic Books.

Lambert, M. J., Bergin, A. E., & Collins, J. L. (1977). Therapist induced deterioration in psychotherapy. In A. S. Gurman & A. M. Razin (Eds.), *Effective psychotherapy: A handbook of research*. New York: Pergamon Press.

Lambert, M. J., & Ogles, B. M. (2004). The efficacy and effectiveness of psychotherapy. In M. J. Lambert (Ed.), *Bergin and Garfield's handbook of psychotherapy and behavior change* (5th ed., pp. 139–193). New York: Wiley.

Lambie, R. (2008). *Family systems within educational and community contexts: Understanding students who are at risk or have special needs* (3rd ed.). Denver, CO: Love.

Lauer, J. C., & Lauer, R. H. (1986). *'Til death do us part: A study and guide to long-term marriages*. New York: Harrington Park.

Lazarus, A. (1971). *Behavior therapy and beyond*. New York: McGraw-Hill.

Lazarus, A. (1981). *The practice of multimodal therapy*. New York: McGraw-Hill.

Leboyer, F. (1975). *Birth without violence*. New York: Knopf.

Levant, R. (1978). Family therapy: A client-centered perspective. *Journal of Marriage and Family Counseling, 4*(2), 35–42.

Levant, R. (1984). *Family therapy: A comprehensive overview*. Englewood Cliffs, NJ: Prentice Hall.

Lewin, K. (1951). *Field theory and social science*. New York: Harper.

Lewis, R., & Spanier, G. (1979). Theorizing about the quality and stability of marriage. In W. Burr, R. Hill, F. I. Nye, & I. Reiss (Eds.), *Contemporary theories about the family* (Vol. 2). New York: Free Press.

Liberman, R. P. (1970). Behavioral approaches to couple and family therapy. *American Journal of Orthopsychiatry, 40,* 106–118.

Liddle, H., & Halpin, R. (1978). Family therapy training and supervision: A comparative review. *Journal of Marriage and Family Counseling, 4,* 77–98.

Liddle, H., Davidson, G., & Barrett, M. (1988). Pragmatic implications of live supervision: Outcome research. In H. A. Liddle, D. C. Breunlin, & R. C. Schwartz, (Eds.), *Handbook of family therapy training and supervision*. New York: Guilford Press.

Liddle, H. A. (1991). Training and supervision in family therapy: A comprehensive and critical analysis. In A. S. Gurman & D. P. Kniskern (Eds.), *Handbook of family therapy* (Vol. 2). New York: Brunner/Mazel.

Liddle, H. A., & Dakof, G. A. (1995). Efficacy of family therapy for drug abuse: Promising but not definitive. *Journal of Marital and Family Therapy, 21*(4), 511–544.

Liddle, H. A., & Rowe, C. L. (2004). Advances in family therapy research. In M. P. Nichols & R. C. Schwartz (Eds.), *Family therapy: Concepts and methods* (6th ed.), Boston: Pearson.

Lowe, R. N. (1982). Adlerian/Dreikursian family counseling. In A. M. Horne & M. M. Ohlsen (Eds.), *Family counseling and therapy*. Itasca, IL: Peacock.

Luborsky, L., Singer, B., & Luborsky, L. (1973). Comparative studies of psychotherapies. *Archives of General Psychiatry, 29,* 719–729.

Lyddon, W. J. (1990). First and second order change: Implications for rationalist and constructivist cognitive therapies. *Journal of Counseling and Development, 69,* 122–127.

Lyddon, W. J. (1992). A rejoinder to Ellis: What is and is not RET? *Journal of Counseling and Development, 70,* 452–454.

Mace, N. L. & Rabins, P. V. (2001). *The 36 hour day: A family guide to caring for persons with Alzheimer Disease, related dementing illnesses, and memory loss in later life.* Clayton, VIC: Warner Books.

Mackey, R. A., & O'Brien, B. A. (1995). *Lasting marriages: Men and women growing together.* Westport, CT: Praeger.

Mahler, M. (1968). *On human symbiosis and the vicissitudes of individuation, Vol. 1, Infantile psychosis.* New York: International Universities Press.

Mahler, M. S., Pine, F., & Bergman, A. (1975). *The psychological birth of the human infant.* New York: Basic Books.

Margolin, G. (1982). Ethical and legal considerations in family therapy. *American Psychologist, 7,* 788–801.

Margolin, G. (1987). The multiple forms of aggressiveness between marital partners: How do we identify them? *Journal of Marital and Family Therapy, 13*(1), 77–85.

Maslow, A. (1968). *Toward a psychology of being* (2nd ed.). New York: Van Nostrand Reinhold.

McClendon, R. (1977). My mother drives a pick-up truck. In G. Barnes (Ed.), *Transactional analysis after Eric Berne.* New York: Harper & Row.

McFarlane, W. R., Dixon, L., Lukens, E., & Lucksted, A. (2003). Family psychoeducation and schizophrenia: A review of the literature. *Journal of* Marital *and Family Therapy, 29*(2), 223–245.

McGoldrick, M., & Rohrbaugh, M. (1987). Researching ethnic family stereotypes. *Family Process, 1,* 89–100.

McGoldrick, M., Pearce, J. K., & Giordano, J. (1982). *Ethnicity and family therapy.* New York: Guilford Press.

McGoldrick, M., Preto, N. G., Hines, P. M., & Lee, E. (1991). Ethnicity and family therapy. In A. S. Gurman & D. P. Kniskern (Eds.). *Handbook of family therapy* (Vol. 2). New York: Brunner/Mazel.

Meichenbaum, D. (1977). *Cognitive behavior modification.* New York: Plenum.

Minuchin, S. (1974). *Families and family therapy.* Cambridge, MA: Harvard University Press.

Minuchin, S., & Fishman, C. (1981). *Family therapy techniques.* Cambridge, MA: Harvard University Press.

Minuchin, S., Montalvo, B., Guerney, B. G., Jr., Rosman, B. L., & Schumer, F. (1967). *Families of the slums: An exploration of their structure and treatment.* New York: Basic Books.

Minuchin, S., Rosman, B., & Baker, L. (1978). *Psychosomatic families: Anorexia nervosa in context.* Cambridge, MA: Harvard University Press.

Mitchell, K. M., Bozarth, J. D., & Kraft, C. C. (1977). A reappraisal of the therapeutic effectiveness of accurate empathy, nonpossessive warmth, and genuineness. In A. S. Gurman & A. M. Razin (Eds.), *Effective psychotherapy: A handbook of research.* New York: Pergamon Press.

Mittleman, B. (1948). The concurrent analysis of married couples. *Psychoanalytic Quarterly, 17,* 182–197.

Mittleman, B. (1956). Analysis of reciprocal neurotic patterns in family relationships. In V. W. Eisenstein (Ed.), *Neurotic Interactions in Marriage.* New York: Basic Books.

Montalvo, B., & Thompson, R. F. (1988). Conflicts in the caregiving family. *The Family Therapy Networker,* July–Aug., 30–35.

Moreno, J. L. (1951). *Sociometry, experimental method and the science of society.* Boston: Beacon.

Moreno, J. L. (1983). Psychodrama. In H. Kaplan & B. Sadock (Eds.), *Comprehensive group* (2nd ed.). Baltimore: Williams & Wilkins.

Morgan, L. A. (1990). The multiple consequences of divorce: A decade review. *Journal of Marriage and the Family, 52,* 911–924.

Mosak, H. H. (2005). Adlerian Psychotherapy. In R. J. Corsinsi & D. Wedding, (Eds.), *Current psychotherapies* (7th ed.). Belmont, CA: Books/Cole–Thomson Learning.

MST Services, Inc. (2010). *Program in formation for multisystemic therapy.* Retrieved from www.mstservices.com

Murdock, N. L. (2009). *Theories of counseling and psychotherapy: A case approach.* Upper Saddle River, NJ: Merrill.

Murphy, J. P. (1984). Substance abuse and the family. *Journal for Specialists in Group Work, 9,* 106–112.

Murstein, B. I. (1976). *Who will marry whom?* New York: Springer.

Murstein, B. I. (1987). A clarification of the SVR theory of dyadic pairing. *Journal of Marriage and the Family, 49,* 929–933.

Napier, A. Y., & Whitaker, C. A. (1978). *The family crucible.* New York: Harper & Row.

Nathan, P. E. & Gorman, J. M. (2007). *A guide to treatments that work* (3rd ed.). New York: Oxford University Press.

Nichols, M. P. (2009). *Family therapy: Concepts and methods.* Boston: Allyn & Bacon.

Nichols, M. P., & Schwartz, R. C. (2001). *Family therapy: Concepts and methods* (5th ed.). Boston: Allyn & Bacon.

Noler, P., & Fitzpatrick, M. A. (1990). Marital communication in the eighties. *Journal of Marriage and the Family, 52,* 832–843.

Northey, W. F. (2002). Characteristics and clinical practices of marriage and family therapists: A national survey. *Journal of Marital and Family Therapy, 29,* 487–494.

Norton, A. J., & Mooreman, J. E. (1987). Current trends in marriage and divorce among American women. *Journal of Marriage and the Family, 49,* 3–14.

Nylund, D., & Thomas, J. (1994). The economics of narrative. *The Family Therapy Networker, 18*(6), 38–39.

O'Hanlon, B. (1994). The third wave. *The Family Therapy Networker, 18*(6), 18–29.

O'Leary, C. J. (1989). The person-centered approach to family therapy: A dialogue between two traditions. *Person-Centered Review, 4,* 308–323.

Oberdorf, C. P. (1938). Psychoanalysis of married people. *Psychoanalytic Review, 25,* 453–475.

Olin, G. V., & Fenell, D. L. (1989). The relationship between depression and marital adjustment in a general population. *Family Therapy, XVI,* 11–20.

Olson, D. (2011). FACES IV and the circumplex model: Validation study. *Journal of Marital and Family Therapy, 3,* 64–80.

Olson, D. H., & DeFrain, J. (2006). *Marriages & families: Intimacy, diversity and strengths.* Boston: McGraw-Hill.

Olson, D. H., Russell, C., & Sprenkle, D. H. (1980). Marriage and family therapy: A decade review. *Journal of Marriage and the Family, 42,* 973–993.

Olson, D. H., Russell, C. S., & Sprenkle, D. H. (1989). *Circumplex model: Systemic assessment and treatment of families.* New York: Haworth Press.

Olson, D. H., Sprenkle, D. H., & Russell, C. (1983). Circumplex model of marital and family systems IV: Theoretical update. *Family Process, 22*(1), 69–83.

Pais, S., Piercy, F., & Miller, J. (1988). Factors related to family therapists' breaking confidence when clients disclose high-risks-to-HIV/AIDS sexual behaviors. *Journal of Marital and Family Therapy, 24,* 457–472.

Paolino, T. J., Jr., & McCrady, B. S. (Eds.) (1978). *Marriage and marital therapy: Psychoanalytic, behavioral and systems theory perspectives.* New York: Brunner/Mazel.

Papp, P. (1980). The Greek chorus and other techniques of paradoxical therapy. *Family Process, 19,* 45–57.

Parsons, B. V., & Alexander, J. F. (1973). Short-term family intervention: A therapy outcome study. *Journal of Consulting and Clinical Psychology, 41,* 195–201.

Patterson, G. (1971). *Families: Application of social learning in family life.* Champaign, IL: Research Press.

Patterson, G. (1976). *Families: Application of social learning in family life.* Champaign, IL: Research Press.

Patterson, G., Reid, J., Jones, R., & Conger, R. (1975). *A social learning approach to family intervention: Families with aggressive children.* Eugene, OR: Castalia.

Patterson, J. E., Miller, R. B., Carnes, S., & Wilson, S. (2004). Evidence based practice for marriage and family therapists. *Journal of Marital and Family Therapy, 30,* 183–195.

Pattison, E. M. (1982). Family dynamics and interventions in alcoholism. In A. S. Gurman

(Ed.), *Questions and answers in the practice of family therapy* (Vol. 2). New York: Brunner/Mazel.

Paul, G. L. (1967). Strategy of outcome research in psychotherapy. *Journal of Consulting Psychology, 31,* 109–118.

Perls, F. (1969). *Gestalt therapy verbatim.* Moab, UT: Real People Press.

Pinsof, W. M., & Wynne, L. C. (1995a). The effectiveness and efficacy of marital and family therapy: Introduction to the special issue. *Journal of Marital & Family Therapy, 21*(4), 341–343.

Pinsof, W. M., & Wynne, L. C. (1995b). The efficacy of marital and family therapy: An empirical overview, conclusions, and recommendations. *Journal of Marital & Family Therapy, 21*(4), 585–613.

Popenoe, D. & Whitehead, B. D. (2004). *The state of our unions.* New Brunswick, NJ: National Marriage Project, Rutgers University.

Prince, S. E., & Jacobson, N. S. (1995). A review and evaluation of marital and family therapies for affective disorders. *Journal of Marital and Family Therapy, 21*(4), 377–402.

Psychotherapy Networker (2007). The top 10: The most influential therapists of the past quarter century. *Psychotherapy Networker, 31*(2), 24–68.

Rabin, M. (1980). *The field of family therapy: A paradigmatic classification and presentation of the major approaches.* Paper presented at the annual meeting of the American Personnel and Guidance Association, Atlanta, GA.

Raskin, N., & Van der Veen, F. (1970). Client-centered therapy: Some clinical and research perspectives. In J. Hart & T. Tomlinson (Eds.), *New directions in client-centered therapy.* Boston: Houghton Mifflin.

Reid, J., & Patterson, G. (1976). The modification of aggressive behavior in boys in the home setting. In A. Bandura & E. Ribes (Eds.), *Behavior modification: Experimental analysis of aggression and delinquency.* Hillsdale, NJ: Erlbaum.

Robbins, M. S., & Szapocznik, J. (2005.) Brief strategic family therapy. *Family Therapy Magazine, 4*(5), 18–21

Roberto, L. G. (1991). Symbolic-experiential family therapy. In A. S. Gurman & D. P. Kniskern (Eds.), *Handbook of family therapy* (Vol. 2). New York: Brunner/Mazel.

Robinson, L. C., & Blanton, P. W. (1993). Marital strengths in enduring marriages. *Family Relations, 42,* 38–45.

Rogers, C. R. (1957). The necessary and sufficient conditions of therapeutic personality change. *Journal of Consulting Psychology, 21,* 95–103.

Rogers, C. R. (1961). *On becoming a person: A therapist's view of psychotherapy.* Boston: Houghton Mifflin.

Rogers, C. R. (1980). *A way of being.* Boston: Houghton Mifflin.

Rosenfeld, M. J. (2010). The independence of young adults in historical perspective. *Family Therapy Magazine, 9*(3), 16–19.

Rowe, G. P., & Meridith, W. H. (1982). Quality in marital relationships after twenty-five years. *Family Perspective, 16*(4), 149–155.

Rudestam, K. E. (1982). *Experiential groups in theory and practice.* Pacific Grove, CA: Brooks/Cole.

Saldana, L., & Sheidow, A. J. (2005). Multisystemic therapy: Origins, empirical results, and current efforts. *Family Therapy Magazine, 4*(5), 26–29.

Satir, V. (1983). *Conjoint family therapy* (3rd ed.). Palo Alto, CA: Science and Behavior Books.

Satir, V. (1988). *The new peoplemaking.* Palo Alto, CA: Science and Behavior Books.

Schumm, W. R. (1985). Beyond relationship characteristics of strong families: Contrasting a model of family strengths. *Family Perspective, 19*(1), 1–9.

Schwartz, R. C. (1995). *Internal family systems therapy.* New York: Guilford Press.

Schwartz, R. C. (2001). *Introduction to the Internal Family Systems Model,* Oak Park, IL: Trailheads.

Segal, L. (1991). Brief therapy: The MRI approach. In A. S. Gurman & D. P. Kniskern (Eds.), *Handbook of family therapy* (Vol. 2). New York: Brunner/Mazel.

Serovich, J. M., & Mosack, K. E. (2000). Training issues for supervisors of marriage and family therapists working with persons living with HIV. *Journal of Marital and Family Therapy, 26,* 103–111.

Sexton, T. L. & Alexander, J. F. (2002). Family-based, empirically supported interventions. *The Counseling Psychologist, 30,* 238–261.

Sexton, T. L., & Alexander, J. F. (2002). *Functional Family Therapy: For at risk adolescents and their families.* Wiley Series in Couples and Family Dynamics and Treatment, Comprehensive Handbook of Psychotherapy Volume II: Cognitive–behavioral approaches (T. Patterson, Ed.). Wiley: New York.

Sexton, T. L., & Alexander, J. F. (2003). Functional family therapy: A mature clinical model for working with at-risk adolescents and their families In T. L.Sexton, G. R. Weeks & M. S. Robbins (Eds.), *Handbook of family therapy. The science and practice of working with families and couples* (pp. 323–350). New York: Brunner-Routledge.

Sexton, T. L., & Ridley, C. R. (2004). Implications of a moderated common factors approach: Does it move the field forward? *Journal of Marital and Family Therapy, 30*(2), 159–164.

Sexton, T. L., Ridley, C. R., & Kleiner, A. J. (2004). Beyond common factors: Multi-level-process models of therapeutic change in marriage and family therapy. *Journal of Marital and Family Therapy, 30*(2), 131–149.

Shadish, W. R., & Baldwin, S. A. (2003). Meta-analysis of MFT interventions. *Journal of Marital and Family Therapy, 29*(4), 577–570.

Shapiro, A. F., Gottman, J. M., & Carrere, S. (2000). The baby and the marriage: Identifying factors that buffer against decline in marital satisfaction after the first baby arrives. *Journal of Family Psychology, 14,* 59–70.

Shea, M. T., Elkin, I., Imber, S. D., Sotsky, S. M., Watkins, J. T., Collins, J. F., … Parloff, M. B. (1992). Course of depressive symptoms over follow-up: Findings from the National Institute of Mental Health Treatment of Depression Collaborative Research Program. *Archives of General Psychiatry, 49,* 782–787.

Sheidow, A. J., Henggeler, S. W., & Schoenwald, S. K. (2003). Multisystemic therapy. In T. L. Sexton, G. R. Weeks & M. S. Robbins (Eds.), *Handbook of family therapy: The science and practice of working with families and couples* (pp. 303–321). New York: Brunner-Routledge.

Smith, B. (2010, February 22). Sobering statistics: Army struggles to meet needs of soldiers with alcohol issues. *Army Times,* p. 6.

Smith, M. L., & Glass, G. V. (1977). Meta-analysis of psychotherapy outcome studies. *American Psychologist, 32,* 752–760.

Smith, M. L., Glass, G. V., & Miller, T. I. (1980). *The benefits of psychotherapy.* Baltimore: John Hopkins University Press.

Spanier, G. (1976). Measuring dyadic adjustment: New scales for assessing the quality of marriages and similar dyads. *Journal of Marriage and the Family, 38,* 15–28.

Sperry, L., Carlson, J., & Peluso, P. (2006). *Couples therapy: Integrating theory and technique* (2nd ed.). Denver, CO: Love.

Spitz, R. (1965). *The first year of life.* New York: International Universities Press.

Sporakowski, M., & Hughston, G. A. (1978). Prescriptions for happy marriage: Adjustments and satisfactions of couples married 50 years or more. *Family Coordinator, 27,* 321–327.

Sprenkle, D. H. (1990). Continuity and change. *Journal of Marital and Family Therapy, 16,* 337–340.

Sprenkle, D., & Blow, A. J. (2004). Common factors and our sacred models. *Journal of Marital and Family Therapy, 30,* 113–129.

Stanton, M. D. (1978). Some outcome results and aspects of structural family therapy with drug addicts. In D. Smith, S. Anderson, M. Buxton, T. Chung, N. Gotlieb, & W. Harvey (Eds.), *A multicultural view of drug abuse.* Cambridge, MA: Schenkman.

Stanton, M. D., & Todd, T. (1979). Structural family therapy with drug addicts. In E. Kaufman & P. Kaufman (Eds.), *The family therapy of drug and alcohol abuse.* New York: Gardner Press.

Stanton, M. D., & Todd, T. (1981). Family treatment approaches to drug abuse problems. *Family Process, 18,* 251–280.

Stevens, P., & Smith, R. L. (2001). *Substance abuse counseling: Theory and practice* (2d ed.). Upper Saddle River, NJ: Prentice Hall.

Stinett, N., & Sauer, K. H. (1977). Relationship characteristics of strong families. *Family Perspective, 11*(4), 3–11.

Storm, C. L. (1991). Placing gender at the heart of MFT masters programs: Teaching a gender sensitive systemic view. *Journal of Marital and Family Therapy, 17,* 45–52.

Strupp, H. H., & Hadley, S. W. (1979). Specific vs. nonspecific factors in psychotherapy: A controlled study of outcome. *Archives of General Psychiatry, 36,* 1125–1136.

Stuart, R. (1980). *Helping couples change: A social learning approach to marital therapy.* New York: Guilford Press.

Substance Abuse and Mental Health Services Administration (SAMHSA). (2010). *Recovery Month Survey Results.* Retrieved from http://www.samsa.gov

Sullivan, H. S. (1947). *Conceptions of modern psychiatry.* Washington, DC: William Alanson White Psychiatric Foundation.

Sullivan, H. S. (1953). *The interpersonal theory of psychiatry.* New York: Norton.

Sullivan, H. S. (1954). *The psychiatric interview.* New York: Norton.

Swensen, C. H., Eskew, R. W., & Kohlhepp, K. A. (1984). Five factors in long-term marriages. *Lifestyle: A Journal of Changing Patterns, 7,* 94–106.

Tallman, K., & Bohart, A. C. (1999). The client as a common factor: Clients as self-healers. In M. A. Hubble, B. L. Duncan, & S. D. Miller (Eds.), *The heart and soul of change: What works in therapy* (pp. 91–131). Washington, DC: American Psychological Association.

Tan, M. (2009, Dec. 18). 2 million troops have deployed since 9/11. *Marine Corps Times.*

Tan, M. (2010, June 6). 2009 worst year yet for soldier suicides. *Army Times,* p. 29.

Thayer, L. (1991). Toward a person-centered approach to family therapy. In A. M. Horne & J. L. Passmore (Eds.). *Family counseling and therapy* (2nd ed.). Itasca, IL: Peacock.

Thomas, D., & Rogharr, H. B. (1990). Postpositivist theorizing: The case of religion and the family. In J. Sprey (Ed.), *Fashioning family theory: New approaches.* Newberry Park, CA: Sage.

Tilghman, A., & McGarry, B. (2010, March 8). Medicating the military. *Army Times,* p. 24.

Toman, W. (1961). *Family constellation.* New York: Springer.

Training of clinical psychologists. (1981). *Psychology Today, 16*(2), 85.

Truax, C. B., & Carkhuff, R. R. (1967). *Toward effective counseling and psychotherapy: Training and practice.* Chicago: Aldine.

Truax, C. B., & Mitchell, K. M. (1971). Research on certain therapist interpersonal skills in relation to process and outcome. In A. E. Bergin & S. L. Garfield (Eds.), *Handbook on psychotherapy and behavior change: An empirical analysis.* New York: Wiley.

US Bureau of the Census (2001). *Statistical abstract of the United States* (121st ed.). Washington, DC: US Government Printing Office.

US Bureau of the Census (2010, November 10). *Men and women wait longer to marry.* Retrieved from www.census.gov

Usher, M. L., & Steinglass, P. J. (1981). Responding to presenting complaints in an alcoholic family. In A. S. Gurman (Ed.), *Questions and answers in the practice of family therapy.* New York: Brunner/Mazel.

Van der Veen, F. (1977). *Three client-centered alternatives: A therapy collective, therapeutic community and skills training for relationships.* Paper presented at annual meeting of the American Psychological Association.

Visher, E. B., & Visher, J. S. (1979). *Stepfamilies: A guide to working with stepparents and stepchildren.* New York: Brunner/Mazel.

von Bertalanffy, L. (1968). *General systems theory: Foundation, development, applications.* New York: Brazillier.

Wachtel, E. F. (1999). *We love each other, but....* New York: Golden Books.

Waite, L. J., & Gallagher, M. (2000). *The case for marriage.* New York: Doubleday.

Wallerstein, J. S. (1992). Children after divorce. In O. Pocs (Ed.), *Marriage and Family.* Guilford, CT: Dushkin.

Wallerstein, J. S., & Blakeslee, S. (1995). *The good marriage: How and why love lasts.* Boston: Houghton Mifflin.

Wallerstein, J. S., Lewis, J. M., & Blakeslee, S. (2000). *The unexpected legacy of divorce: A twenty-five year landmark study.* New York: Hyperion.

Wampold, B. E. (2001). *The great psychotherapy debate: Models, methods and findings.* Mahwah, NJ: Erlbaum.

Watson, R. (1977). An introduction to humanistic psychotherapy. In S. Moore & R. Watson (Eds.), *Psychotherapies: A comparative casebook.* New York: Holt, Rinehart, & Winston.

Watzlawick, P., Weakland, J. H., & Fisch, R. (1974). *Change: Principles of problem formation and problem resolution.* New York: Norton.

Weiner-Davis, M. (1992). *Divorce busting.* New York: Summit Books.

Weinhold, B. K., & Hendricks, G. (1993). *Counseling and psychotherapy: A transpersonal approach.* Denver, CO: Love.

Weishaus, L., & Field, D. (1988). A half century of marriage: Continuity or change. *Journal of Marriage and the Family, 50,* 763–774.

Wells, R. A., & Dezen, A. E. (1978). The results of family therapy revisited: The nonbehavioral methods. *Family Process, 17,* 251–274.

Whitaker, C. A. (1976). The hindrance of theory in clinical work. In P. J. Guerrin, Jr. (Ed.), *Family therapy: Theory and practice.* New York: Gardner Press.

Whitaker, C. A., & Keith, D. V. (1981). Symbolic–experiential family therapy. In A. S. Gurman & D. P. Kniskern (Eds.), *Handbook of family therapy.* New York: Brunner/Mazel.

White, M. (1986). Negative explanation, restraint, and double description: A template for family therapy. *Family Process, 25,* 169–184.

White, M., & Epston, D. (1990). *Narrative means to therapeutic ends.* New York: Norton.

Wilcoxon, S. A., & Fenell, D. L. (1983). Engaging the nonattending spouse in marital therapy through the use of a therapist-initiated written communication. *Journal of Marital and Family Therapy, 9,* 199–203.

Wilcoxon, S. A., & Fenell, D. L. (1986). Linear and paradoxical letters to the nonattending spouse: A comparison of engagement rates. *Journal of Marital and Family Therapy, 12*(2), 191–193.

Winch, R. (1958). *Mate selection: A study of complimentary needs.* New York: Harper & Row.

Wolpe, J. (1958). *Psychotherapy by reciprocal inhibition.* Stanford, CA: Stanford University Press.

Wolpe, J. (1969). *The practice of behavior therapy.* New York: Pergamon Press.

Woody, S. R., Weisz, J., & McLean, C. (2005). Empirically supported treatments: 10 Years later. *Clinical Psychologist, 58,* 5–11.

Wynne, L. C., (Ed.) (1988). *The state of the art in family therapy research: Controversies and recommendations.* New York: Family Prouss Press.

Wynne, L. C., McDaniel, S. H., & Weber, T. T. (1987). Professional politics and the concepts of family therapy, family consultation and systems consultation. *Family Process, 26,* 153–166.

Wynne, L. C., Ryckoff, I. M., Day, J., & Hirsch, S. I. (1958). Pseudomutuality in the family relationships of schizophrenics. *Psychiatry, 21,* 205–220.

Youssef, N. A. (2010, March 17). Military sexual assault cases up. *Denver Post,* p. 5A.

Zur, O., & Smith, T. (2011). *Codes of ethics regarding competence and limits of confidentiality in treatment of clients with HIV/AIDS.* Retrieved from http://www.zurinstitute.com/codesofethicsofhiv-aids.html

Name Index

Subject Index